The Middle East
after the
Israeli Invasion of Lebanon

Contemporary Issues in the Middle East

The Middle East
after the
Israeli Invasion of Lebanon

edited by

Robert O. Freedman

SYRACUSE UNIVERSITY PRESS

1986

Library of Congress Cataloging-in-Publication Data

The Middle East after the Israeli invasion of Lebanon.

(Contemporary issues in the Middle East)
Bibliography: p.
Includes index.
1. Near East—Politics and government—1945–
I. Freedman, Robert Owen. II. Series.
DS63.1.M4845 1986   956'.04   86-14475
ISBN 0-8156-2388-7 (alk. paper)
ISBN 0-8156-2389-5 (pbk. : alk. paper)

Contents

Preface

T HE MIDDLE EAST has long been one of the most volatile regions on
the globe. Wars, coups détat, rapid shifts in alliances and alignments, numerous intra-Arab and regional conflicts, and constant superpower intervention have wracked the region since the first Arab-
Israeli war of 1948. In an effort to increase public understanding of
this complex region, the Center for the Study of Israel and the Contemporary Middle East of the Baltimore Hebrew College has held a series of conferences bringing together Middle Eastern specialists from
various perspectives to analyze and discuss the region.

The first conference, held in 1978, examined the impact of the
Arab-Israeli conflict on the Middle East, and the papers were later
published as *World Politics and the Arab-Israeli Conflict* (Robert O.
Freedman, ed., New York: Pergamon, 1979). The second conference,
held in 1979 (two years into the administration of Israeli Prime Minister Menahem Begin), made a preliminary analysis of the dynamics
of the Begin regime. Following the Israeli election of 1981, the conference papers were updated and published as *Israel in the Begin Era*
(Robert O. Freedman, ed., New York: Praeger, 1982). The third conference, which took place in 1982, dealt with Middle Eastern developments in the period between the Camp David agreements of 1978
and the Israeli invasion of Lebanon in 1982. The conference papers
were published as *The Middle East Since Camp David* (Robert O.
Freedman, ed., Boulder, Colo.: Westview Press, 1984). Just as the
Camp David agreements marked a major turning point in the Middle
East, so too did the Israeli invasion of Lebanon. For this reason, three
years after the invasion, a fourth conference was held at the Baltimore
Hebrew College to analyze the impact of the invasion on the Middle
East. This volume contains the papers presented at that conference.

This book was made possible through the help of a number of individuals and institutions. The initiating conference was cospon-
sored by the Baltimore Jewish Community Relations Council and the

Peggy Meyerhoff Pearlstone School of Graduate Studies of the Balti-
more Hebrew College. Dr. Leivy Smolar, President of the Baltimore
Hebrew College, has provided strong support for the Institute for the
Study of Israel and the Contemporary Middle East since its founding
in 1977. The Baltimore Hebrew College Library staff, and its director,
Dr. Schmuel Hirschfeld, and its periodical specialist, Mrs. Jeanette
Katkoff, provided invaluable research services, and my secretary,
Elise Baron, did a masterful job of typing the manuscript while also
helping to manage the college's graduate program. Special thanks
also go to my research assistant, Elaine Eckstein, who helped to keep
the clipping files of the Center up to date, and to Diane Kempler for
preparing the manuscript for the computer. I would also like to express my deep appreciation to the Meyerhoff Philanthropic Fund for
the financial support that enabled the Baltimore Hebrew College to
hold the conference that served as the basis for this book.

Finally, a word about the transliteration system used in this book.
Every editor dealing with a Middle East topic must decide between
using the exact transliteration of Arabic names, including the initial
hamza, or using a system that reflects the more common Western
transliteration. To aid those readers who do not know Arabic, we have
chosen the latter system, which renders the names of Arab leaders
and places in a form that English-speaking audiences will recognize.
Thus, for example, the reader will find Gamal Nasser (instead of Abd-
al-Nasir), Hafiz Assad for Hafiz al-Asad, Muammar Kaddafi for al-
Qadhafi, and King Hussein for Husayn, and such place names as Dho-
far and Oman (for Dhufar and 'Uman, respectively). In addition, given
the often bitter controversy over the name of the body of water lying
between Iran and Saudi Arabia—known to the Iranians as the Persian Gulf and to the Arabs as the Arab Gulf—most of the authors
have chosen to employ the neutral term *Gulf.*

Baltimore, Maryland   Robert O. Freedman
December 1985

Contributors

LOUIS J. CANTORI is chairman of the political science department of the University of Maryland (Baltimore County). He is the author of a number of books and articles on Egypt and the Middle East, notably *Local Politics and Development in the Middle East*. Dr. Cantori is also a consultant to the American Agency for International Development relative to its projects in Egypt.

JOHN DEVLIN is a former Middle East analyst for the Central Intelligence Agency and is currently a consultant on Middle Eastern Affairs. He is the author of *Syria: Modern State in an Ancient Land* and *The Ba'ath Party: A History from its Origins to 1966*.

ROBERT O. FREEDMAN is professor of political science and dean of the Peggy Meyerhoff Pearlstone School of Graduate Studies at Baltimore Hebrew College. He has written a number of books and articles on the Middle East, among them *Soviet Policy Toward the Middle East Since 1970* (now in its third edition) and is the editor of *The Middle East Since Camp David, Israel in the Begin Era*, and *World Politics and the Arab-Israeli Conflict*.

ROBERT E. HUNTER is director of European studies and senior fellow in Middle Eastern Studies at the Georgetown University Center for Strategic and International Studies. Among his numerous books are *Security in Europe, Presidential Control of Foreign Policy*, and *Grand Strategy for the Western Alliance*.

SHIREEN T. HUNTER is deputy director of the Middle East project at the Georgetown University Center for Strategic and International Studies. Her publications include *OPEC and the Third World: Politics of Aid* and *The Gulf Cooperation Council: Problems and Prospects*.

RASHID KHALIDI is associate professor of History and a member of the Middle East Institute at Columbia University. Among his many books are *British Policy Towards Syria and Palestine 1906–1914* and *Un-*

der Siege: PLO Decision-making During the 1982 War. He is also co-editor of *Palestine and the Gulf.*

AARON DAVID MILLER is a senior analyst on Lebanon and the PLO for the Intelligence and Research Section of the Department of State. He is the author of a number of publications on Middle Eastern politics, including *Search for Security: Saudi Arabian Oil and American Foreign Policy.*

WILLIAM OLSON is regional security affairs analyst of the Strategic Studies Institute of the Army War College. He served as a Fulbright Scholar in Iran in 1974 and is the author of a number of publications on Iran and Iraq, including *Anglo-Iranian Relations During World War I* and *Britain's Elusive Empire in the Middle East, 1900–1921.*

DAVID POLLOCK is Near East research analyst for USIA and former visiting lecturer in government at Harvard University. Among his numerous publications are *The Politics of Pressure: American Arms and Israeli Policy Since the Six-Day War* and *The Iranian Revolution: Implications for the Middle East.*

ROUHALLAH K. RAMAZANI is the Harry F. Byrd Professor of government and foreign affairs at the University of Virginia. He is the author of ten books on the Middle East, including the forthcoming *Oil, War and Revolution in the Middle East.* Dr. Ramazani also serves on the board of governors of the Middle East Institute.

BARRY RUBIN is currently international affairs fellow of the Council on Foreign Relations and the author of a number of major books on the Middle East, including *Paved with Good Intentions: The American Experience and Iran.* His most recent book is *Secrets of State.*

Introduction

T HE ISRAELI INVASION OF LEBANON in June 1982 was in some ways a turning point in Middle Eastern politics. To begin with, it spurred the United States to get reinvolved in a major way in the Arab-Israeli peace process, while at the same time weakening the position of PLO leader Yasser Arafat and exacerbating his conflict with Syrian President Hafiz Assad. This, in turn, impelled Arafat to turn to Jordan's King Hussein to try to work out a framework for peace talks with Israel. Meanwhile, at least in part because of the war, the hard-line Likud government of Israel fell, to be replaced by a government of National Unity. Composed of representatives of both Israel's Labor and Likud parties, the National Unity government for the first two years was led by Labor Party leader Shimon Peres, who was far more amenable to territorial compromise with Jordan than the Likud's Shamir, and who soon began to explore the prospects of peace with Jordan. Finally, as another result of the war Egypt, by championing the PLO cause, was able to regain some standing in the Arab world after having been ostracized because of its 1979 peace treaty with Israel.

Another effect of the invasion was the decision of the United States to become heavily involved in the internal politics of Lebanon, a morass from which it rather ignominiously extracted itself in February 1984—with, however, surprisingly little loss to its Middle East position or to the domestic political standing of President Ronald Reagan, who was easily reelected six months later. Ironically, neither the Soviet Union, which had looked on rather passively as Israel invaded Lebanon in June 1982, nor its Arab ally, Syria, was able to profit greatly from the U.S. debacle in Lebanon, as first the escalation of fighting in the Gulf and then the formation of a bloc of Syria's enemies (Egypt, Jordan, and the Arafat wing of the PLO) reinvigorated the peace process and seemed to catch Moscow off-stride.

If the policies of the United States, USSR, Jordan, Egypt, the PLO, Israel, and Syria were affected in a major way by the Israeli invasion of Lebanon, the other major conflict taking place at this time in the

Middle East—the war between Iran and Iraq—was surprisingly unaffected, although Iraq sought to exploit the Israeli invasion as a de-
vice to get Iran to end a war that Iraq had unwisely started in September 1980.

In sum, as might be expected, the war had a greater effect on the
policies of the core actors in the Middle East than on the policies of
the peripheral ones—although this is not to say that such peripheral
actors as Iran and Iraq had no impact on the core area. Indeed, Iran
(by aiding the Islamic fundamentalists in Lebanon) and Iraq (by giving tacit support to the Mubarak-Hussein-Arafat alignment) did play
important roles in the core area during this period, even though their
primary energies were devoted against each other.

It is the purpose of this book to analyze these developments, as
case studies in the foreign policies of each of the main actors involved. Where domestic forces have played a major role in the foreign
policies of the main actors, these will be examined as well. Yet it is
hoped that the book itself is more than merely the sum of its parts,
however excellent the analysis in each of the chapters. Instead, since
the book examines Middle East dynamics from three different levels—that of extraregional forces (the United States, the Soviet Union
and Western Europe); regional politics (intra-Arab relations, and the
Iran-Iraq war); and local politics (Jordan, Israel, the Palestinians,
Syria, and Egypt)—the reader will be able to come away with a multidimensional view of Middle Eastern political dynamics. That is, not
only will the reader be able to observe the impact of domestic politics
on a given country's foreign policy, he will also be able to see the role
of regional politics and the impact of extraregional forces. Indeed, if
there is one lesson that can be learned from the sorry history of Lebanon from the outbreak of civil war in 1975 through the Israeli invasion of 1982, it is that in the Middle East there is a constant interaction of local, national, regional, and extraregional forces, and that it
is impossible to understand the politics of the Middle East without examining developments at each of these levels.

Finally, since the book presents case studies that encompass the
period from June 1982 to June 1985, each author has provided a background analysis giving the main thrust of the forces affecting his or
her subject's policies in the period before the Israeli invasion of June
1982. It is hoped that both the multidimensional nature of the presentation and these background analyses to the various case studies
will elevate this book beyond what might otherwise be viewed as a

"period piece" covering the 1982–1985 period, however pregnant that period with major Middle Eastern events.

In the first chapter of the book, Robert O. Freedman describes the essentially reactive nature of Soviet policy toward the Middle East in the aftermath of the Israeli invasion of Lebanon. Quiescent during the invasion itself, the USSR helped Syria to recover from its war-time losses and also added two new weapons systems to the Syrian arsenal for its confrontation with Israel: the SAM-5 antiaircraft missile system and the SS-21 ground-to-ground missile system. While Moscow greeted with great satisfaction Syria's successes in confounding U.S. and Israeli policy in Lebanon, Freedman shows how Moscow was far less enthusiastic about both Syrian behavior in the September and November-December 1983 crises in Lebanon (which held out the possibility of a U.S.–Soviet confrontation) and Syrian efforts to control the PLO. Freedman also indicates how such events as the escalation of the Gulf war and the resumption of the Middle East peace process worked against Soviet interests in the region.

If Soviet policy in the aftermath of the Israeli invasion of Lebanon appeared essentially reactive in nature, that of the United States can best be described as confused. This is the primary message one receives from the chapter on U.S. policy toward the Middle East by Barry Rubin. Frequent personnel changes in the positions of secretary of state, national security advisor, and Middle East special representative, as well as policy conflicts among the secretaries of state and defense and the national security advisor, hindered U.S. policy— especially during the period of the U.S. intervention in Lebanon. Nonetheless, Rubin concludes that U.S. policy came full circle during this period: from an initial emphasis on close ties with Israel, through the Reagan plan that sought to draw in Arab moderates to force a solution of the Arab-Israeli conflict, and back toward a close tie with Israel in the aftermath of the U.S. experience in Lebanon as American policymakers became discouraged about the reliability of the Arab moderates.

While the United States and, to a lesser degree, the Soviet Union were the primary external actors in the Middle East in the aftermath of the Israeli invasion of Lebanon, the various states of Western Europe, despite their continued dependence on Arab oil, played a very minor role. This is the main conclusion one can draw from the paper prepared by Robert Hunter, who also highlights areas of tension between the United States and Western Europe over Middle East policy.

Hunter warns that while there was relatively little conflict between the United States and Western Europe over the Middle East during the 1982–85 period, the possibility of renewed conflict remains a real one, given the differing interests of the two sides in the region. Indeed, the confrontation between the United States and Italy over the Achille Lauro hijacking in October 1985 was an example of just such a conflict.

In moving from the role of external actors to the area of regional politics, two major themes are seen. As Shireen Hunter notes in her chapter on inter-Arab politics, these themes are 1) the continuation—indeed, the escalation—of the Iran-Iraq war, and 2) the re-alignment in Arab politics as Syria, despite its victory over the United States and Israel in Lebanon, did not go on to become the leader of the Arab world but rather found itself confronted with an Arab alignment of its enemies: the Arafat wing of the PLO, Jordan, and Egypt. Hunter concludes that, despite the war in Lebanon, the Arab world remains as divided as ever, with major constraints affecting the policies of all the major Arab states.

While the Arab world remains badly divided, the revolutionary regime of the Ayatollah Khomeini of Iran has consolidated its power and continues to reject all outside calls to end its war with Iraq unless the regime of Saddam Hussein is ousted. R. K. Ramazani, in his chapter on Iranian policy, discusses both the continuities and changes in Iranian foreign policy since the ouster of the Shah. While the general goals of territorial integrity and political independence remain paramount, Ramazani describes how an essentially pro-Western, anti-Soviet orientation has changed to a generally antisuperpower orientation, and how past alignments with Egypt and Israel have disintegrated while an alliance with Syria has been formed. He also notes, however, that these changes "have not been written in stone," and hints that the improved relations between Iran and the pro-Western states of Turkey and Pakistan in the face of the Soviet threat may foreshadow an improvement of ties with the United States in the future as well.

While the Iran-Iraq war has preoccupied the regime of the Ayatollah Khomeini, for the regime of Saddam Hussein of Iraq the war has been all-encompassing. William Olson, in his chapter on Iraq, outlines the main factors which influence that country's foreign policy, and he demonstrates the impact of the war on Iraqi policy—particularly on its relations with the other Arab states and with the two su-

perpowers. He concludes by predicting that the way the war progresses and ultimately ends will have a profound impact on future
Iraqi foreign policy.

Iraq's strongest Arab ally during the Iran-Iraq war has been Jordan. But, as Aaron David Miller indicates in his chapter, Iraq's weakening during the war has affected Jordan negatively, both in terms of
shortfalls in economic aid promised to Jordan by Iraq (and other Gulf
states) and because a weakened Iraq is less able to counter Syrian
pressure on Jordan. Indeed, in discussing Jordan's role in the peace
process, Miller emphasizes the major constraints on Jordanian policymakers, which range from economic dependency, through a large
Palestinian constituency which limits how far King Hussein can go
without the PLO's endorsement, to fear of Syrian military action.
Miller outlines how, despite these constraints, King Hussein has
nonetheless skillfully manipulated the weakening of Arafat after his
expulsions from Lebanon in 1982 and 1983 (and Jordan's rapprochement with Egypt in 1984) to position himself for a possible breakthrough in the Middle East peace process.

If, on balance, Jordan's position was strengthened by the invasion
of Lebanon, the position of the PLO, and its Chairman, Yasser Arafat,
was weakened. Rashid Khalidi, in his contribution to this volume,
shows how the PLO went from a position of possessing a state-within-
a-state in south Lebanon with a certain amount of deterrent capability vis-à-vis Israel, to one of disordered dispersion throughout the
Arab world after being forced out of Lebanon—first by Israel and then
by Syria. He also demonstrates, however, how Arafat sought to cope
with this difficult situation by embracing the "Jordanian option," and
how Arafat was able to gain the support of the majority of the Palestinians for his viewpoint despite Syrian efforts to split Fatah and oust
him from the PLO leadership.

If the elimination of the PLO from South Lebanon was the one
major gain from its invasion that Israel could point to, there were also
a number of problems that may be traced to the invasion, including
the deep divisions within the Israeli polity that helped bring down the
Likud government in 1984. David Pollock discusses these developments in his chapter on Israel, but also notes that the invasion did relatively little harm to Israel's relations with its most important ally,
the United States. Pollock also analyzes the major constraints facing
Israel's National Unity government, which continues to be split between the Labor party led by Prime Minister Shimon Peres (which

seeks a peace agreement with Jordan based on a territorial compromise on the West Bank) and the Likud party, which opposes any peace settlement involving the surrender of West Bank territory.

While Jordan, the PLO, and Israel have been groping their way toward a peace settlement, the government of Hosni Mubarak has been actively encouraging the process. As Louis Cantori indicates in his chapter on Egypt, Mubarak skillfully exploited the Israeli invasion to improve Egypt's standing in the Arab world by aiding the PLO (whose leader, Arafat, reciprocated the Egyptian assistance by going to Egypt following his expulsion from Syria). Cantori also shows how the close cooperation with the PLO, the resumption of diplomatic relations with Jordan, a chilling of relations with Israel, and the distancing of Egypt somewhat from the United States also helped Mubarak to legitimize his position domestically, although Egypt continued to abide by the military provisions of the Egyptian-Israeli agreement and continued to cooperate militarily with the United States.

As might be expected, Syria looked with displeasure on the formation of an alignment among King Hussein, Mubarak, and Arafat. John Devlin, in his article on Syria, analyzes that country's role in the Arab world, the guiding principles behind its foreign policy, and its relations with the two superpowers. Devlin also shows how Syria was able to recover both from its military defeat at the hands of Israel in June 1982 and from internal problems caused by the illness of Syrian president Hafiz Assad to score a major political victory over both the United States and Israel in Lebanon.

In sum, the authors of this book have presented an encompassing analysis of the major developments in Middle East politics in the three-year period following the Israeli invasion of Lebanon. It is hoped that this volume will serve to aid in the understanding of this highly complex period.

I

The Role of External Powers

I

Soviet Middle East Policy After the Israeli Invasion of Lebanon

Robert O. Freedman

Introduction

T HE ISRAELI INVASION OF LEBANON had, at first, a very negative impact on Soviet diplomacy in the Middle East. While the United States seized the diplomatic initiative in the region, Moscow came in for heavy Arab criticism for not giving military support to the hard-pressed Syrian and PLO forces. Subsequently, however, when Moscow sent sophisticated weapons systems to Syria and the United States became enmeshed in the Lebanese morass, the Soviet position improved. Nonetheless, due to developments in the Gulf and new alignments in Arab politics, Moscow proved unable to exploit the American diplomatic failure in Lebanon to achieve any major improvement in its Middle East position. In order to place Soviet diplomacy in the aftermath of the Israeli invasion of Lebanon in proper perspective, however, it is necessary first to briefly analyze both Soviet goals in the Middle East and the underlying assumptions that motivate Soviet policy planners in the region.

As far as the question of Soviet goals in the Middle East is concerned, there are two major schools of thought.[1] While both agree that the Soviet Union wants to be considered as a major factor in Middle Eastern affairs, if only because of the USSR's propinquity to the region, they differ on what they see as the ultimate Soviet goal in the Middle East. One school of thought sees Soviet Middle Eastern policy as being primarily defensive in nature, that is, aimed at preventing the region from being used as a base for military attack or political subversion against the USSR. The other school of thought sees Soviet policy as primarily offensive in nature, with its goal the limitation and

3

ultimate exclusion of Western influence from the region and its replacement by Soviet influence. It is the opinion of the author that Soviet goals in the Middle East, at least since the mid-1960s, have been
primarily offensive in nature, and that in the Arab segment of the
Middle East, the Soviet Union appears to have been engaged in a zero-
sum game competition for influence with the United States.

In its efforts to weaken and ultimately eliminate Western influence from the Middle East (particularly from the Arab world) while
promoting its own influence, the Soviet leadership has employed a
number of tactics. First and foremost has been the supply of military
aid to its regional clients.[2] Next in importance comes economic aid:
the Aswan dam in Egypt and the Euphrates dam in Syria are prominent examples of Soviet economic assistance, although each project
has had serious problems. In recent years Moscow has also sought
to solidify its influence through the conclusion of long-term Friendship and Cooperation treaties, such as the ones concluded with Egypt
(in 1971), Iraq (1972), Somalia (1974), Ethiopia (1978), Afghanistan (1978), South Yemen (1979), Syria (1980), and North Yemen
(1984)—although the repudiation of the treaties by Egypt (in 1976)
and Somalia (1977) indicates that this has not always been a successful tactic. Moscow has also attempted to exploit both the lingering
memories of Western colonialism and Western threats against Arab
oil producers, and has—as in the case of the assassination of Indira
Ghandi—deliberately used "disinformation" to discredit American
policy.[3] The USSR has also sought influence through the establishment of ties between the CPSU (Communist Party of the Soviet Union) and such Arab ruling political parties as the Syrian Ba'ath and
the Algerian FLN. Still another tactic aimed at gaining influence has
been the provision of security infrastructure assistance to countries
like South Yemen and Ethiopia. Finally, Moscow has offered the Arabs
aid of both a military and diplomatic character against Israel, although that aid has been necessarily limited in scope since Moscow
continues to support Israel's right to exist—both for fear of unduly
alienating the United States (with whom the Russians desire additional strategic arms agreements and improved trade relations), and
because Israel serves as a convenient rallying point for potentially
anti-Western forces in the Arab world.[4]

While the USSR has used all these tactics, to a greater or lesser
degree of success, over the last two decades, it has also run into serious problems in its quest for influence in the Middle East. First, vis-à-

vis the numerous inter-Arab and regional conflicts (Syria-Iraq; North Yemen–South Yemen; Ethiopia-Somalia; Algeria-Morocco; Iran-Iraq; and so on) in that period, it has usually been the case that when the USSR has favored one party it has, ipso facto, alienated the other—often to the point of driving it over to the West. Second, the existence of Middle Eastern Communist parties has proven to be a handicap for the USSR, as internal Communist activities have on occasion caused a sharp deterioration in relations between Moscow and the country in which the Communist party has operated. (The Communist-supported coup d'état in the Sudan in 1971, Communist efforts to organize cells in the Iraqi army in the mid and late 1970s, and the activities of the Tudeh party in Khomeini's Iran are recent examples of this problem.[5]) Third, the wealth which flowed to the Arab world (or at least to its major oil producers) due to the quadrupling of oil prices in late 1973 has enabled the Arabs to buy quality technology from the West and Japan, and this has helped weaken the economic bond between the USSR and such Arab states as Iraq. Fourth, since 1967 and particularly since the 1973 Arab-Israeli war, Islam has been resurgent throughout the Arab world, and the USSR—identified as it is in the Arab world with atheism—has been hampered as a result, particularly since the Soviet invasion of Afghanistan in 1979 where Moscow has been fighting against an essentially Islamic resistance force. Fifth, in the diplomacy surrounding the Arab-Israeli conflict, Moscow is hampered by its lack of diplomatic ties with Israel, a factor which enables the United States alone to talk to both sides of the conflict. Finally, the United States (and to a lesser extent, China and France) has actively opposed Soviet efforts to achieve a predominant influence in the region, and this has frequently enabled Middle Eastern states to play the extraregional powers off against each other, thereby preventing any one of them from securing predominance.

To overcome these difficulties, Moscow has evolved one overall strategy: the development of a bloc of "anti-imperialist" states within the Arab world. In Moscow's view, these states should bury their potentially internecine rivalries and join together, along with such political organizations as the Arab Communist parties and the PLO, in a united front against what the USSR has called the "linchpin" of Western imperialism in the Middle East: Israel. Under such circumstances it is the Soviet hope that the Arab states would then use their collective pressure against Israel's supporters, especially the United

States.[6] The ideal scenario for Moscow—and one that Soviet commentators have frequently referred to—was the situation during the 1973 Arab-Israeli war when virtually all the Arab states supported the war effort against Israel while at the same time imposing an oil embargo against the United States. As is well known, not only did the oil embargo create domestic difficulties for the United States, it caused serious problems within the NATO alliance—a development that was warmly welcomed in Moscow. Unfortunately for the USSR, however, this "anti-imperialist" Arab unity was created not by Soviet efforts, but by the diplomacy of Egyptian President Anwar Sadat; and when Sadat changed his policies and turned toward the United States, the "anti-imperialist" Arab unity sought by the USSR fell apart. Nonetheless, so long as Soviet leaders continue to think in terms of such Leninist categories of thought as "united fronts" ("anti-imperialist" Arab unity, in Soviet parlance, is merely another way of describing a united front of Arab governmental and nongovernmental forces), and so long as there is a deep underlying psychological drive for unity in the Arab world, Moscow can be expected to continue to pursue this overall strategy as a long-term goal.

At the time of the Israeli invasion of Lebanon in June 1982, the Arab world was divided into three major groups as a result of such events as the Egyptian-Israeli peace treaty, the Soviet invasion of Afghanistan, and the Iran-Iraq war.[7] On the one hand was the pro-Western contingent led by Egypt and including the Sudan, Oman, and Somalia. This Arab group supported Camp David, opposed the Soviet invasion of Afghanistan, supported Iraq in its war with Iran, and cooperated with the United States in joint military exercises. On the other side of the Arab spectrum was the so-called Front of Steadfastness and Confrontation, led by Syria and including Libya, the Peoples Democratic Republic of Yemen, the PLO, and Algeria. This Arab contingent opposed Camp David and—with the exception of Algeria—supported Soviet activity in Afghanistan, and Iran against Iraq. In the center of the Arab spectrum was the group of Arab states composed of Saudi Arabia, Jordan, Kuwait, the United Arab Emirates, Morocco, Iraq, North Yemen, Tunisia, Bahrein, and Qatar. These "centrists" opposed Camp David, but also opposed the Soviet invasion of Afghanistan and tended to back Iraq in its war with Iran. From the Soviet viewpoint, the diplomatic goal was to move the centrist Arab grouping as close as possible to the Steadfastness Front, so as to isolate Egypt and other members of the pro-Western Arab bloc. Conversely, from the U.S. standpoint it was essential to try to move the centrist Arabs in the direction of the Egyptian-led Arab states.

Consequently, the Soviet inactivity during the period from the Israeli invasion in June 1982 until the American-engineered PLO exodus from Beirut in August could only damage Moscow's Middle East position. Soviet policy during this period has already been discussed in detail elsewhere and need only be summarized here.[8] Suffice it to say that—despite the existence of the Soviet-Syrian treaty and the fact that Israel shot down eighty-five Syrian planes and destroyed the SAM bases Syria had established in Lebanon in 1981—Moscow, contrary to its behavior during the Yom Kippur war of 1973, provided no military help during the course of the fighting. At the same time, its verbal warnings to Israel and the United States were of only a very general nature (and singularly ineffectual) until the announcement of the possible deployment of U.S. troops to Beirut, and even then Brezhnev quickly backed down from his warning after it became clear that the United States was going ahead with the deployment. While Moscow did mount a resupply effort to Syria once the fighting had ended, Moscow took no substantive actions once it became clear that Israel was not going to invade Syria but was restricting its efforts to destroying the PLO infrastructure in Lebanon (although battering Syrian troops stationed in Lebanon in the process)—thus demonstrating that the Soviet-Syrian treaty did not cover Syrian activities in Lebanon. To be sure, Moscow did appeal to the Arabs to unite to confront Israel and to use their oil weapon against the United States, but the badly divided Arab world, threatened on the east by Iran, was to take neither action. Indeed, the Arab states were unable even to convene a summit conference until after the PLO left Beirut.

Needless to say, Soviet inactivity during the crisis precipitated a great deal of Arab criticism, including some highly negative comments from its Middle East client, Libya,[9] while the United States for its part exploited the enhanced U.S. diplomatic position in the Middle East following the PLO withdrawal from Beirut to try to win over the centrist Arabs. Thus the "Reagan plan" issued on September 1 included a number of provisions with which both centrist Arabs and those in the Egyptian camp could agree. These included no Israeli sovereignty over the West Bank and Gaza, a stop to the building of Israeli settlements there, and a link between a West Bank–Gaza entity and Jordan—something King Hussein had long wanted.[10] The Arab states, finally convening their long-postponed summit (in Fez, Morocco), issued their peace plan one week later.[11] With both the U.S. and Arab peace plans now on the table, the USSR hastened to issue its plan in a speech delivered by Brezhnev in mid-September. While a number of its points were repetitions of previous Soviet proposals (including Moscow's basic three-point peace plan calling for a total Israeli withdrawal to the pre-1967 war boundaries, a Palestinian state on the West Bank and Gaza, and the right to exist of all states in the Middle East, including Israel), other points seem to have been added in order to emphasize the similarity between the Fez and Soviet plans.[12] In modeling the Soviet peace plan on Fez, Brezhnev evidently sought to prevent the Arabs from moving to embrace the Reagan plan. Nonetheless, with the United States clearly possessing the diplomatic initiative in the Middle East after the PLO pullout from Beirut, and with both Jordan's King Hussein and PLO leader Arafat (along with other Arab leaders) expressing an interest in the Reagan plan, Moscow was on the diplomatic defensive. Given this situation, it is not surprising that Brezhnev seized upon the massacres in the Sabra and Shatilla refugee camps to point out to Arafat that "if anyone had any illusions that Washington was going to support the Arabs ... these illusions have now been drowned in streams of blood in the Palestinian camps...."[13]

Nonetheless, despite the massacres, Arafat evidently felt that there was some value in pursuing the Reagan plan and he began to meet with his erstwhile enemy, King Hussein of Jordan, to work out a joint approach to the United States. Such maneuvering infuriated Syria, which sought to use pro-Syrian elements within the PLO to pressure Arafat into abandoning his new policy, a development which further exacerbated relations between Assad and Arafat. In addition, Moscow—evidently fearing the weakening of the Steadfastness Front and the possibility of the PLO (or at least Arafat's followers) defecting from it—continued to warn the Arabs about what it termed U.S. efforts to split the PLO and to draw Jordan and Saudi Arabia into supporting the Reagan plan (which the USSR termed a cover for Camp David).

It was at this point, in mid-November, that Brezhnev passed from the scene. His successor, Yuri Andropov, faced the task of rebuilding the Soviet position in the Middle East—a position that had suffered a major blow during the Israeli invasion of Lebanon.

Soviet Policy toward the Middle East under Andropov

Policy toward Syria

Essentially Andropov faced three major problems. In the first place, due to its inactivity during the Israeli invasion of Lebanon and the siege of Beirut in 1982, Soviet credibility as an ally of the Arabs had been called into question. Second, due to the poor performance of Soviet-made weaponry in the hands of Syria, the quality of Soviet military equipment had become suspect. This was a major problem for Moscow for two reasons: 1) the provision of modern weaponry was the single most important element of Soviet influence in the Middle East; and 2) the sale of weapons earned Moscow badly needed hard currency. A final Middle East problem for Andropov at the start of 1983 was the fact that the United States, which at the beginning of January had established a new "Central Command" to oversee its Rapid Deployment Force (RDF) in the Middle East, was clearly holding the diplomatic initiative in the region. By contrast, Moscow's own peace plan had received little support. In addition, Moscow's principal allies—Libya, South Yemen, Syria, and the PLO—seemed to have little clout in Arab politics, and had serious disagreements among themselves, with both Libyan leader Muammar Kaddafi and Syrian President Hafiz Assad at odds with the PLO's Yasser Arafat, who was publicly flirting with the Reagan plan.

Andropov was to receive additional evidence of Moscow's diminution of influence in the Middle East (and the concomitant rise of American influence) when Arafat journeyed to Moscow in mid-January 1983. The PLO leader, who had long been a close Soviet ally in the Arab world, was now openly praising some aspects of the Reagan plan, and had stated that he was resigned to dealing with the United States as the dominant superpower in the Middle East.[14] As a result, his visit to Moscow revealed a number of major Soviet-PLO differences. Thus, where in the past Arafat had supported Soviet plans for an international conference to solve the Arab-Israeli conflict, he now conceded only that such a conference "might open a road to a settlement."[15] Even more discouraging for Moscow must have been the PLO leader's announced agreement to the establishment of a confederation between Jordan and "an independent Palestinian state after its creation." While Moscow was itself in favor of the creation of an independent Palestinian state, the fact of its linkage to Jordan, a centrist state, not only seemed to align the PLO at least partially with the philosophy of the Reagan plan, but also appeared to prove its defection from the Steadfastness Front, which had already been badly weakened by the Israeli invasion. Consequently, the USSR expressed only its "understanding" of the PLO position—a diplomatic way of demonstrating its opposition.[16]

Under these circumstances, and with Soviet influence in the Middle East at a low ebb, Andropov took action to rebuild the Soviet position in the region. His first action was the deployment of several batteries of SAM-5 missiles to Syria, along with sufficient Soviet soldiers to operate and guard them.[17] This Soviet move went far beyond the Soviet resupply effort of tanks and planes to Syria that had been going on since the end of the Israeli-Syrian fighting in 1982. Indeed, by sending Syria a weapons system that had never been deployed outside the USSR itself—a system that had the capability of engaging Israel's EC-2 aircraft system that had proven so effective during the Israeli-Syrian air battles in the first week of the Israeli invasion of Lebanon—Moscow was demonstrating to the Arab world, and especially to Syria, that it was willing to stand by its allies.[18] Nonetheless, by manning the SAM-5 missiles with Soviet soldiers, Moscow was also signalling that the USSR, and not Syria, would determine when the missiles would be fired.[19] Given the fact that in both November 1980 and April 1981 Assad had tried to involve the USSR in his military adventures, this was probably a sensible precaution.[20] Yet another cautionary element in the dispatch of the missiles was that Moscow never formally announced that its own troops were involved in guarding the missiles, thus enabling the USSR to avoid a direct confrontation with Israel (and possibly the United States) should Israel decide to attack the missile sites.

Policy toward Libya

At the same time he was moving to bolster the USSR's primary Arab ally, Syria, with new weaponry, Andropov also sought to strengthen the position of Libya, another key Soviet client state, which had once again found itself in a posture of confrontation with the United States. Acting in response to reports of a planned Libyan-supported coup in the Sudan in mid-February, the United States sent four AWACS aircraft to Egypt for what were first described as "training maneuvers," and also dispatched the aircraft carrier *Nimitz* from Lebanon to a position near Libya (although outside the disputed Gulf of Sidra where the United States had shot down two Libyan planes in

1981).[21] Following these American moves, no Libyan coup attempt took place and U.S. Secretary of State George Shultz bluntly stated that Kaddafi had been "put back into his box where he belonged."[22]

While Moscow kept a low profile during the crisis itself (just as it had in the 1981 Gulf of Sidra incident), the Soviet leadership evidently felt that if the USSR was to rebuild its Middle East position, something more than a mere denunciation of U.S. policy was called for. Thus, Moscow took a significant (but not irreversible) step toward deepening relations with Libya by coming to "an agreement in principle" to conclude a treaty of friendship and cooperation with Libya one month after the Libyan–U.S. confrontation.[23] The agreement was reached during the mid-March Moscow visit of the number two man in the Libyan hierarchy, Abdel Salam Jalloud, who was a frequent visitor to the USSR. However, Moscow was not yet ready to fully endorse all of Kaddafi's adventures. Thus, although Soviet Prime Minister Tikhonov noted in a dinner speech welcoming Jalloud that the Soviet Union wanted to see Libya "as an economically developed state playing a weighty, positive role in international affairs and capable of repulsing all outside encroachments on its independence," the Soviet Prime Minister went on to say that "the all around assistance given by us to your country, the fulfillment of a number of promising projects of much importance for the development of Libya's economy, are called upon to facilitate the attainment of this aim."[24] Tikhonov's emphasis was clearly on the Soviet-Libyan economic relationship (Soviet-Libyan trade had passed the one billion ruble mark for the first time in 1982),[25] while it would appear that the Libyans were more interested in a strong military relationship.[26]

This difference in emphasis was reflected in a joint communiqué that described the talks as taking place in a spirit of "frankness and mutual understanding" and including a "thorough exchange of opinions" on the international situation.[27] While Moscow condemned the "provocative and dangerous [U.S.] aggressive actions against Libya," it issued no direct threats against the United States, stating only that "actions of this kind were aimed at undermining the universally accepted principles of relations between sovereign states."[28] In addition, while both Libya and the USSR condemned the establishment of the U.S. Central Command as well as Israeli actions in Lebanon, the only detailed areas of cooperation mentioned in the communique were in the economic sphere, thus indicating that Moscow's emphasis had prevailed. In any case, while at the close of the communiqué mention was made of the agreement "in principle" to conclude a Treaty of Friendship and Cooperation, the failure of the Soviet press to report any further progress toward concluding such a treaty during the remainder of 1983 may well have been an indication that Moscow had had second thoughts about even appearing to give a military guarantee to Kaddafi. The latter's mercurial behavior was well known in Moscow, especially since—in the aftermath of the Jalloud visit—Libya had again become enmeshed in Chad, where it almost precipitated a confrontation with France.[29]

The March–May Crisis in Lebanon

Nonetheless, when Moscow consented in mid-March 1983 to the "agreement in principle" it was still in an assertive mood as it sought to rebuild its Middle East position, and it followed up its promise to Libya with a public warning to Israel not to attack Syria. This Soviet warning, issued on March 30, came after a series of similar Syrian warnings, but it was limited in nature.[30] Thus, while Moscow warned that Israel was "playing with fire" by preparing to attack Syria, it made no mention of the Soviet-Syrian treaty. Indeed, in listing those on Syria's side in its confrontation with Israel, the Soviet statement merely noted that "on the side of the Syrian people are Arab patriots, the Socialist countries, and all who cherish the cause of peace, justice and honor." (The statement also emphasized the need to settle the Arab-Israeli conflict politically, rather than through war.)

This rather curious Soviet wording can perhaps be understood if one assumes that Moscow did not seriously expect an Israeli attack on Syria. With the more cautious Moshe Arens as Israel's new defense minister, and with rising opposition to Israel's presence in Lebanon being registered in Israel's domestic political arena, it appeared unlikely that Israel would attack Syria, even to take out the newly installed SAM-5 missiles. Indeed, even the hawkish Israeli chief of staff, General Rafael Eitan, in an interview on Israeli Armed Forces radio, stated that Israel had no intention of starting a war.[31] But if Moscow assumed that Israel would not go to war, why the warning? Given the fact that Moscow's credibility in the Arab world had dropped precipitously as a result of the warnings it had issued during the Israeli invasion of Lebanon in the June/July 1982 period—warnings that had been routinely ignored by both Israel and the United States—Moscow possibly saw a chance to increase its credibility in the region. Thus if Moscow, acting on the assumption that Israel would not attack

Syria in any case, issued a warning to Israel not to attack Syria, and Israel then did *not* attack Syria, Moscow could perhaps take credit for the non-attack and could sell the Arab world the fiction that Soviet diplomacy was effective vis-à-vis Israel, at least as a deterrent force. If this was, in fact, Moscow's thinking, however, not all the Arab states were taken in. Indeed, the Saudi paper *ArRiyad* expressed a lack of trust in the Soviet warning, noting that the limited validity of Soviet pronouncements had been proven during the Israeli invasion of Lebanon "which dealt a sharp and severe blow to the Kremlin when the Soviet missiles became no more than timber towers in the face of the sophisticated weapons the United States had unconditionally supplied to Israel."[32]

In any case, only three days after the Soviet warning to Israel Soviet Foreign Minister Andrei Gromyko, newly promoted to deputy prime minister, held a major press conference in Moscow.[33] While the main emphasis of Gromyko's press conference was on strategic arms issues, he also took the opportunity to make two major points about the Middle East situation. In the first place, in response to a question from a correspondent of the Syrian newspaper *Al-Ba'ath*, Gromyko stated that "the Soviet Union is in favor of the withdrawal of all foreign troops from the territory of Lebanon, all of them. Syria is in favor of this."[34] Second, Gromyko noted once again that the USSR was in favor of Israel's continued existence as a state: "We do not share the point of view of extremist Arab circles that Israel should be eliminated. This is an unrealistic and unjust point of view."[35] The thrust of Gromyko's remarks was clear: the Soviet leader, by urging the withdrawal of all foreign troops (including Syrian troops) from Lebanon and by reemphasizing the Soviet commitment to Israel's existence, seemed to be telling Syria that, despite the provision of the SAM-5 missiles, Moscow was not desirous of being dragged into a war in Lebanon on Syria's behalf. If this was indeed the message Gromyko was trying to get across, the rapid pace of Middle Eastern events was to pose new challenges, as well as opportunities, for Soviet policy.

On the one hand, Moscow had to be pleased by those developments within the PLO that challenged Arafat's opening to Washington and the subsequent slowing of the momentum in support of the Reagan plan. Indeed, Moscow's interest in preventing a PLO tilt to the United States was shared by Syria and Libya, both of which actively tried to undermine Arafat's position.[36] The efforts of the anti-Arafat forces were to prove successful when the Palestine National Council, after a number of postponements, finally convened in mid-February in Algiers and formally stated its refusal to consider the Reagan plan "as a sound basis for a just and lasting solution to the Palestinian problem and the Arab-Israeli conflict."[37] Needless to say, Moscow viewed this development positively, with *Pravda* correspondent Yuri Vladimirov praising the council's policy document as a welcome reaffirmation of the organization's determination to continue the struggle against imperialism and Zionism.[38]

As sentiment within the PLO hardened against the Reagan plan, King Hussein of Jordan, who on January 10 had stated that he would make his decision about joining peace talks with Israel by March 1, began to back away. Indeed, on March 19, after delaying any official statement, the King indicated during a visit to London that unless the United States succeeded in getting all foreign troops out of Lebanon and got Israel to stop building settlements on the West Bank, the talks could not get started.[39] Under these circumstances, and having linked (perhaps unwisely) progress on a troop-withdrawal agreement in Lebanon to the Reagan plan, the United States stepped up its efforts to keep the plan alive. Thus, President Reagan, on the one hand tied the promised sale to Israel of seventy-five F-16 fighter bombers to an Israeli agreement to withdraw from Lebanon, and on the other promised King Hussein that if Jordan joined the Middle East peace talks, the United States would try to bring about a halt to the building of Israeli settlements on the West Bank.[40]

Despite these U.S. actions, by the end of March it appeared that the Reagan plan was in deep trouble. On March 30, speaking at a Palestinian rally in Damascus, Arafat himself rejected the Reagan plan.[41] The Arafat rejection cast a predictable pall on the final round of the Arafat-Hussein talks in Jordan, and it was not surprising when on April 10 King Hussein, claiming that Arafat had reneged on an earlier agreement, stated that Jordan would not enter into the peace negotiations.[42] Hussein's statement was greeted with great relief by Moscow, which had long feared that Jordan would be attracted to the Reagan plan (which the Soviet leadership saw as an extension of Camp David). As *Pravda* correspondent Pavel Demchenko noted on April 13:

> The authors of the "Reagan Plan" have especially been counting on Jordan. The government of that country has announced, however, that it would make a final decision only after meeting with the lead-

ers of the Palestine Liberation Organization and would act only in concert with it. And now, after those meetings have ended, Amman has published a statement saying that, as in the past, Jordan will not hold talks on behalf of the Palestinians and refuses to take separate action to establish peace in the Middle East.

As the *New York Times* writes, Jordan's answer "killed President Reagan's plan."[43]

The American diplomatic position deteriorated still further in mid-April when, one week after King Hussein had announced his refusal to enter into peace negotiations, the U.S. embassy in Beirut was blown up by a car bomb, with a massive loss of life. Reacting to both events, President Reagan dispatched Secretary of State George Shultz to salvage the stalled Israeli-Lebanese talks and regain the momentum for the United States in Middle East diplomacy. As Shultz toured the region, shuttling back and forth between Beirut and Jerusalem, prospects for a Lebanese-Israeli agreement began to improve. Both Moscow and Damascus, for different reasons, wanted to see the Shultz mission fail. The USSR did not want to see any more Arab states following in Egypt's footsteps and agreeing to a U.S. blueprint for Middle East peace. Syria, for its part, had long sought the dominant position in Lebanon, and feared that any Lebanese-Israeli agreement would strengthen the Israeli position in Lebanon at Syria's expense. In addition, Syria also did not wish to see any more Arab states moving toward peace with Israel, since this would leave Syria increasingly isolated among the Arab confrontation states facing Israel. The end result was a rise in tension and a war scare in which Moscow was to play a role—albeit perhaps a somewhat unwilling one.

Less than a week after King Hussein refused to enter the peace talks, the Syrian government raised its price for a Lebanese troop withdrawal. While as late as January Syria had been willing to have a simultaneous withdrawal of Israeli, Syrian, and PLO forces, on April 16 the Syrian government, strengthened both by its new Soviet weapons and by the Soviet warning to Israel, stated that Syria would not even discuss the withdrawal of its troops from Lebanon until all Israeli troops had left the country.[44] While the United States sought to assuage Syrian opposition in a letter from Reagan to Assad in which the U.S. president indicated that the United States was still pressing for Israeli withdrawal from the Golan Heights,[45] the U.S. ploy was not successful. Indeed, Syria appeared to step up the tension by allowing guerrillas to infiltrate Israeli lines to attack Israeli troops while simultaneously accusing the Israeli government of reinforcing its troops in Lebanon's Bekaa Valley and of staging "provocative" military exercises on the Golan Heights.[46] Although Israeli Foreign Minister Shamir described the Syrian-induced tension as "artificial,"[47] Israeli Defense Minister Arens, concerned about Soviet and Syrian intentions, put Israeli troops on alert and indicated that Israel would not leave Lebanon until Syria did.[48] Syria then stepped up its pressure on April 26 when Syrian forces opened fire on an Israeli bulldozer near the cease-fire line.[49]

Meanwhile, despite the rise in Syrian-Israeli tension, U.S. Secretary of State Shultz continued to work for an Israeli-Lebanese troop withdrawal agreement, and on May 6 his efforts were crowned with success when the Israeli government accepted, in principle, a troop-withdrawal agreement that had already been agreed to by Lebanon.[50] The next U.S. goal was to try to gain general Arab support for the agreement, so as to pressure Syria into withdrawing its forces from Lebanon. As might be expected, though, neither Moscow nor Syria was in favor of a rapid Syrian withdrawal. Moscow, although interested in Syria ultimately withdrawing its troops from Lebanon, did not want any precipitate withdrawal in the aftermath of the Israeli-Lebanese agreement lest the United States reap the obvious diplomatic benefits. Syria, for its part, complained that Israel had profited too much from the treaty, and Damascus Radio asserted that Lebanon had "capitulated to the Israeli aggressor."[51]

As Syria was opposing the Israeli-Lebanese agreement, Moscow was cautiously supporting its Arab ally. Thus, on May 9, three days after Israel had agreed in principle to the accord, the Soviet Union issued an official statement denouncing the agreement, and in a gesture of support for Syria demanded that "first and foremost" Israeli troops be withdrawn from Lebanon. The statement added, however, that "American and other foreign troops staying in Lebanon also must be withdrawn from it"—an oblique reference to Moscow's continuing desire to see Syrian troops leave the country.[52] At the same time, perhaps to enhance the atmosphere of crisis, Soviet dependents were withdrawn from Beirut, although the Soviet ambassador to Lebanon was careful to state that the departure of the dependents was due to the beginning of summer camp in the USSR.[53] In helping to thicken the atmosphere of crisis, Moscow may also have been seizing the opportunity to once again play a role in the Middle East peace process, after having been kept on the diplomatic sidelines since Sadat's trip to Jerusalem in 1977. Indeed, on May 10, Shultz openly urged Moscow to use its influence to get Syria to withdraw its troops, adding that he might be willing to meet with Soviet Foreign Minister Gromyko to discuss the Middle East, along with other international issues.[54] Shultz, however, indicated that the United States was not yet ready for an international conference on the Middle East, still a cardinal goal of Soviet diplomacy.[55]

Nonetheless, in giving Syria even a limited degree of support, Moscow had to be concerned as to the possibility of war erupting, especially as Syria began to issue a series of increasingly bellicose threats—threats that included Soviet support for Syria in case of war.[56] Thus, on May 9 Syrian Foreign Minister Khaddam noted in an interview that in the event war between Israel and Syria broke out, "we believe that the USSR will fulfill its commitments in accordance with the [Soviet-Syrian] treaty."[57] The next day, Syrian Radio warned that any Israeli attack against Syrian forces anywhere, even in Lebanon, would mean an "unlimited war."[58] Syrian bellicosity, however, may have overstepped the bounds of propriety insofar as Moscow was concerned: in a broadcast over Beirut Radio, Soviet Ambassador to Lebanon Alexander Soldatov, when asked about Khaddam's assertion that Moscow would fully support Syria if war with Israel broke out, replied that "the USSR does not reply to such hypothetical questions."[59] (Soldatov added that the USSR continued to support the withdrawal of all foreign forces from Lebanon, however.) These themes of caution were repeated during the visit of a Soviet delegation to Israel in mid-May to attend ceremonies marking the thirty-eighth anniversary of the defeat of Nazi Germany. One of the leaders of the delegation, the well-known Soviet journalist Igor Belayev, took the opportunity to state upon his arrival at Ben Gurion Airport that Syria's recent military moves in the Bekaa Valley were purely defensive and that Syria had no aggressive intent toward Israel.[60]

Meanwhile, Syria continued to escalate the political and military pressure calculated to undermine the Israeli-Lebanese agreement. On the political front, it formed an alignment with a group of Lebanese leaders opposed to the agreement including former Lebanese premier Rashid Karami, former president Suleiman Franjieh, Druze leader Walid Jumblatt, and Lebanese Communist party first secretary George Hawi.[61] Given the fact that Jumblatt had a powerful militia behind him, Assad may have felt that he now had sufficient military, as well as political, support to sabotage the implementation of the agreement—or at least to maintain Syrian influence in Lebanon, should Syrian troops one day be withdrawn.

While moving to strengthen his political position in Lebanon, Assad also stepped up the political and military pressure in the Bekaa. After refusing to see U.S. Envoy Philip Habib, Assad on May 23 predicted a new war with Israel in which Syria would lose 20,000 men.[62] Two days later, Syrian planes fired air-to-air missiles against Israeli jets flying over the Bekaa Valley—the first such encounter since the war in 1982.[63] Assad followed this up by conducting military exercises in the Golan and Bekaa, and the risk of war appeared to heighten.[64] Nonetheless, except for a limited countermobilization, Israel kept very cool during the crisis, while for its part Moscow kept a very low profile (although it did send a new aircraft carrier into the Mediterranean)—supporting Syria politically but issuing no threats against the United States or Israel, while again appealing for full withdrawal of all foreign forces from Lebanon. In any case, by the end of May the crisis had subsided and the dangers of a Syrian-Israeli war in Lebanon for the time being at least, seemed to have lessened.

Moscow and the Gulf

While Moscow was pleased that the crisis ended without an escalation of the Syrian-Israeli conflict (and with U.S. efforts to gain centrist Arab support for the May 17 treaty apparently stymied), it faced a very sharp deterioration of its position in Iran. The Soviet-Iranian relationship had been deteriorating since 1982,[65] despite Soviet efforts to cultivate the regime of Ayatollah Khomeini. This had occurred in part because of an increase in the supply of Soviet military equipment to Iraq—a development publicly noted by Iraqi Foreign Minister Tariq Aziz in late February;[66] however, another major irritant in the relationship was the Communist party of Iran, the Tudeh, which Khomeini and the majority of his followers held in deep suspicion. In February, the First Secretary of the Tudeh, Nureddin Kianuri, and a number of other top party leaders were arrested on charges of espionage. Moscow vehemently denied the charge with a *Pravda* article on February 19 that blamed the arrest on the increased activity of "reactionary conservative forces in Iran which are trying to deal a blow against the progressive patriotic forces and at the same time damage Iranian-Soviet relations." The *Pravda* article went on to list the areas in which the Soviet Union had been aiding Iran since the fall of the shah, but also pointedly cited the comments by the late Soviet Party Secretary Leonid Brezhnev on the need for reciprocity in the Soviet-Iranian relationship.[67] If the *Pravda* article and its call for reciprocity were aimed at deterring the Khomeini regime from moving further against the Tudeh, the ploy was not to prove successful. On April 30 Kianuri made a public confession on Iranian television of having spied for the Soviet Union.[68] Four days later Iran expelled eighteen Soviet diplomats and dissolved the Tudeh party, declaring that "any activity on behalf of the party is now illegal."[69] Further clouding the anti-Soviet atmosphere in Iran were such slogans as "Britain is bad; America is worse than Britain; and the Soviet Union is worse than both of them."[70]

The first Soviet response to the Iranian action came in the form of a *Pravda* editorial on May 6 that not only denied that Tudeh members had been spying for the USSR, but also asserted that their confessions had been extracted by torture. In addition, the editorial noted that the USSR had lodged a "resolute protest" against the Iranian government's "arbitrary" and "groundless" expulsion of the Soviet diplomats. Nonetheless, it was still in Moscow's interest to preserve some ties with Iran, lest Iran begin to gravitate toward the West (a possibility noted in the *Pravda* editorial). For this reason, Moscow's counteractions against Iran were limited to 1) editorial denunciations of the Iranian authorities as a whole, without mentioning Khomeini by name; 2) a more sympathetic purview of the Iraqi position in the Iran-Iraq war (which Moscow continued to deplore, as it had since the war erupted in 1980); and 3) the expulsion of three Iranian diplomats from Moscow.[71]

At the same time Moscow was seeking to prevent any further deterioration of Soviet-Iranian ties, it also had to be concerned about a tilt of Iraq toward the West. Thus, as Iraq's position in the Iran-Iraq war worsened, Baghdad not only signed an oil-for-arms deal with France—in January, in a *Le Monde* interview, Iraq's Foreign Minister Tariq Aziz stated that France was Iraq's "main political, economic, military, and trading partner"[72]—and improved relations with Egypt, but also began to cautiously cultivate the United States. Thus, in early January President Saddam Hussein of Iraq, in a major policy change, publicly indicated that "it was necessary to have a state of security for the Israelis" in any peace settlement.[73] This was followed in May by a meeting between Iraqi Foreign Minister Aziz and U.S. Secretary of State Shultz in Paris for what the Iraqi leader later said were "useful talks."[74] Despite continuing U.S.–Iraqi friction over the presence of Palestinian terrorist Abu Nidal in Iraq,[75] Iraqi–U.S. relations continued to improve: an Iraqi foreign ministry representative visited Washington in early September[76] and the new U.S. Middle East envoy, Donald Rumsfeld, visited Baghdad in December—the first visit of such a senior U.S. official to the Iraqi capital since the June 1967 Arab-Israeli war.[77]

As Franco-Iraqi and U.S.-Iraqi relations improved, the USSR moved to improve its relations with Iraq to counterbalance the Iraqi tilt toward the West. Thus, while continuing to both maintain official neutrality in the Iran-Iraq war and to call for as rapid as possible an end to the conflict from which it claimed "only the imperialists" benefited, Moscow stepped up its arms shipments to Iraq and began to more openly criticize Iran for continuing the war. Thus, while praising Iraq's ceasefire proposal of June 1983, a commentary in *Pravda* by Yuri Glukhov on November 14 criticized Iran's rejection of it, blaming the rejection on "chauvinistic attitudes" in Tehran. In addition, Moscow publicized a visit by Tariz Aziz to the Soviet Union in late November, during which the USSR again called for a rapid end to the Iran-Iraq war, adding that Moscow would continue to work for a political settlement of the conflict. Nonetheless, the visit was clearly marked by disagreement on a number of issues: the *Pravda* report described the talks as having taken place in a "frank and friendly atmosphere," observing that there had been "an exchange of views" on the situation in the Middle East and on Soviet-Iraqi relations.[78]

Moscow and the Split in Fatah

While Moscow continued to be concerned about the weakening of its position in both Iran and Iraq, it was also confronted by a serious split in the PLO that occurred in mid-May when Syria moved to undermine Arafat's authority within the most important of the PLO's numerous factions, Fatah, by aiding a rebel movement in that organization. The revolt was led by Abu Musa, a hardliner who not only vehemently opposed any settlement with Israel[79] but was also outspoken in his opposition to a Jordanian-PLO negotiating arrangement.

The revolt against Arafat underlined the PLO leader's weakened position in the aftermath of the Israeli invasion of Lebanon, which had eliminated his main base of operations. While he was supported by the bulk of Palestinians living outside Syria and Syrian-controlled regions in Lebanon, and while both Iraq and Algeria gave him support

in the Arab world's diplomatic arena, he had no real power to resist
Syria's crackdown against him. Thus, as the summer wore on, the positions of Arafat's supporters in the Bekaa Valley of Lebanon were
overrun, and Arafat himself was expelled from Syria. In early August,
the Palestine Central Council, meeting in Tunis, called for an "immediate dialogue" to rebuild relations with Syria.[80] However, this effort, along with others attempted during the summer, proved to no
avail and in early September Arafat, who had once again begun to
meet with Jordanian officials, admitted that all attempts at negotiations with Syria had failed.[81]

As the revolt within Fatah accelerated, Moscow was faced by another of its serious problems of choice. On the one hand, a victory of
Fatah hardliners would make it even more difficult for Moscow to succeed in promoting its Middle East peace plan. In addition, the very
split within Fatah, and the fact that Iraq and Algeria, key Arab countries, were backing Arafat against the Syrian-supported opposition,
further underlined the disunity in the Arab world—one more obstacle in the way of the "anti-imperialist" Arab unity Moscow had sought
for so long. On the other hand, however, Moscow could not have been
too unhappy with the fact that Arafat was being punished for his flir-
tation with the Reagan plan. In any case, in any showdown between
Assad and Arafat the imperatives of realpolitik impelled Moscow to
side with Assad, who in the aftermath of the Israeli invasion of Lebanon headed the most important Arab state opposing U.S. diplomacy
in the Middle East, and who had granted to Moscow the use of Syrian
naval and air force facilities as well.[82]

Given this situation, about all Moscow could do was deplore the
divisions within the PLO while continuing to plead for Palestinian unity and PLO cooperation with Syria.[83] Nonetheless, a procession of
PLO officials, including Salah Khalaf, Naef Hawatmeh, and Farouk
Kaddoumi, journeyed to Moscow in June and July in an apparent effort to get the USSR to intervene, but to no avail. While PLO media
frequently reported that the USSR was backing Arafat,[84] no public
statement of support from Moscow was forthcoming. The most Moscow would do was denounce the split within the PLO, as the *Pravda*
description of Kaddoumi's talks in Moscow noted:

> The Soviet side expressed its firm opinion about the impermissibil-
> ity of strife and internecine dissension among the Palestinians faced
> with the Israeli aggressor, for they weaken the forces of the Palestin-

ians and decimate the ranks of the Arabs. Discord within the PLO
can and should be overcome by political means, through a dialogue.[85]

The fact that the talks were described as having taken place in an
atmosphere of "mutual understanding" indicates that the two sides
remained far apart, and this may have been the reason that Arafat did
not undertake a rumored visit to Moscow after Kaddoumi's trip.[86]
About the only positive development Moscow could have seen from
the conflict within the PLO was the decision by Naef Hawatmeh's
Democratic Front for the Liberation of Palestine and George Habash's
Popular Front for the Liberation of Palestine to establish a single military and political leadership, since this was a step (albeit a small one)
toward Palestinian unity.[87]

One of the reasons Moscow was standing on the sidelines during
the clash between Assad's forces and those of Arafat may have been
that the Soviet leadership was concerned lest the unpredictable Assad yet strike a deal with the United States over Lebanon. While Syria
indicated that long-time U.S. mediator Philip Habib was persona non
grata in Damascus, it did receive U.S. Secretary of State George
Shultz in July, and Habib's replacement, Robert McFarlane, in August
for talks about a Syrian troop withdrawal from Lebanon. In addition,
although Assad continued to denounce the May 17 Israeli-Lebanese
agreement and to assert that Syria would not pull its forces out of Lebanon unless all Israeli forces left "without any political gains," he did
agree to establish a working group with the United States to consider
restoration of Lebanon's unity and independence.[88] He also helped secure the release of the kidnapped president of the American University of Beirut, David Dodge, who had been abducted in the summer of
1982.[89]

While maintaining contact with the United States, Assad was also
strengthening Syria's position in Lebanon. In addition to bringing Arafat's forces in the Bekaa under his control, he was profiting from the
growing war-weariness of Israel, which was planning a unilateral
withdrawal of its forces from the Chouf Mountains and seemed in no
mood to go to war to throw the Syrians out of Lebanon. Indeed, on
June 1 Prime Minister Begin had stated that Israel was not preparing
to attack Syria,[90] and a week later Israel's Deputy Foreign Minister Ye-
huda Ben-Meir ruled out the use of military action to remove Syrian
forces from Lebanon.[91] One month later Shultz stated that U.S. Marines would not fill any vacuum created by a unilateral withdrawal of
Israel from Lebanon.[92]

Under these circumstances Assad was able to fill the vacuum with
Syrian-backed forces, in large part because of mistakes by the Lebanese government. By July, the Lebanese government of Amin Gemayel had alienated two of the major forces within Lebanon, the
Druze and the Shiites. In part because he did not establish an equi-
table power-sharing system, and in part because Phalangist policies
in the Chouf Mountains and in Shiite areas of Beirut angered the
Druze and Shiites, they entered into an alignment with Syria. Druze
leader Walid Jumblatt assumed the leadership of the newly proclaimed "National Salvation Front," whose members included Rashid
Karami (a Sunni Muslim) and Suleiman Franjieh (a Christian opponent of Gemayel), while Shiite leader Nabih Berri gave tacit support
to the organization.[93]

The strengthening of the Syrian position in Lebanon was, on balance, a plus for Moscow, since by the end of August U.S. diplomatic
efforts to secure a troop-withdrawal agreement from Lebanon had all
but collapsed and Moscow was again raising the possibility of a joint
U.S.–Soviet effort to bring about a Middle East peace settlement.[94]
Yet the situation also had its dangers for the USSR. As Israel prepared
to withdraw its troops from the Chouf Mountains, the possibility that
new fighting would erupt became increasingly strong—particularly
since no agreement had been reached between the Druze and Gemayel about deploying the Lebanese army in the Chouf to replace the
departing Israelis. Exacerbating the situation was the Syrian government statement on August 27 to the effect that it would defend its allies against the Lebanese army.[95] The danger for Moscow lay in the
fact that the United States was backing the Gemayel government;
consequently, a direct U.S.–Syrian confrontation could occur, in
which case Moscow would again face the problem of how to react to a
military conflict in which its principal Arab ally was involved. This
time, however, the opponent would most likely not be Israel (backed
by the United States), but the United States itself. In short, Moscow
faced the prospect of a superpower confrontation over Lebanon;
when the crisis did occur, however, the USSR adopted a very cautious
policy designed to avoid any direct involvement.

The September 1983 Crisis in Lebanon

The crisis began at the end of August when warfare broke out between the Lebanese government and the Shiites of western and southern Beirut; the latter resisted a Lebanese army push into their neighborhoods on August 30 and 31. The scale of fighting escalated sharply,
however, after the Israeli redeployment of September 3, with Syrian-

support Druze forces clashing with both the Maronite (Phalange) militia and the Lebanese army. While the Phalangist forces were all but
driven from the Chouf Mountains, the Lebanese army proved a
tougher opponent for the Druze, and a major battle was fought for the
strategic mountain town of Souk el-Gharb, which overlooked Beirut.
While Israel held off from intervening both because of pressure from
its Druze minority and because of assurances from Druze leader
Walid Jumblatt that he would not permit the PLO to occupy positions
in Druze-controlled areas, the United States decided to play an active
role in the fighting in support of the Lebanese army (which it was
training). (United States involvement in the conflict had actually begun before the Israeli withdrawal, when U.S. helicopters fired on sniper and mortar positions that had harassed the Marines.) The U.S.
role escalated during the fighting in the Chouf as guns from U.S. warships in Beirut harbor were fired both in support of Lebanese army
troops fighting in Souk el-Gharb,[96] and against artillery positions that
were firing on or near U.S. positions.[97] After at first holding aloof from
the fighting, France also got involved when its forces came under
fire.[98] As the fighting escalated, Syria felt constrained to issue threats
against the United States in support of its clients in the Chouf
Mountains[99]—particularly as the U.S. battleship *New Jersey,* whose
sixteen-inch guns had the capability of seriously damaging Syrian positions, neared Beirut.

As the crisis developed, Moscow reacted very cautiously. A Tass
statement published in *Pravda* on September 1, noting that the Soviet Union was "deeply concerned" over U.S. armed intervention in
Lebanon, called for an end to that intervention as well as for the unconditional withdrawal of Israeli forces from Lebanon and the withdrawal of U.S. troops and any "foreign troops that arrived with them."
Interestingly enough, there were no Soviet threats against the United
States, although Moscow may have balanced its caution with the implicit support of Syria's right to remain in Lebanon, since there was
no mention of any Syrian withdrawal in the Tass statement—a clear
shift from earlier Soviet policy.

The rapid escalation of the crisis, however, posed both problems
and opportunities for the USSR. Moscow seized on the U.S. involvement in the fighting to discredit American policy in the Middle East
by asserting that the United States was now directly fighting the
Arabs. Vladimir Kudravtzev, one of *Izvestia*'s more colorful commentators, emphasized this Soviet propaganda line with the statement,

"By shedding the blood of Arab patriots, the United States has de facto declared war on the Arabs."[100] In addition, Soviet commentators also seized on the intervention to discredit the U.S. Rapid Deployment Force (RDF), whose forces, it claimed, were fighting in Lebanon.[101] Moscow also sought to exploit the Lebanese fighting to divert attention from its shooting down of a Korean airliner in early September. Nonetheless, as American participation in the fighting grew, Moscow faced the dilemma of whether or not it should get directly involved, particularly as Syrian positions came under American fire. The Soviet press, perhaps to prepare the Soviet public for a heightened crisis, noted the escalation of the fighting, and also noted Syria's warning to the United States that it would fire back if fired upon.[102]

Nonetheless, on September 20—the day after *Pravda* published the Syrian warning—the same Soviet newspaper published a Tass statement that carefully avoided any hint of Soviet involvement in the fighting. While it accused the United States of trying to intimidate Syria, and of seeking to establish its own hegemony in the Middle East, it issued no warning to the United States other than to state that Washington would not "evade responsibility" for the consequences of the escalated fighting.[103] To be sure, Moscow did not deny reports in the Kuwaiti press that the USSR had placed its forces in the southern part of the country on alert, and that a joint Soviet-Syrian operations room was monitoring the situation in Lebanon.[104] In addition, Moscow rejected a U.S. request to cooperate in limiting Syrian participation in the conflict.[105] Nonetheless, Moscow refused to formally offer military support to Syria—nor did it react to statements by Syrian officials that Damascus might turn to the USSR for help.[106] It also ignored the leftist Lebanese newspaper *As-Safir*'s report that Assad had made a secret trip to Moscow in mid-September.[107] Perhaps most important of all, throughout the crisis Moscow failed to publicly comment on the Soviet-Syrian treaty. In sum, Soviet behavior during the crisis was very cautious indeed, and it is not surprising that Moscow, which feared a superpower confrontation over Lebanon (an area of only tertiary interest to the USSR), warmly welcomed the ceasefire that finally ended the crisis.[108]

Looking back upon the September 1983 crisis, it is clear that it differed substantially from the one four months earlier. In May, Assad had been basically in control of the situation and had maneuvered accordingly. Since that crisis centered on what was essentially a *political* issue (the Israeli-Lebanese treaty), Syrian mobilizations and threats of war were essentially political acts, and as such unlikely to get out of control. In September, by comparison, the crisis was essentially a military one, and one that escalated rapidly. Under these circumstances, it is not surprising that the USSR refrained from giving Syria any overt support during the crisis.

Syria did not complain publicly about the lack of Soviet aid (thus repeating the strategy it followed during the Israeli invasion of June 1982), although Damascus could not have been too happy with the situation. Syria expressed its anger more openly against its fellow Arabs, intimating that whatever the position of the Arab governments, the Arab masses supported Syria.[109] The lack of Soviet and Arab support, coupled with the U.S. Congress's agreement to extend the stay of U.S. Marines in Beirut for an additional eighteen months and the arrival near Beirut of the U.S. battleship *New Jersey,* seem to have persuaded Assad that at least a temporary compromise was in order; he therefore agreed to a Saudi-mediated ceasefire plan that held out the possibility of a new distribution of power in Lebanon.[110] No sooner had the ceasefire been achieved, however, than Assad moved to further strengthen Syria's position in Lebanon by expelling the remaining troops loyal to Arafat from the Bekaa Valley, forcing them to go over the mountains to Tripoli where Arafat had suddenly appeared in mid-September.

In the aftermath of the ceasefire, the Soviet Union adopted what, on the surface, appeared to be a contradictory policy toward Syria. On the one hand, perhaps to assuage Syrian unhappiness at the lack of support during its confrontation with the United States in September, Moscow dispatched to Syria modern SS-21 ground-to-ground missiles with a range of seventy miles—enough to strike deep into Israel—and with greater accuracy than either the SCUD or Frog missiles previously supplied.[111] On the other hand, perhaps out of concern that Syria might become involved in a major confrontation with the United States if the Lebanese ceasefire should break down, Moscow downplayed its military relationship with Syria. With Andropov ill, a major Soviet campaign to prevent the deployment of U.S. Pershing II and cruise missiles underway in Western Europe, and Moscow still trying to overcome the negative effects of the Korean airliner incident, the time was not opportune for the USSR to become involved in a Middle Eastern war. Thus, Soviet treatment of the third anniversary of the Soviet-Syrian treaty was very low-key as far as Soviet military aid was concerned. A *New Times* article commemorating the treaty, for example, emphasized that Soviet aid had enabled Syria to enhance its defense potential, and that the Syrian leaders had themselves repeatedly stressed that they possessed the means to repulse an aggressor.[112] Similarly, a *Pravda* commentary by Yuri Glukhov on October 8 cited the Syrian prime minister's statement that Syria relied on its own efforts first, and only then on the assistance of its friends. Perhaps to reinforce the point that the first friends Syria should look to for help were its fellow Arabs, an Arabic language broadcast commemorating the tenth anniversary of the 1973 Arab-Israeli war asserted that the effectiveness of aid from the Socialist countries would have increased manyfold had the Arab states themselves united to fight the aggressor.[113]

In addition, as if to disassociate Moscow from the possibility of intervening, a major Arabic language broadcast on November 3 minimized the Soviet military presence in Syria, borrowing the by now familiar Soviet practice of citing Syrian statements to the effect that "Syria has enough means at its disposal to defend itself." The broadcast also asserted that "there is no Soviet military presence in Syria at all, only experts helping Syria bolster its defense capability," and that Syria had "repeatedly replied vehemently to the lie of the alleged Soviet military presence on its soil."[114]

The December 1983 Crisis in Lebanon

Nonetheless, as tensions rose in Lebanon following the blowing up of the U.S. Marine headquarters (and the subsequent U.S. invasion of Grenada), Moscow evidently felt constrained to issue another warning to the United States, if only to show its support for the "progressive" Lebanese forces backed by Syria. Thus, on November 4 a Soviet government Tass statement, citing remarks by Reagan, Weinberger, and Shultz, stated that the United States was planning a "massive strike against Lebanese national patriotic forces," and warned the United States "with all seriousness" against taking such action.[115] As had been the case with the March 30 warning to Israel, however, the Soviet warning of November 4 was very limited. Not only was there no mention of Syria (let alone of the Soviet-Syrian treaty), there was not even the usual Soviet statement pointing out that the Middle East lay close to the southern borders of the USSR. Likewise, when *Pravda* commentator Pavel Demchenko two days later stated specifically that the United States was preparing "an act of retribution against Syria," he omitted any Soviet warning to the United States as well as any reference to the Soviet-Syrian treaty.[116]

While Moscow was thus seeking to limit its involvement during this period of mounting tension, Assad was exploiting the possibility of an escalated U.S.–Syrian confrontation to crack down on the last redoubt of Arafat's supporters: the refugee camps north of Tripoli. At the same time, it was announced that Syrian Foreign Minister Abdul Khaddam would shortly visit the Soviet Union.[117] It is not known whether the Khaddam visit was at the initiative of Moscow (which was unhappy with Assad's crackdown on Arafat's forces) or of Damascus. Whoever initiated it, it was clearly Damascus that exploited the atmosphere surrounding the visit. Thus, despite American and Israeli statements that they were not going to attack Syria, Assad mobilized his army on November 8.[118] While Moscow noted the Syrian mobilization in an Arabic language broadcast on November 9, adding that Syria was exerting its additional defense efforts with the help of the USSR on the basis of their bilateral treaty, the broadcast also stated that "the substance of this treaty is very well known."[119] The purpose of this qualification to the treaty may well have been to remind the Arabs that the treaty did not cover Syrian activities in Lebanon. Indeed, the latter part of the broadcast was devoted to a call for the Arabs to strengthen their unity and act collectively in the face of the U.S. threat. Interestingly enough, in a possible backhand slap at Syria, the broadcast also noted Soviet support "for the efforts of some Arab states aimed at healing the rift in the ranks of the Palestinian resistance movement and at consolidating the ranks of the Arabs."

While Moscow was urging the Arabs to unite on an "anti-imperialist" basis, Assad appeared to be painting his Soviet allies into a corner in which they had no choice but to support him, regardless of what he did to Arafat's forces. Thus, on the eve of Khaddam's visit to the USSR, Syrian forces opened fire on four American reconnaissance planes.[120] At the same time, the Syrian ambassador to Britain was stating in a television interview that a conflict caused by U.S. "aggression" against Syria would not be confined to one area, but would be "large scale because of the help which we are supposed to get from our brothers and friends."[121]

Thus, Syrian Foreign Minister Khaddam flew on to Moscow in the midst of a crisis which, like the one in May, seemed to have been orchestrated by Assad (who, at this critical moment, suddenly became seriously ill). For its part, Moscow could not have been too pleased either with Syrian claims to Soviet aid in a widened conflict or to Syria's crackdown on Arafat's forces in the Tripoli area: Moscow still ap-

peared to wish to see Arafat, and the PLO, as independent actors in
the Middle East who would eventually need Soviet support, rather
than as a dependent element of Syria. A sentence in Gromyko's
luncheon speech to Khaddam made this point very clear:

> We regard as highly important and urgent the need for overcoming
> strife and restoring unity within the ranks of the liberation move-
> ment of the Arab people of Palestine which must remain an active
> and effective factor of the anti-imperialist struggle in the Middle
> East.[122]

Gromyko also pointedly called for increased Arab unity, stating "the
fact is that the enemies of the Arabs seek, in no small measure, to rely
on their aggressive policy precisely on this disunity."
   While Gromyko also condemned U.S. and Israeli threats against
the Lebanese National Patriotic Forces and Syria, he pointedly refrained from mentioning the Soviet-Syrian treaty. Khaddam, in his
return speech, totally ignored the Palestinian issue while pointedly
mentioning, in a segment of his speech ignored by *Pravda* but reported by Damascus Radio, that Soviet support "helped Syria in its
steadfastness" and "enabled it to confront aggression."[123] Khaddam
did, however, state Syrian aims in Lebanon that seemed to coincide
with those of the Soviet Union: the renunciation of the May 17 agreement; the full withdrawal of Israeli and multinational forces; and the
achievement of national unity and the restoration of security in Lebanon. The joint communiqué issued at the conclusion of the talks reflected the clearly differing viewpoints of the two sides as it reported
an "exchange of opinions"—the usual Soviet code words for *disagreement*—"regarding the U.S. and Israeli threats against Syria and
the danger of aggression against Syria in this connection."[124] Moscow
did, however, give a general statement of support for Syria against
"the intrigues of imperialism and Zionism," and "confirmed its adherence" to its commitments under the terms of the Soviet-Syrian
treaty.
   If Moscow felt that it had succeeded in getting Syria to moderate
its pressure on Arafat as a result of the Khaddam visit to Moscow, developments soon proved otherwise. Indeed, soon after Khaddam's return to Damascus, Syrian-backed troops stepped up their attacks on
Arafat's forces, driving them out of the two Palestinian refugee camps
north of Tripoli and into the city itself. It is possible that Assad felt

equal to withstanding Soviet pressure because at the same time his
forces were fighting Arafat's followers near Tripoli, U.S. National Security Adviser Robert McFarlane was warning Syria that the United
States would retaliate if Syria continued to fire on U.S. reconnaissance planes (he specifically reminded Damascus of what the United
States had done in Grenada),[125] and French and Israeli planes were
attacking purported terrorist bases in parts of Lebanon under Syrian
control.[126] Indeed, at the height of the fighting in Tripoli, Syrian Defense Minister Mustafa Tlas was threatening suicide attacks against
U.S. warships and proclaiming that the USSR would never allow Syria
to be defeated.[127] At the same time, Assad, in a Syrian telecast of his
interview with the American columnists Evans and Novak, was
stressing the possibility of a Soviet-American confrontation if a new
war broke out.[128]

As the twin Lebanese crises escalated, Moscow increased its rhetorical activity. An article by Demchenko in *Pravda* on November 17
cited McFarlane's comments on Grenada, noting that the United
States and Israel counted "on deriving the maximum advantage from
the present situation in the region, which is complex enough as it is,
with the senseless Iran-Iraq war continuing, inter-Arab discord exacerbated, and the PLO's internal differences having led to bloody
clashes between rival groupings." He then appealed for cooperation
among all "anti-imperialist" forces, to counter the "dangerous development of events" and the U.S.–Israeli threats. Two days later, a
Pravda editorial discussing the fighting in Tripoli made the point
even more stongly:

> It is no accident that the inter-Palestinian discord is being exploited
> in the framework of the anti-Syrian campaign unleashed by impe-
> rialist circles. In these conditions, the senseless and perverse na-
> ture of the fratricidal clashes in northern Lebanon are particularly
> vivid.[129]

The editorial also quoted from Gromyko's luncheon address during
Khaddam's visit where the Soviet foreign minister had stressed that
the PLO "had to continue to operate as an active and effective factor
of the antiimperialist struggle in the Near East." The editorial went on
to say that Moscow was taking "active political steps to end the conflict."

As the Tripoli fighting escalated still further despite Soviet pleas,

Moscow stepped up the level of its public complaints with an appeal from the Soviet Afro-Asian Peoples Solidarity Organization. Reminiscent of similar pleas at the time of Syrian-PLO fighting during the Syrian intervention in Lebanon in 1976,[130] the AAPSO called for an end to the "senseless bloodshed," the restoration of unity in the ranks of the Palestinians; and the consolidation of all Arab anti-imperialist forces "in the face of the mounting military and political pressure on the part of the USA, Israel and their allies."[131]

Perhaps as a gesture to Arafat, Gromyko received Farouk Kaddoumi, one of Arafat's closest allies in the PLO, on November 23. The fact that *Pravda* described the talks as having taken place in a "friendly, businesslike atmosphere," however, indicated that little agreement was reached (and that Kaddoumi was probably told Moscow would not take action against Syria), although Gromyko promised to help "in any way possible" to achieve a settlement among the Palestinian factions.[132] Fortunately for Moscow, however, an uneasy ceasefire was achieved in Tripoli several days later—although to what degree Saudi inducement, Soviet pressure, and/or the realization that Arafat continued to have widespread support in the Arab world and among Palestinians influenced Assad to agree to halt the fighting is not yet clear. In any case, Moscow warmly praised the ceasefire in an Arabic language "Window on the Arab World" broadcast on November 26,[133] and three days later a joint Soviet party-government statement on the "international day of solidarity with the Palestinian people" saluted Arafat as the chairman of the PLO executive committee.[134] At the same time, it called for unity within the organization and its "close collaboration" with "those countries that are in the forefront of resistance to the U.S. and Israel" (i.e. Syria), as Moscow continued to try to maintain good relations with both Arafat and Assad.

While Moscow was clearly relieved by the Tripoli ceasefire (however tentative that may have been), it had to be concerned with the rise in U.S.–Syrian tensions. United States Defense Secretary Weinberger had asserted on November 22 that the attack on the Marine headquarters had been undertaken by Iranians with the "sponsorship and knowledge and authority of the Syrian government."[135] While Syria rejected the charge, [136] it again asserted that its planes had driven off U.S. jets flying over Syrian-controlled areas.[137] At this point, with the ceasefire holding in Tripoli, Moscow moved again to champion Syria: a *Novosti* article by Demchenko that was distributed to Western correspondents warned that Syria was an ally of Moscow, with whom it had a Treaty of Friendship and Cooperation, and that aggression against Syria was an "extremely dangerous venture." He also noted that the potential of forces opposing U.S. and Israeli policy in Syria and Lebanon did not compare "in any way with what the Pentagon faced on Grenada."[138] This was the strongest warning given by Moscow to the United States thus far in the Lebanese crisis, and was perhaps aimed at deterring the United States from any strike against Syria—although the fact that it took the form of a *Novosti* article, rather than a Tass statement, indicated it was still low-level. Nonetheless, such a warning again raised questions of Soviet credibility should a Syrian-American confrontation take place, either in the form of an American retaliation for the Marine headquarters explosion or an attack on Syrian positions in Lebanon in retaliation for the firing on the U.S. reconnaissance planes. Syrian government statements such as the one broadcast on Syrian radio on November 29 ("Syria expresses its pride—before the Arab nation and the world—at the fact that it agitates a superpower")[139] appeared to make some form of confrontation even more likely.

The U.S. attack came on December 4, following Syrian antiaircraft fire on U.S. reconnaissance planes the previous day. The fact that the United States lost two planes, with one pilot killed and the other captured, did not detract from the fact that the United States had openly attacked Syria and that a major confrontation was underway. Under these circumstances, Moscow was again faced with the dilemma of either supporting its client's policies in Lebanon—policies that the USSR did not entirely agree with—or losing still more of its diplomatic credibility, particularly since Reagan was threatening to strike Syrian positions again if U.S. forces continued to come under attack.[140]

Once again Moscow was to take a cautious stand, although its diplomatic credibility was to suffer. Thus, a Tass statement noted simply that the Soviet Union "declared its solidarity with the peoples of Lebanon, Syria, and other Arab countries in defending their independence" and that "the aggressive actions of the United States against Syria constitute a serious threat to peace not only in the Middle East region."[141] The Tass statement also sought a propaganda advantage by tying the U.S. attack to the strategic cooperation agreement concluded between Reagan and Israeli Prime Minister Yitzhak Shamir a week earlier, and claimed that by its attack the United States no longer qualified as an "honest broker" in the Middle East. However, the failure of the Tass statement to mention the Soviet-Syrian treaty indicated that Syria could not expect more than Soviet moral support in its confrontation with the United States—so long as the confrontation was limited to Lebanon.

While Moscow was not willing to aid Syria militarily in its confrontation with the United States, the USSR did seek to use the American attack against Syria to undermine the U.S. position in the Middle East. Thus, a *Pravda* editorial on December 10 repeated the Tass themes that the United States no longer qualified as a mediator in the Arab-Israeli conflict and that the U.S. attack was the outgrowth of U.S.–Israeli strategic cooperation. The editorial went on to assert that the United States was now out of favor even in conservative Arab countries, and that Moscow once again appealed for Arab unity on an "anti-imperialist" basis. An Arabic language broadcast on December 12 carried this theme still further, asserting that when the United States signed its "strategic alliance" with Israel it challenged "all Arabs without exception, the progressives and moderates alike."[142] Interestingly enough, however, the broadcast mentioned Soviet support for Syria only in passing, again calling on the Arabs to unite and use their economic pressure against the United States. It seems clear that Moscow, unwilling to use force to aid Syria, had gone back to the course of action it had pursued since the September crisis: an appeal to the Arabs themselves to help Syria. Unfortunately for the USSR, however, which hoped that the U.S. attack would force the centrist Arabs to again rally around Syria and what was left of the Steadfastness Front, this was not to happen. With Syria's ally, Iran, again threatening to close the Straits of Hormuz, the centrist Arabs—and particularly the members of the Gulf Cooperation Council—had no choice but to rely on the United States for help. Syria, to its apparent bitter disappointment, also realized this soon after the U.S. attack as the Syrian media bewailed the lack of Arab support. As *Al Ba'ath* noted on December 8:

It is illogical to have Arab resources remain idle, waiting for the circle of aggression to reach them. It is also illogical to restrict the role of this or that Arab country to mere condemnation or denunciation of the aggressor.[143]

The end result was that Syria, with neither Soviet nor Arab support against the United States, and with its efforts to topple Arafat as leader of the PLO only moderately successful (the PLO leader, who continued to command widespread Palestinian support, left Tripoli under the United Nations flag), moved to deescalate the tension. Thus, it returned the body of the dead U.S. airman to the United States; agreed to talk to U.S. mediator Donald Rumsfeld (despite the fact that the battleship *New Jersey* was firing on Syrian positions after U.S. reconnaissance planes had again been fired upon); and, finally, in a gesture which it said was aimed at "creating a circumstance conducive to the withdrawal of U.S. forces from Lebanon," released the captured U.S. airman, Lieutenant Goodman.[144] This was a major Syrian concession, given the fact that Syrian leaders had earlier said that he would not be released until after the "war" was over and U.S. forces had withdrawn from Lebanon.[145]

It is clear that Assad, now recovered from his illness, was trying to exploit the rising tide of opposition in the United States to the Marine presence in Lebanon; nonetheless, to release the airman at a time when U.S. naval guns were still pounding Syrian positions indicated that the Syrian leader realized that his confrontation with the United States held the danger of getting out of control at a time when he could count on neither Soviet nor Arab support. Fortunately for Assad—and for Moscow—the release of Lieutenant Goodman increased the clamor in the United States for a pullout of the Marines from Lebanon, a clamor that was reflected in the U.S. Congress.[146] At the same time, the position of Amin Gemayel weakened considerably as negotiations for a disengagement plan among the various warring Lebanese factions broke down at the end of January. The diplomatic impasse was followed by heavy fighting in the Beirut area between the Lebanese army and Druze and Shiite forces, a development that led to the virtual collapse of the Lebanese army, the resignation of Prime Minister Wazzan, and the seizure of West Beirut by Moslem militias. As chaos appeared to reign in Beirut, President Reagan suddenly announced the "redeployment" of U.S. Marines to Navy ships off the coast of Lebanon.[147] The U.S. redeployment, which was soon to be followed in kind by the other members of the multinational force, was accompanied by American naval shelling of anti-Government positions in the vicinity of Beirut, although the rationale for the shelling was never clearly explained by the Reagan administration.[148] Indeed, the general course of U.S. policy during this period seemed confused at best, and whatever mistakes the United States had made in backing the Gemayel government up until this point, the hurried exodus of the Marines from Beirut, and what now appeared to be indiscriminate artillery fire into the Lebanese mountains could only hurt the U.S. image—not only in Lebanon, but in the Middle East as a whole. Naturally, such a weakening of the U.S. position was welcomed by Moscow, which moved to coordinate policy directly with Syria following the Moslem takeover of West Beirut. On February 8, *Pravda* announced that Geydar Aliyev, the only Politburo member of Shii Muslim extraction, would be going to Syria for a "working visit." Just before Aliyev was to depart, however, Andropov became the second Soviet leader to die during the Lebanese crisis.

Soviet Policy toward the Middle East Under Chernenko

The Collapse of the U.S. Position in Lebanon

The succession to power of Konstantin Chernenko was quite rapid, and the new Soviet leader soon moved to exploit the U.S. defeat in Lebanon. The first issue pertaining to the Lebanese crisis facing Chernenko was a French proposal to replace the multinational force in Beirut with a United Nations force. The Soviet leadership vetoed the French plan, ostensibly because it would not prevent the United States from continuing to shell Syrian and pro-Syrian forces in Lebanon behind the screen of the U.N. troops. It would appear, however, that the primary reason for the Soviet veto of the French proposal was to prevent the United States from using the insertion of a U.N. force as a cover for the American retreat from Lebanon, a development which might dull the impact of the U.S. defeat.[149]

Moscow was to achieve another success for its Lebanese policy when Amin Gemayel, now virtually bereft of U.S. military support, was forced to turn to Assad for aid in staying in power. Assad, at least in the short term, proved willing to do so—for a price. The price was the abrogation of the May 17 Israeli-Lebanese agreement, and Gemayel duly announced its abrogation on March 5. Yet even as Moscow was hailing this development (Soviet commentators were to call it a major blow to the entire Camp David process); even as Aliyev was getting ready again to journey to Damascus, there remained a number of problems that the new Soviet leadership had to face despite the collapse of the U.S. position in Lebanon. In the first place, a power struggle had erupted in Damascus over the succession to President Hafiz Assad, who had apparently not fully recovered from his heart attack. Second, despite its victory in Lebanon (which the Syrian media were hailing as equivalent to Nasser's nationalization of the Suez Canal),[150] Syria remained in diplomatic isolation in the Arab world, while Egypt continued to improve its ties to the various centrist Arab states. Egypt's rapprochement with the centrist Arabs was reinforced by the surprise visit of Arafat to Cairo after his expulsion from Lebanon in December 1983 (Arafat later went also to Jordan, where he resumed discussions with King Hussein), and was highlighted by the decision of the Islamic Conference to readmit Egypt to its ranks in mid-January—a development Moscow attributed to the "pressure of conservative Moslem regimes."[151] Nonetheless, the fact that Libya, Syria, and South Yemen walked out of the conference indicated the continuing isolation of Moscow's closest Arab allies, while the USSR had to be concerned about the possible formation of a new Arab front that would move to reincorporate Egypt into the Arab League and possibly revive the Reagan plan. Indeed, following the Arafat visit to Cairo, *Izvestia* noted unhappily that

> behind the scenes some "moderate" Arab regimes are using all kinds of tricks and lies to induce the PLO leadership to adopt the Reagan plan for the resolution of the Palestinian problem. . . . This is why out of necessity, they are playing up to Cairo which, as a participant in Camp David, is trying to urge other Arab countries onto this path.[152]

Soviet concern with such a development could only have increased with Mubarak's visit to King Hassan of Morocco—the first official visit to an Arab country by the head of the Egyptian state since the 1979 peace treaty, as Moscow television noted unhappily[153]—and by Mubarak's meeting with King Hussein in Washington in mid-February as the two Arab leaders prepared for talks with President Reagan.

Meanwhile, as Egypt's relations with the centrist Arab nations improved, Syria, despite its victory in Lebanon, appeared to remain isolated. Not only was its influence insufficient to prevent the Islamic Conference from readmitting Egypt, but it was further isolated when the Arab League Foreign Ministers, in a mid-March meeting that Syria and Libya boycotted, took a stongly anti-Iranian position, condemning that country for its continuing "aggression against Iraq" and warning Iran that the continuation of the war would force the Arab states to reconsider their relations with it.[154] For its part, Moscow must have been concerned with Syria's continuing isolation, not to mention that of Libya, whose heavy-handed actions against Jordan (the storming of the Jordanian embassy in Tripoli) had served only to alienate a regime Moscow was seeking to win over.

Compounding Moscow's difficulties in exploiting the U.S. failure in Lebanon was the situation in the Gulf. Iran had again undertaken a major offensive against Iraq and was threatening the key southern Iraqi city of Basra, while at the same time repeating its threats to close the Straits of Hormuz if Iraq used its newly acquired Super-Entendard bombers to interfere with Iranian oil exports. Moscow, at a time when its relations with Iran were at a low ebb (in part because of the Khomeini regime's persecution of the Tudeh party), was clearly concerned that the United States, which had again pledged to keep the Straits open, and which had increased the size of its fleet near the Gulf, might exploit the Iranian threats to reinforce its position in the Arab states of the Gulf, and thereby divert attention from its failure in Lebanon. As *Krasnaya Zvezda* noted on March 4, "Washington is trying (in the Persian Gulf) to compensate at least somehow for its political and military errors in Lebanon."[155] In a counter move to the stepped-up U.S. deployment near the Gulf, the Soviet government issued a statement on March 8 denouncing U.S. activity in the Gulf as a "grave threat to peace and international security," and stating that the USSR would not abide by any restrictions imposed by the U.S. in the Gulf region.[156]

Thus, when Geydar Aliyev arrived in Damascus the overall Middle East picture was not as bright as Moscow could have wished, despite the failure of U.S. policy in Lebanon. In addition, the dinner speeches during Aliyev's visit reflected continued tension in Soviet-Syrian relations. Khaddam, for example, while hailing the defeat of American and Israeli policy in a dinner speech welcoming Aliyev, gave more credit to Syrian action than to Soviet aid, and praised those Palestinian "patriotic forces who courageously opposed the policy of sliding, fragmentation, and departure from the decisions of the Palestine National Council, pursued by some Palestinian leaders to satisfy the Americans and Israelis."[157] In his speech in response, Aliyev praised the Lebanese National Patriotic Forces for resisting U.S. pressure before mentioning the Syrian role, although he did have some words of praise for the Soviet-Syrian treaty. He also called for the Arab people of Palestine, "under the leadership of the PLO, its sole legitimate representative, to be given an opportunity to establish its own state."[158]

In the final communiqué issued after Aliyev's talks with Syrian leaders, Moscow made special mention of Aliyev's meeting with Rifa'at al-Assad, who was "heartily congratulated" on his appointment as vice president—perhaps as a gesture intended to show that Moscow had confidence in Rifa'at.[159] The communiqué also referred to a "spirit of friendship and mutual understanding"—the usual Soviet code words for disagreement.[160] Thus, while the two sides hailed the abrogation of the May 17 Israeli-Lebanese agreement as a great victory, and also expressed their mutual aspirations to further strengthen Soviet-Syrian relations, the final communiqué noted "an exchange of opinions" regarding U.S. and Israeli threats against Syria. As in the visit of Khaddam to Moscow in November of 1983, this probably indicated disagreement over the degree of Soviet support Syria might expect if it became involved in a war with the United States or Israel.[161] An even more serious Soviet-Syrian disagreement over the Palestinian issue was revealed by the communiqué's notation that "a thorough exchange of opinions took place on questions relating to the state of affairs in the Palestinian Resistance movement." Nonetheless, perhaps reflecting Moscow's displeasure with the Arafat-Mubarak meeting and the resumption of Arafat's talks with Hussein, the communiqué also noted that

> the Soviet Union and Syria are convinced of the need to preserve the unity of the Palestinian resistance movement and to overcome as speedily as possible the disagreement within the PLO, which is the sole legitimate representative of the people of Palestine, on a *progressive-patriotic and anti-imperialist basis.*
>
> The sides believe that the implementation of the Palestinian National aspirations is impossible without observance of the Palestine National Council's decision aimed at countering the Israeli aggression and the Camp David policy of separate deals, including the "Reagan Plan" and without close cooperation by the PLO with Syria, all progressive Arab states, and patriotic forces of the Arab world.[162] (Emphasis added)

Another area of Soviet-Syrian disagreement was almost certainly Syria's continuing support for Iran at a time when Moscow was trying to end the Iran-Iraq war. While no mention of this dispute was made in the joint communiqué, the Kuwaiti periodical *al-Qabas* asserted that such differences had surfaced during the discussions.[163]

On balance, however, Aliyev's visit appeared to help solidify Soviet-Syrian relations following the succession in Moscow and the power struggle in Damascus. As might be expected, Soviet broadcasts to the Arab world highlighted the visit, citing Syrian newspaper declarations of praise for Soviet-Syrian (and Soviet-Arab) relations.[164] Nonetheless, as far as Lebanon was concerned, Moscow did not appear ready to cede it to Syria as a satrapy. In the first place, despite the departure of the U.S. Marines and the abrogation of the May 17 agreement, Syria was not yet in a position to fully control events in Lebanon, as the failure of the Lausanne National Reconciliation Conference, which had been held under Syrian auspices, indicated. Indeed, while both Druze leader Walid Jumblatt and Shii leader Nabih Berri had cooperated with Syria against Amin Gemayel, neither was a Syrian stooge. (According to some reports, Jumblatt's father had been killed by Syria.) In any case, both men might behave in an increasingly independent manner if a genuine power-sharing system were ever worked out in Lebanon. Under these circumstances, Moscow evidently felt it useful to develop its own ties with the key Lebanese groups. For example, Walid Jumblatt, whose father had had close ties to Moscow before his assassination, was invited to visit the Soviet capital in January 1984,[165] and there were frequent meetings between Soviet leaders and Lebanese Communist party officials. Also, at the end of March, Karen Brutents, deputy chief of the CPSU Central Committee's International Department, journeyed to Lebanon where he met Berri, Jumblatt, Lebanese Foreign Minister Elie Salim, Lebanese Communist party leader George Hawi, and Lebanese President Amin Gemayel.

Moscow's goal in Lebanon at this time appeared to be to gain firsthand knowledge of the complex political situation there in order to help consolidate the victory of those Lebanese forces opposed to American influence (and thus keep Lebanon out of the U.S.-directed peace process). To be sure, the United States at this time was having more than its share of difficulties with its Middle East diplomacy. Not only had it suffered a debacle in Lebanon, but the Reagan plan suffered a major blow in mid-March when King Hussein of Jordan announced he would not enter into talks with Israel, even if the Israelis froze the construction of settlements in occupied territories, because the United States had lost its credibility and was no longer a trusted mediator.[166] Needless to say, Moscow was delighted with this development, with some Soviet commentators attributing the king's action to the failure of U.S. policy in Lebanon.[167] Syrian commentators dismissed the king's speech as insignificant given his ties with the United States,[168] and they may well have been closer to the mark: at a March 30 press conference the king expressed interest in a possible Labor Party victory in the suddenly-announced Israeli elections—a development that might once again breathe life into the Reagan plan and the U.S.-mediated peace process.[169]

All in all, though, despite the collapse of U.S. policy in Lebanon and Washington's other diplomatic difficulties in the Arab world,[170] by the end of March it did not appear that either Moscow or Syria would be able to convert the recent events in Lebanon into larger victories in the Arab world. Essentially, then, Moscow had two major problems in the spring of 1984: 1) dealing with an escalating Iran-Iraq war in such a way as to prevent the United States from improving its position in the Middle East, and 2) preventing any further moves toward the reintegration of Egypt into the Arab world, which would risk the expansion of the Camp David process.

Moscow and the Gulf Crisis of 1984

As far as the situation in the Gulf was concerned, Moscow moved quickly to exploit the sudden chilling of U.S.–Iraqi relations caused by U.S. accusations that Iraq had employed poison gas in its war against Iran. While denying reports that it had supplied chemical weapons to Iraq (and castigating the Iranian government for spreading the rumors),[171] Moscow sought to strengthen its ties with Iraq by signing an intergovernmental agreement on economic and technical cooperation that involved Soviet assistance in the construction of two major projects in Iraq: a heat and power station and a hydroelectric complex.[172] A month later, Iraq's Deputy Prime Minister Taha Ramadan was invited to Moscow for talks. The fact that in addition to meeting with Prime Minister Tikhonov, Ramadan met also with both Soviet Deputy Defense Minister and Chief of Staff Nikolai Ogarkov and the chairman of the State Committee on Foreign Economic Relations, Yaakov Ryabov (who is responsible for foreign arms sales) would seem to suggest that the Iraqi leader was interested in securing more arms from the USSR.[173] Subsequent reports of increased Soviet arms shipments indicate that Ramadan may well have been successful in his quest, although it is interesting to note that while the *Pravda* description of the talks stated that Ramadan had criticized U.S. "imperialist intrigues,"[174] the Iraqi news agency description cited no such statement.[175] Iraq clearly had no wish to alienate the United States unnecessarily, since Iran—whose February offensive had scored some costly gains—was reportedly preparing yet another major offensive.

Another purpose of Ramadan's visit may have been to alert the USSR to Iraq's plan to wage a war of attrition against Iranian oil exports so as to weaken Iran's ability to finance its war effort. Having proclaimed a fifty-mile air and sea blockade around Iran's main oil export terminal on Kharg Island in February, Iraq now began to attack oil tankers and other vessels that entered the zone. Iran responded by using its air force to attack Kuwaiti and Saudi tankers, and the Gulf war escalated further. Moscow's continuing concern during the war's escalation was that the United States would exploit the situation to improve its ties with the Gulf states, which might be forced to turn to the U.S. for protection.[176]—and indeed, just such a development was to take place in the case of Saudi Arabia.

As a result of U.S. policy in Lebanon; the increasingly close U.S. ties with Israel; the U.S. Congress's opposition to the sale of Stinger antiaircraft missiles to Saudi Arabia; and the possible move of the U.S. embassy in Israel to Jerusalem, Saudi–U.S. ties had cooled considerably by April 1984.[177] Such incidents as the Saudi decision to negotiate for a $4.5 billion air defense system from France (rather than the United States) and the invitation of Soviet Ambassador Anatoly Dobrynin to a dinner at the Saudi embassy in Washington were cited in some quarters as evidence of Saudi Arabia's tilt away from the United States.[178] Nonetheless, the Iranian attack on a Saudi oil tanker in mid-May quickly reversed this trend. Two days after the tanker was hit, Saudi Ambassador Bandar Bin Sultan met with U.S. Secretary of State George Shultz, reportedly to obtain a U.S. commitment to come to Saudi Arabia's aid in case a crisis occurred.[179] The United States was quick to respond: President Reagan sent a letter to King Fahd reportedly reaffirming U.S. support for the kingdom as well as for freedom of navigation in the Gulf, and pledging that the United States would back up its commitment with military power if requested to do so by friendly nations in the area.[180] Reagan, citing the demands of "national security" (which obviated the need for congressional approval), then sent 400 Stinger missiles and 200 launchers to Saudi

Arabia, along with a KC-10 tanker aircraft to augment the three
KC-135 tankers already there. The U.S. thinking was to enable Saudi
F-15s and the Saudi-based U.S. AWACS to stay in the air for longer periods, thereby—in the words of State Department spokesman Alan
Romberg—"to lower the risk of a broader conflict by providing a deterrent against hostile activities."[181] Thus strengthened, and perhaps
angered by comments in the United States and elsewhere that they
would not fight even to defend their own interests (except perhaps
against Israel), the Saudi leaders sent up their F-15s against Iranian
F-4s hunting for oil tankers near the Saudi coast, and shot down one
Iranian plane while driving off a number of others. The fact that the
Saudis had acted with U.S. AWACS assistance, and that more American assistance was on the way in the form of extra fuel tanks for the
F-15s and more advanced AWACS capable of detecting slow-moving
ships and aircraft,[182] clearly improved U.S.–Saudi relations, and the
Saudis were to reciprocate soon afterwards by including many of the
Americans held in Saudi jails in a general amnesty.[183] The Saudi–U.S.
relationship improved still further in August when the United States
promptly responded to Saudi requests to clear the Red Sea of mines
(apparently laid by Libya), which hampered not only maritime trade
in the Red Sea and through the Suez Canal but also the *Hajj*, which
Saudi Arabia—as keeper of the holy places of Mecca and Medina—
took great pride in hosting.

   While the USSR could do little to prevent the United States from
exploiting the escalation of the Iran-Iraq war to improve its ties to
Saudi Arabia, Moscow was to work energetically to prevent a similar
development in U.S.–Kuwaiti relations. As the most steadfastly neutralist of all the Gulf Cooperation Council states (and the only one at
the time to have diplomatic ties and a military purchase relationship
with the Soviet Union), Kuwait occupied a special place in Soviet
strategy toward the GCC. Because of the USSR's invasion of Afghanistan and of the pattern of Iranian victories in the Iran-Iraq war, Moscow had long feared that the GCC might gravitate to the United States
for protection; the Soviet leadership sought to cultivate Kuwait's neutralist leanings (and its basically anti-American press) to prevent
such a development. On the eve of the escalation of the tanker war in
mid-May, a Kuwaiti delegation headed by Undersecretary of the Foreign Ministry Rashid ar-Rashid visited Moscow for discussions on the
Gulf war, and to arrange the visit to Moscow of Kuwaiti Defense Minister Sheikh Salem as-Sabah.[184] The delegation met also with Yaakov

Ryabov (possibly for a preliminary discussion on new arms sales), and also signed an agreement on cultural cooperation. It was at this time, however, that the Saudi and Kuwaiti tankers were hit, and questions were raised in Kuwait about the desirability of its non-alignment policy in the face of the escalating Iranian threat. Possibly noting that Reagan had been willing to buck congressional opposition to send Stinger missiles to Saudi Arabia, Kuwaiti Foreign Minister Sheikh Sabah al-Sabah also asked the United States for missiles.[185] Unfortunately for Kuwait, however, its refusal to accept an American ambassador the year before (because of his previous service in the U.S. consulate in East Jerusalem) and the generally anti-U.S. tone of the Kuwaiti press, had not particularly endeared the Kuwaitis to President Reagan, who in addition had no desire to alienate Congress further by sending another batch of Stingers to an Arab country. (Other arguments against the sale were the relatively small U.S. stockpile of Stingers and fears in the United States that the Stingers might wind up in the hands of terrorists.)[186] The end result was that the United States announced, in the words of State Department spokesman John Hughes, that while "no final decision had been made on the sale, we don't contemplate a sale at this time."[187] However, the United States did offer to improve the quality of the U.S.–made Hawk antiaircraft missiles that Kuwait already possessed (a U.S. team that had made a survey of Kuwait's defense needs had recommended this), while also offering to share with Kuwait the information gathered by U.S. AWACS based in Saudi Arabia. On the eve of the trip to Moscow by its Defense Minister, Kuwait made no formal response to the U.S. offer to improve the Hawks; Sheikh Sabah did announce, however, that Kuwait was already making use of the AWACS-gathered information.[188]

These were the circumstances as Sheikh Salem as-Sabah, the Kuwaiti defense minister, journeyed to Moscow in early July. The Soviet leadership was aware, of course, that the Kuwaitis had not only been denied the weapons system they wanted, but had been embarrassed in the process (the Kuwaiti foreign minister, after having been privately denied the missiles, had made a public appeal to the U.S. Congress, going so far as to say that the missiles were only for defensive purposes and not "to declare war" against Israel).[189] Moscow, therefore, was anxious to demonstrate that the USSR could treat a client far better than the United States. Thus, Sheikh Salem, in addition to being reportedly offered a wide variety of weapons,[190] was taken on a tour of Leningrad, Tbilisi, Sevastopol, Tashkent, and Samarkand, where he not only witnessed live-fire exercises (including a combined land, air, and naval exercise) but was also shown a number of archeological sites and Soviet museums.[191] The Soviet leadership seems to have gone out of its way to demonstrate warm hospitality to the Kuwaiti official, and while the end result of the visit appears not to have been on the order of the $347 million arms deal initially rumored, the Kuwaiti defense minister ultimately did agree not only to purchase Soviet air-defense missiles,[192] but also to invite a small number of Soviet advisers to Kuwait (the first time this had ever happened) to train Kuwaitis in the use of the antiaircraft missiles.[193]

Nonetheless, despite the decision to buy the weapons from Moscow Kuwait was clearly keeping its lines to Washington open, and in the fall an agreement was made with the United States both to train 150 Kuwaiti pilots in the United States and for the United States to establish a pilot training school in Kuwait.[194] At the same time, the Kuwaiti government reportedly gave red-carpet treatment to the new U.S. Ambassador to Kuwait, Anthony Quinton, and also toned down the traditionally anti-U.S. Kuwaiti press.[195] Finally, in the course of the hijacking of a Kuwaiti plane bound from Iran, the Kuwaiti government stood firm and refused to accede to the highjackers' demand that it free a number of imprisoned terrorists accused of attacks on the U.S. and French embassies in December 1983. The stance earned warm praise from President Reagan.

While the escalation of the Iran-Iraq war was, somewhat paradoxically, to lead to an improvement in Kuwait's ties to both the USSR and the United States, on balance Washington gained more—much to the displeasure of a Moscow that continued (and continues) to see the Arab world as a zone of zero-sum game competition with the United States. Nonetheless, Moscow must have been heartened by the fact that the Gulf Cooperation Council—thanks at least in part to Kuwait's opposition and to the somewhat lessened fear of Iran attributable to the prolonged postponement of the expected Iranian offensive—did not move to establish a joint defense treaty or even a joint air-defense system at its meeting in late November (although its constituent members did agree to earmark troops for a GCC Rapid Deployment Force).[196] As *Literaturnaya Gazeta* commented on December 5th: "This means that the GCC will remain an economic organization as its founders intended and will not become a military organization, a kind of defensive pact, over which the United States seeks to gain control."[197]

While Moscow proved unable to incline Saudi Arabia away from the United States, and while it had only limited success in reinforcing Kuwait's neutralist leanings, it continued to be frustrated by the Iran-Iraq war, and, in particular, by the Khomeini regime in Iran. Moscow's relationship with Iran had reached a new low on the eve of 1984, as shown by an extensive article in *Pravda* that criticized the regime for arresting 8,500 Tudeh members, went on to note that anti-Soviet circles in Iran were trying to entice the Iranian government "onto a path of blind fanaticism," and concluded by warning the Khomeini regime to stop the "filthy campaign of slander" against the USSR.[198] Similarly, a feature article in *New Times* analyzing the record of the first five years of the new Iranian government complained that the political revolution had not developed into a social revolution, and blamed Iran for the continuation of the Iran-Iraq war. It also noted the growing trade ties between Iran and the United States and other NATO members, and the antisocialist hostility that "the conservative wing of the Iranian religious and political leadership has always harbored." The article also condemned Iran for its support of "Afghan counterrevolutionaries" and for arresting and imprisoning Tudeh members as terrorists.[199] Interestingly enough, both the *Pravda* and *New Times* articles also appealed to Iran for an improved relationship, much as Moscow had previously done at times of Soviet-Iranian conflict.

If Moscow's ties with Tehran were strained, however, U.S.–Iranian relations—except in the area of trade which had risen to $1.2 billion in 1983—were far worse. The United States blamed Iran for the terrorist attack on the Marine headquarters in Lebanon in October 1983, and had officially classified Iran as an exporter of terrorism, thus necessitating a close scrutiny of all exports to Iran[200] and possibly making the country a target for a U.S. retaliatory strike. Nevertheless, as in the past, this hostile relationship with the United States did not drive Iran any closer to the USSR; despite Soviet warnings, for example, Iran announced the execution of ten Tudeh members in late February.[201] Moscow grew increasingly angry as Iran went on the offensive in its war with Iraq the same month, fearing that such a development would push the Gulf Arabs toward the United States. *Krasnaya Zvezda* noted in its review of the war on April 21 that the escalation of the war created "a pretext (though a false one) for a further build up of the U.S. military presence in the Gulf."

The outbreak of the tanker war, however, and a possible split in

Iran's ruling elite over the desirability of Iran's continuing its "go it alone" policy may have caused Iran to partially adjust its policy toward the USSR in June. In its first major diplomatic gesture toward Moscow since the expulsion of eighteen Soviet diplomats the year before, on June 6 Tehran sent Seyed Mohamed Sadr, the director general of the Iranian Foreign Ministry, to Moscow, where he met with Soviet Foreign Minister Andrei Gromyko.[202] Commenting on the trip, Iran's newly reelected speaker of Parliament, Hashem Rafsanjani, stated that the visit was "unrelated to the war" but that it helped improve relations. He also observed that Iran did not want its relationship with the USSR to become "darkened."[203] Following the visit, there did seem to be something of a warming of Soviet-Iranian relations: there were reports that Moscow's allies Bulgaria, Czechoslovakia, and North Korea had stepped up their shipments of arms to Iran,[204] and on June 21 the Soviet Union's Deputy Power and Electricity Minister Aleksei Makukhin led a delegation to Iran—the highest level Soviet delegation to Iran in more than a year.

Moscow's purpose in sending the delegation (in addition to reciprocating the earlier visit of the Iranian foreign ministry official) seems to have been to try to build upon its economic relationship with Tehran, hoping perhaps that this might be the foundation for improved political relations in the future. One of the central themes of Moscow radio's Persian-language broadcasts to Iran ever since the Khomeini regime took power had been the benefits that would accrue to Iran from increased trade with Moscow. One broadcast went so far as to urge Iran to allow the rebuilding of the bridges on the border rivers "which were built in the early years of World War II and are now old"[205]—as if the Iranians might have forgotten how the bridges were used to facilitate Soviet occupation of northern Iran at the time! Another goal of the Soviets may have been to try to save the lives of imprisoned Tudeh leaders, as a Persian-language broadcast to Iran on the eve of the Soviet delegation's visit cited the appeal of the Arab Communist and workers parties to free them.[206]

Nonetheless, even as it was moving to improve its ties with Moscow somewhat, Iran was making gestures to the West as well. Hans Dietrich Genscher, the West German foreign minister, said after his late July visit to Tehran that the Iranian government had expressed a "clear wish" to gradually reestablish contacts with the West.[207] In addition, despite the fact that France was known to be harboring many exiles opposed to Khomeini, Rafsanjani was quoted as saying that "not all doors with France were closed."[208]

In the following months, the issues placing the greatest strain on Soviet-Iranian relations were fourfold: the persecution of the Tudeh party; the proliferation of anti-Soviet propaganda in Iran; continued Iranian aid to the Afghan guerrillas; and—centrally—the continuation of the Iran-Iraq war. The Soviet press, observing the fifth anniversary of the outbreak of the war in September 1984, continued to call for the war's end as soon as possible, since the conflict "only benefits the imperialists."[209]

As Moscow was encountering difficulties with Iran (and with the fundamentalist Islam encouraged by the Khomeini regime), it could at least draw some comfort from the fact that U.S.–Iranian relations appeared to be worsening. Thus, the U.S.–Iranian claims panel was suspended after two Iranian judges physically attacked a Swedish judge whom they accused of pro-American bias,[210] and Iranian Foreign Minister Ali Akhbar Velayati noted in an interview that he saw no hope of improving ties with the United States.[211] Interestingly enough, Velayati also stated—possibly in a gesture toward Moscow at a time when Iran was undertaking a minor offensive against Iraq— "Our relations with the USSR are exactly what relations between two neighboring states should be. The Tudeh party is an internal problem for us that had absolutely nothing to do with any foreign government."[212]

If the Soviet leadership could perhaps take some small comfort from these words of Velayati, it was less positively inclined to developments in Iraq. Despite the increase in Soviet shipments of arms, especially tanks and planes, the Iraqi regime had also been receiving sophisticated aircraft from France (Super Entendards and Mirage F-1s) and had evidently decided to renew its strategy of seeking a balance between the superpowers.[213] In an interview in early October of 1984, Iraqi Foreign Minister Tariq Aziz noted that "a very agreeable atmosphere" existed in U.S.–Iraqi relations, and hinted that full diplomatic relations would be restored after the impending U.S. presidential elections.[214] It was perhaps for this reason that, on his visit to Moscow two weeks later, the discussions which Aziz had with Gromyko were described as having taken place in a "frank and friendly atmosphere."[215] At the end of November, the United States and Iraq announced the restoration of full diplomatic relations, a development that Iranian Prime Minister Hussein Mousavi stated could only increase anti-U.S. sentiment in Iran.[216] Less than a week later, however, it was reported that Iran had agreed to replace the two Iranian judges who had physically abused their Swedish colleague at the U.S.–Iran claims tribunal[217]—a development that enabled Iran to keep at least one line of negotiations with the United States open, while at the same time resuming the process of regaining its creditworthiness in the Western world.

All in all, the Gulf proved to be a major problem area for Soviet policy in 1984. For one thing, the Soviet leadership, headed now by the aged and infirm Chernenko, tended to be reacting to events caused by the Iran-Iraq war, rather than formulating new initiatives of its own. Moscow would take more of an initiative, however, in trying to deal with a possible rivival of the Reagan plan.

The New Soviet Peace Effort

As far as the Reagan plan was concerned, the centerpiece of Moscow's concern was King Hussein of Jordan. Hussein's acquiescence, along with that of the Israeli government, was essential if the Reagan plan were to have any hope of being put into effect. So long as the Likud party ruled Israel, there was little likelihood of progress on the Reagan plan, since both Prime Minister Menahem Begin and his successor, Yitzhak Shamir, opposed it. By the end of February 1984, however, the Likud government had fallen, and the rival Labor party soon assumed a commanding lead in the Israeli public-opinion polls. This presented a problem for Moscow, since not only had Labor party leader Shimon Peres welcomed the Reagan plan but King Hussein, in commenting on the collapse of the Likud government, had stated that a Labor victory would be a healthy change[218]—an indication that the Jordanian monarch was, as always, keeping his options open.

For this reason, during the spring and summer of 1984 Soviet Middle Eastern diplomacy had a uniquely Jordanian focus. Moscow assiduously wooed King Hussein, with numerous Soviet delegations visiting Jordan (and Jordanian delegations visiting the USSR).[219] The Soviets hoped to keep Jordan from embracing the Reagan plan in the event that, as the polls predicted, the Labor party scored a major victory in the upcoming Israeli elections. In addition, the Soviet leadership prepared a new edition of its Middle East peace plan—one that might prove more amenable to King Hussein than had previous Soviet peace plans. While the Jordanian monarch had long shared the Soviet goal of an international conference to settle the Arab-Israeli conflict, he also insisted upon a link between any Palestinian entity or state on the West Bank and Jordan, whose population was more than sixty percent Palestinian. The inclusion of such a link in the Soviet peace plan of July 29, can therefore be considered a major gesture toward Hussein.

The new plan was modeled on the Brezhnev peace plan of September 15, 1982, which had combined the basic three-point Soviet peace plan (total Israeli withdrawal to 1967 boundaries; a Palestinian state on the West Bank and Gaza; and the right of all states in the region to exist) with the major components of the Arab program announced at Fez in 1982.[220] The new Soviet plan had one additional key element: an acknowledgment that the new Palestinian state could decide to form a confederation with a neighboring country.[221] Given the clash with Arafat over this issue during the PLO leader's visit to Moscow in January 1983, the Soviet leadership's inclusion of this element in its peace plan may therefore also be seen as a gesture to Arafat— who, in the summer of 1984, was engaged in a prolonged political battle to win over the Marxist elements of the PLO (the so-called Democratic Alliance of the PFLP, DFLP, and Palestine Communist party),[222] while at the same time struggling to isolate the so-called National Alliance of Palestinian factions controlled by Syria.

As interesting as was the new content of the Soviet peace plan of July 29th, its timing was also significant. Apparently prepared to coincide with the July 23 Israeli elections, Moscow evidently hoped to use the plan to help keep King Hussein from joining the Reagan plan. Contrary to expectations, however, the Labor victory was so narrow that it appeared unlikely that Peres, even if he were able to manage to form a narrow Parliamentary majority, would be able to make the concessions that the Reagan plan would require. This was a bonus for the USSR, as Moscow now used the plan as a rallying point for centrist and Steadfastness Front Arabs, to draw them not only together but also away from the United States and its Egyptian-camp allies.

Not unexpectedly, Israel quickly rejected the Soviet peace initiative. In addition to refusing to participate in any international conference where the PLO would be present, Israel also opposed the Soviet concept of an international conference on the Middle East because it feared that at such a conference the Arabs would be reduced to their lowest common denominator: opposition to Israel's right to exist. The United States, whose Reagan administration was deeply suspicious of Soviet motivations in the Middle East, also rejected the Soviet proposal.

Much to Moscow's satisfaction, however, its peace initiative was warmly received in the Arab world, especially by such centrist Arab states as Jordan and Kuwait. Arafat's wing of the PLO also accepted the plan, as did Lebanon, and it also received favorable comment from North and South Yemen, Saudi Arabia, and—to a lesser degree—Syria. Arab League Secretary General Chedli Klibi called it a "positive approach for solving the crisis," and in line with the (Fez) Arab peace plan.[223] Moscow was buoyed by the generally positive Arab reaction for the plan, although the various Arab states tended to be more supportive of the Soviet recommendation of an international conference on the Middle East than for the specific elements of the Soviet proposal; in any case, Moscow moved ahead during the summer to garner increased backing for the plan. In following this policy it appears doubtful that the Soviet leadership really thought a Middle East conference was a viable option in the near future, given the opposition of both Israel and the United States; rather, it seems likely that Moscow was capitalizing on their opposition as it put forth a basic framework on which both the Steadfastness Front and centrist Arab groupings in the Arab world might agree. This might not reunite the two Arab camps, but it might at least slow the pace of rapprochement between Egypt—which was at best lukewarm about the Soviet plan[224]—and the centrist Arab states, while at the same time highlighting the United States as the opponent of the Arab consensus on the peace program. Indeed, Radio Damascus in its commentary on the Soviet plan seemed to follow this interpretation:

> It becomes clear from the viewpoint of world observers and politicians that the Soviet peace program in the Middle East will frankly expose the stands of the enemies of peace, particularly the stand of the United States.... The Soviet peace program in the Middle East gives all the Arab states an opportunity to put the U.S. and USSR in the Arab balance.[225]

In its effort to gain support for its peace plan (and to isolate the United States and Israel), Soviet propaganda also exaggerated the close ties between Israel and the United States, going so far as to allege that Israel was going to deploy Pershing missiles on its soil to enable it "to intimidate Arab countries."[226] Interestingly enough, though, there were numerous hints in the Israeli press of Soviet feelers to get Israel's acceptance of an international conference on the Middle East—feelers that included the prospect of a resumption of diplomatic relations between the two countries; however, these came to naught.

Moscow continued its efforts to gain support for its peace plan in the late summer and early fall, as the leaders of North and South Yemen journeyed to Moscow along with the president of Syria and the deputy prime minister of Iraq. The first three Arab leaders give a general endorsement to the Soviet peace plan. (The visit of the president of North Yemen was highlighted by the signing of a Soviet-Yemeni treaty of friendship and cooperation.) Chedli Ben Jedid of Algeria followed suit during a visit to Algiers by Politburo member Boris Ponamarev in mid-October. In the case of Syria, however, there was continuing disagreement on the Palestinian question, although the fact that Gromyko, in a meeting with Arafat in East Berlin in late September, had convinced the PLO leader to strongly back the Soviet peace initiative may have inclined Assad to at least give lip service to it.[228] Nonetheless, the fact that the communiqué issued after Assad's visit referred to "an atmosphere of friendship and mutual understanding" and an "in-depth exchange of opinions on questions concerning the state of affairs in the Palestine Resistance Movement" probably indicates that Moscow and Damascus remained far apart on this issue, although the two states jointly condemned the attempts to "activate" the policy of Camp David-type separate accords.[229]

Despite Moscow's tactical success in garnering at least verbal support for its peace plan from most of the Arab world, the pace of Middle Eastern events once again seemed to confound Soviet strategy. In late September—soon after President Reagan, from the rostrum of the United Nations, had again emphasized the Reagan plan as U.S. policy in the Middle East, while a Peres-led National Unity government had taken office in Israel—King Hussein, whom Moscow had been courting, suddenly reestablished full diplomatic relations with Egypt. This move marked the final stage of a steady improvement of Jordanian-Egyptian relations since December 1983, and appeared to be a major step in the rapprochement between the centrist Arab camp and Egypt. To be sure, Moscow may have hoped—given the continuing tension in U.S.–Jordanian ties, and the steady development of Soviet-Jordanian relations—that Jordan might pull Egypt away from its close tie to the United States (rather than being itself pulled by Egypt toward the Reagan plan). Nevertheless, despite having resumed full diplomatic relations on the ambassadorial level with the Soviet Union in July [230] and making such small gestures to the USSR as allowing the reopening of a Soviet bookstore in Cairo, Egypt continued its close military and economic relationship with the United States. This was exemplified by Mubarak's call for U.S. aid in the clearing of mines

from the Red Sea in August, as well as by the joint military exercise
"Sea Wind" in early November. Indeed, the low-level treatment that
the Soviet press gave to the resumption of Egyptian-Jordanian diplomatic relations seems to indicate that Moscow was trying to play
down that development while continuing to cultivate Jordan. An
Izvestia editorial of October 14 by Vladimir Kudravtsev seemed
to indicate Moscow's true feelings about the Jordanian monarch's
activities:

> The U.S. press is devoting a great deal of attention to Jordan's re-
> establishment of diplomatic relations with Egypt (all Arab countries
> severed diplomatic relations with Egypt by decision of the Baghdad
> conference of those countries' heads of state and government, in re-
> sponse to Cairo's Camp David capitulation). Amman's step was
> viewed in the Arab countries as a flagrant violation of Arab unity....
> In its aggressive plans, the U.S. is trying to make the most of Am-
> man's violation of the Arab decision on Egypt, while disregarding
> (for the time being) Jordanian representatives' statements specifi-
> cally opposing U.S. policy in the Middle East, including its policy on
> the Palestinian problem....[231]

Despite resuming diplomatic relations with Egypt, however, Hussein appeared to go out of his way to demonstrate that by doing so he
was not succumbing to the blandishments of the United States or Israel. Thus, in a speech at the opening of the Jordanian parliament on
October 1, he characterized Peres's call to join in peace negotiations
as "an exercise in subterfuge and deception," and repeated his approval of the Soviet Union's call for an international conference on the
Middle East.[232] One month later, in an interview with the London-
based Saudi newspaper *al Sharq al Awsat,* Hussein announced that
he would go to Moscow for weapons.[233]

Such statements notwithstanding, the resumption of diplomatic
relations with Egypt was not to be the only action taken by King Hussein that was to discomfit the Soviet Union (not to mention Moscow's
chief ally, Syria, which bitterly attacked Hussein for reestablishing
ties with Egypt). In November, King Hussein agreed to the convening
of the Palestine National Council in Jordan. Arafat was eager to convene this meeting in a friendly capital (he had previously been turned
down by Algeria and South Yemen), and managed to achieve a quorum in Amman despite the boycott of the session by the Syrian-
backed Palestinian National Alliance and by the Marxist Democratic

alliance, which included the pro-Soviet Palestinian Communist party. Moscow's displeasure with the meeting was exemplified not only by the failure of the Palestine Communist party to attend, but also by the failure of the Soviet Ambassador to Jordan to attend the session as well as by the pro-Soviet Israeli Communist party's opposition to it.[234] In addition, both PFLP leader George Habash and DFLP leader Naef Hawatmeh announced their opposition to the PNC meeting after hurried visits to Moscow,[235] and both a *Pravda* article marking Palestinian Solidarity Day on November 29 and a Tass report on the Palestine National Council meeting held the following day contained muted criticisms of the meeting. The Tass report noted that,

> as is known, a number of the Palestinian organizations did not attend the Amman session of the National Council of Palestine. They published statements pointing out that the time for the convention of the session was not suitable due to the lack of unity among the Palestinians and [that the convention] did not meet the interests of the Arab people of Palestine.[236]

The PNC meeting was orchestrated by Arafat, to demonstrate his control over the PLO while also offering a renewed tie to both the Democratic and National Alliances. For precisely that reason, however, the meeting did not make any dramatic moves toward peace. (Indeed, Arafat emphasized the need for armed struggle.)[237] The very fact that the meeting took place when and where it did, however, held out the possibility of a final split in the PLO between Arafat's backers and those of Syria.[238] Both Assad's speech at the Syrian Ba'ath Congress in January 1985, in which he implied that Syria would take command of the Palestinian Movement,[239] and the assassination of PLO executive committee member Fahd al Qawasmeh (which Arafat blamed on Assad)[240] seemed to hasten such a split. Such a development could mean that Moscow might be faced by an alignment of Egypt, Jordan, and Arafat's wing of the PLO—and possibly Iraq (which had just resumed diplomatic relations with the United States) as well. Under these circumstances, Moscow had to be concerned that Arafat might yet move again toward the Reagan plan, much as he appeared to be doing in the fall of 1982 prior to the Syrian-engineered plot in the PLO against him. This would certainly breathe new life into the U.S. initiative, given both Egypt's preference for the United States playing a major role in the peace process and the avowed position of Israeli Prime Minister Shimon Peres. Peres, long a supporter of the "Jordanian option," had begun to consolidate his position in Israel, and had started to withdraw Israeli troops from Lebanon. Indeed, Moscow received further evidence that just such a development was underway when Arafat and Hussein signed an "agreement" on February 11, 1985, that laid out a framework for negotiating a Middle East settlement.[241] While Syria denounced the Hussein-Arafat agreement, Moscow—perhaps still hoping to win over Jordan, or possibly to gain entrance to the peace process at some stage so that it could be manipulated for Soviet purposes—at first limited itself to citing the strong opposition to the Hussein-Arafat agreement by Syria, South Yemen, and a number of anti-Arafat Palestinian leaders.[242] However, Soviet unhappiness was soon to be made more clear.

Soviet Policy under Gorbachev

When Egyptian President Mubarak threw his support behind the Hussein-Arafat agreement and Israeli Prime Minister Peres also reacted positively, Moscow came out in shrill opposition to the agreement. At this point, however, the ill Chernenko died, to be replaced by Mikhail Gorbachev. Just as Andropov had inherited a weakened Soviet position, so too did Gorbachev, who had to contend with the increasing momentum toward a Middle East settlement reflected in the visits to the Middle East of Deputy United States Secretary of State Richard Murphy and then of Secretary of State George Shultz. Meanwhile, as the peace process accelerated, Moscow again became increasingly dependent on Syria as its only strong ally in the Middle East opposing U.S. policy. In many ways, the situation closely resembled that of November 1983, when Assad had exploited Soviet dependence to strike at Arafat's supporters in the PLO in Tripoli; this time, however, the target was to be Arafat's supporters in the Palestinian refugee camps in Beirut, and Syria's instrument was to be Nabih Berri's Shiite Moslem Militia Amal (which had its own score to settle with the PLO). In any case, with at least tacit Syrian support, Amal soldiers attacked the refugee camps, causing what Arafat himself later called the "second massacre" of Sabra and Shatilla.[243] As in November 1983, Moscow protested, but rather ineffectually: the highest-level public protest was a statement from the Soviet Afro-Asian Peoples Solidarity Organization.[244] In addition, Moscow complained that only Israel and other enemies of the Arabs profited from the

fighting.[245] After all of the Sabra camp and most of the Shatilla camp
were captured by Amal, a ceasefire was worked out. While Moscow
gave the credit for the ceasefire to Syria, it was more likely brought
about as a result of the pro-Syrian Palestinians switching sides and
fighting Amal, as well as because even Syria's allies Libya and Iran, to
say nothing of its Arab enemies, severely criticized Syria. In any case,
the Amal-PLO clash left Assad even more isolated than before, although Syria would regain some of its prestige as a result of the TWA
aircraft hijacking that occurred soon after the Beirut ceasefire.

When Syria's ally, Nabih Berri and his Amal Militia, took control
of the hijacking situation, Syria gained a certain amount of leverage
over what was happening. For its part, Moscow downplayed the significance of the hijacking, emphasizing that the hijackers had a legitimate grievance since Israel held their countrymen captive[246]; yet
Moscow had to be concerned. In the first place, the United States was
finally out of Lebanon and the Soviet leadership had no desire to see
a return of U.S. military power to the area. Second, the fact that the
United States had moved elements of its fleet opposite Beirut held out
the possibility of a military confrontation between the United States
and Amal, and therefore the possibility of such a confrontation's escalation to a U.S.–Syrian clash—with the resultant dilemma for
Moscow, which it had faced twice before in 1983, of whether or not to
get involved. Third, Israel had completed a unilateral withdrawal
from Lebanon in early June,[247] and this development further
strengthened Syria's position in Lebanon.

Under these circumstances, then, Moscow had no desire to upset
what—despite the internal clashes—was generally a favorable trend
of events in Lebanon. It is quite possible, therefore, that Moscow
might have suggested to Assad that the hostages be freed.[248] In any
case, Assad flew to Moscow several days after the hijacking took place
for meetings with the new Soviet leader, Mikhail Gorbachev. Once
again, while the two countries noted their satisfaction about the development of Soviet-Syrian relations, and while Assad thanked the
USSR for its economic and military assistance and voiced its support
for Soviet plans for an international peace conference to solve the
Middle East conflict, Pravda described the talks as taking place in an
atmosphere of "mutual trust and frankness." Other indications of
continued disagreement in key issues were reflected in the communiqué's statements to the effect that "there was an exhaustive exchange of views pertaining to the Middle East situation, Soviet-Syrian

relations and the international situation," and that "during an exchange of views on questions concerning the state of affairs in the Palestine Resistance Movement, the Soviet side laid special emphasis on
the importance of preserving the PLO's unity and of quickly overcoming differences among the Palestinians on a fundamentally anti-
imperialist platform."[249] Whether or not Moscow used its influence
with Damascus to free the prisoners is not yet known (Assad had his
own reasons, of course, to maintain some positive links to Washington), but the prisoners were in fact released ten days after Assad's
visit to Moscow, and the chances of another U.S.–Syrian clash, with
the possibility it held of a U.S.–Soviet confrontation, were thereby
lessened—something that had to gratify Moscow.

Meanwhile, as Moscow was seeking to cope with the hijacking situation, it could take comfort from developments in the Sudan. The
strongly pro-Western Jaafar Nimeri had been overthrown in April,
and the new regime—an uneasy mixture of military officers and ci-
vilians—was rapidly moving the country toward a more non-aligned
posture.[250] While remaining heavily dependent on the United States
for the food needed to resist its famine, the new Sudanese Government resumed diplomatic relations with Libya. That country, in turn,
promised to end support for southern Sudanese rebel leader Joseph
Garang. The Sudan also moved toward improving its ties with Ethiopia, now a full-fledged Marxist regime. Should this trend continue,
the pro-Western Egyptian camp would be seriously weakened, a circumstance that would at least partially compensate Moscow for the
damage to the Steadfastness Front caused by the clash between Assad
and Arafat. In any case, however, developments in the Sudan provide
a useful point of departure toward a final evaluation of the course
of Soviet policy toward the Middle East since the Israeli invasion of
Lebanon.

Conclusions

Looking at Soviet foreign policy in the Middle East in the aftermath of the Israeli invasion of Lebanon, one central conclusion can
be drawn. Despite the fact that there were no fewer than four Soviet
leaders during this period (Brezhnev, Andropov, Chernenko, Gorbachev) there was an essential continuity in Soviet policy as the

USSR sought to cope with American military and political intervention in Lebanon, the escalation of the Iran-Iraq war, and the ups and downs of the American-sponsored Middle East peace process.

In the case of the Lebanese crisis, Moscow managed to muddle through successfully—not so much because of any actions of its own, but rather because of a misguided U.S. policy, the growing war-weariness in Israel, major mistakes by Amin Gemayel, and the steadfastness of Syrian President Hafiz Assad. To be sure, the provision of SAM-5 and SS-21 missiles to Syria aided Assad in standing up to both Israel and the United States. Nonetheless, while benefiting from the abrogation of the May 17, 1983, Israeli-Lebanese agreement, Moscow ran a number of risks in its Lebanese policy as Syria sought to gain Soviet support for its policy in Lebanon, not only against Israel but also against the United States, almost to the point of a major military confrontation. On two separate occasions in 1983 (September and November-December) Moscow faced a possible confrontation with the United States because of Syrian actions in Lebanon, and on both occasions Moscow chose not to back its Syrian ally, thus rekindling memories of Moscow's credibility problem during the Israeli invasion of Lebanon. Yet another problem facing Moscow in the Lebanese crisis was that Syria exploited it to force Arafat and his supporters to leave Lebanon—a development that would lead to an Egyptian-PLO rapprochement, and to the emergence of Egypt from isolation in the Arab world.

While the American debacle in Lebanon was clearly a major defeat for the United States vis-à-vis its influence competition with the Soviet Union, events in the Gulf and in the Arab-Israeli peace process prevented Moscow from making any major Middle Eastern gains as a result of the American failure in Lebanon. At the same time the United States was making its ignominious departure from Lebanon, Iraq was bombing tankers en route to and from Iran, and this escalated the Gulf crisis. When Iran responded by bombing Saudi and Kuwaiti tankers, both Saudi Arabia and Kuwait called on the United States for help, thereby mitigating the impact of the American failure in Lebanon as world attention rapidly shifted to the Gulf. Meanwhile, frustrated by its inability to profit from the continued anti-American feelings in Iran—in fact, Soviet-Iranian relations deteriorated in the 1982–85 period—Moscow saw its influence remain at a low level in Iraq as well, as Baghdad moved closer to both Paris and Washington, finally restoring diplomatic relations with the United States in November 1984.

It was in the Arab-Israeli peace process, however, that Moscow encountered its most serious problems. Kept on the sidelines since 1973, Moscow became concerned lest the U.S.-orchestrated Camp David peace process gain momentum after the United States arranged for the exodus of PLO forces from Beirut in August 1982 and President Reagan issued his Middle East peace plan (which Moscow saw as an extension of Camp David). While little came of the Reagan plan in 1983 due to the U.S. preoccupation with Lebanon, the plan was reinvigorated in 1984 when the Likud government of Israel, which opposed the Reagan plan, fell, to be replaced by a National Unity government led by Labor party leader Shimon Peres who supported the plan.

While Moscow sought to keep both Arafat's wing of the PLO and Jordan out of the peace process by amending the Soviet peace plan in July 1984, to more nearly conform with Jordanian desires for a link between a Palestinian entity and Jordan, the Soviet move did not meet with much success. Indeed, less than two weeks after the formation of the National Unity government in Israel, King Hussein reestablished diplomatic ties with Egypt, thereby legitimizing the Camp David agreement—and several months later Hussein hosted the Palestine National Council meeting in Amman. Here, he appealed to Arafat, whose own PLO faction, Fatah, had been split by Syria, to join him in the peace process. The end result was the Hussein-Arafat agreement of February 11, 1985, which was denounced both by Syria and the USSR. Moscow grew increasingly concerned that the joint Palestinian-Jordanian negotiating team called for by the Hussein-Arafat agreement, which had been strongly endorsed by Egypt and cautiously welcomed by both the United States and Israel, might succeed in working out a settlement with Israel.

In sum, Soviet policy toward the Middle East in the three-year period following the Israeli invasion of Lebanon was a highly reactive one as Moscow found itself in the position of primarily responding to events caused by other actors on the Middle East scene. Its one major initiative, the 1984 peace plan, met with little success as the United States, despite its debacle in Lebanon, continued to dominate the Middle East peace process. All in all, the aftermath of the Israeli invasion of Lebanon shows that Soviet influence in the Middle East remains, as it was in the years preceding the invasion, quite limited.

NOTES

1. For studies of Soviet policy in the Middle East, see Robert O. Freedman, *Soviet Policy Toward the Middle East Since 1970*, 3rd ed. (New York: Praeger, 1982); Jon D. Glassman, *Arms for the Arabs: The Soviet Union and War in the Middle East* (Baltimore: Johns Hopkins, 1975); Galia Golan, *Yom Kippur and After: The Soviet Union and the Middle East Crisis* (London: Cambridge University Press, 1977); Yaacov Ro'i, *From Encroachment to Involvement: A Documentary Study of Soviet Policy in the Middle East* (Jerusalem: Israel Universities Press, 1974); and Adeed Dawisha and Karen Dawisha, eds., *The Soviet Union in the Middle East: Policies and Perspectives* (New York: Holmes & Meier, 1982). See also Yaacov Ro'i, ed., *The Limits to Power* (London: Croom Helm, 1979). For an Arab viewpoint, see Mohamed Heikal, *The Sphinx and the Commissar* (New York: Harper and Row, 1978), and for a Soviet view see E. M. Primakov, *Anatomiia Blizhnevostochnogo Konflikta* (Moscow: Mysl', 1978).

2. For studies of Soviet military aid, see Glassman, *Arms,* and George Lenczowski, *Soviet Advances in the Middle East* (Washington: American Enterprise Institute, 1972). See also Amnon Sella, *Soviet Political and Military Conduct in the Middle East* (New York: St. Martin's, 1981) and Bruce D. Porter, *The USSR in Third World Conflicts* (New York: Cambridge, 1984).

3. See Richard H. Shultz and Roy Godson, *Dezinformatsia: Active Measures in Soviet Strategy* (New York: Pergamon-Brassey's, 1984).

4. For a view of the role of Israel in Soviet Middle East strategy, see Arthur Klinghoffer, *Israel and the Soviet Union* (Boulder, Colo.: Westview Press, 1985).

5. For studies of Soviet policy toward the Communist parties of the Arab world, see Robert O. Freedman, "The Soviet Union and the Communist Parties of the Arab World: An Uncertain Relationship," in Roger E. Kanet and Donna Bahry, eds., *Soviet Economic and Political Relations with the Developing World* (New York: Praeger, 1975), pp. 100–134; John K. Cooley, "The Shifting Sands of Arab Communism," *Problems of Communism* 24, no. 2 (1975):22–42; and Arnold Hottinger, "Arab Communism at a Low Ebb," *Problems of Communism* 30, no. 3 (1981):17–32.

6. For a Soviet view of the importance of such an "anti-imperialist" Arab unity, see the comments by Soviet Foreign Minister Andrei Gromyko to PLO chairman Yasser Arafat during Arafat's visit to the Kremlin in 1979. (The minutes of the conversation were captured during the Israeli invasion of Lebanon in 1982.) See Raphael Israeli, ed., *PLO in Lebanon: Selected Documents* (New York: St. Martin's Press, 1983), p. 47.

7. These events are discussed in Robert O. Freedman, ed., *The Middle East Since Camp David* (Boulder, Colo.: Westview Press, 1984).

8. The central reasons for Soviet inactivity during the Israeli invasion would appear to be 1) the failure of the other Arab states to aid Syria and the PLO; 2) Israeli air supremacy in the region; and 3) uncertainty over the possible U.S. reaction to Soviet intervention. The reasons for Soviet inactivity are discussed in Robert O. Freedman, "The Soviet Union and the Middle East: Failure to Match the United States as a Regional Power," in *Middle East Contemporary Survey*, vol. 6, *1981–82*, ed. Colin Legum, Haim Shaked, and Daniel Dishon (New York: Holmes & Meier, 1984), pp. 40–48; and Karen Dawisha, "The USSR in the Middle East: Super Power in Eclipse," *Foreign Affairs* (Winter 1982–83):438–52.

9. *Jana* (Tripoli), 26 June 1982 (*Foreign Broadcast Information Service Daily Report: The Middle East* [hereafter *FBIS:ME*], 26 June 1982, pp. Q-2, Q-3).

10. For a description of the Reagan plan, see Barry Rubin, "The United States and the Middle East from Camp David to the Reagan Plan," *Middle East Contemporary Survey 1981–82, op.cit.,* pp. 30–31.

11. For a description of the Fez Plan, see *The Middle East Journal* 37, no. 1 (Winter 1983):71.

12. *Pravda,* 16 September 1982. For an analysis of the status of the Soviet Middle East peace plan on the eve of the Israeli invasion of Lebanon, see Robert O. Freedman, "Moscow, Washington and the Gulf," *American-Arab Affairs* 1 (Summer 1982):132–34.

13. *Pravda,* 21 September 1982.

14. Cited by Loren Jenkins, *Washington Post,* 13 November 1982.

15. *Pravda,* 13 January 1983.

16. Ibid.

17. Edward Walsh, *Washington Post,* 5 January 1983, and Thomas L. Friedman, *New York Times,* 21 March 1983.

18. It is also possible that the Soviet move was in part a response to the emplacement of U.S. troops in Beirut, as well as a means of hampering U.S. air operations in the Eastern Mediterranean near Lebanon.

19. For an analysis of the military implications of the Soviet-Syrian arms-supply relationship, see Cynthia A. Roberts, "Soviet Arms-Transfer Policy and the Decision to Upgrade Syrian Air Defenses," *Survival* (July/August 1983):154–64.

20. For a discussion of these events, see Robert O. Freedman, "Soviet Policy Toward Syria Since Camp David," *Middle East Review* (Fall/Winter 1981–82): 31–42.

21. For an analysis of the alleged coup attempt in the Sudan, see the report by Lou Cannon and George Wilson, *Washington Post,* 19 February 1983.

22. Cited in report by Bernard Gwertzman, *New York Times,* 21 February 1983. For a Soviet view of the crisis, see "Sabre Rattling," *New Times,* no. 9 (1983):11.

23. *Pravda,* 30 March 1983.

24. Tass report, cited in *Foreign Broadcast Information Service Daily Report: The Soviet Union* [hereafter *FBIS:USSR*], 18 March 1983, p. H-1.

25. Tass report, 17 March 1983 (*FBIS:USSR,* 18 March 1983):H-3, H-4.

26. Following the 1981 Gulf of Sidra incident, Kaddafi, speaking on Tripoli radio on the anniversary of the Libyan revolution, had stated: "We desperately need to be in military alliance with any ally who will stand by us against the United States." (Tripoli Domestic Service, 1 September 1981, cited in Ellen Laipson, "Libya and the Soviet Union: Alliance at Arms Length," unpublished paper, p. 6).

27. *Pravda,* 30 March 1983.

28. Ibid.

29. For a detailed analysis of the crisis in Chad, see Edouard Bustin, "Chad: Escalation Leads to Impasse," *The Middle East Annual,* vol. 3, *1983* (Boston: G. H. Hall, 1984), pp. 171–80.

30. *Pravda,* 31 March 1983.

31. *Christian Science Monitor,* 30 March 1983.

32. *SPA* (Riyadh), 2 April 1983 (*FBIS:ME,* 4 April 1983):C-6.

33. For the text of Gromyko's press conference, see *FBIS:USSR*, 4 April 1983:AA-1–AA-17.

34. Ibid.:AA-15.

35. Ibid.:AA-16.

36. The rise in opposition to Arafat within the PLO is discussed by Twefik Mishlawi, *Wall Street Journal*, 12 January 1983 and 19 January 1983. See also the chapter by Rashid Khalidi in this volume.

37. Thomas L. Friedman, *New York Times*, 23 February 1983. The fact that PLO moderate Issam Sartawi, who publicly advocated a compromise between Israel and the PLO, was forbidden to speak at the meeting was a further indication of the erosion of Arafat's position. (Sartawi was subsequently assassinated in April while attending the Socialist International Congress in Portugal.) For general discussions of the PNC session, see Judith Perera, "Hammering Out a Compromise," *The Middle East*, no. 101 (March 1983): 8–9; and Cheryl A. Rubenberg, "The PNC and the Reagan Initiative," *American-Arab Affairs* 4 (April 1983): 53–69. For an analysis of trends within the PLO, see Aaron David Miller, "Palestinians in the 1980s," *Current History* (January 1984):17–20, 34–36; and "The PLO Since Camp David," in Robert O. Freedman, ed., *The Middle East Since Camp David* (Boulder, Colo.: Westview Press, 1984); and the article by Rashid Khalidi in this volume.

38. *Pravda*, 25 February 1983.

39. Peter Osnos, *Washington Post*, 20 March 1983.

40. Bernard Gwertzman, *New York Times*, 9 April 1983.

41. Reuters report, *Washington Post*, 31 March 1983.

42. Herbert H. Denton, *Washington Post*, 11 April 1983. For a provocative interpretation of Hussein's decision, see the articles by Karen Elliott House in the *Wall Street Journal*, 14 April 1983 and 15 April 1983. For an analysis of Jordan's position vis-à-vis the Palestinians, see Adam M. Garfinkle, "Jordanian Foreign Policy," *Current History* (January 1984):21–24, 38–39.

43. *Pravda*, 13 April 1983 (translated in *Current Digest of the Soviet Press* [hereafter *CDSP*] 35, no. 15:9).

44. Reuters report, *New York Times*, 17 April 1983.

45. David Landau, *Jerusalem Post*, 20 April 1983.

46. Herbert Denton, *Washington Post*, 22 April 1983.

47. *Jerusalem Post*, 24 April 1983.

48. Ibid., 26 April 1983.

49. Ibid., 27 April 1983.

50. For an analysis of the dynamics of the process leading to the Israeli-Lebanese agreement, see the report by Bernard Gwertzman, *New York Times*, 10 May 1983.

51. Herbert Denton, *Washington Post*, 7 May 1983.

52. Tass report, 9 May 1983 (*FBIS:USSR*, 10 May 1983:H-1).

53. Thomas Friedman, *New York Times*, 10 May 1983; and Nora Boustany, *Washington Post*, 10 May 1983.

54. Bernard Gwertzman, *New York Times*, 11 May 1983.

55. John Goshko, *Washington Post*, 11 May 1983.

56. *SANA* (Damascus), 9 May 1983 (*FBIS:ME*, 9 May 1983:H-2).

57. Ibid.

58. *New York Times,* 11 May 1983.

59. Beirut Domestic Service in Arabic, 10 May 1983 (*FBIS:ME,* 16 May 1983:H-8).

60. *Jerusalem Post,* 15 May 1983.

61. Robin Wright, *Christian Science Monitor,* 17 May 1983.

62. *Jerusalem Post,* 24 May 1983.

63. William E. Farrell, *New York Times,* 26 May 1983.

64. Hirsh Goodman, *Jerusalem Post,* 27 May 1983.

65. For a Soviet view of the causes of the deterioration in Soviet-Iranian relations, see *Pravda,* 23 March 1983. See also Dmitry Volsky, "The Revolution at the Crossroads," *New Times,* no. 2 (1983):13–14.

66. Reuters report, *New York Times,* 25 February 1983.

67. Brezhnev had made these comments at the 26th CPSU Party Congress in February 1981.

68. *Washington Post,* 5 May 1983.

69. AFP report, *Washington Post,* 5 May 1983. The Soviet diplomats who were expelled included two minister counsellors, four first secretaries, and three military attachés.

70. For a description of the anti-Soviet atmosphere in Iran at this time, see Shireen T. Hunter, *Christian Science Monitor,* 27 July 1983.

71. *Christian Science Monitor,* 26 May 1983.

72. Eric Rouleau, *Le Monde,* 8 January 1983 (trans. *Manchester Guardian Weekly,* 23 January 1983).

73. This was done by making public a 25 August 1982 conversation between Saddam Hussein and U.S. congressman Steven Solarz (*Washington Post,* 3 January 1983).

74. *New York Times,* 19 May 1983.

75. Drew Middleton, ibid., 21 July 1983.

76. Ian Black, *Washington Post,* 9 September 1983.

77. Reuters report, ibid., 21 December 1983.

78. *Pravda,* 22 November 1983.

79. Herbert Denton, *Washington Post,* 5 July 1983.

80. *FBIS:ME,* 5 August 1983:A-1.

81. *Al-Watan al-Arabi,* cited by INA (*FBIS:ME,* 2 September 1983:A-1).

82. For a description of Soviet military facilities in Syria, see *Near East Report* 27, no. 23 (10 June 1983):2.

83. Moscow Radio Peace and Progress, 26 May 1983 (*FBIS:USSR,* 1 June 1983:H-3). See also A. Stepanov, "To Safeguard Palestinian Unity," *New Times,* no. 28, *1983*:14–15.

84. WAFA, 4 June 1983, cited in *Jerusalem Post,* 5 June 1983.

85. *Pravda,* 14 July 1983.

86. Loren Jenkins, *Washington Post,* 3 August 1983. See also reports in the *Baltimore Sun,* 10 July 1983; *New York Times,* 15 July 1983; and *Washington Post* (AFP report), 17 July 1983.

87. Stepanov, "To Safeguard Palestinian Unity" p. 14.

88. Don Oberdorfer, *Washington Post,* 7 July 1983. For a European view of the Shultz visit, see the *Economist,* 9 July 1983:31.

89. AP report in the *Washington Post,* 24 July 1983.

90. David Shipler, *New York Times*, 2 June 1983.

91. Reuters report, *Baltimore Sun*, 8 June 1983.

92. Don Oberdorfer, *Washington Post*, 8 July 1983.

93. Nora Bustany, ibid., 24 July 1983.

94. *Novosti* article by Pavel Demchenko, cited in AP report in the *Jerusalem Post*, 3 August 1983. (*Novosti* reports are often used as a direct means of trying to influence Western nations.) See below, pp. 31–32.

95. *Tishrin* editorial, cited in Reuters report, *Washington Post*, 28 August 1983.

96. E. J. Dionne, Jr., *New York Times*, 20 September 1983.

97. David Ottaway, *Washington Post*, 18 September 1983.

98. Thomas L. Friedman, *New York Times*, 23 September 1983.

99. Trudy Rubin, *Christian Science Monitor*, 19 September 1983.

100. *Izvestia*, 4 September 1983 (*FBIS:USSR*, 7 September 1983:H-4).

101. Editorial, *New Times*, no. 38, *1983*, p. 1.

102. *Pravda*, 19 September 1983.

103. Ibid., 20 September 1983.

104. Cf *Al-Qabas* (Kuwait), 20 September 1983 (*FBIS:USSR*, 22 September 1983:H-1).

105. Bernard Gwertzman, *New York Times*, 23 September 1983.

106. *Tishrin*, 12 September 1983, cited on Radio Monte Carlo (*FBIS:ME*, 13 September 1983:H-1).

107. Radio Monte Carlo, 23 September 1983 (*FBIS:ME*, 23 September 1983:H-1).

108. Andropov himself praised the ceasefire (*Pravda*, 30 September 1983) in a page one report of his meeting with Peoples Democratic Republic of Yemen (PDRY) leader Ali Nasser Mohammed. A Tass statement published in *Pravda* on September 29 noted that the ceasefire had been "favorably received" in the Soviet Union, and then went on to editorialize against both the Israeli and American troop presence in Lebanon and the May 17 Israeli-Lebanese agreement.

109. Damascus Domestic Service, 15 September 1983 (*FBIS:ME*, 15 September 1983:H-1); 18 September 1983 (*FBIS:ME*, 19 September 1983:H-3); and 14 September 1983 (*FBIS:ME*, 20 September 1983:H-1, H-2).

110. For the text of the ceasefire agreement, see the AP report, *New York Times*, 27 September 1983.

111. Michael Getler, *Washington Post*, 7 October 1983. A report in the Arabic language *Al-Majallah* asserted that Moscow had told Damascus that the missiles could only be used in self-defense (*FBIS:ME*, 31 October 1983:ii).

112. A. Stepanov, "Consistent Support," *New Times*, no. 42, *1983*, p. 13.

113. Moscow Radio in Arabic, commentary by Alexander Timoshkin, 6 October 1983 (*FBIS:USSR*, 7 October 1983:H-2, H-3).

114. Moscow Radio in Arabic, Rafael Artonov commentary, 3 November 1983 (*FBIS:USSR*, 4 November 1983:H-3).

115. *Pravda*, 5 November 1983.

116. Ibid., 6 November 1983.

117. Tass, 4 November 1983 (*FBIS:USSR*, 8 November 1983:H-2).

118. Bernard Gwertzman, *New York Times*, 8 November 1983.

119. *FBIS:USSR*, 10 November 1983:H-2.

120. Thomas Friedman, *New York Times,* 11 November 1983.

121. *FBIS:ME,* 9 November 1983:i.

122. *FBIS:USSR,* 15 November 1983:H-2.

123. *FBIS:ME,* 14 November 1983:H-2.

124. *Pravda,* 13 November 1983.

125. AP report, *New York Times,* 14 November 1983.

126. For Moscow's reaction, see *Pravda,* 18 and 19 November 1983.

127. Radio Free Lebanon, 19 November 1983 (*FBIS:ME,* 21 November 1983: H-1).

128. Damascus television, 15 November 1983 (ibid., 16 November 1983:H-1).

129. *Pravda,* 19 November 1983 (*CDSP* 35, no. 46:8).

130. Freedman, *Soviet Policy,* pp. 255, 261.

131. Tass, 20 November 1983 (*FBIS:USSR,* 21 November 1983:H-2).

132. *Pravda,* 24 November 1983.

133. *FBIS:USSR,* 29 November 1983:H-8. There was some indication that Arafat was publicly angry with the lack of Soviet aid, but he moved quickly to deny the report published to that effect in the Egyptian newspaper *al-Akhbar* (*KUNA* (Kuwait), 29 November 1983 [*FBIS:USSR,* 29 November 1983:H-1]).

134. *Pravda,* 29 November 1983.

135. Richard Halloran, *New York Times,* 23 November 1983.

136. UPI report, *Washington Post,* 24 November 1983.

137. David Ottaway, ibid., 27 November 1983.

138. AP report, *New York Times,* 27 November 1983.

139. Damascus Domestic Service, 29 November 1983 (*FBIS:ME,* 30 November 1983:H-2).

140. *New York Times,* 5 December 1983.

141. *FBIS:USSR,* 6 December 1983:H-1.

142. Ibid., 14 December 1983:H-1.

143. The article was read on Damascus Radio 8 December 1983 (*FBIS:ME,* 8 December 1983:H-4).

144. Damascus Domestic Service, 3 January 1984 (ibid., 3 January 1984:H-2).

145. This point had been repeatedly emphasized by Defense Minister Mustapha Tlas, while Syrian Foreign Minister Khaddam only a few days earlier had linked the airman's release to the suspension of U.S. reconnaissance flights over Syrian positions (Radio Monte Carlo, 1 January 1984) (*FBIS:ME,* 3 January 1984:H-1, H-2).

146. House Speaker Thomas P. ("Tip") O'Neill was especially vocal. See Philip Taubman, *New York Times,* 30 December 1983.

147. For an analysis of U.S. behavior at this time, see Thomas L. Friedman, "America's Failure in Lebanon," *New York Times Magazine,* 8 April 1984.

148. E. J. Dionne, *New York Times,* 12 February 1984, and David Hoffman, *Washington Post,* 12 February and 15 February 1984.

149. For a Soviet explanation of the veto, see Moscow World Service in English, 2 March 1984 (*FBIS:ME,* 5 March 1984:H-2).

150. Damascus Domestic Service, 29 February 1984 (ibid., 1 March 1984: H-3).

151. Tass, 20 January 1984 (*FBIS:USSR,* 23 January 1984:H-5).

152. Konstantin Geyvandov, *Izvestia,* 5 January 1984 (ibid., 6 January 1984: H-7).

153. Moscow television service, 8 February 1984 (ibid., 9 February 1984:H-6).

154. INA (Baghdad), in Arabic, 14 March 1984 (*FBIS:ME*, 15 March 1984: p. A-2).

155. Translated in *FBIS:USSR*, 7 March 1984:H-4.

156. *Krasnaya Zvezda*, 8 March 1984 (ibid., 8 March 1984:H-1).

157. For a translation of the speeches, see *FBIS:USSR*, 13 March 1984:H-3, H-4.

158. Ibid.

159. *Pravda*, March 15, 1984.

160. Ibid., 14 March 1984 (translated in *FBIS:USSR*, 14 March 1984:H-1 to H-2).

161. See text pp. 42–43.

162. *Pravda*, 14 March 1984 (translated in *FBIS:USSR*, 14 March 1984:H-1, H-2). Emphasis added.

163. *Al-Qabas* (Kuwait), 19 March 1984 (*FBIS:ME*, 21 March 1984:H-2). The article also asserted that the USSR had promised to "revolutionize" the Syrian air force to allow it to go on the offensive, as well as to improve the electronic defense system of Syria to compensate it for a reported Israeli link to the U.S. satellite system.

164. Moscow Radio, in Arabic, to the Arab world, 14 March 1984 (*FBIS:USSR*, 15 March 1984:H-2).

165. For the Soviet view of the Jumblatt visit, see *Pravda*, 15 January 1984.

166. Hussein's statement is part of an interview in the *New York Times* of 15 March 1984 in which he also called for a Soviet role in the peace talks.

167. *Izvestia*, 28 March 1984.

168. *Al Ba'ath* (Damascus), 18 March 1984 (*FBIS:ME*, 22 March 1984:H-1).

169. Ibid., 2 April 1984:ii.

170. In March 1984, a major effort had been mounted in the U.S. Congress to move the U.S. embassy in Israel from Tel Aviv to Jerusalem—a development that aroused considerable Arab anger.

171. *Krasnaya Zvezda*, 22 March 1984.

172. *Pravda*, 20 March 1984. According to a report by David Ottaway in the 21 July 1984 issue of the *Washington Post*, the agreement involved two billion dollars in Soviet credits.

173. *Pravda*, 26 April 1984. See also Dusko Doder, *Washington Post*, 28 April 1984.

174. *Pravda*, 26 April 1984.

175. *FBIS:ME*, 26 April 1984:i.

176. Cf *Izvestia*, 23 May 1984.

177. For a Saudi evaluation of Saudi–U.S. relations at this time, see the Reuters interview with Prince Bandar Bin Sultan, Saudi ambassador to the United States, *Washington Post*, 11 April 1984.

178. For a description of the Saudi-French arms deal, see the article by Paul Lanier, *New York Times*, 17 January 1984.

179. Bernard Gwertzman, *New York Times*, 18 May 1984.

180. Don Oberdorfer, *Washington Post*, 22 May 1984.

181. David Ignatius, *Wall Street Journal*, 30 May 1984.

182. *Ibid.*

183. Judith Miller, *New York Times*, 4 August 1984.

184. *Kuna*, 14 May 1984 (*FBIS:USSR*, 16 May 1984:H-1). For a Soviet view of Kuwait at this time, see V. Yuryev, "Kuwait Facing the Future," *International Affairs* (Moscow), March 1984:141–47.

185. Jonathan Randal, *Washington Post*, 5 June 1984.

186. John Gosko and Rick Altison, ibid., 20 June 1984.

187. Bernard Gwertzman, *New York Times*, 20 June 1984.

188. David Ottaway, *Washington Post*, 19 June 1984.

189. Bernard Gwertzman, *New York Times*, 20 June 1984.

190. *Kuna*, 9 July 1984 (*FBIS:USSR*, 10 July 1984:H-2).

191. *Krasnaya Zvezda*, 15 July 1984 (*FBIS:USSR*, 17 July 1984:H-3); and *Kuna*, 15 July 1984 (ibid., 16 July 1984:H-3).

192. The agreement was signed in mid-August (*Kuna*, 15 August 1984 [*FBIS:USSR*, 16 August 1984:H-2]). Although the Kuwaitis did not reveal the type of weapons system they purchased from the USSR, it is possible that they were promised the SAM-8, which in some ways is similar to the U.S. Stinger.

193. *Kuna*, 18 July 1984 (*FBIS:USSR*, 19 July 1984:H-1).

194. David Ottaway, *Washington Post*, 1 December 1984.

195. *Ibid.*

196. David Ottaway, ibid., 30 November 1984, and Judith Miller, *New York Times*, 30 November 1984.

197. Translated in *FBIS:USSR*, 5 December 1984:H-1.

198. *Pravda*, 31 December 1983.

199. V. Komarov, "Highways and Byways," *New Times*, no. 2, *1984*:18–21.

200. Gerald Sieb, *Wall Street Journal*, 23 January 1984.

201. Iranian news agency report, cited in *Washington Post*, 24 February 1984.

202. *Pravda*, 7 June 1984.

203. *FBIS:ME*, 12 June 1984:i.

204. Jack Anderson, *Washington Post*, 4 August 1984.

205. Radio Moscow, in Persian, to Iran, 12 April 1984 (*FBIS:USSR*, 18 April 1984:H-4).

206. Radio Moscow, in Persian, to Iran, 19 June 1984 (Ignor Sheftunov commentary) (*FBIS:USSR*, 22 June 1984:H-7).

207. AP report, *New York Times*, 22 July 1984.

208. Robert Duby, *Baltimore Sun*, 3 August 1984.

209. *Izvestia*, 24 September 1984.

210. William Pruzik, *Washington Post*, 3 October 1984.

211. Elaine Scolino, *New York Times*, 4 October 1984.

212. *Ibid.*

213. Drew Middleton, ibid., 18 October 1984.

214. Don Oberdorfer, *Washington Post*, 7 October 1984. As part of the growing U.S.–Iraqi relationship, the U.S. Information Office was reopened in Baghdad for the first time since the Iraqi revolution of 1958 (ibid., 24 October 1984) and the U.S. increased its agricultural exports to Iraq.

215. Tass, 19 October 1984 (*FBIS:USSR*, 22 October 1984:H-1).

216. Don Oberdorfer, *Washington Post*, 29 November 1984.

217. Ibid., 5 December 1984.

218. *FBIS:ME*, 2 April 1984:ii.

219. The head of Jordan's armed forces visited Moscow at this time, as did delegations from the Jordanian-Soviet Friendship Society and the Jordanian National Assembly.

220. See note 11, above.

221. For the text of the 1984 peace plan, see *Pravda*, 30 July 1984 (translated in *Current Digest of the Soviet Press* 36, no 30:9–10).

222. Arafat had signed an agreement with them in Aden in July that included a provision calling for the strengthening of ties with the USSR. For the text of the agreement, see *FBIS:ME*, 13 July 1984:A-1.

223. *INA* (Baghdad), 1 August 1984 (*FBIS:ME*, 2 August 1984:A-2).

224. Cairo Radio on July 30 called it a "constructive addition to efforts being executed by the U.N. to solve the crisis, but seven years too late" (ibid., 31 July 1984:D-1).

225. Damascus Radio, 30 July 1984 (ibid., 31 July 1984:H-1).

226. Radio Moscow, in Arabic, 30 September 1984 (*FBIS:USSR*, 5 October 1984:H-3).

227. Prime Minister Shamir in *Maariv*, 15 July 1984; and *Hadashot*, 22 June 1984.

228. *Pravda* on 8 October 1984 noted that Gromyko had met with Arafat in East Berlin at the latter's request, at which time the PLO leader strongly praised the Soviet stand on a Middle East peace settlement.

229. *Ibid.*, 19 October 1984. There was, however, apparent agreement on arms shipments to Syria.

230. Egyptian Prime Minister Kamal Hassan Ali stated in an interview at the time that this would not affect U.S.–Egyptian ties. (see AP report, *New York Times*, 24 July 1984.)

231. *Izvestia*, 14 October 1984 (translated in *CDSP* 36, no. 41:19).

232. Judith Miller, *New York Times*, 2 October 1984.

233. UPI report, *Washington Post*, 31 October 1984.

234. *Jerusalem Post*, 20 November 1984.

235. It is unclear whether Habash and Hawatmeh used the opportunity of the trip to Moscow to play for time so as to avoid a final decision on the PNC until the last possible moment. From the Soviet perspective, however, consultation with the members of the Democratic Alliance was important at a time that marked a major turning point in PLO fortunes.

236. Tass, 30 November 1984 (*FBIS:USSR*, 4 December 1984:H-1).

237. The speeches and resolutions of the PNC may be found in *FBIS:ME* issues of 23–30 November 1984.

238. Another blow to Assad was the transfer of the PNC headquarters from Damascus to Amman, where the new PNC speaker resided. The warm reception at the Congress for the large Egyptian delegation must have also angered the Syrian President. Indeed, the Syrian-backed Palestine Liberation Front was particularly vituperative in describing the evolving ties between Arafat and the leaders of Jordan and Egypt as "an alliance with the Black September butcher's regime in Amman and the Camp David regime in Egypt" (*FBIS:ME*, 3 January 1985:A-3).

239. For the text of Assad's address of 5 January 1985, see *FBIS:ME*, 7 January 1985: H-1–H-5. By stating "we are sure that those capitulationists and conspirators

will never represent the Palestinian Arab people (p. H-4), Assad implied that he would back his own Palestinian leadership and, in effect, seek to take over the PLO.

240. *FBIS:ME*, 31 December 1984:i.

241. For the text of the agreement, see the AP report in *New York Times*, 24 February 1985.

242. *Pravda*, 20 February 1985. It should be noted that the USSR and the United States had a high-level meeting on the Middle East at this time as part of a series of superpower meetings on regional problems. See ibid., 21 February 1985.

243. Rabat Domestic Service, 7 August 1985 (*FBIS:ME*, 8 August 1985:A-4).

244. *New Times* editorial "Senseless Bloodshed," by D. Zgorsky (*New Times*, no. 23, *1985*, p. 11). It will be remembered that the Soviet Afro-Asian Solidarity Committee also complained at the time of Syrian clashes with the PLO in 1976 and 1983.

245. *Pravda*, 3 June 1985.

246. *Izvestia*, 24 June 1985.

247. Israel maintained a small "security zone" on its northern border with the help of Antoine Lahad's South Lebanese Army.

248. *Al-Qabas* (Kuwait) contended that the USSR advised Syria to use its influence with Berri to end the hijacking "because the United States and Israel are planning a major military operation in Lebanon." (*FBIS:ME*, 24 June 1985:i).

249. *Pravda*, June 20, 1985.

250. *Izvestia*, 10 July 1985.

2

The United States and the Middle East

Barry Rubin

Introduction

U.S. MIDDLE EAST POLICY between 1981 and 1985 came full circle, back to some of the concerns and orientations that marked the Reagan administration's first days in office. The September 1982 Reagan peace plan was finally rejected by Jordan's King Hussein in April 1983, a development that discouraged Washington both about prospects for settlement of the Arab-Israeli conflict and about the reliability of Arab moderates. Consequently, the U.S.–Israel alliance was strengthened, recovering from the blows it suffered during Israel's 1982 intervention in Lebanon, and Syria was again singled out by the United States as the prime obstacle to regional stability.[1]

Parallel with the U.S. efforts to promote the Reagan plan were attempts to remove foreign forces from Lebanon and to reconstitute a viable and pro-Western government there. The presence of U.S. Marines as part of a multinational force in Beirut was intended as a symbol of U.S. commitment to these goals, but that presence became highly controversial at home in proportion to the rising toll of U.S. casualties. Ambassador Philip Habib successfully negotiated a Lebanon-Israel agreement in April 1983, but failed to shake Damascus in its determination to hang on to its sizeable foothold in eastern and northern Lebanon.

The Reagan administration, during its first eighteen months in office, sought to create a "strategic consensus" among Arab states in the Gulf that would be directed against potential Soviet aggression. Emphasis was put on development of a U.S. rapid deployment force (RDF) and on arms sales to countries in the area in response to both the Iranian revolution and the Soviet invasion of Afghanistan. Seeing little prospect for progress on the Arab-Israeli conflict, Washington put a low priority on those issues.

By mid-1982, however, this conception was under serious challenge. Arab states were reluctant to become identified with U.S. objectives and were more worried about actual Israeli and Iranian actions than a potential Soviet assault. Behind the scenes, though, much progress was made toward improving the defense of the Gulf region against threats to stability. Strategic cooperation proved useful as a basis for technical and military coordination, but as a public and political policy strategic consensus enjoyed but little success.

At the same time, a series of armed clashes in Lebanon turned administration attention to that troubled country and, by extension, to the Arab-Israeli conflict. In a cycle of escalation beginning in 1981, Syria introduced antiaircraft missiles in the Bekaa Valley, an act followed that summer by heightened PLO artillery attacks against northern Israel. Ambassador Habib, the president's Middle East envoy, obtained a ceasefire but tensions were dangerously raised. Despite U.S. efforts, Israeli forces crossed into Lebanon in June 1982 and proceeded toward Beirut. While Washington was fairly sympathetic toward a limited, forty-kilometer incursion, the overwhelming Israeli victory (and the negative reaction to it in the Arab world) caused many officials to worry about possible disastrous effects on U.S.-Arab relations. The U.S. media also presented Israeli actions in an extremely negative light, producing some major (albeit temporary) shifts in public opinion.[2]

The United States and the Arab-Israeli Conflict

With the June 1982 resignation of Secretary of State Alexander Haig, a leading advocate of close U.S.-Israeli relations, the stage was set for an experiment by sectors in the State Department, supported by incoming Secretary of State George Shultz and by National Security Adviser William Clark, that favored both a pro-Arab tilt and a top-priority effort to reach a negotiated settlement of the Arab-Israeli conflict. Influenced by the State Department's Bureau of Near East Affairs, under the leadership of Assistant Secretary of State Nicholas Veliotes, they argued that there was a major opportunity for a breakthrough to peace.[3] Jordan was believed ready to enter negotiations, possibly with the permission and hopefully even with the participation of the PLO. In addition Syria, Habib assured Shultz, was ready to negotiate its withdrawal from Lebanon. All of these assertions proved to be erroneous during 1983.

President Ronald Reagan's September 1, 1982, speech explicitly prescribed, in a more detailed way than ever before, a proposed solution for the Arab-Israeli conflict.[4] The President labeled his position as the "next step" in the Camp David "autonomy talks to pave the way for permitting the Palestinian people to exercise their legitimate rights." The Lebanon war, "tragic as it was, has left us with a new opportunity for Middle East peace," Reagan continued. "The military losses of the PLO have not diminished the yearning of the Palestinian people for a just solution of their claims.... While Israel's military successes in Lebanon have demonstrated that its armed forces are second to none in the region, they alone cannot bring just and lasting peace to Israel and her neighbors." The question is "how to reconcile Israel's legitimate security concerns with the legitimate rights of the Palestinians. This must be done through diplomacy rather than on the battlefield and would involve concessions by both sides."

The United States, Reagan continued, had a "special responsibility.... No other nation is in a position to deal with the key parties to the conflict on the basis of trust and reliability." Israel deserved Arab recognition and, Reagan implied, some revision of the pre-1967 boundaries. Up to that point, he said, Israel had lived in narrow borders, within artillery range of hostile Arab armies, and "I am not about to ask Israel to live that way again."

The president advocated, in line with the Camp David accords, a five-year transition period after the election of a self-governing Palestinian authority. In addition, "The immediate adoption of a settlement freeze by Israel, more than any other action, could create the confidence needed for wider participation in these talks." But what specifically was Reagan proposing? "Peace cannot be achieved," he stated, "by the formation of an independent Palestinian state—nor is it achievable on the basis of Israeli sovereignty or permanent control over the West Bank and Gaza." The preferred U.S. solution was "self-government by the Palestinians of the West Bank and Gaza in association with Jordan."

The Reagan plan's approach proceeded from the belief that the United States must show progress toward solving the Arab-Israeli issue—or at least continue to make energetic attempts in that direction—in order to retain U.S. influence in the Arab world. The policy was meant to show the Arabs that America was sympathetic and trying to respond to their grievances. There was also an important domestic component, since dramatic action was deemed necessary to prove that the administration had Middle East policy under control. It was therefore hoped that a broad consensus at home could be built on behalf of the proposals.

The administration hoped that Israel's continuing integration of the West Bank and the PLO's Lebanon defeat had so chastened the PLO and convinced Jordan of the need for haste that the two would cooperate lest the territories be lost to Israel forever. As had happened in the past, the administration was overoptimistic about a supportive Saudi response. Israel itself, however, had not been consulted, since Washington feared a leak and a probable rejection. (The U.S. handling of the issue would make both of these circumstances inevitable.)

At the Arab summit meeting in Fez, Morocco, only a week after Reagan's speech, the results were even more discouraging. Behind the scenes, Washington asked Saudi Arabia to work for a final resolution that would not attack the Reagan plan and, preferably, might even endorse it. Washington reacted optimistically to the meeting's general statement, which did not mention the U.S. proposal but rather adopted a watered-down version of the Fahd plan[5]—although clearly King Hussein had not received the hoped-for mandate to negotiate over the territories' fate. Vice President George Bush said the Fez resolution meant implicit Arab recognition of Israel, while Shultz thought the Arab League Fez summit could be a genuine breakthrough and might even produce an implied recognition of Israel.[6]

Meanwhile, the U.S. Marines who had come to Lebanon as part of a multinational force to supervise the PLO's departure left Beirut on September 10, despite local expressions of concern over the safety of the West Beirut population. After the assassination of Lebanon's President Bashir Gemayel, Israeli troops entered West Beirut and several hundred Palestinian refugees were murdered by Christian Phalange troops in the Sabra and Shatilla camps.

The U.S. government reacted angrily to the Israeli advance, which it criticized as conflicting with the agreement worked out by Habib. Israeli prestige in the United States was further eroded by the massacre, with several dozen members of Congress writing Begin to demand a full-scale investigation. The 1200 Marines again returned to Beirut, despite some domestic concern over the commitment.

Washington called on the Lebanese government to safeguard Palestinian rights, and voted at the United Nations to condemn the Israeli incursion and the massacre. However, the United States generally defended Israel before that international body, opposing strong resolutions condemning the invasion of Lebanon, vetoing a ban on military aid to Israel, and fighting any attempt to revoke Israel's membership in the organization. Nevertheless, Shultz told the General Assembly in late September that Israel must yield territory in order to gain peace, and that the Palestinians had an "undeniable claim" to some form of self-rule.

The question of foreign troops in Lebanon and of continued Israeli settlements in the occupied territories assumed particular importance as King Hussein had designated progress on these issues as preconditions for his participation in negotiations. He hinted at a possible Jordanian-Palestinian delegation including West Bank notables responsive to, though not members of, the PLO. The United States tried to encourage Hussein's participation by linking his decision with future supplies of U.S. arms to Jordan.

United States aid to Israel was untouched by the political frictions. At the end of 1982, not only did Israel obtain $2.5 billion in economic and military assistance from the 1983 U.S. budget ($1.7 billion for the former and $785 million for the latter), but in addition some $510 million that the White House had proposed as loans were converted into outright grants. (United States military aid to Israel had remained steady at around $1 billion a year between 1977 and 1980.) This last step was taken despite the opposition of the White House and of four powerful chairmen of key congressional committees: Senators Charles Percy and Mark Hatfield of the Senate Foreign Relations and Apropriations committees, respectively, and Representatives Clement Zablocki and Jamie Whitten of the House of Representatives Foreign Affairs and Appropriations committees, respectively.

But clearly, mutual credibility in the bilateral relationship had declined. President Reagan, who remained his government's strongest supporter of Israel, was dismayed over bilateral differences on Lebanon; Secretary of Defense Caspar Weinberger was hostile to the U.S.–Israel alliance; and Secretary of State George Shultz and National Security Adviser William Clark were hopeful of a major breakthrough for peace made possible by a tilt toward Saudi Arabia, Jordan, and other Arab states. For their part, Israeli leaders were baffled by changing U.S. signals on Syria, the PLO, and Israeli action in Lebanon. The feeling in Israel was that the invasion benefited the United States by weakening its enemies and enhancing its leverage in the Arab world; in addition, the Reagan plan was believed to be in conflict with the Camp David accords. Defense Minister Ariel Sharon, before his removal in February 1983, was also hostile toward Washington, accusing the United States of attempting to divide Israel politically and to force a return to the 1967 borders.

The years 1981–1982, then, saw swings in both U.S.–Israeli relations and in Washington's hopes for a resolution of the Arab-Israeli conflict. At the end of the period, Lebanon had emerged as a focal point of U.S. involvement, while the absence of a major crisis in the Gulf had eased somewhat some of the keenest U.S. fears of the post-Iranian revolution era. Hopes on the first two points were shattered in the following two years. At the same time, however, the absence of any severe regional crisis avoided the need for any major policy shifts or interventions.

The years 1983–84 were disillusioning ones for U.S. Middle East policy. President Reagan's September 1982 Arab-Israeli peace plan was rejected by all sides, while U.S. intervention in Lebanon suffered a bloody and embarrassing series of setbacks. At the same time, Washington's regional position remained strong as Reagan began his second term in January 1985: the lesson of his first four years was taken evidently to be that less activism there might be both politically safer and better for U.S. interests. During the early months of 1983, American attention was fixed on trying to gain Jordanian acceptance of the Reagan plan, and on helping Israel and Lebanon to reach an agreement that would lead to the withdrawal of Israeli troops. The former effort failed in April; the latter led to the May 1983 Israel-Lebanon accord (although Syrian pressure kept this a dead issue). Only in January 1985 did Israel announce plans for complete withdrawal from Lebanon, after all efforts to reach a diplomatic agreement had broken down.

In the second half of 1983, the U.S. Marines in Lebanon came under increasingly heavy attack. Casualties from spectacular terrorist truck bombings of the Marine headquarters and U.S. embassy in Beirut, growing domestic pressure, inability to outlast a determined Syria, and the lack of a political solution to internal Lebanese quarrels combined to force the withdrawal of U.S. forces in February 1984. (Although this failure was said to have brought lower U.S. credibility in the region, the episode has in reality had little apparent lasting effort on American policy.)

The Iran-Iraq war in the Gulf remained deadlocked, although Iraqi attacks on oil tankers and occasional Iranian reprisals heightened international concern. Washington tilted somewhat more openly toward Iraq, but remained relatively uninvolved in the conflict. The United States continued to sell arms to and attempt to coordinate defensive efforts with the Gulf Arab monarchies.

During the closing months of 1982 and throughout 1983, the United States sought to negotiate the removal of all foreign troops from Lebanon. Shultz accepted the State Department's argument that if arrangements were made for an Israeli withdrawal, the Syrians and PLO would quickly follow suit; hence, Habib devoted relatively little time to working toward an internal Lebanese settlement. Further, progress on Lebanon was deemed essential to King Hussein's entry into peace negotiations. In the Lebanon-Israel talks, Washington argued that the Lebanese government could not sign a peace treaty due to domestic and Arab pressures; Israel disagreed, and Sharon claimed that the United States was blocking a political arrangement. The talks dragged on for months. In the meantime, the United States provided $82 million for emergency relief in Lebanon and $30 million to supplement housing and services, as well as military supplies and training for the Lebanese army.

United States–Israeli tensions reached a peak in February–March 1983, both because of Washington's desire to signal Hussein its willingness to pressure Israel and because of differences over Lebanon. President Reagan stated that it would be wrong for Israel to wait for a peace treaty with Lebanon before withdrawing, while on the Palestinian issue, the President reiterated his belief that the United States had to provide something in the nature of a homeland, but not necessarily a state. He also said that some moderate Arab nations "do want peace and this would involve recognition of Israel's right to exist."

The particular acrimony between the two defense ministers was reflected in some minor confrontations between the two countries' military forces in Beirut. On one much-publicized occasion, a U.S. Marine officer drew his pistol while stopping Israeli tanks from crossing into what was deemed the U.S.–controlled sector. (Such differences were partly due to a refusal of the United States to agree on clear demarcation lines or to carry out proper liaison.) In March 1983, the U.S. Defense Department made public a letter from the Marine Corps commandant to Weinberger saying that Israeli troops had involved U.S. forces in "life-threatening situations" and provocations.

At about the same time, Undersecretary of State Lawrence Eagleburger said that the two countries were working very hard to try to establish a situation in which (confrontations) will not happen again. Washington also obstructed Israeli efforts to build the new Lavi fighter-bomber by holding up licenses, and delayed sales of the U.S.–built F-16. The breakdown in communications also prevented the exchange of military information gained by Israel in the course of the fighting in Lebanon.

When Israel's Kahan commission issued its critical report on Israeli mistakes leading up to the Sabra-Shatilla massacres, Sharon was forced to resign as defense minister and the situation was eased. Sharon's replacement, Moshe Arens, had been highly regarded as Israel's ambassador to the United States, and seemed determined both to resolve the earlier difficulties and to negotiate an agreement in Lebanon.[7] In addition, Israel's image was also getting better in the area of American public opinion. A March 1983 *Washington Post* survey showed that while 29 percent of Americans believed Arab leaders sincerely wanted peace, fifty-two percent thought otherwise. Of those polled, 52 percent sympathized with Israel while 16 percent preferred the position of the Arab nations. In addition, 45 percent rated Israel as the best Middle East ally of the United States, compared with 28 percent who ranked Egypt first. (A September 1982 poll had showed Egypt preferred by a 46 percent-36 percent margin.) Thus, while there were undeniably lasting scars, much of the conflict over the 1982 Lebanon offensive seemed to have dissipated.

The atmosphere was further improved as the United States sought to convince Israel to make concessions in its accord with Lebanon. During his visit to tie up the loose ends of the agreement in April, Shultz predicted success because Jerusalem's withdrawal was "in both the Israeli and Lebanese interests.... And anyway, as a negotiator and mediator you have to be very optimistic. You have to think it will succeed. Otherwise you won't get anywhere." The trip was a success. After two weeks in the region in May, Shultz obtained the agreement ending the state of war and providing security arrangements for southern Lebanon. The agreement was signed May 17.[8]

Shultz announced he was "confident" that Syria would withdraw its troops in the future, despite Damascus's strong opposition to the new bilateral treaty. "Lebanon will again have a chance to be a sovereign country, to decide for itself how it wants to live," the secretary of state proclaimed. This optimism, conditioned partly by the reports

Shultz was receiving from his negotiating team, was not to be fulfilled, however. Within a few days of the treaty's conclusion, the United States was already noting an accelerated Syrian military buildup as well as stepped-up Soviet arms aid to Syria as dangerous. Damascus refused to participate in any further talks with Ambassador Habib, the leading architect of the agreement. Also, Arab pressure on Syria, which it had been hoped would be one of the main props of the U.S. effort, failed to live up to expectations. Further, the course of Lebanon negotiations, the intensified focus on the Lebanon-Israeli talks, and the improvement of U.S.–Israeli relations were also conditioned by developments on the other track of U.S. Middle East policy: the Reagan plan. During the spring of 1983, the PLO rejected the proposal and King Hussein announced his inability to join negotiations.

The United States had pushed to secure an Israeli withdrawal from Lebanon in response to one of King Hussein's conditions. During the months between September 1982 and April 1983 assurances on other matters—including forthcoming U.S. military aid, and the willingness to press Israel for a freeze on settlements—proceeded from Reagan to Hussein. The president also sent a letter to Syrian President Hafiz al-Assad urging Syrian participation in negotiations that would include the matter of the Golan Heights. The U.S. embassy in Amman reported optimistically about the king's intentions, while in Washington the State department was remarkably confident, both in public and in private, about the prospects for a breakthrough.[9]

By March 1983, however, U.S. impatience with the king's postponements was beginning to show. Secretary of State Shultz said on March 13 "I think it's time" for the king to decide on entering negotiations.[18] But Hussein could not obtain PLO cooperation, and would not join the talks on his own. A February Palestine National Council meeting had rejected the plan, and Yasser Arafat could not deliver the necessary backing even after Hussein made further concessions. The absence of Saudi and other Arab support and the king's apparent belief that the United States could not secure the necessary Israeli concessions were no doubt other factors in his decision. While Israel's own opposition to the plan can be cited as a further discouraging point, that position would not have prevented—in fact, it would have enhanced—the king's opportunity to use diplomatic means to drive a wedge between Israel and the United States, to Jordan's (and, generally, Arab) advantage. Nevertheless, on April 11 Hussein announced his decision not to accept the Reagan plan.[10]

Understandably, President Reagan continued to insist that his plan was still alive; and while there was an element of political and diplomatic expediency in such pronouncements (which continued throughout the following months), the program's poor prospects did not negate its persistent importance. The objective of a West Bank and Gaza Strip federated to Jordan was now official U.S. policy, and would for some time to come remain the linchpin of Washington's efforts to resolve the Arab-Israeli conflict.

The most immediate effect of King Hussein's decision, however, was to amplify American denunciations of the PLO and sharply improve relations with Israel. Only a week after Hussein's announcement, for example, Washington reversed an earlier decision and agreed to allow Israel to buy U.S.–designed components for its new Lavi aircraft. Two months later, Undersecretary of State Eagleburger announced that U.S.–Israeli relations were "back on an even keel," and two days after that Secretary of Defense Weinberger signaled his willingness to reinstate the bilateral memorandum of understanding that had been suspended following Israel's extension of its law to the Golan Heights in December 1981. If Hussein had agreed to enter negotiations, the Reagan Administration had been prepared to pressure Israel for concessions—but the Arab failure to take up the U.S. offer opened a new period of greatly heightened U.S.–Israel cooperation. One reason for this development was Washington's attempt to threaten Syria enough to convince it to make a deal over Lebanon. Such an objective required the United States to show the determination to stay in Lebanon and a willingness to escalate, if necessary, the conflict with Syria (with the implicit threat of potential Israeli military efforts, too)—in other words, to frighten Damascus without becoming involved in a shooting war.

Obviously, given Syria's awareness of the domestic opposition to remaining in Lebanon in both Israel and the United States, it was difficult for such a bluff to succeed. In addition, Syria continued to have many more incentives for staying in, rather than withdrawing from, that country. Shultz's July visit to Syria made no headway, even as Washington supported Gemayel's suspension of the Lebanon-Israel pact in a futile attempt to keep the door open for developments that might win Syrian acceptance.

During those months, however, Israel was moving toward a partial pullback in Lebanon. The issues leading Jerusalem toward this step included continuing casualties, domestic pressure, disillusionment with the Beirut government's unwillingness to accept bilateral normalization of relations (and its inability to control the country), and frustration with U.S. policy. The last-mentioned problem developed out of a paradox in the American position—or, rather, from conflicts in the successive and contradictory stands emanating from Washington. From January to April 1983, for example, the United States had pressed for a rapid Israel-Lebanon accord to be followed by the withdrawal of Israeli troops. Once the Reagan plan was rejected and the United States adopted a tough policy toward Syria, however, there was a complete turnabout. From June 1983 on, the United States wanted Israel to stay in Lebanon—perhaps even to initiate threats against Syria—and urged Beirut to suspend the bilateral agreement worked out by Washington itself only weeks earlier.

The United States was worried that a partial Israeli pullback from the hotly contested Chouf mountains would be the first step toward the permanent partition of Lebanon, and could only further encourage Syrian intransigence. Washington therefore tried to convince Israel to hold the line, winning two postponements of the shift to give U.S. negotiators more time in their efforts to make headway with Damascus. But continued U.S. failure to make progress caused Washington to finally accept the Israeli move in August. With the Chouf now under the control of pro-Syrian Druze forces, the U.S. Marines guarding the airport in Beirut's southern suburbs came under increasing artillery and sniper fire. They had originally arrived in August 1982 to monitor the PLO's retreat from Beirut. That accomplished, the U.S. forces left on September 10, but 1600 U.S. Marines returned nineteen days later after the Sabra and Shatilla massacres. At that time President Reagan stated that there was no intention or expectation that U.S. armed forces would become involved in hostilities.

The Lebanon Debacle

At first, the Marines were left alone by the local forces, although the U.S. embassy in Beirut was hit by a suicide car-bomb on April 18, 1983, with a loss of forty lives—mostly Lebanese employees. A month later, the United States and Israel signed a confidential agreement recognizing Israel's right to retaliate against terrorist attacks and accepting a delay in Israeli withdrawal until Syria and the PLO did the same. During July and August, shelling and sniper attacks escalated against the Marine positions near the Beirut airport; about a dozen U.S. soldiers were killed during this period. Reacting to this problem, President Reagan ordered an additional 2000 Marines onto U.S. ships off Lebanon's coast and permitted U.S. artillery to wage "aggressive defense" tactics against harassing gun positions. In mid-September, U.S. Navy guns fired in support of Lebanese army forces defending against advances by the pro-Syrian Druze militia.

The casualties and slightly escalating U.S. strategy provoked much debate in Congress. After heated debate, a compromise was reached giving the president eighteen months to maintain U.S. forces in Lebanon. This timing was important: two weeks later, on October 23, a suicide truck-bomb destroyed the Marine barracks and killed 241 American soldiers. The strong reaction in the United States greatly increased domestic political opposition to a continued U.S. presence. An investigation by the congressional Long Commission criticized the handling of the Marines' security and the alleged lack of political direction for the operation. Public opinion, however, remained mixed. A *New York Times* poll taken just after the heavy casualties showed that 48 percent of the respondents supported the Marines going to Lebanon, and 34 percent thought the government had adequately explained why the Marines were there. About 50 percent thought the Marines could not keep the peace, while 37 percent were more optimistic. More than 35 percent of those polled favored withdrawal, as against only 21 percent who wanted to continue the present mission.[22] Meanwhile, congressional Democrats were developing a resolution seeking a "prompt and orderly withdrawal" of the Marines.[23]

A December 1983 air raid against Syrian positions after U.S. reconnaissance flights were fired upon resulted in the shooting down of two U.S. planes by the Syrians, with one airman killed and the other, Lieutenant Robert Goodman, captured. The latter officer was freed with the help of Democratic presidential candidate Jesse Jackson during a dramatic trip to Damascus in January 1984. Naturally, with 1984 a presidential election year, partisan and popular criticism had more effect. The Reagan administration continued to argue against a pullout, but was obviously ready to find some face-saving way out of Lebanon. For one thing, it no longer maintained that U.S. troops would be kept until either stability was reestablished or foreign troops removed. In early February, President Reagan announced the pullout of 1600 Marines; they departed without further incident, although amid some final shelling of Druze positions. The American naval units, finally, sailed away from the Lebanon coast in March.

Given the loss of U.S. leverage in Lebanon, the State department could only hope that Damascus might play some constructive role in putting together an internal political settlement or making a behind-the-scenes agreement that would facilitate Israeli withdrawal. These expectations were again disappointed, however. In September 1984, the U.S. embassy was moved before proper security arrangements were in place and another car bomb attack registered heavy losses. Again, administration handling was criticized by, among others, Democratic presidential candidate Walter Mondale.

Yet while U.S. efforts in Lebanon between 1982 and 1984 seemed to end in a debacle, the political fallout was quite limited. At home, once the Marines had been withdrawn the issue largely disappeared, and would not seriously recur during the ensuing presidential campaign. Moreover, while there was much talk of damage to U.S. credibility in the region, there seemed to be no long-range effect—nor did Lebanon come under complete Syrian or radical control, as the administration had earlier warned.

U.S.–Israeli Relations

A number of factors combined to improve the state of U.S.–Israeli relations from mid-1983 onward. To begin with, Syrian pressure and Syrian- and Iranian-assisted terrorism struck at the U.S. position in Lebanon, bringing together Washington and Jerusalem. Israel's May 1983 accord with Lebanon showed a way out for Israel's military presence in Lebanon (which had provoked some Reagan administration hostility), but then Syria was seen as blocking implementation of the agreement and hence of the Israeli withdrawal.

The rejection of the Reagan plan by Jordan, Syria, and the PLO also closed a door in the face of administration peace efforts. Israel's earlier opposition to the plan had been expected, since the proposal was intended as a concession to the Arab side; but King Hussein's statements critical of U.S. policy stirred real resentment in the White House and Congress. Some officials, including Secretary of State Shultz and National Security Adviser McFarlane, who had entered office willing to pressure Israel toward a settlement, were by now skeptical of Arab willingness to negotiate seriously to this end. Finally, the departure of Prime Minister Menahem Begin and Defense Minister Ariel Sharon, whose personal relationship with U.S. leaders had been marked by friction, also eased matters. (The coming of the 1984 U.S.

elections, to the extent that it increased pro-Israel activity among many American political figures, also played a role, though not to the degree usually attributed to such considerations.)

The November 1983 bilateral strategic cooperation agreement provided for a joint commission to coordinate military planning, maneuvers, and stockpiles of U.S. equipment in Israel. That accord remained mostly symbolic, however, since there was little implementation. Materially, U.S. aid levels continued to climb and, for the 1984 budget, monies previously charged as loans were now transformed into grants. Aid was also provided for building Israel's new Lavi plane, in spite of the fact that some U.S. aircraft companies claimed it would compete with their product lines on the export market. Congress also passed a bill in 1984 providing for the establishment of a free-trade zone in Israel. That year's budget provided $2.6 billion in aid for Israel, $1.4 billion of it in the form of military aid. However, Washington demanded certain budget cutbacks and antiinflation measures in Israel's economy as a prerequisite for increasing aid in 1985; given U.S. budget deficits, there was an inclination to freeze aid levels.

One controversy that spanned most of 1984 concerned a bill introduced by Senator Daniel Moynihan and Congressman Tom Lantos in late 1983 proposing that the U.S. embassy in Israel be moved from Tel Aviv to Jerusalem. The administration opposed this measure, warning that Arab objections might lead to turmoil and anti-Americanism in the region. Supporters responded that the refusal to recognize Israel's long-functioning capital was a foolish anomaly in U.S. policy. Reagan threatened to veto the proposal, although the administration said it could accept a nonbinding resolution. Given this controversy, the bill never came up for a final vote.

Arab-Israeli Peace Process

In September 1982 Reagan launched an initiative that came to be known as the Reagan plan. The plan favored Jordanian rule over the West Bank in a federation with the local Palestinians. In exchange, the Arab states would recognize and make peace with Israel, and there would be some unspecified border modifications in the West Bank. The U.S. State department confidently explained that King Hussein would accept the plan and negotiate with Israel, possibly with PLO-approved Palestinians in his delegation.

In March 1984, however, King Hussein rejected this plan in a speech attacking U.S. policy. Although the king stressed his interest in diplomacy in meetings with and in communications to high U.S. officials, his unpredictability convinced important elements in the administration of a general Arab inability or unwillingness to act constructively. Similarly, Saudi Arabia's failure to provide leverage over Syria on Lebanon or to help Jordan be more forthcoming on the Reagan plan also disillusioned U.S. officials on the role and potential of that Arab state. Consequently, despite Arab calls for more initiatives or efforts, there was by now little American interest in striving to go beyond the earlier proposal. As Shultz told the *New York Times* on March 20, 1984: "We have to get over this notion that every time things don't go just to everybody's satisfaction in the Middle East, it's the United States's fault or it's up to the United States to do something about it." The Reagan plan continued to be the official U.S. policy toward the issue.

Egyptian President Hosni Mubarak suggested that the United States put a high priority on peace efforts by helping amend United Nations Resolution 242 and trying to bring the PLO into negotiations. There was little American enthusiasm for this approach, however, which had been tried by President Carter in 1977. On the other hand, Washington was pleased with Egypt's progress toward reintegration in the Arab mainstream without having to abandon either Camp David or its strong relationship with the United States. The United States also contributed to a Jordan-Egypt rapprochement by bringing Hussein and Mubarak together in Washington in February 1984. The U.S. was further encouraged by the formal resumption of diplomatic relations between the two countries in September 1984. In February 1985, an agreement between Hussein and Arafat calling for a joint Palestinian-Jordanian negotiating team seemed to once again open up the prospects of an Arab-Israeli peace settlement, and the United States sent both Deputy Secretary of State for Middle East Affairs Richard Murphy and Shultz to the region to try to reinforce what appeared to be a newly emergent peace process.[11]

The Gulf

Jordanian rejection of the Reagan plan, both in itself and because of the resulting sentiment in Congress, led the administration to withdraw in March 1984, a request for funding a Jordanian rapid deployment force for use in the Gulf. The plan had been to supply two

Jordanian brigades, totaling about 8000 men, with 1600 Stinger anti-aircraft missiles, a number of C-130 transport planes, and other equipment.

In dealing with the Gulf region, U.S. interests were defined as promoting stability, minimizing Soviet influence, and assuring the continued free flow of oil. These interests were read to mean support for the Gulf Arab monarchies against direct or indirect Iranian aggression and against internal upheaval. At the same time, however, there was a feeling that U.S. opposition to Iran was constrained by the wish to prevent Tehran from turning toward its powerful northern neighbor, the USSR, or of becoming so unstable as to open the way to a pro-Soviet regime or to disintegration. The Pentagon's Defense Guidance statement—its five-year master plan for the 1984–88 period—ranked the defense of Southwest Asia as second only to the defense of North America and Western Europe. In the statement's words: "Our principle [sic] objectives are to assure continued access to Persian Gulf oil and to prevent the Soviets from acquiring political-military control of the oil directly or through proxies. It is essential that the Soviet Union be confronted with the prospect of a major conflict should it seek to reach oil resources of the Gulf. Whatever the circumstances, we should be prepared to introduce American forces directly into the region should it appear that the security of access to Persian Gulf oil is threatened."

The RDF had 230,000 Army, Navy, Marines and Air Force personnel theoretically available to a "Central Command" force in time of emergency. The RDF's jurisdiction covered U.S. activities in the Gulf and in twenty countries (not including Israel). In practice, however, the United States was still a long way from having an effective regional strike force. United States–Egyptian maneuvers, identified as Bright Star 83, were held in August 1983; the two countries were unable to agree, though, on terms for upgrading the Egyptian base at Ras Bannas for U.S. use in regional contingency planning. In February 1983 a Congressional Budget Office report warned that reinforcement of the U.S. Rapid Deployment Force (RDF) would leave gaps in Europe that would weaken NATO in the event of a conflict there. The RDF as currently constituted, the report pointed out, had little chance of stopping a major Soviet thrust but "could probably serve successfully in support of friendly Arab states involved in regional conflicts, which are not unlikely."

A fresh concern for the United States in 1983–1984 was concern over potential dangerous turns in the Iran-Iraq war. First, there were reports that Iraq might collapse due to Iran's continuing military pressure or as a result of internal economic pressures. Second, Baghdad was using its new French-built Super-Etendard planes, equipped with anti-ship Exocet missiles, to attack tankers carrying Iranian oil. For its part, the Iranians threatened to close the Gulf to all oil tankers. The United States made it clear that in such a contingency its military forces would make sure that the Gulf remained open to shipping. In October 1983 Secretary of State Shultz stated that Washington would not accede to the blackmail implicit in closing the Gulf.

To avoid even the need for such military action—and responding to reports that Iraq might crumble under the Iranian attack—the Reagan administration carefully considered a greater tilt toward Iraq. Such ideas were bolstered when, in the middle of the policy reassessment, terrorist attacks organized by Iranian forces struck against U.S. Marines in Lebanon and the U.S. embassy in Kuwait. The upshot was that in December 1983 the U.S. Middle East special negotiator, Ambassador Donald Rusmfeld, became the highest-ranking U.S. official to visit Baghdad in six years. Yet the United States cautiously avoided involvement in the Iran-Iraq war. A policy evaluation had concluded in the spring of 1984 that Iraq was not in imminent danger of military collapse. As for the economic problems, these could be dealt with through providing credits—as the United States and a number of other countries did—and by the implementation of Iraq's plans for new or expanded oil export pipelines through Turkey, Saudi Arabia, and Jordan. (There were hints that Washington had assured Baghdad that Israel would not attack its projected pipeline to Jordan's Gulf of Aqaba.)

Otherwise, U.S. capabilities for helping Iraq were limited. Direct and indirect economic assistance was granted, U.S. construction companies worked on planning new pipelines, and the administration struggled to keep Congress from returning Iraq to the list of countries aiding terrorism. (The administration had removed it in October 1983.) Between 1982 and 1984, Washington granted Iraq $2 billion in commodity credits, and some intelligence information was already being shared. Washington also put pressure on a number of friendly nations, including South Korea, Brazil, and Israel, to stop arms exports to Iran, and tightened its own licensing procedures in January 1984. Shipments of U.S. military equipment had already been banned, and those seeking to circumvent the boycott were prosecuted.

After the attack on Marine headquarters in Beirut, U.S. officials charged Iranian forces with backing the terrorists, although they stopped short of blaming the Tehran government. There was also great concern that light planes provided by Iran might be used to attack U.S. ships off Lebanon. Iran, along with Syria, Libya, and South Yemen, was on the list of countries considered to be aiding terrorism.

The United States maintained fifteen warships, led by the carrier *Midway,* in the Arabian Sea, as well as four small vessels in the Gulf itself. In February 1984 the U.S. destroyer *Lawrence* fired warning shots at an Iranian patrol plane and frigate that approached it near the Straits of Hormuz. The U.S. Navy also escorted oil tankers chartered to supply these ships with fuel to petroleum terminals in Bahrain.

The U.S. tilt toward Iraq, however, was not only constrained by strategic factors but was also partly offset by other U.S. actions. For example, U.S.–Iranian trade increased in 1983, while U.S.–Iraqi trade declined. Also, in March 1984, the U.S. government criticized Baghdad for its use of poison gas. The reestablishment of U.S.–Iraqi diplomatic relations in November 1984 was a symbolic gesture inclining toward more cooperation, but the overall extent of the U.S. tilt should not be exaggerated—nor are there any indications that it will increase markedly in the near future.

Saudi Arabia and the Gulf Arabs

Concern that Iran's battlefield frustration might be taken out against Gulf Arab monarchies prompted continued U.S. arms sales to Saudi Arabia and its allied sheikdoms.[12] When Iranian planes attacked Saudi tankers in May 1984, Washington dispatched KC10 tankers to allow Saudi F-15 fighters to stay aloft, while U.S.-manned AWACS early-warning planes that had been supplied earlier monitored the skies. Finally, some 400 Stinger anti-aircraft missiles were also sent, to protect ground installations.[13]

In all cases, the confidence-building aspects of these weapons supplies were deemed as important as—perhaps even more important than—their military utility. The administration also sought to send an additional 1200 portable Stingers, valued at $140 million, thus reinstating a Saudi order that had earlier been cancelled at the same time as certain proposed arms sales to Jordan; however, Congress was reluctant to proceed on this matter. Similarly, the administration was not forthcoming on a Kuwaiti request for Stingers, due both to U.S. concern over proper protection for the technology involved and to a distaste for Kuwait's ongoing criticism of close relations with the United States in defense of Gulf security. However, when Kuwait bought some arms from the USSR, planning to blend it with U.S. warning equipment, Washington took the news quite calmly.

In May 1984, President Reagan wrote King Fahd affirming support for Saudi Arabia in any confrontation with Iran and urging cooperation in advanced defensive planning; the Saudis were reluctant, however, to commit themselves to such an involvement. Washington also supported an Arab resolution in the United Nations that condemned Iranian attacks on Gulf shipping while remaining silent on similar Iraqi actions. The administration was also very pleased by the shooting down of an Iranian fighter by Saudi F-15s, aided by U.S. AWACS and aerial tankers, in June. Some sixty-two F-15s were delivered by the United States to Saudi Arabia between 1981 and 1983. The sale of more F-15s to that country was a major arms-sale project to be presented to Congress in 1985.

While U.S.–Saudi relations remained important for Washington, the relative leverage of the Arab oil producers fell with economic shifts and because of an oil-supply glut. United States exports to Arab countries dropped 9.1 percent from the first half of 1982 to the first half of 1983, while imports declined by 53.4 percent. Saudi oil exports to the United States were down 41.5 percent during the same period, while imports from the United States declined by only 4.3 percent. Thus, Saudi exports declined by $3.1 billion while the overall U.S. balance of trade with Arab oil producers showed a surplus.

As the funds of Arab states fell due to reduced production and lower prices, the volume of U.S. business with the Gulf Arab states began to follow suit. The oil boom that had begun in 1973 was over— or at least its first phase was over. While the Gulf continued to be an important priority for U.S. foreign policy, there were visible signs that it was playing a less important role than in earlier years.

Terrorism

Assaults on American installations in Lebanon and Kuwait, along with related attacks in Europe that were apparently Middle East in origin, further heightened U.S. consciousness over the dangers of terrorism stemming from regional issues. Not only was terrorism seen as a threat in itself, but also increasingly as an extension of political and military struggles. In Lebanon, for instance, it had proven an effective means of leverage in defeating U.S. policy objectives.

Iran, Libya, and Syria were identified as countries promoting anti-American terrorism. The Reagan administration remained particularly vocal on the dangers of Libyan-supported subversion. United States aid to the Sudan was based to a large extent on Washington's concern over real and alleged Libyan efforts at destabilization of that neighboring state. Washington sought to persuade European countries to impose economic sanctions on Libya, but with little success. United States export controls already denied Libya most products, and trade between the countries fell from $800 million in 1981 to less than $200 million in 1983.

In February 1983, four U.S. AWACS reconnaissance planes were sent to Egypt after Washington charged Kaddafi with planning a coup in the Sudan. United States Ambassador to the United Nations Jean Kirkpatrick stated that the United States had a strong strategic interest in assuring that Kaddafi was not able to upset neighboring governments or to intervene militarily in other countries. Similarly, when mysterious mines appeared in the Red Sea in August 1984, Washington blamed Libya. Egypt's request for American mine-sweeping helicopters and other equipment to clear the mines was seen as evidence of U.S. power's continuing prestige and importance in the area.

Given Washington's attitude toward Libya, the announcement of a Morocco-Libya merger in September 1984 provoked horror in the administration—particularly since it had not known of the move in advance. Although the plan never amounted to much, the fact that such a close U.S. ally as Morocco would dally with Libyan leader Muammar al-Kaddafi emphasized how difficult it was going to be to isolate him.

In December 1984 a Kuwaiti airliner was hijacked to Iran where Shi'a Muslim terrorists murdered two American A.I.D. officials before being finally captured by Iranian authorities. There was a great deal of suspicion that, at worst, Tehran was implicated in the operation and, at best, was slow to react against it. United States officials demanded the trial or extradition of the terrorists, as U.S.–Iranian relations remained totally frozen. Secretary of State Shultz called for retaliation after the murder of the two State Department employees, but the Defense department was reluctant to act. It was clear that, although the Reagan administration had come to office in 1981 emphasizing its high priority on antiterrorism, it had been unable to formulate any effective deterrent to such deeds.

The Policy Process

United States Middle East policy during the Reagan administration was marked by a number of internal disputes during 1981–1982. The resignation of Secretary of State Alexander Haig was partly related to disagreements with other high officials, most notably National Security Adviser Clark, over the handling of Lebanon, and with Secretary of Defense Weinberger over whether to tilt toward Israel or toward the Arabs. When Shultz replaced Haig in mid-1982, he was determined to make a high-priority initiative on the Arab-Israeli conflict. The result was the Reagan plan, which Shultz had been urged to adopt by the Near East bureau of the State department, headed by Assistant Secretary of State (and former U.S. ambassador to Jordan) Nicholas Veliotes. Veliotes insisted privately and publicly that King Hussein would accept the Reagan plan in some form and come forward for negotiations. Similar perceptions—and a belief in the ability to enlist Syrian cooperation over Lebanon—were echoed by U.S. negotiator Philip Habib and his deputy, Ambassador Morris Draper.

This trio proved incorrect on all points. The Syrians dug in their heels against any deal—even refusing to allow Habib to come to Damascus—while Jordan rejected the president's plan in extremely strong language. Both the White House and Shultz were disillusioned with this team: Habib returned to retirement, while Veliotes and Draper were moved to other posts.

During 1983 there was a rapid rotation of key policymakers. Robert McFarlane, a Marine colonel who had served as the administration's original State Department counselor, became first Clark's deputy at the National Security Council, then Habib's replacement as Lebanese negotiator, and finally Clark's successor as the President's assistant for national security affairs. Shultz and McFarlane favored the sending of U.S. troops to Lebanon, and a tough policy designed to force Syria to back down there. This position, in turn, pushed them closer to Israel, as did the Reagan plan's gloomy fate. By contrast, Weinberger—and CIA Director William Casey in a secondary role—

was opposed to the presence of U.S. forces in Lebanon, and against any escalation of pressure there. The resulting friction created a great deal of bitterness at State and the NSC, whose leaders saw Weinberger as undermining their policy. The eventual withdrawal of the Marines, as well as the dispute over the handling of terrorism, made them more angry with the Defense department's performance.

The position of McFarlane and Shultz had, in some ways, brought the administration full circle to its original policy of 1981. They were for a strong alignment with Israel and a posture that saw Syria as a major obstacle to U.S. interests. At the same time, they did not over-estimate Soviet power in the region and were much less worried— about security issues in the Gulf.

Despite Democratic criticisms of Lebanon, U.S. Middle East policy was on a relatively bipartisan basis at this time. On covert U.S. aid to Afghan guerrillas—an operation Democrats oppose in regard to Nicaragua—they tended to support increased help along the administration's lines. Equally, there was little congressional controversy over Gulf policy (although there was some concern that Reagan was getting too close to intervention) or over Arab-Israeli policy. Most important, while there continued to be many within the career bureaucracy who felt that major, urgent initiatives were needed on the Arab-Israeli conflict (among other issues), top policymakers were rather disillusioned concerning the possibility of any dramatic break-throughs, and unconvinced of the need for U.S. action. They were far more willing to wait and see if the regional actors would take steps toward resolving their own problems.

NOTES

1. For a more detailed discussion of the Reagan policy process and the early period of administration policy, see Barry Rubin, "The Reagan Administration and the Middle East," in Ken Oye et al., *The Eagle Defiant* (New York, 1982), and *Secrets of State* (New York: Oxford University Press 1985). See also Christopher Madison, "U.S. Balancing Act in the Middle East," *National Journal*, 28 November 1981.

2. See Itamar Rabinovich, *The War for Lebanon* (Ithaca, N.Y.: Cornell University Press, 1984), and Alexander Haig, *Debacle* (New York, 1984).

3. See Shultz's testimony of 12 July 1982, Walter Laqueur and Barry Rubin, *The Israel-Arab Reader* (New York, 1984), pp. 656–63.

4. Text in ibid, pp. 650–52.

5. For a discussion of the Fahd plan, see *The Middle East Contemporary Survey* 6 (1981–82):202–207.

6. The text of the Fez Plan is to be found in Laqueur and Rubin, *Israel-Arab Reader*, pp. 663–664.

7. For the Kahan Commission report, see *The Beirut Massacre* (New York: Karz-Cohl Pub., 1983).

8. Laqueur and Rubin, *Israel-Arab Reader*, pp. 691–95.

9. Karen Elliot House, *Wall Street Journal*, 14 and 15 April 1983.

10. Hussein's statement is reproduced in Laqueur and Rubin, *Israel-Arab Reader*, pp. 686–691.

11. The revival of the peace process in 1985 is discussed in pp. 51–54 of this volume.

12. President Reagan said of the Saudis: "Saudi Arabia is a leader of the moderate Arab states. I believe the Saudis are the key to spreading the peace throughout the Mideast instead of just having it confined to Israel and Egypt." *Washington Post*, 1 November 1981.

13. For a detailed examination of the escalation of the Gulf war, see pp. 40–44 of this volume.

3

Western Europe and the Middle East Since the Lebanon War

Robert E. Hunter

OR THE UNITED STATES, events in Lebanon in 1982–85 had a highly chastening effect on policymakers who had been ambitious for U.S. activity in the Middle East. The Lebanon experience colored and conditioned virtually all U.S. Middle East policy for sometime thereafter. This has ranged from caution in Arab-Israeli peacemaking to the American tilt toward Iraq against Iran, the supposed progenitor of Shi'a terrorism in Lebanon. By contrast, basic European attitudes toward the Middle East were not vitally affected by events in Lebanon. There has been no "sea change" over Lebanon, no neuralgic response to all things Middle Eastern, although, as will be discussed below, other factors have influenced both thinking and policy in Western Europe.

There is, however, a conceptual problem in analyzing European policy toward the Middle East, because—for many purposes concerning events in the outside world—there is no such thing as "Western Europe." Instead, there is a collection of independent sovereign states, each with its particular viewpoint on, interests in, and independent policies toward the Middle East—and all colored by past associations. Thus, any statement about "European" attitudes and policies will be at best incomplete. In fact, even talk about a collective "European" attitude toward the Middle East began to be heard only after the 1973 crisis. Moreover, while in the last decade or so a "European" approach has indeed developed on a few underlying Middle East issues, considerable differences still exist in the policies of individual European states toward the region.

Nevertheless, all is not anarchy from the standpoint of analysis. In fact, since 1973 enough similarity of position, interest, and outlook on the two underlying issues of the Middle East—the Arab-Israeli conflict at one end and Gulf security and oil at the other—has emerged in most West European countries to permit a number of useful generalizations. (Of course, it remains important to be aware of nuances and difference in the policies of individual countries.)

Thus, any survey of European policy toward the Middle East in the post-Lebanon period should be conducted on two levels: collective and individual. Also, West European views of, and policy toward, the Middle East in the period after the Israeli invasion of Lebanon can only be understood by reference to what went before. This discussion will therefore begin with a brief history of European policy toward the Middle East between 1973 and June 1982.

Europe and the Middle East 1973–1982

The year 1973 marked the beginning of a collective European policy toward the Middle East. Before then, individual West European countries had pursued almost totally independent policies that were, at times, in conflict with each other. There were two basic factors behind the development of a collective European policy: the dynamics of intra-European cooperation and events in the Middle East.

European Political Cooperation

Among the member states of the European Community (EC), a loose form of cooperation on a limited range of "foreign" policy problems has grown up during the past decade-and-a-half. This process, which is not expressly sanctioned by the Treaty of Rome, is known by the formal title European Political Cooperation (PoCo), and has steadily increased in importance. Indeed, it can be seen in part as an effort to compensate for some of the political elan lost by the community as various economic and political problems have sapped much of its idealism and even a good deal of its purpose.

It should not be remarkable that the area in which European Political Cooperation has been most active over much of its lifetime has been the Middle East. The latter is a region of critical importance to West European nations because of its oil, the role of the Soviet Union, its proclivity for conflict (including a terrorism that at times spills over onto the Continent), and—to a greater or lesser degree—sheer proximity. The Middle East has two other characteristics that have led to its being singled out by European Political Cooperation: 1) it does not involve the direct interests of any one EC country to the extent that placing Middle East issues in a wider political context would lead to the unacceptable goring of European oxen; and 2) it is a region in which, during the past two decades, Western leadership has been exercised by the United States. Indeed, while it is rarely stated so baldly, one of the central purposes of European Political Cooperation has been to develop a foreign policy personality, however fledgling and conditioned, whose distinction from the policies of the United States is an end in itself.[1]

Regional Events

Events in the Middle East have also had an important impact on the development of a collective West European policy. Most significant, of course, have been the Arab-Israeli war of 1973 and the ensuing oil crisis. In this connection, events of 1973 had two important consequences: 1) they dramatically highlighted the vulnerability of Europe's energy supplies to hostile actions by Middle Eastern states (threatening in turn significant balance-of-payments and other economic problems for most European countries); and 2) they gave the Arab oil producers tremendous financial power and generated a new wave of Arab activism vis-à-vis the Arab-Israeli conflict, calculated to gain sympathy for the Palestinian cause and to find a solution favorable to the Arab position.

Western Europe needed the Arabs, then, in order both to secure its energy supplies and to finance its mounting trade deficits, both through greater access to Arab markets and through the investment in Europe of part of the so-called petrodollars. For their part, the Arabs concluded that they could effectively exploit the Europeans' new vulnerability in order to change the latter's attitudes toward the Arab-Israeli conflict and the Palestinian issue. (Such a change would obviously be a tremendous victory for the Arab cause.) Most important, however, the Arabs thought that they could use the Europeans to pressure the United States into changing its policies. This linkage between economics and politics thus became the basis for the so-called Euro-Arab dialogue, and the beginning of a dramatic change in European attitudes toward the Arab-Israeli issue.[2]

In November 1973, the EC issued a declaration that set the framework for its Middle East policy. The declaration's principal points were as follows:

[The EC members] consider that a peace agreement should be
based particularly on the following points:
1. the inadmissibility of the acquisition of territory by force;
2. the need for Israel to end the territorial occupation which it
has maintained since the conflict of 1967;
3. respect for the sovereignty, territorial integrity, and independence of every State in the area and their right to live in peace
within secure and recognized boundaries;
4. recognition that, in the establishment of a just and lasting
peace, account must be taken of the legitimate rights of the Palestinians.
      They recall that, according to Resolution No. 242, the peace
settlement must be the object of international guarantee. They consider that such guarantees must be reinforced, among other means,
by the dispatch of peace-keeping forces to the demilitarized zones
envisaged in Article 2(c) of Resolution No. 242. They are agreed
that such guarantees are of primary importance in settling the overall situation in the Middle East in conformity with Resolution No.
242, to which the Council refers in Resolution No. 338. They reserve the right to make proposals in this connexion.[3]

Since this first declaration, there has been periodic talk of European
initiatives regarding the Middle East.
      However, in addition to sharing these occasional common posi-
tions on the Arab-Israeli conflict, individual West European countries
have proceeded to develop extensive and independent sets of economic and political relations with individual Middle Eastern countries. Britain, for example, has continued to build on its long-standing
relations with the Arab states of the Persian Gulf; France has developed a special relationship with Iraq; while Italy, West Germany, and
a number of other European countries have developed new links with
individual Middle Eastern countries.[4] An important point to bear in
mind here, however, is that European activism in the Middle East, especially as regards the Arab-Israeli conflict, has been in direct proportion to two basic factors: economic considerations, especially the
availability and price of oil; and political considerations, especially
the degree of U.S. involvement in Arab-Israeli peacemaking and the
level of Arab pressure.
      Thus, during 1977–78, after the shock of the oil crisis had sub-
sided and the United States was involved in the Camp David process,
the level of European diplomatic activity subsided. But during 1979–

1980, when the Iranian revolution led to an upsurge in oil prices and as the second stage of the Camp David peace process (addressing the West Bank and Gaza) became bogged down, there was another flurry of European activity on the Arab-Israeli conflict. Most notably, the European summit at Venice in the summer of 1980 produced recommendations that the Americans believed were directly at variance with the Camp David accords. The EC called for the "association" of the Palestine Liberation Organization with negotiations—a position that went well beyond Washington's tolerance as well as its stated commitments. So did the EC's recommendation in the Venice Declaration for "self-determination" on the West Bank, which was generally recognized as a code phrase for an independent Palestinian state.[5]

U.S.–European Tensions

A byproduct of greater West European involvement in Middle East diplomacy during the past decade or so has been increasing irritation between Europe and the United States. For example, the EC's activities at the Venice Summit did not sit well with the United States. Nevertheless, no totally unbridgeable gulf has developed across the Atlantic on the conduct of Arab-Israeli peacemaking diplomacy. Indeed, at times the Europeans and the United States have cooperated in the region, although this has not always been easy.

For example, the United States in 1980–81 sought support from its European allies and certain other states for the creation of a Multinational Force and Observers (MFO) in the Sinai Desert as a necessary condition for Israel's withdrawal and the separation of the Egyptian and Israeli armies. After considerable political difficulty, four members of the European Community (Britain, France, Italy, and the Netherlands) did agree to take part in the MFO. Several factors accounted for European acquiescence. First, the initial stage of the Camp David process was indeed a success; it would have been very difficult, therefore, for the Europeans not to lend some support to a successful effort that had brought peace between Egypt and Israel. Second, at this time the Arab oil producers were preoccupied by the aftermath of the Iranian revolution and with the Iran-Iraq war; thus, they were incapable of focusing on the Arab-Israeli conflict, and of bringing enough pressure to bear on the Europeans to keep them out of the MFO. Finally, there was the emotional and political impact in Western Europe of President Sadat's assassination.

The tortured diplomacy required to get these four West European states to take part in the MFO was still considerable, since they—like the Community as a whole—sought a formula that would avoid the appearance of a blanket endorsement of the Camp David Accords. Such an endorsement was considered likely to earn the enmity of those Arab states that opposed both this venture and the Egyptian-Israeli peace treaty.

The Venice Summit in 1980 has so far proved to be the high-water mark in the European Community's collective diplomatic activism in the Middle East, especially regarding the Arab-Israeli conflict. Again, the tailing off of EC efforts reflected a combination of European and regional factors.

European Factors: Presidency of François Mitterand

The ascendency of the French socialists to political power in 1981 signaled a change in France's policy toward the Middle East—a change which, given France's active role in the European Community's Middle East diplomacy, affected the policies of the Community as a whole.

During the French presidential election campaign, France's Middle East policy had become a major issue. This was especially true of France's close identification with the Arabs at the expense of relations with Israel. The socialists were highly critical of the policies of President Giscard d'Estaing. Their alternative was a more balanced policy and an improvement in Franco-Israeli relations. A number of reasons accounted for this change in French policy: 1) the links between the French socialists and the Israeli Labor party within the Socialist International; 2) François Mitterrand's personal proclivity to undo General de Gaulle's legacy, of which France's Middle East policy was a major part;[6] 3) Mitterrand's desire to assuage France's Jewish population, which had been alienated by the previous government's rather cold and detached treatment;[7] and 4) Mitterrand's more "moral" approach to foreign policy issues.[8]

Thus, the changes in France's Middle East policy had significant symbolic dimensions within the context of its domestic politics. However, there were also a number of important, but contradictory, changes in French policy. For example, during a press conference attended by Arab journalists on December 19, 1981, French Foreign

Minister Claude Cheysson presented the underlying principles of France's new Middle East diplomacy in the following terms:

> The right of all states of the region to live in peace and within secure and recognized borders, all states . . . the state of Israel as well as the Palestinian state; the same rights for all peoples . . . namely the right to a homeland, the right to self-determination, the right to a state; there should not be any unilateral violation of international decisions; all solutions should result from negotiations among regional forces.[9]

A few of these points merit special attention. First, by accepting the principle of a Palestinian state the Mitterrand government went far beyond the previous French government and the Venice declaration, which advocated only a "Palestinian homeland" and remained silent on the political and legal status of this homeland.[10] Second, the new government declared that any solutions to the conflict should result from direct negotiations among the regional countries. This attitude, in turn, contradicted the Venice Declaration and the idea of a possible European initiative on the Middle East. The latter aspect of the new French position had a significant impact in slowing the pace of European diplomacy in the Middle East.[11]

Yet despite these significant changes in the underlying principles of France's position, in practice its Middle East policy remained fairly stable. For example, France took great pains to protect its extensive economic and diplomatic links with the Arab world—especially the oil-rich countries of the Gulf.

Regional and International Factors

As important as they unquestionably were, the changes in France's government and in its Middle East policy were not the only factors that tended to slow the pace of European diplomacy in the Middle East. A number of regional and international developments were also important. At the regional level, for example, the Iranian revolution, followed by the outbreak of war between Iran and Iraq, had greatly preoccupied the Gulf states. Thus, they were no longer actively pursuing the Europeans on the Palestinian issue and on Middle East peacemaking. As to the latter, Sadat's assassination and the preoccupation of Egypt's new president with issues of domestic stabilization and the problem of reintegrating Egypt into the Arab fold had effectively brought efforts at Middle East peacemaking to a halt.

Meanwhile, the administration of President Reagan in the United States had adopted a nonactivist approach towards the Middle East. Thus, since in many respects the Europeans have traditionally defined their Middle East policy in relation to that of the United States, the lack of any consistent U.S. posture contributed to European inactivity as well. Of course, individual European countries have on occasion taken some initiative, but there has been no concerted European diplomatic effort.

Developments in the Gulf

At the same time that the European Community was taking its boldest stance regarding the Arab-Israeli conflict, the Gulf (not coincidentally) was emerging as a serious concern for all Western nations. In fact, events in the Gulf—the oil crisis, ensuing financial developments, and the political activism of the Gulf Arab states—were instrumental in the development of West European diplomacy. And again, a consequence of new developments was disagreement and tension between the United States and Europe.

For most of the 1970s, the Gulf was not an area of controversy between Europe and the United States. By the end of the decade, however, some differences developed within the Western alliance over views of the source and seriousness of certain threats to Western security, plus the best means for dealing with them. For example, the United States was clearly more preoccupied with the Gulf than were its West European allies. This preoccupation was intensified first by the Iranian revolution—in large part because of the special political and strategic relationship with Iran that America had inherited from Britain—and then by the Iranian hostage crisis. Indeed, the latter event produced some hard feelings across the Atlantic, as the United States sought to coordinate economic sanctions against the regime of the Ayatollah Ruhollah Khomeini. With a good deal of truculence (and some patent efforts to circumvent declared sanctions), most of the West European allies eventually did follow the U.S. lead—although none to the same degree.

What transformed the politics of the situation was the event that followed closely upon the hostage crisis: the Soviet invasion of Afghanistan that began at the end of December 1979. Most West European states once more, followed the U.S. lead by imposing sanctions—with mixed emotions, however, about the key symbol: the boycott of the 1980 Moscow Olympics. Yet there was a sharp division of views that placed in opposition two very different concepts of what was happening.

Events in the Gulf and elsewhere in southwest Asia were important to West European states primarily because of their need to import Arab oil. Vis-à-vis the hostage crisis, the possibility that the oil flow would be interrupted was of more pressing concern than the fate of the American hostages (although it was conceded in Western Europe that the two factors could not be entirely separated, and that any country was vulnerable to hostage-taking). At the same time, events in Afghanistan also brought the oil question to European minds, whereas the United States saw in the Soviet invasion far broader implications and assessed its policies in terms of a global perspective on East-West relations. Few, if any, of the West European allies shared that perspective. In fact, there was some concern on the Continent that the United States would, following this line of reasoning, overreact and thus jeopardize a hard-won and greatly prized detente in Europe. There was also deep concern in Western Europe that the Afghanistan crisis would be seen in Washington as falling within the purview of the so-called linkage doctrine and thus cripple attempts to enact the SALT II treaty.[12]

In view of these concerns, it was striking that so little attention was paid in Western Europe, as in the United States, to the enunciation in early 1980 of the so-called Carter Doctrine. This committed the United States to defend the Gulf region against any outside threat (meaning the Soviet Union) by all means necessary. The thinking on the Continent, however, was that this was an unlikely contingency—although there was an element here of the wish being father to the thought. To the extent that the United States was prepared to take the lead, though: so much the better.

Nevertheless, since 1980 a debate that antedates the Lebanese crisis has raged within the Western alliance—although with far less intensity since about 1983, for reasons that will be developed below. And there have been differences of view *within* the allied countries as well as between them. Again, there is some risk in generalization. In the main, however, governmental opinion in Western Europe has seen threats to Western interests in the Gulf/southwest Asia region as emanating primarily from regional and internal problems, including but not limited to the Arab-Israeli conflict, whereas the U.S. government has tended to focus on the Soviet role. Similarly, concerning the character of these threats, the West Europeans have focused more on political and economic factors and the Americans on military considerations.

On these issues, the Iran-Iraq war that began in September 1980 seemed to produce a compromise of analysis within the alliance: it was patently a regional threat to Western interests and not something produced by Moscow, however much the Soviets might like to exploit the various turns of events in the conflict; however, the threat to Western interests was very much military in character. At the same time, though, the Iran-Iraq war did not produce the intense concern in Western Europe that might have been expected, since it was not directed against Western interests per se. That is, any cutoff of oil supplies that proceeded from the conflict would be for tactical reasons related to the conflict itself, rather than because of general opposition to the Western position.

Nonetheless, during the last several years there have been striking differences in the attitudes of individual European countries toward the war and toward the two combatants, as well as differences in viewpoint between the Europeans collectively and the United States. For example, France has taken a staunchly pro-Iraq position, whereas other European countries have tried to maintain links with Iran. However, there has been an underlying agreement both among the Europeans and between the Europeans and the United States on the need to prevent a victory by Iran.[13]

There has also been considerable disagreement across the Atlantic on the kinds of responses required to meet threats in the Gulf, and on who should take responsibility for them. The United States has, in general, placed greater emphasis on military responses, including the development of a Rapid Deployment Force and the provision of equipment (such as the AWACs airborne warning stations sold to Saudi Arabia). The West Europeans, meanwhile, have looked more to political and economic responses. The debate on methods was reflected, for example, in the proposal made by West German Chancellor Helmut Schmidt (with U.S. prompting) for a "division of labor" within the alliance concerning the security of the Middle East, by means of which each ally would do that which it was best suited to accomplish.[14]

In the debate concerning which allied countries should take responsibility for protecting Western interests, the breakdown was highly predictable. Britain and France were prepared to maintain some naval units in the Indian Ocean/Gulf area; both had the capability, as well as some vestiges of an extra-European political attitude. The West Germans were inhibited by law from following suit, although they were in a position to use economic instruments. Other West European states remained relatively aloof.

The Aftermath of Lebanon

When Israel invaded Lebanon in June 1982, the Middle East peace process had long since come to a complete standstill.[15] The Lebanon crisis ended this lull in Middle East diplomacy. Inevitably, the West European countries also had to react to the new circumstances. Middle East diplomacy in the post-Lebanon period was focused primarily on reshaping Lebanon's internal structure as well as on defining the nature of new regional relationships.

For reasons presented earlier, basic West European attitudes toward the Middle East were not fundamentally changed by the Lebanon crisis. To be sure, no European state was oblivious to what was happening there. One country (France) was at pains to indicate its historical interest in Lebanese cultural and religious as well as political developments. There was also considerable grumbling in Western Europe that America's continuing close involvement with Israel had been a factor in the invasion of Lebanon. In European eyes, at least, the lack of U.S. interest in the peace process prior to the Israeli invasion vindicated the views expressed within European Political Cooperation that the peace process should be recast.

Whatever reservations the Europeans may have had about Israel's actions in Lebanon and about the U.S. response, they did not verbalize them. In general, the Europeans waited to see whether Israel's gamble in Lebanon would pay off; some, however, did express concern over the fate of the PLO.[16] For various reasons, though, most European countries supported U.S. efforts, tacitly if not actively. Thus, the United States was successful in enlisting three West European states in the Multinational Force (MNF) stationed in Lebanon from the fall of 1982 until February 1984. Each state had its reasons: France had its historical involvement in the area; Italy was basking in a new-found special relationship with the United States that was at marked contrast with its earlier status as the unconsulted "fifth wheel" of the NATO core countries; while Britain, finally, was con-

cerned about its own special relationship with the United States and
about the possibilities of affecting the course of U.S. policy. (Nevertheless, its contribution to the MNF was never more than token.)[17]

The other aspect of Middle East diplomacy was President Reagan's peace plan, presented in September 1982. Here, too, the Europeans basically supported U.S. policy. It was only when the situation
in Lebanon began to deteriorate that the Europeans began to distance
themselves from the United States. These pressures became particularly strong after the bombing of the U.S. Marine barracks and
French troops in Beirut in October 1983.[18] Yet even though the Europeans began to distance themselves from the United States, this did
not lead to expanded European diplomatic activity. By and large, the
European states followed the U.S. lead in responding to the Lebanese
crisis and to the broader issue of Arab-Israeli peacemaking.

The reasons for this lack of a major European reaction are important. To a degree, the Lebanese crisis distracted attention from more
central preoccupations in the Middle East. For example, many commentators—and not just in Western Europe—argued that nothing
would be possible in the broader framework of Arab-Israeli peacemaking until Lebanon was sorted out. But just as many commentators seem to have seen in Lebanon's plight a need to get on with efforts
within a broader framework, among other things as a means of reliev-
ing Lebanon of intolerable political pressures.

Nor should we be surprised by the apparent coincidence of periods of heightened European Community activity on the Arab-
Israeli conflict and those periods in which the United States has been
most deeply engaged in the area. As noted above, even when there is
a strong and pervading sense in Western Europe that it will be affected, perhaps even vitally, by the turn of events in the Levant, the
United States is still looked to as the Western leader. No European
country is willing (and probably none is able) to replace the United
States in its central role. Among other things, no European state—
including France, notwithstanding its newly improved links under
Mitterrand—has the standing in Israel that would permit it to be a
valid interlocutor in the peace process. Nor does any European state
have the kind of economic and military relationship with Israel that
undergirds Washington's primacy in the peace process. Nevertheless,
when the United States is engaged in Arab-Israeli peacemaking, the
European Community is anxious to help shape the direction of that
effort. Conversely, when the United States is patently not engaged,

there is a general sense in Western Europe that a separate European initiative would be feckless—certainly, that it would have little chance of success. In effect, the audience for European Political Cooperation over the Arab-Israeli conflict has been first and foremost the United States during periods of Washington's own active diplomacy.

There is also an institutional component to the relative lack in recent years of EC activity in the Arab-Israeli conflict. Again, this is a development that is taking place virtually irrespective of events in Lebanon. For a variety of reasons unconnected with the Middle East, there is new interest in Western Europe for creating what is known popularly as a "European defense personality." This has been occasioned by a series of trans-Atlantic debates over both conventional defense and nuclear deterrence. The French and Germans have been groping toward some deeper defense cooperation, while six key allies have been trying to revive the moribund Western European Union—the political vehicle for West Germany's rearmament after 1955. In short, it can be said that the West Europeans have other matters on their minds—concerns related to developments within the Continent that distract attention from European Political Cooperation and its decidedly extra-European focus on the Arab-Israeli conflict.

Most important, however, is the course of West European interests and concerns within the Middle East region. The chancelleries of West Europe are not fundamentally different from those elsewhere: squeaky wheels get the grease—and in certain real senses, the Middle East wheel has not been squeaking lately. This development has had several elements, each reflecting the traditional character of West European concern with the region.

Strategic Change in the Arab-Israeli Conflict

At the level of superpower involvement, Western Europe has benefited from the Egyptian-Israeli peace treaty just as have the United States and the engaged parties. Clearly, this treaty has been of major strategic importance. Classically, a major Arab-Israeli confrontation is an irrational act of policy for any Arab state unless Egypt can be factored in the military balance. And only a war that threatens major military advances against either Israel or an Arab state contains the risk of a U.S.–Soviet political or military confrontation over Arab-Israeli relations. (This has certainly been the historical record, based on the wars of 1956, 1967, and 1973.)

Yet Egypt is no longer a part of the Arab-Israeli military balance, and will not return to it so long as the Egyptian-Israeli peace treaty holds; thus, the risks of U.S.–Soviet confrontation have declined radically. Notably, there was little hint of any U.S.–Soviet confrontation over the Lebanese war and ensuing crisis. While the U.S. diplomatic defeat in that crisis may have increased the ability of the Soviet Union to make political inroads in the region—an issue on which the jury is still out as of this writing—this has not so far proved to be a world-class development threatening key Western interests. More to the point in terms of this discussion, the West Europeans are less concerned about the U.S.–Soviet dimension of the Arab-Israeli conflict than they were before the Egyptian-Israeli peace treaty. This includes recurring fears on the Continent that developments outside of Europe will strike at East-West relations in Europe. There has also been some lessening of the (perhaps uncharitable) European concern that the United States will somehow mess things up with the Soviets in an extra-European setting.

The Oil Factor

Most Western Europeans, like their counterparts in the United States, have been affected by developments in the Gulf. And for the Europeans, the linkage between the two ends of the region has been far tighter than has been the case for the United States. To be sure, Washington has pursued Arab-Israeli peacemaking with one eye on developments in the Gulf, but that has been a secondary motivation as compared with the American relationship to Israel, the inherent risks of conflict in the Middle East generally, and the (now greatly reduced) U.S. concern with a possible U.S.–Soviet confrontation over the Arab–Israeli conflict. For the West Europeans, the oil factor has always been of paramount concern; by contrast, for the United States the oil factor is an indirect interest. Except for a brief period at the end of the 1970s and beginning of the 1980s, the importance of Gulf oil has remained below the threshold of U.S. vital interest. True, if there were a serious oil stoppage, the American economy would perforce be damaged and U.S. security undercut by the inevitable damage to the West European and Japanese economies; but Gulf oil is still a derivative, not a direct, interest for the United States.

The oil factor is perhaps most important in explaining the intensity of West European concern over the Arab-Israeli conflict at the beginning of this decade. Indeed, it is striking that West European concern with regional threats to Gulf oil supplies has never—not even during such feverish interludes as the hostage crisis and various periods of intensification of the Iran-Iraq war—reached the level of concern with which Western Europeans followed the course of the Arab-Israeli conflict and its impact on Western access to Arab oil. This may be a somewhat atavistic attitude, since the unrealized threat of an Arab oil embargo endured for so many years until it materialized, at least in theory, during the 1967 and 1973 Arab-Israeli wars. Thus, the fear of a future oil embargo—perhaps even one engineered in peacetime, for political reasons, to affect Western diplomacy and/or U.S. support for Israel— has continued to cloud the West European view even after regional politics and economics has moved on. (This development was symbolized by the Fez declaration of the Arab summit in 1982, which, however flawed, at least talked about peace rather than war.)

A series of developments has reduced both U.S. and West European fears concerning the security of oil supplies from the Gulf. (Whether or not this relative optimism is genuinely merited is another story that need not delay us here.) In the early 1980s, the worldwide recession and ensuing glut of oil on world markets significantly depressed the price; on its own strength, this development took much of the day-to-day anxiety out of West European perspectives on Gulf oil. Of course, this attitude has begged two questions. First, the very real dependence of virtually all West European states (save only Britain and Norway) on energy supplies from the Gulf region remains essentially unchanged. At the margin, dependence has gone down (and with it, the oil price that is set at the margin); but there remains no doubt that any serious, sizeable, and sustained cutoff of Gulf oil to Western Europe would nevertheless have a devastating effect. The oil-sharing provisions of the International Energy Agency, the stockpiling of oil (as in the Federal Republic), some diversification of sources of supply, and energy conservation are all comforting achievements, but they do not detract from the simple fact that the Continent is virtually dependent on Gulf oil and will continue to be at least well into the twenty-first century.

Second, the disarray introduced into OPEC by price shifts has reduced its capacity to act as a cartel, with all the political as well as economic ramifications of this position. Of course, that statement does not necessarily apply with equal force to OAPEC (the Organization of Arab Petroleum Exporting Countries), whose effectiveness has always been open to question. But it should not be automatically assumed that OAPEC cannot be revived under the right (or wrong) circumstances. Still, this may be largely a quibble. In any case, the oil glut has affected the political perceptions and self-perceptions of OAPEC members, as well as those of the broader-membership OPEC. It is also true that, throughout the post-Shah period and especially during the war between Iran and Iraq and the period of recession-induced oil glut, the Arab states of the Gulf have been more preoccupied with matters closer to home than the Arab-Israeli conflict.

This last point is, indeed, the key to a shift in West European attitudes and behavior toward the Arab-Israeli conflict. Simply put, these countries are under less political pressure than they were before. Their stake in oil appears to have diminished, along with the commercial opportunities to recoup petrodollars in the Arab oil-producing countries; the producers have, in fact if not in theory, downgraded the Arab-Israeli conflict from first place on their political agenda.

Living with Instability

There is a closely related point, especially concerning West European interests directly in the Gulf region: this is the fact that the West has in general learned to live with shifting developments there. The Soviet Union remains in Afghanistan, but it has so far not pushed beyond to Pakistan and the Arabian Sea. (Nevertheless, under the new Soviet leader, Mikhail Gorbachev, a serious effort to "discipline" the Pakistani government must be considered a possibility.) In addition, the United States no longer demands that its West European allies join it in demonstrations against Soviet activities in the region: the question of linkage is not now being invoked, and "going to Geneva" for arms-control talks has once again come to characterize East-West relations. At least in the region of the Middle East/southwest Asia, there has been no serious West European concern that the United States might do something untoward vis-à-vis the Soviet Union that would jeopardize hopeful East-West developments in Europe. Indeed, in 1985 Washington and Moscow held bilateral talks on the region.

Meanwhile, Moscow has shown a disinclination to move against Iran—the very contingency that produced the Carter Doctrine. Iran's forty-two million Muslims might only complicate the Soviets' existing problems with their Asiatic populations, although here too the possibility of a dramatic policy reversal cannot be ruled out in the event Iran were to collapse militarily under the force of Iraqi assault. It continues to be true that an Iran dominated by the Soviet Union, even through "peaceful" means, would represent the worst strategic setback for the West since the (since recouped) "loss" of China in 1949. Furthermore, it also remains true that it would be difficult if not impossible for U.S. military forces, operating from 8,000 miles away, to contain any Soviet military venture in Iran, and that circumstances could arise in which certain unpalatable alternatives would have to be considered. As clearly understood in NATO planning circles if not publicly, these alternatives center on either horizontal escalation (an extreme form of linkage to East-West relations elsewhere in the world, perhaps involving military conflict) or vertical escalation, which means the use of tactical nuclear weapons.

These considerations seem very remote from Western Europe today, and that fact reinforces the reluctance of several West European allies, vocally led by France, to keep the geographic limits of the North Atlantic Treaty from being extended to cover the Middle East.[19] This lack of plausibility may also help to explain the extent to which various West European countries have been prepared to exploit the opportunities for arms sales in the region—to Iraq especially, but in late 1985 also to Saudi Arabia and Jordan. There are risks in any imprudent flow of arms to Iraq, however—especially if Iran thereby becomes directly vulnerable to Soviet inroads, or simply to a collapse that will inevitably increase instabilities overall in the region.

At the same time, the West has adapted itself to the course of the Iran-Iraq war and even to its occasional escalation. During 1984, there was some short-term panic when Iraq embarked on a policy of trying to enlist the assistance of outside powers in its struggle against Iran by launching attacks on oil tankers in the Gulf. Here, however, the United States was able to prevail upon its two key West European allies, Britain and France, to prepare for common naval action in the event this would be required to guarantee passage through the Strait of Hormuz. (There was also broad international cooperation in sweeping the Red Sea of the mysterious mines that damaged several merchant ships.) In short order, however, calmer nerves prevailed in the West; contingencies planned for did not come to pass, and the willingness of America's allies to take military action did not have to be tested. Whether or not this reduction of anxiety was a legitimate reaction in view of the risks and the stakes, it has henceforth dominated Western attitudes.

Conclusions

In sum, a variety of factors have led to a relative decline in West European preoccupation with the Middle East, whether in terms of the Arab-Israeli conflict or developments in the Gulf. It would be foolhardy, however, to argue that this situation will necessarily continue indefinitely, in terms of either provocation or West European response. In terms of oil—the linchpin of the European attitude toward the Middle East—the end of global recession should see some increase in price and thus of perceived West European dependence on the Gulf. As noted above, the Soviet dimension of the future of southwest Asia is by no means clear, nor is the potential impact of the continuing Iraq-Iran war on Western interests. In the Arab-Israeli conflict, meanwhile, logical analysis argues that relative quiet will prevail, at least in terms of the conflict's impact on Western interests. But this analysis can again be confounded. Indeed, much of the impetus for continued U.S. involvement in Arab-Israeli peacemaking is based on a policy of insurance against the unexpected and untoward. Thus, it would also be wrong to predict that European Political Cooperation will not return boldly to the consideration of the Arab-Israeli conflict, or that European-American disputes over this corner of the Middle East—as well as over the Gulf—will not reemerge with full force.

Finally, the governments of Western Europe do not appear to be any more advanced than the U.S. government in either understanding or reacting to the emergence of Islamic fundamentalism. There is general agreement that this intensely unsettling phenomenon takes many forms, and that it has not run its course. But how much of a challenge it (in its various forms) will pose for Western interests produces no consensus: for Europeans as well as for Americans, this may be the central conundrum in the Middle East during the next several years.

NOTES

1. One of the most difficult issues to be resolved within European Political Cooperation has been the extent to which the EC member states could consult with the United States on their common decisions. This matter was tentatively resolved in

1974 with agreement that the country in the chair of the European Council could brief Washington on PoCo deliberations—after the fact.

2. The Euro-Arab dialogue was a product of the crisis atmosphere of the 1970s and Western Europe's growing economic and financial links with the Arab oil producers. For the Europeans, the dialogue was meant to secure continued access to Arab oil, markets, and financial resources, while the Arabs sought to change European attitudes on the Arab-Israeli conflict. (There were other, more grandiose, plans for Euro-Arab cooperation as well.) The dialogue succeeded in a limited sense, but with the passing of crisis it began to falter, and by the late 1970s was moribund for all practical purposes. See J. P. Cassadio, *The Economic Challenge of the Arabs*, (Farnborough, England: Westmead, 1976). See also Saad Allah Hallabra, "The Euro-Arab Dialogue," *American-Arab Affairs*, no. 10, (Fall 1984):44—59.

3. See *European Political Cooperation*, published by the Press and Information Office of the Federal Government of Germany, 1982.

4. For details see various special reports published by *The Middle East Economic Digest* during the period 1979–1985 on the relations of individual European countries with the Middle East.

5. *Text of Venice Declaration*

Resolution by the EEC pointing out the need to implement two universally acknowledged principles: that of the right to security of all states in the Middle East and that of the right of the Palestinian people to self-determination and of the PLO to be associated in peace negotiations.

Venice, June 13, 1980

1) The Heads of State and Government and the Ministers of Foreign Affairs held a comprehensive exchange of views on all aspects of the present situation in the Middle East, including the state of negotiations resulting from the agreements signed between Egypt and Israel in March 1979. They agreed that growing tensions affecting this region constitute a serious danger and render a comprehensive solution to the Israeli-Arab conflict more necessary and pressing than ever.

2) The nine Member States of the European Community consider that the traditional ties and common interests which link Europe to the Middle East oblige them to play a special role and now require them to work in a more concrete way towards peace.

3) In this regard, the nine countries of the Community base themselves on Security Council Resolutions 242 and 338 and the positions which they have expressed on several occasions, notably in their Declarations of 29 June 1977, 19 September 1978, 26 March and 18 June 1979 as well as in the speech made on their behalf on 25 September 1979 by the Irish Minister of Foreign Affairs at the 34th United Nations General Assembly.

4) On the bases thus set out, the time has come to promote the recognition and implementation of the two principles universally accepted by the international community: the right to existence and to security of all the States in the region, including Israel, and justice for all the peoples, which implies the recognition of the legitimate rights of the Palestinian people.

5) All of the countries in the area are entitled to live in peace within secure, recognized and guaranteed borders. The necessary guarantees for a peace settle-

ment should be provided by the U.N. by a decision of the Security Council and, if necessary, on the basis of other mutually agreed procedures. The Nine declare that they are prepared to participate within the framework of a comprehensive settlement in a system of concrete and binding international guarantees, including [guarantees] on the ground.

6) A just solution must finally be found to the Palestinian problem, which is not simply one of refugees. The Palestinian people, which is conscious of existing as such, must be placed in a position, by an appropriate process defined within the framework of the comprehensive peace settlement, to exercise fully its right to self-determination.

7) The achievement of these objectives requires the involvement and support of all the parties concerned in the peace settlement which the Nine are endeavouring to promote in keeping with the principles formulated in the declaration referred to above. These principles apply to all the parties concerned, and thus the Palestinian people, and to the PLO, which will have to be associated with the negotiations.

8) The Nine recognize the special importance of the role played by the question of Jerusalem for all the parties concerned. The Nine stress that they will not accept any unilateral initiative designed to change the status of Jerusalem and that any agreement on the city's status should guarantee freedom of access for everyone to the Holy Places.

9) The Nine stress the need for Israel to put an end to the territorial occupation which it has maintained since the conflict of 1967, as it has done for part of Sinai. They are deeply convinced that the Israeli settlements constitute a serious obstacle to the peace process in the Middle East. The Nine consider that these settlements, as well as modifications in population and property in the occupied Arab territories, are illegal under international law.

10) Concerned as they are to put an end to violence, the Nine consider that only the renunciation of force or the threatened use of force by all the parties can create a climate of confidence in the area, and constitute a basic element for a comprehensive settlement of the conflict in the Middle East.

11) The Nine have decided to make the necessary contacts with all the parties concerned. The objective of these contacts would be to ascertain the position of the various parties with respect to the principles set out in this declaration and in the light of the results of this consultation process to determine the form which such an initiative on their part could take.

6. See Dominique Moisi, "La France de Mitterrand et Le Conflict du Proche Orient: Comment Concilier Emotion et Politique," *Politiques Étrangères* 2 (June 1982):395–402.

7. Some observers have even interpreted Mitterrand's actions as " ... posthumous reparations for the Vichy government's policy towards France's Jews" (*ibid.*, p. 397).

8. Ibid. Thus, on moral grounds Mitterrand believed that, as long as the PLO did not recognize Israel's right to exist, it could not sit at the negotiating table.

9. Ibid., p. 396.

10. The Mitterrand government's position on the Palestinian issue also derived

from the generally "moral" tone of its diplomacy as well as from certain characteristics of the Socialist Party. The pro-Arab—and especially pro-Palestinian—sentiments of the younger generation of Socialist Party members were particularly important.

11. France's emphasis on the principle that a peaceful solution to the conflict should come about as a result of direct negotiations among the regional countries meant that France would no longer push such ideas as a European initiative for the Middle East.

12. The doctrine of linkage holds that Soviet behavior in one part of the world—e.g., Afghanistan—should be countered by denying the Soviets something they want in another part of the East-West relationship. For example, the Soviets might be denied the showcase of successful Olympic games or the benefits of arms control. This doctrine is highly controversial; some critics argue, for example, that arms control is either in the U.S. interest and should be pursued or it is not and should not; in other words, it is not a favor done to—or withheld from—the Soviet Union. This is the prevailing West European view. Nevertheless, there is an implicit linkage between different aspects of Soviet behavior, because of U.S. domestic politics. These can produce constraints, as in this case when President Carter had to ask the Senate to end its consideration of the SALT II treaty. Of course, it is debatable whether the treaty could have passed the U.S. Senate in any case, even without the Soviet invasion of Afghanistan.

13. In the United States, memories of humiliation during the hostage crisis of 1979–81 have inhibited clear thought about the strategic importance to the United States and the West of Iran's independence, territorial integrity, and relative stability. Indeed, there is no comparison between Iran and Iraq in terms of their importance to the West, especially as pawns in East-West competition. In spite of the failure of the U.S. government to keep these facts uppermost in mind, however, the West European states continue to look to the United States for leadership in the Gulf, and have not been particularly forthcoming with any strategic analyses of their own.

14. Secretary of Defense Harold Brown, March 6, 1980: "While we seek allied support in the region, we must realize that direct contributions are not the only way they can help."

15. The only exception was the plan presented by King Fahd of Saudi Arabia to the Arab summit meeting in Fez, Morocco, in November 1981.

16. France was one of these countries, apparently as a result of pressure by Saudi Arabia and Egypt. See Robert Swan, "Mitterrand's Interventions," *Middle East International,* 16 July 1982:6.

17. These attitudes were also reflected in reactions to terrorist bombings. France, for example, delayed the departure of its contingent in the MNF until after the United States left, in order to register a point about its special concern for Lebanon.

18. See "Beirut Bombs Shatter Allies' Resolve," *Washington Post,* 27 December 1983.

19. This reluctance was apparent even in the early 1980s when threats to Western interests seemed more palpable. For the French, in particular, the limits of alliance must be maintained. In fact, the cohesion of NATO could be threatened by attempts to broaden its formal compass. European states that would become involved in Gulf security in the presence of a NATO commitment would also become involved in its absence—or vice versa.

II

Regional Political Dynamics

4

Inter-Arab Politics

Shireen Hunter

T HE MIDDLE EAST has always been a region of sudden and violent change, of rapidly shifting alliances and fortunes, odd partnerships and often unpredictable twists and turns. The decade of the 1980s has been no exception; in fact, it has so far proved particularly true to these long-standing Middle Eastern traditions.

As the 1970s were drawing to a close, the Islamic revolution in Iran shattered the military equilibrium in the Gulf. The dawn of the 1980s witnessed the Iraqi invasion of Iran in September 1980, and the assassination of Egypt's President Anwar al-Sadat. Both of these developments had significant impacts on Middle East politics, the full implications of which have yet to be realized. Finally, in June of 1982 Israel invaded Lebanon, setting in motion a process which has deeply affected the political landscape of the Arab world, while the impact on the Israeli public and political body has been no less significant.

The main focus of this essay is on intra-Arab politics since the Israeli invasion of Lebanon. However, any adequate analysis and assessment of developments in intra-Arab relations since June 1982 would require at least a brief summary of the state of these relations at the time of the Israeli invasion of Lebanon. It is to this summary we shall turn first.

The Middle East Political Landscape in June 1982

Before sketching the political landscape of the Middle East in 1982, a few points about regional subdivisions, and the extent and nature of interaction between these subdivisions and their periphery, need to be made. Modern students of Middle East affairs have generally divided the region into two principal zones of concern: the Arab-Israeli conflict and the Gulf. In the last two decades, however, a number of developments, such as greater involvement of Gulf Arabs in intra-Arab politics (including the questions of peace and war with Israel), have blurred these distinctions.

In addition, as a result of closer interaction and integration, not only have subregional divisions become blurred but the Arab world's interaction with such non-Arab Middle Eastern actors as Iran and with the peripheral regions has also intensified. Thus intra-Arab politics have become increasingly sensitive to the actions and policies of other, non-Arab and peripheral actors. Similarly, socioeconomic and political events in the Arab world have increasingly been affected by developments in peripheral areas.[1]

The observations above notwithstanding, what was the state of Middle Eastern affairs when Israel invaded Lebanon in June of 1982? First, by 1982 the Camp David era had come to an end, and the peace process between Israel and the Arab countries was at a standstill. This situation was partly due to U.S. policies. The Carter administration in its last year in office was preoccupied with the Iranian hostage crisis and the presidential campaign; thus, the United States was no longer pushing Arab-Israeli negotiations, which at the time were focused on autonomy for the Palestinians of the West Bank and the Gaza Strip.

The Reagan administration that came to power in January 1981 was not enthusiastic about pursuing the Camp David process, and initially focused its attention on developing a framework for a so-called strategic cooperation among Israel, the United States, and the moderate Arabs. It was only after the failure of this approach and the Israeli invasion of Lebanon that the United States in September 1982 presented a revised version of the Camp David formula designed to resolve the Palestinian problem: the Reagan plan.[2]

Egypt for its part was experiencing the shock of Sadat's assassination, which many people attributed in part to his identification with the United States and his peace policy, which had led to Egypt's isolation in the Arab and Islamic worlds. Thus, Egypt's new president, Hosni Mubarak, had immediately after assuming power embarked on a process of de-Sadatization of Egyptian policy, and had tried to distance himself from Sadat's legacy in the hope that this would bring Egypt back into the Arab fold. In turn, Egypt's new policy meant that it was no keener than the United States about reviving the Camp David process.

Parallel with the change in Egypt's policies, a number of developments in the Arab world—especially in the Gulf region—had created fertile conditions for Egypt's reintegration into the Arab fold. Most of these developments derived from the Iran-Iraq war. When Iraq invaded Iran in September 1980, Iraq was the up-and-coming power in the Gulf and in the Arab world. The Iranian revolution; Egypt's isolation—in which, incidentally, Iraq had played a significant role; and the vulnerability of the Gulf Arab states were all contributing factors to Iraq's emergence as the new Arab power.[3]

Iraq's expectation was that the war with Iran would be a kind of blitzkrieg, from which, of course, Iraq would come out victorious; however, these expectations proved unrealistic. The blitzkrieg turned into a trench war, and by June 1982 not only were Iraqi troops forced to withdraw from Iran, but Iraq seemed to be vulnerable to Iranian counterattack. Iraq's miscalculations in its war against Iran not only cost Iraq its chances of becoming the new leader of the Arab world, but also made it doubly dependent—on the financial assistance of the Gulf Arabs, and on the technical and military assistance of certain other Arab countries, notably Egypt. This situation in turn meant that Iraq was no longer in a position to prevent Egypt's reintegration into the Arab fold. Quite to the contrary, Iraq was the first Arab country to resume links, albeit unofficial, with Egypt, a trend which was soon to be followed by other Gulf Arabs. (The case for the Gulf Arabs welcoming Egypt's reintegration was even stronger, since they needed Egypt as a counterweight to both Iran and Iraq—although in 1982 Iran seemed the more immediate threat.)

The Iran-Iraq war had affected the Gulf and Arab politics in yet another way. The war had brought the Gulf countries closer together and had led to the formation of the Gulf Cooperation Council in May 1981. Efforts to create some form of cooperative framework in the Gulf date back to the 1960s. But intraregional conflicts and rivalries—including those between Iran and the two key Gulf Arab states of Iraq and Saudi Arabia—had prevented them from coming to fruition. But in 1981 the Iran-Iraq war had eliminated the restraining impact of Iraqi and Iranian obstruction to intra-Gulf cooperation. More important, heightened internal and external security threats, plus the realization of the need for intra-Gulf economic coordination and cooperation, had convinced the Gulf states of the need for closer cooperation.[4]

The Iran-Iraq war had also affected the relations of a number of Arab countries with the peripheral states (especially Iran), and had contributed to the further polarization of intra-Arab politics. The most significant development from that perspective was the formation of an alliance between Iran and Syria. The primary impetus behind the Syrian-Iranian alliance was, of course, their common animosity towards Iraq, although other factors were also important—significantly, considerations of intra-Arab balance of power.[5] The trend toward Egypt's reintegration in the Arab world, the improvement in Egyptian-Iraqi and Iraqi–Gulf states relations, and the close cooperation between Jordan and Iraq had all strengthened the moderate forces and had led to Syria's isolation. Thus, cooperation with Iran and Libya was a way for Syria to create a counterforce to the emerging moderate Arab coalition. In sum, when Israel invaded Lebanon in 1982, the Arab world was as polarized as ever. However, despite uncertainty about the future of Iraq and the still persistent threat of an expansion of the Gulf war, the position of the moderate forces had improved. The Gulf Arab states had managed to survive the threat of Islamic militancy, and had even begun to cooperate in the coordination of their security efforts. Reconciliation between Egypt on the one hand and Iraq and the other Gulf Arabs on the other (plus the latter's new cooperation, albeit unofficial) had improved the moderates' position.

However, the shift in the balance of power in the moderates' favor was not strong enough to enable them to take any bold initiatives, particularly with regard to the peace process; the radicals continued to maintain their restraining power. Thus, the major Arab effort to come up with an alternative to the Camp David process and the Reagan plan resulted in the Fez formula of September 1982, which not only failed to explicitly recognize Israel's right to exist but also contained provisions for the creation of an independent Palestinian state and the return of Jerusalem to the Arabs.[6] Needless to say, these conditions were totally unacceptable to Israel, and the Fez formula was not a viable base for Arab-Israeli negotiations.

Israel Invades Lebanon

Some longtime observers of Middle East affairs have argued that, when there is not an on-going peace process in the Middle East, the strong likelihood is that the region will drift toward war. As noted earlier, by the time of the Israeli invasion of Lebanon in June of 1982 the peace process in the Middle East had come to a standstill, and the

temptation to resolve problems through violence had reached alarming proportions. Israel's declared objective in the invasion of Lebanon
was to clear southern Lebanon of Palestinian guerrillas and thereby
secure Israel's northern border. It is, of course, very difficult to determine with certainty any state's real objectives, and Israel's goals in
Lebanon are no exception. In fact, some argue that from the very beginning Israel's main goal was to change the shape of Lebanese politics by bringing to power Lebanese Christian allies and then forcing
this newly constituted Lebanon to sign a peace treaty with it.[7] Whatever Israel's real objectives, once it launched its operations in Lebanon it did not confine them to the south but instead began to move
towards Beirut, where the bulk of the Palestine Liberation Organization forces had gathered. However, under international—especially
American and European—pressure, Israel was forced to let the PLO
forces withdraw from Beirut, and to leave Lebanon to the supervision
of a multinational force.

Following the PLO withdrawal, however, Israeli forces accompanied by their Lebanese Christian allies entered the Muslim (western) sector of Beirut. The Christian militiamen then dealt violently
with the Palestinian refugees, who no longer had the protection of the
PLO, culminating in the massacres of the Sabra and Shatila refugee
camps. However, as transpired later, the Christian forces were not capable of bringing order to Lebanon and tightening their grip on the
country. In fact, sectarian strife intensified anew, with violence and
chaos reaching an unprecedented level even for Lebanon, with its
long history of internal turmoil.

The inability of the Christian forces to establish themselves
firmly in power also made the peace with Lebanon that Israel had
hoped for impossible. To be sure, Lebanon and Israel had, with U.S.
mediation, signed an agreement on May 17, 1983 that normalized relations and provided for security arrangements in the south and the
withdrawal of all foreign forces, including the Syrians. However, before the ink on the agreement was dry the opposition of Muslim forces
and Syrian pressure vitiated the impact of the agreement, and it was
formally abrogated in March 1984 following the U.S. withdrawal from
Lebanon.[8] The cancellation of the agreement in turn reflected the ascendancy of Syria in determining Lebanon's fate and heralded the
end of the Israeli era in Lebanon. Since then, the turn of events has
forced Israel to begin withdrawing its forces from Lebanon, although
Syrian forces are still present in that country.

The war in Lebanon has had significant implications for the balance of power among regional states, while at the same time causing interesting shifts in intra-Arab alliances. However, two developments resulting from the Lebanese war—the military disintegration of the PLO and the enhancement of Syria's regional influence—have had the deepest impact on the Middle East's political landscape, and these will now be analyzed in some detail.

PLO after Lebanon: Military Disintegration and Political Division

When in June of 1982 Israel invaded Lebanon, the PLO had created what amounted to almost a Palestinian state within a state in Lebanon.[9] This situation, plus the fact that Lebanon provided a logical territorial base of operations against Israel, had given the PLO both considerable power within the Arab world and a certain freedom of action. Of course, the internal divisions of the PLO and the manipulation of these divisions by various Arab countries had traditionally limited the Palestinian leadership's capabilities—especially its ability to take bold actions. Nevertheless, the PLO's position in Lebanon had enhanced its ability to resist Arab pressures and had enabled it to maintain at least a modicum of independence.[10]

The most devastating consequence of the Israeli invasion of Lebanon for the PLO was the loss of its territorial base of operations. In this regard, the final expulsion of the PLO forces from Tripoli in December 1983 under Syrian pressure was even more significant than its evacuation from Beirut.[11] The second most serious outcome was the military disintegration of the PLO, with its forces scattered in such far-off places as South Yemen, Tunisia, and Algeria. (Needless to say, such loss of military muscle also reduced the PLO's political weight in the Arab world.) The third consequence of the Lebanese war for the PLO was a rebellion within the ranks of the PLO's mainstream Fatah—an open challenge to Yasser Arafat's leadership.

Of course, the PLO has always been a hodgepodge of different groups with different and often opposed ideologies and alliances; in fact, as one scholar of Palestinian affairs has said, the membership of the various groups in the PLO reads like an "alphabet soup."[12] Nevertheless, Fatah, the largest and the most moderate of the PLO groups, has generally been more coherent. More important, Fatah has traditionally provided the backbone of Arafat's support as the group's founder. Thus, a split within Fatah was a much more serious matter

than the PLO's other divisions. The rebellion within Fatah was originated by one Colonel Abu-Musa, and was generally blamed on the
Syrians, and without doubt Syria wanted to weaken the PLO and Arafat and bring the organization under its control. But other factors
were also involved, including grievances against Arafat's handling of
the seige of Beirut, his appointments of PLO military commanders,
and his general style of leadership.

Other reasons aside, however, the rebellion within Fatah would
not have reached the level it did without Syria's moral and material
support. In fact, in the fighting between the PLO rebels and the regular PLO forces, Syrian troops interfered in support of the rebels. Despite these challenges, however, Fatah and Arafat have survived, for a
number of reasons. First, the majority of the PLO, including those
who were unhappy with certain aspects of the leadership, did not
want the organization to fall under Syrian control. Second, despite
events in Beirut, Arafat retained his popularity among the Palestinians of the occupied territories. (These Palestinians were incensed by
the actions of the rebel group.)[13] Third, most Palestinian groups, including even those ideologically opposed to Fatah and Arafat, thought
that any change in leadership after the debacles of Beirut and Tripoli
would only weaken the organization further and reduce its maneu-
verability within the Arab world. Despite the considerable unhappiness with his leadership, then, Arafat survived the rebels' challenge,
and his leadership was confirmed at the meeting of the PLO National
Council in Algeria in February 1983.

The fourth consequence of the Lebanese war for the PLO was the
breach between the organization—and especially of its leader, Arafat—and Syria. Relations between Syria and the PLO had never been
cordial, and in fact they had fought each other in Lebanon in the
past;[14] nevertheless, neither side had heretofore let their differences
lead to an irreversible breach. However, the events in Lebanon and
Syria's open support of the rebels finally led to what some consider to
be an irreversible split between Syria and the PLO.

What Option for the Future?

Given the extent of the changes caused by the events in Lebanon,
both within the PLO itself and in its relations with Syria in the last
two years, the question most frequently asked focuses on what these

changes mean for the PLO's political future, and in particular whether or not these changes will cause the PLO to be more forthcoming on the issue of peace with Israel. Needless to say, expert opinion on this issue has been divided. One group has generally argued that the breach with Syria would enable the PLO leadership to form a coalition with moderate Arab states and develop a joint negotiating strategy with Israel within the framework of a prospective peace process. This group argues that, given the depth and openness of intra-PLO division, there is less compulsion on the part of the PLO leadership to continue with the politics of consensus. Therefore, Arafat, with the support of only part of the PLO, will, be able to develop a common strategy with moderate Arabs. The other group of experts argues that despite the breach with Syria the PLO must still be aware of the Syrian factor, given its influence with Palestinian groups and its position both in Lebanon and vis-à-vis Israel. Moreover, they argue that without the ability to play the Syrian card the PLO's bargaining position vis-à-vis the moderate Arabs would suffer. Thus, they argue that recent changes will not have a significant impact in terms of the PLO's ability to change course, and that future PLO politics will continue to be much the same as in the past—a situation which bars any bold action by the organization.

The experience of the last two years has proven proponents of these views both right and wrong. First, after efforts at reconciliation with Syria failed, Arafat began to move closer to the moderate Arab states. Jordan was the first country Arafat approached, with the purpose of developing a joint response to the Reagan peace plan by incorporating elements of the American plan and the Fez formula. After some initial success, however, the hopes raised by the Arafat-Hussein discussions were dashed when the PLO executive council meeting in Kuwait in April 1983 rejected a tentative agreement worked out between the PLO leader and the king. Understandably, this rebuff irritated King Hussein who, in an angry moment said that he was washing his hands of the Palestinian problem, and that from that point on the PLO would have to bear the main responsibility for the West Bank and Gaza.[15]

After the failure of the first round of talks with Hussein, Arafat returned to Tripoli in September 1983 to try to salvage the remaining PLO positions in Lebanon; however, he was forced out of Lebanon again, this time by Syria and Syria-backed PLO rebels. Having lost all hope of retaining any kind of position in Lebanon, and seeing no chance of reconciliation with Syria, Arafat once more turned to the moderate Arabs. This time he chose Egypt, and—in a bold gesture—he met with President Mubarak on December 19, 1983. Following that meeting, and possibly with Egyptian mediation, Arafat and Hussein resumed a second round of negotiations that finally, on February 11, 1985, led to an agreement on a common position on the Palestinian issue and negotiations with Israel.[16] The language of the accord, however, is very vague. It neither gives a mandate to King Hussein to negotiate on behalf of the Palestinians, nor does it provide for the kind of Palestinian participation in a joint Jordanian-Palestinian negotiating team that would make it acceptable to Israel and the United States.[17]

Thus, despite the Lebanese experience, the PLO's predicament is the same as it has been in the past—namely, an inability to reach a decision that could break the deadlock on Arab-Israeli peace negotiations. The factors behind this situation are many, and relate both to the PLO's internal structure and politics and to external conditions. Among external factors, Syrian opposition has been of great importance, Syria, after all, is the only country actually bordering on Israel that shelters armed PLO members on its territory. In addition, immediately after PLO-Jordanian talks began in March–April 1983, Syria embarked on a campaign of terror. Jordanian embassies abroad were attacked and a number of moderate Palestinian personalities, including Dr. Hisham Sartawi, a member of the Palestine National Council, and Fahd Kawasemeh, an ex–West Bank mayor expelled by the Israelis and living in Jordan, were murdered in April 1983 and January 1985, respectively.

Internally, there was not even consensus within Fatah as to the terms of an agreement, and, of course, without consensus any Arafat-Hussein agreement would be devoid of legitimacy and thus doomed to failure.

But perhaps even more important has been the real divergence of any long-term interest between the PLO and Jordan. Jordan has a long-standing interest in extending its authority over whatever Palestinian entity emerges in the West Bank. Thus, unless the terms of Palestinian participation in the peace process and the nature of the relationship between the prospective Palestinian entity and Jordan are clearly defined, the PLO's goal of establishing an independent Palestinian state (and Arafat's personal dream of becoming its first president) are in vain.[18] What the foregoing implies, therefore, is that in the foreseeable future the PLO will continue to operate under the same limiting factors as in the past—and the fate of the Arab-Israeli peace process will be determined by other factors than by any bold action on the part of the PLO leadership.

Syria's Regional Ascendency

The second important consequence of the Lebanon war was the major enhancement of Syria's regional importance. Initially, the Israeli invasion of Lebanon had weakened Syria both militarily and politically. Militarily, Syrian armed forces and their Russian-supplied equipment performed dismally against Israeli troops using American weapons, and Syria suffered heavy losses in equipment. Politically, as late as one year after the Israeli invasion the danger still existed that the Christian forces would formalize their grip on the country and implement a peace treaty with Israel. Such a circumstance would not only have virtually eliminated Syrian influence in Lebanon, but would also have posed a serious problem for Syria at home. (Still another factor that weakened Syria at this time, although unrelated to Lebanese events, was President Assad's health problem, which had sparked a power struggle between his brother Rifat and Defense Minister General Mustafa Tlas.)

The situation, however, was soon reversed. First, the USSR replaced Syria's military equipment losses, and—in order to spare itself and Syria future embarrassment—dispatched trained advisers to man some of the more sophisticated weaponry it provided. Second, Israeli expectations about their Christian allies' ability to control Lebanon proved unrealizable as well as unrealistic. Syria, drawing on its proximity, its military power, and the expertise drawn from a long history of involvement in Lebanese politics, was able to manipulate Lebanon's internal problems to its own advantage. This, coupled with U.S. miscalculations and outright mistakes in handling the negotiations leading to the May 17 agreement between Lebanon and Israel, finally led to the agreement's unravelling.

Later, Shi'a activism and opposition to Israeli occupation, the growing cost to Israel of its Lebanese adventure, and increasing opposition at home forced Israel to withdraw from Lebanon. In addition, these Lebanese events served to partially undermine the moral standing of the moderate Arabs, since many in the Arab world now argued that Lebanon's invasion was the direct result of the Camp David process.

As a result of these developments Syria emerged as the new regional power. However, it is important to note that Syria's power has been more negative than positive. In other words, Syria has been very successful in foreclosing certain options, but it has been less successful in terms of making things go exactly its own way. For example, Syria has not been able to bring peace to Lebanon, or to unseat Arafat from the PLO's leadership. It did not even succeed in preventing the convening of the PLO National Council meeting in Jordan in November 1984.

Egyptian-Jordanian Rapprochement: Counterforce to Syria

As noted earlier, one of the principal objectives of Egypt's foreign policy since Mubarak's assumption of power has been the reintegration of Egypt into the Arab fold. The realization of this objective was to some degree facilitated by the regional developments referred to earlier. Nevertheless, Egypt's reconciliation with its Arab cousins has remained essentially unofficial. For example, none of the Gulf Arab states have resumed diplomatic relations with Egypt, nor has Egypt been readmitted into the Arab League.[19]

The reestablishment of diplomatic relations between Egypt and Jordan in September 1984 was therefore a significant development. The primary rationale for Jordan, of course, was a desire to counterbalance Syria's regional influence. Another reason was King Hussein's wish for a supporter of his policy of trying to strike a deal with the Palestinians. Nor was King Hussein wrong in his calculations: not only has Egypt supported the Hussein-Arafat accord, but Egyptian support has also enabled Jordan to follow a policy opposed to Syria's views, and at times even to defy the Syrians—as, for example, with the convening of the PLO National Council in Amman. However, there is a certain limit beyond which Jordan dare not go in antagonizing Syria without running the serious risk of retaliation by Damascus. In fact, in the last few months (perhaps in an effort to cover his flank) King Hussein has been trying to improve relations with Syria, and to that end has appointed as prime minister Zaid al-Rifai, known for his good relationship with Damascus.[20]

The Egyptian-Jordanian coalition has been further strengthened by the close relations between these countries and Iraq. However, Jordan's effort to improve relations with Syria, if carried too far, might negatively impact on its relations with Iraq. This should not be too serious a problem for King Hussein, though, since at present Iraq is more in need of Jordanian cooperation than vice versa.

Saudi Arabia: A Power in Decline

Since the oil revolution of 1973 saw the transfer of massive financial resources to Saudi Arabia, that country has become an important and influential actor in the Middle East, and to some degree in international politics. In the last ten years, however, most Middle East observers have tended to exaggerate Saudi Arabia's ability to influence events based on the power of the purse string.[21] Events in Lebanon, for example, clearly demonstrated the serious limits of Saudi power; as a matter of fact, miscalculation of the degree of Saudi influence led to some serious mistakes on the part of the United States in its Lebanese diplomacy. For instance, in negotiating the May 17 agreement between Israel and Lebanon, the United States relied heavily on Saudi Arabia's ability to convince Syria to withdraw its troops from Lebanon. Many U.S. officials mistakenly believed that the Saudis could "play a key role because of their dominant position in the Arab world in general and their influence in Syria in particular."[22] However, it transpired that Saudi Arabia could not influence Syria; to the contrary, when Syria set out to undo the May 17 agreement the Saudis lobbied the United States and Lebanon to agree to its cancellation.

Nor should this Saudi policy have been surprising. Not only do the Saudis have little influence in Syria (despite their large financial contributions to its budget), they feel themselves to be highly vulnerable to a variety of Syrian pressures. Thus, throughout the series of events in Lebanon the Saudis' principal concern was not to antagonize the Syrians. The Saudis are also ambivalent about recently emerging political patterns and new Arab alliances; for example, they welcome Egypt's return to the Arab fold, and its potential there as a counterweight to Syria and perhaps even to Iraq. (On the other hand, they do not want to see Egypt become too powerful, either.) Thus, by and large, the Saudis have followed their traditional policy of counterbalancing different forces so as to maximize their own influence and freedom of action. Consequently, they have not gone out of their way to help Egypt and have maintained their close links to Syria.[23]

In general, though, Saudi Arabia has been seeing regional events slipping from its control and evading its influence. This situation has in turn led the Kingdom to become even more cautious in its regional policies and to avoid any bold actions, concentrating its attention on internal affairs. Events in the Gulf, especially those proceeding from the Iran-Iraq war, are also demanding Saudi attention. Thus, as far as the central power struggle in the Arab world is concerned—that between Syria on the one hand and Egypt on the other—Saudi Arabia has "retreated to the diplomatic sidelines."[24] (However, the Saudis did make a show of power in the Gulf when they downed an Iranian jet fighter in the summer of 1984.)

Many of these changes, of course, have resulted from events other than the Lebanese war, such as the fall in oil prices and instability in the Gulf. But the war in Lebanon, by enhancing Syria's power and helping Egypt's reemergence, has contributed to the Saudi decline. However, this relative decline in Saudi power should not affect deeply such central issues in the Arab world as the Arab-Israeli conflict and the peace process, since the importance of the Saudi factor has been exaggerated in the past. Of course, with the decline in their power and their preoccupation closer to home, the Saudis have been even more cautious in their regional policy—particularly in regard to the issues of war and peace. At the same time, their ability to affect the actions of such major actors as Jordan has continued to diminish.

Conclusions

The most important conclusion to be drawn on the state of intra-Arab politics is that, in the Middle East the French dictum *plus ca change plus c'est la meme chose* holds true. After three years of bloody war in Lebanon and shifting fortunes and alliances, the Arab world remains as divided as ever. Similarly, all the dramatic events of the past three years, including the military disintegration of the PLO and the multiple realignments, have not altered the underlying balance of power in the Arab world, and most Arab countries continue to operate under the same constraining factors as before.

Thus King Hussein, despite his alliance with Egypt and in the face of the PLO's misfortunes, is yet not capable of defying Arafat and engaging in direct negotiations with Israel. Likewise, although Egypt's position has improved because of its rapprochement with Jordan and Iraq, it has not been readmitted to the Arab League; nor has it been able to persuade Jordan and the PLO to be forthcoming on the issue of peace negotiations with Israel. As for Syria, its position and influence have indeed been enhanced in the last two years, but its power remains limited. For example, Syria has not been able to unseat Yasser Arafat from the chairmanship of the PLO, nor has it been able to prevent PLO-Jordanian and PLO-Egyptian rapprochement. Meanwhile, further to the east, the Gulf Arabs, including Saudi Arabia, remain preoccupied with the Iran-Iraq war and their immediate security problems, and are thus on the sidelines of the central power struggle in the Arab world.

What does this situation mean, then, for future Arab politics, especially vis-à-vis the central issues of war and peace with Israel? The persistence of the polarized state of Arab politics and the underlying balance of power within the Arab world means that the Arab world will, most probably, remain paralyzed as regards the pivotal question of peace with Israel. Of course, there will be considerable agitation on the part of some Arab actors, but the chances that this will lead to any bold departures from past behavior seem slim, as do the chances for the initiation of a meaningful peace process with any solid hope of success.

With the stalemate in the peace front, the danger of the region once again drifting toward violence—and not necessarily toward a war that will pit Israel against one or more Arab countries—increases. Also, with the growing conviction in many quarters that without a drastic shift in the intra-Arab balance of power the Arab world's paralysis cannot be remedied, pressure for internal change in many Arab countries will probably increase. The net result of this situation would be increased danger of political instability and unpredictability throughout the entire region.

NOTES

1. For a more detailed treatment of these points see Shireen T. Hunter and Robert E. Hunter, "The Post Camp David Arab World," in Robert O. Freedman, ed., *The Middle East Since Camp David* (Boulder, Colo.: Westview Press, 1984), pp. 79–99.

On Iran's interaction with the Arab world, see Shireen T. Hunter, "Arab-Iranian Relations and Stability in the Persian Gulf," *Washington Quarterly* 7, no. 3 (Summer 1984):67–76.
2. The salient points of the Reagan plan are the following, as expressed in the president's words:

In the Camp David talks thus far, both Israel and Egypt have felt free to express openly their views as to what the outcome should be. Understandably, their views have differed on many points.

The United States has thus far sought to play the role of mediator, we have avoided public comment on the key issues. We have always recognized—and continue to recognize—that only the voluntary agreement of those parties most directly involved in the conflict can provide an enduring solution. But it has become evident to me that some clearer sense of America's position on the key issues is necessary to encourage wider support for the peace process.

First, as outlined in the Camp David accords, there must be a period of time during which the Palestine inhabitants of the West Bank and Gaza will have full autonomy over their own affairs. Due consideration must be given to the principle of self-government by the inhabitants of the territories and to the legitimate security concerns of the parties involved.

The purpose of the five-year period of transition, which would begin after free elections for a self-governing Palestinian authority, is to prove to the Palestinians that they can run their own affairs and that such Palestinian autonomy poses no threat to Israel's security.

The United States will not support the use of any additional land for the purpose of settlements during the transition period. Indeed, the immediate adoption of a settlement freeze by Israel, more than any other action, could create the confidence needed for wider participation in these talks. Further settlement activity is in no way necessary for the security of Israel and only diminishes the confidence of the Arabs that a final outcome can be freely and fairly negotiated.

I want to make the American position well understood: the purpose of this transition period is the peaceful and orderly transfer of authority from Israel to the Palestinian inhabitants of the West Bank and Gaza. At the same time such a transfer must not interfere with Israel's security requirements.

Beyond the transition period, as we look to the future of the West Bank and Gaza, it is clear to me that peace cannot be achieved by the formation of an independent Palestinian state in those territories. Nor is it achievable on the basis of Israeli sovereignty or permanent control over the West Bank and Gaza.

So the United States will not support the establishment of an independent Palestinian state in the West Bank and Gaza, and we will not support annexation or permanent control by Israel.

There is, however, another way to peace. The final status of these lands must, of course, be reached through the give and take of negotiations. But it is the firm view of the United States that self-government by the Palestinians of the West Bank and Gaza in association with Jordan offers the best chance for a durable, just and lasting peace.

We base our approach squarely on the principle that the Arab-Israeli conflict should be resolved through negotiations involving an exchange of territory for peace. This exchange is enshrined in U.N. Security Council Resolution 242, which is, in turn, incorporated in all its parts in the Camp David agreements. U.N. Resolution 242 remains wholly valid as the foundation stone of America's Middle East peace effort.

It is the United States position that—in return for peace—the withdrawal provision of Resolution 242 applies to all fronts, including the West Bank and Gaza.

When the border is negotiated between Jordan and Israel, our view on the extent to which Israel should be asked to give up territory will be heavily affected by the extent of true peace and normalization and the security arrangements offered in return.

Finally, we remain convinced that Jerusalem must remain undivided, but its final status should be decided through negotiations.

In the course of the negotiations to come, the United States will support positions that seem to us fair and reasonable compromises and likely to promote a sound agreement. We will also put forward our own detailed proposals when we believe they can be helpful. And, make no mistake, the United States will oppose any proposal—from any party and at any point in the negotiating process—that threatens the security of Israel. America's commitment to the security of Israel is ironclad. And, I might add, so is mine.

Israel-Arab Reader, ed. Walter Laqueur and Barry Rubin (New York: Penguin, 1984), pp. 660–62.

3. See Claudia Wright, "Iraq: New Power in the Middle East," *Foreign Affairs* 58, no. 2 (Winter 1979–80):257–77.

4. See Shireen T. Hunter, ed., "Gulf Cooperation Council: Problems and Prospects," Significant Issues Series VI, No. 15, Center for Strategic and International Studies, Georgetown University, 1984.

5. On Syrian-Iranian relations, see Shireen T. Hunter, "Syrian-Iranian Relations: An Alliance of Convenience or More?' *Middle East Insight*, May/June 1984.

6. The main points of the Fez formula are the following:

1. Israel's withdrawal from all Arab territories occupied in 1967, including Arab Jerusalem.

2. The removal of settlements set up by Israel in the Arab territories after 1967.

3. Guarantees of the freedom of worship and the performance of religious rites for all religions at the holy places.

4. Confirmation of the right of the Palestinian people to self-determination and to exercise their firm and inalienable national rights, under the leadership of the PLO, its sole legitimate representative, and compensation for those who do not wish to return.

5. The placing of the West Bank and Gaza strip under U.N. supervision for a transitional period, not longer than several months.

6. The creation of an independent Palestinian state with Jerusalem as its capital.

7. The drawing up by the Security Council of guarantees for peace for all the states of the region, including the independent Palestinian state.

8. Security Council guarantees for the implementation of these principles. (*Foreign Broadcasting Information Service, Middle East and Africa,* 10 September 1982:A17–18.)

7. For a detailed study of Israeli-Lebanese relations, see Jonathan C. Randal, *Going All the Way: Christian Warlords, Israeli Adventurers, and the War in Lebanon* (New York: Viking Press, 1983). See also Ze'ev Shiff and Ehud Ya'ari, *Israel's Lebanon War* (New York: Simon & Schuster, 1984).

8. The most important (and most controversial) part of the 17 May 1983 Israel-Lebanon agreement related to the security arrangements: According to the agreement, Lebanon would have been divided into two security zones: one running from the Israeli border approximately to the Zahrani River; the other, from the Zahrani to the Awali River. The southern zone would have been patrolled by a "territorial brigade" composed of Major Hadad's (since dead) militia and other locally recruited people, whereas the northern zone would have been patrolled by the regular Lebanese army. (See *New York Times,* 10 May 1983.)

9. For a discussion of the Palestinian community in Lebanon before the Israeli invasion, see Rashid Khalidi, "The Palestinians in Lebanon: Social Repercussions of Israel's Invasion," *The Middle East Journal* 38, no. 2 (Spring 1984):255.

10. For a discussion of the impact of internal divisions and Arab pressures on the PLO's ability to act effectively and independently, see Aaron David Miller, *The PLO and the Politics of Survival* (New York: Praeger, 1983).

11. See *Washington Post,* 21 December 1983.

12. Helena Cobban, "The 1983 Inter-Palestinian Fighting in Tripoli and the Future of the Palestinian Movement," in Shireen T. Hunter, ed., *The PLO After Tripoli,* Significant Issues Series VI, no. 10, Center for Strategic and International Studies, Georgetown University, 1984, p. 3.

13. For example, rebel Abu-Musa's own mother, living in the West Bank, denounced her son. See "On Occupied West Bank, Support for Arafat Remains Strong," *The Christian Science Monitor,* 1 July 1983. It is also important to note that given the loss of the PLO's territorial base and the dispersal of the Palestinians across various Arab lands, the Palestinians of the occupied territories remain the only compact group of Palestinians and as such acquire an even greater significance in terms of PLO politics. See Cobban, *1983 Inter-Palestinian Fighting.*

14. See *Le Monde,* 17 April 1985.

15. *Israel-Arab Reader,* op.cit. pp 690–691.

16. The following is the text of the PLO-Jordan agreement as published in the *Washington Post,* 24 February 1985:

Emanating from the spirit of the Fez summit resolutions, approved by Arab states, and from United Nations resolutions relating to the Palestine question, IN ACCORDANCE with international legitimacy, and DERIVING from a common understanding of the establishment of a special relationship between the Jordanian and Palestinian peoples,

The Government of the Hashemite Kingdom of Jordan and the Palestine Liberation Organization have agreed to move together toward the achievement of a

peaceful and just settlement of the Middle East crisis and the termination of Israeli occupation of the occupied Arab territories, including Jerusalem, on the basis of the following principles:

1. Total withdrawal from the territories occupied in 1967 for comprehensive
peace as established in United Nations and Security Council resolutions.
2. Right of self-determination for the Palestinian people: Palestinians will exercise their inalienable right of self-determination when Jordanians and Palestinians will be able to do so within the context of the formation of the proposed con-
federated Arab states of Jordan and Palestine.
3. Resolution of the problem of Palestinian refugees in accordance with United
Nations resolutions.
4. Resolution of the Palestine question in all its aspects.
5. And on this basis, peace negotiations will be conducted under the auspices
of an international conference in which the five permanent members of the Security Council and all the parties to the conflict will participate, including the
Palestine Liberation Organization, the sole legitimate representative of the Palestine people, within a joint delegation (joint Jordanian-Palestinian delegation).

17. The United States and Israel have opposed the participation of known PLO
members in any joint Jordanian-Palestinian delegation.
18. This difference of interest between the PLO and Jordan is clearly reflected
in the differing interpretations made in Jordan of the nature of relations between Jordan and an eventual Palestinian entity. It is expressed by one scholar in the following
terms:

In one conversation, Jordanian officials told me of four different and conflicting
images they held on what would happen to the West Bank if Jordan and the PLO
would work out a formula based on the Reagan Plan. One argued that everything
would revert to the pre-1967 situation. "We're just going to run the West Bank as
a part of Jordan. The central government is going to possess it, and that is all
there is to it." A second view could be called the federation idea: "We are going to
give them a certain amount of autonomy but it's going to be basically on local
matters. We are going to dominate." A third view was the confederation view:
"They're going to be pretty separate on a lot of things. Of course, we'll keep an
overall umbrella. But they will have more than just a nominal amount of power."
And then, fourth, the Palestinian state view: "But, of course, there can't be any
solution to the problem without a Palestinian state."

Barry Rubin, "Yasir Arafat's Tightrope in Arab Politics," in *PLO After Tripoli,*
op.cit., p. 15. See also *Middle East Policy Survey,* no. 126, 19 April 1985.

19. Egypt has, however, been readmitted into the Islamic conference despite
Libyan and Iranian opposition, and has taken part in the meetings of the nonaligned
movement.

20. See *The Middle East Economic Digest* 26, no. 15 (12–18 April 1985):18.

21. The use of Saudi financial power has been more effective in averting threats to its security rather than influencing the policies of other countries. Similarly, Saudi financial power has been most effective when used in conjunction with the military assets of other states. For a detailed study of the use of Saudi financial resources as an instrument of foreign policy, see Shireen T. Hunter, *OPEC and the Third World: The Politics of Aid* (Bloomington, Ind.: Indiana University Press, 1984), pp. 123–44.

22. *New York Times*, 7 May 1983.

23. Frustrated in their own efforts to become the dominant power in the Arab world, the Saudis have tried to prevent other Arab countries from acquiring a predominant position, and have fashioned their alliances to forward this overriding aim. For a treatment of this and other aspects of Saudi foreign policy, see William B. Quandt, *Saudi Security in the 1980s* (Washington, D.C.: Brookings Institution, 1981).

24. David B. Ottaway, "Saudi Leaders Turn Inward as Nation Faces Uncertain Era," *Washington Post*, 25 November 1984.

5

The Impact of Khomeini's Iran

*R. K. Ramazani**

T HE IRANIAN REVOLUTION did not change the geographic, cultural, historical, and economic factors that make the Middle East the region of primary interest to Iranian foreign policymakers. But the taking of American hostages in November 1979 made the conflict with the United States the central issue in Iran's revolutionary foreign policy until the settlement of the hostage dispute in January 1981. The Iraqi invasion of Iran in September 1980, combined with the dire consequences of Western economic and diplomatic sanctions against the Khomeini regime (as well as the shah's death), prompted Iran to settle the dispute. Thereafter, the war with Iraq became the dominant issue in Iranian foreign policy, and has remained so up to this writing.

The central purpose of this essay is to show the continuity and the change in Iran's Middle Eastern policy since the Lebanon war. Toward that end, it will argue that the Middle Eastern policy of the revolutionary regime has been largely a function of its overall orientation toward the superpowers (as it was of course during the shah's regime), but that the revolution has wrought radical changes in the nature of that orientation and hence in the patterns of Iranian regional alignments since 1979.

Revolutionary Reorientation and Realignment

Long before the late shah cast his lot with the United States by signing the American-sponsored, anti-Soviet Baghdad Pact alliance

*The author wishes to acknowledge the research support of the Center for Advanced Studies at the University of Virginia for a large project on which this chapter is partly based.

in 1955, he had become convinced that he could vouchsafe both the survival of his regime and the independence of Iran by means of such an alliance. As early as 1941, in fact, when the twenty-two-year-old shah ascended the throne, he took the initiative to inform the United States of his deep interest in an American alliance.[1] However, he had to weather the opposition of nationalist, communist, and Muslim fundamentalist forces to his rule before he could press on with his youthful dream. The successful coup against the nationalist leader and prime minister Muhammad Musaddiq, engineered in August 1953 and backed by the United States, was followed by the first American acquisition of interest in Iranian oil and by an Iranian alliance with the United States through a bilateral executive agreement. This was four years after the signing of the Baghdad Pact, and was followed by the endorsement of the anti-Soviet Eisenhower Doctrine in 1957. The void created by the British departure from the Gulf region by the end of 1971; Washington's reluctance to act as the British legatee in the oil-rich region; and finally the perception and the reality of Iran's being the strongest pro-Western power in the area at the time made the shah's Iran the Gulf's Western "policeman," as well as the single largest recipient of sophisticated American arms.

The Soviet Union was as much a bete noir for the shah as it had been for his father, Reza Shah. But when the global and regional environment allowed the shah in the 1960s to pursue a policy of "peaceful coexistence" with the Soviets, he moved to ease the longtime cold-war tensions between Tehran and Moscow. In addition to pledging that Iran would not allow the use of its territory as a base for foreign missiles deployed against the Soviet Union, the shah dramatically improved economic, technical, and commercial relations with the Kremlin—without compromising, much less abandoning, his alliance with Washington. His economic rapprochement with Moscow, however, suffered from ideological and political differences to the very end of his rule. From the shah's perspective, certain geopolitical realities made the continuation of a basically pro-Western and anti-Soviet orientation necessary for both the survival of his regime and for the security of Iran. (In his mind, the two were inextricably intertwined.)

The shah's Middle Eastern policies reflected this basic orientation in realpolitik.[2] In the Persian Gulf region, he allied Iran with the pro-Western monarchy in Iraq. He opposed the pretensions of Nasser's regime in the lower part of the Gulf, and sought accommodation with Saudi Arabia in the 1950s.[3] After the Iraqi Revolution of 1958, he opposed the antimonarchical and pro-Soviet regime in Baghdad by every means, including the support of the Iraqi Kurdish rebels. In 1974, finally, he nearly went to war with the Ba'thist regime over the longtime Shatt al-Arab dispute, which would be settled in the following year.[4]

In the eastern Mediterranean, the shah's regime for all practical purposes aligned Iran with Israel. It provided the Jewish state with most of its oil supplies, while receiving Israeli aid in a variety of forms, including intelligence, security, and agriculture. At the same time, Iran fought a protracted cold war with Nasser's revolutionary regime—Israel's most powerful enemy in the Arab and Muslim world. Nasser finally broke all diplomatic relations with the shah's regime in 1960, allegedly because his government recognized the state of Israel. (Actually, Iran had extended de facto recognition early in the 1950s and had never withdrawn it.)[5] Although Nasser resumed diplomatic relations with Iran shortly before his death in 1970, it was the succession of Anwar al-Sadat to leadership that transformed the Irano-Egyptian hostility of more than a decade into an unprecedented rapprochement between Tehran and Cairo. For the shah, the emergence of Egypt as a pro-Western and essentially anti-Soviet country was the most welcome development in the Eastern Mediterranean since 1955, when Soviet influence had increased in Egypt. His personal friendship with Sadat reinforced his sense of common strategic interests between Iran and Egypt, and he both supported the Sadat regime in the October 1973 war and gave it generous financial aid after the war. He hailed Sadat's historic trip to Jerusalem in November 1977 and supported the Camp David accords in 1978, even though his own regime was being increasingly threatened by revolution.

Finally, the shah's overall foreign-policy orientation was reflected in his policies in the Northern Tier. He continued Iran's alliance with Turkey and Pakistan in the Central Treaty Organization (CENTO) after the defection of Iraq from the Baghdad Pact, and committed Iran to the defense of Pakistan after the Indo-Pakistani war of 1971. He tried to woo the non-aligned Daud regime in Afghanistan, using oil money to aid the government and also trying to mediate the longtime dispute between Kabul and Islamabad over Pushtunistan. Although the shah's dissatisfaction with the CENTO alliance increased after the 1965 and 1971 Indo-Pakistani wars and the perceived American failure to help Pakistan, he continued Iran's close relations with its regional allies, increasingly under the umbrella of the Regional Development Cooperation (RCD) that had been created by Iran, Turkey, and Pakistan in 1964.[6]

The Khomeini regime's Middle Eastern policy has also reflected its overall foreign-policy orientation in world politics. That orientation, however, is quite different from the shah's. The revolutionary slogan today is *nah sharq, nah qharb, faqat Jumhury-e Islami:* "neither East nor West, only the Islamic Republic." What does this appellation mean, and how is it reflected in revolutionary Iran's Middle Eastern policy? Does it mean that Iran is committed to a policy of nonalignment between the superpowers? If so, what does "nonalignment" really denote? In seeking the answers to these questions, it might be helpful to consider the causes of change in Iran's foreign-policy orientation—a change, I suggest, that has resulted mainly from Iran's new revolutionary politics and ideology.

Let us first take up the effects of revolutionary politics on the Iranian foreign-policy orientation. Anti-Americanism was used by the opponents of the shah in destroying his regime much as he had used pro-Americanism to maintain it. For decades, the shah had allied himself with the United States to assure the survival of his regime.[7] All of his opponents challenged that alliance. They opposed the shah as much for being a "servile" "American king" as for being an Iranian despot. In the eyes of his disparate opponents on all sides of the political spectrum, these perceived characteristics of the shah's rule were the two sides of the same coin. This apparent commonality of outlook was rooted in the populace's increasing alienation from the shah and his closest ally, the United States. As such, it disguised the wide political and ideological differences among the revolutionary forces opposed to the shah—differences which would emerge only after his dramatic downfall. In their common hatred of the shah's regime, all of the major sociopolitical forces downplayed their ultimate goals: the leftists aimed at a socialist political order; the nationalists wanted a liberal democratic political system; and the Muslim radicals (fundamentalists) pressed for a purely Islamic government. With respect to a new Iranian foreign-policy orientation, the revolutionary regime's first prime minister, Mehdi Bazargan, claimed—after his own fall from power—that Khomeini, like himself, had believed in the principles of equality and reciprocity before the hostage crisis, but that subsequently the Ayatollah chose a confrontational stance—particularly toward the United States.[8]

Even without the benefit of hindsight it is highly questionable whether Bazargan should have taken the pronouncements of Khomeini at face value. As early as 1964, Khomeini had not only fiercely opposed the shah's efforts to extend diplomatic immunities and privileges to American military personnel in Iran, but had also clearly revealed the depth of his hatred of foreign powers—especially the United States. He declared that "the world must realize that all the difficulties faced by the Iranian nation and the Muslim peoples are because of aliens, because of America. The Muslim nations hate aliens in general and Americans in particular...."[9] In the intervening years between his exile by the shah in that same year and his triumphant return to Iran in 1979, Khomeini had not said or done anything to indicate a real change of heart toward the United States. Given this fact, his favorable comments in Paris about the principle of "reciprocity" as the basis of Iran's future policy toward the United States should have been taken for what they were: remarks delivered for purposes of expediency.

In any event, revolutionary political dynamics resulted in a basic change in Iran's foreign-policy orientation. For months—from the time of the seizure of power by the revolutionary forces on February 11, 1979, until the takeover of the American embassy on November 4 of that year—the centrist forces under the leadership of Bazargan tried to pursue what he called a "defensive policy" (*syasat-e defa'i*) in world politics, including normalization of relations with the United States on the basis of "equality." But the extremists on both sides of the political spectrum, seeking to shape a new political order in their own image and under their own exclusionary power and control, combined their efforts to stop the attempted normalization-of-relations process with the United States. Under the leadership of Ayatollah Khoiniha, they seized the American embassy—an act that precipitated the downfall of the Bazargan government. The political demise of the moderate forces followed. Khomeini's ex post facto endorsement of the seizure of the U.S. embassy, enacted without his prior knowledge, was fully compatible with his own well-known anti-American sentiments. It ushered in what he called a "second revolution," even superior to the first one (which he himself had led).

Up to this point in the Iranian revolutionary process, the slogan "neither East nor West" had had quite a "defensive" meaning. It only meant, Bazargan tells us, that Iran would try to realize its "all encompassing independence" (*istiqlal-e hameh-janebeh*) without relying

on foreigners including the superpowers astride the Eastern and
Western blocs, "politically, economically and militarily." But after the
seizure of the U.S. embassy and the fall of the provisional government, the slogan increasingly reflected not only a "confrontational
political dimension" (*janbeh-ye ta'arozy-e syasi*) but also an "anti-
Western mode in cultural and educational fields."[10] In other words,
the basically accommodative orientation in world politics that the
centrist forces had attempted to pursue during the first phase of the
Iranian revolutionary politics (February 11–November 6, 1979) was
increasingly replaced by an essentially confrontational approach advocated by the extremist forces on both sides of the political spectrum.

   This major change in revolutionary Iran's foreign-policy orientation, however, has reflected not only the outcome of the political and
ideological struggle among diverse sociopolitical forces but also the
world view of Ayatollah Khomeini. As the supreme arbiter of all Iranian affairs, domestic and foreign, his precepts have guided the formulation and execution of Iranian foreign policy. Since I have elsewhere analyzed in detail the ideological foundations of Khomeini's
foreign policy precepts,[11] it will suffice here to point out their implications only for Iran's foreign-policy orientation toward the superpowers. Khomeini's world view eschews both pan-Shi'ism and pan-Is-
lamism; it aspires instead to the ultimate establishment of an
"Islamic world order" in place of the existing international system of
modern nation-states. This system, he contends, is flawed because,
among other reasons, it is dominated by the two superpowers. As
such, the United States and the Soviet Union both belong to the camp
of the "oppressors" (*mustakberin*). And as such, they are inevitably
the enemies of all the "oppressed" peoples of the world (*mustaz-
a'fin*).

   Since, in Khomeini's world view, Iran is the vanguard Islamic nation (since it is the only country in the world where the rule of the
faqih [supreme jurisprudent] has been established), it should lead
the fight of the oppressed peoples everywhere against the superpowers. In his own words: "We must settle our accounts with the great
and the superpowers, despite all the painful problems that face us."[12]
In his rhetoric, the United States is the "Great Satan" and the Soviet
Union the "Lesser Satan," and by association all governments that
ally themselves with either of the two superpowers perforce become
their lackeys. In addition, even those that do not enter into any kind

of alliance with the superpowers should not necessarily be considered as truly nonaligned, since most such "nonaligned" nations in fact lean either toward the East or the West.

This skeptical, if not cynical, view reveals the special meaning that revolutionary leaders attach to the purist brand of Iran's own nonalignment—one that rejects pursuing the position of "equidistance" between the two superpowers that was attempted by Musaddiq', for example, with his policy of "negative equilibrium" (*muvazeneh-ye manfi*). (This nationalist brand of nonalignment was closer to the "defensive" variety that Bazargan tried to pursue during the short term of his premiership in 1979.) Khomeini's religious and radical conception of nonalignment, however, differs from these. In Foreign Minister Velayati's words, "neutrality vis-à-vis these two arrogant powers" cannot serve to eliminate their worldwide "domination" (*tahmil*); only the "weapon of faith of the Islamic Revolution," as in Iran, can maintain "its cutting edge against the superpowers' weapons." The phrase "only the Islamic Republic" that is included in the slogan of "neither East nor West" is precisely intended by the revolutionaries to distinguish this absolutist brand of Iranian Islamic nonalignment from all other types of Third World alignment. This encompasses not only those that tilt toward the East or toward the West, but even those that pursue a more genuinely "independent course." Beyond pursuing a "completely independent" foreign policy, Khomeini's conception of nonalignment demands that Iran should strive to restructure the existing international system preparatory to the ultimate establishment of an "Islamic world government" under Imam Mahdi (Messiah).

Toward that lofty end, Iran must actively export its "Islamic revolution." It must not merely try to maintain an Islamic political order within the confines of its own international frontiers, no matter how important the goal of an independent Iran. In Khomeini's own words, "we should try hard to export our revolution to the world.... If we remain in an enclosed environment we shall definitely face defeat."[13] The combination of the religious obligation to export the Islamic revolution to the rest of the world and the inevitability of confrontation with the superpowers everywhere lies at the heart of revolutionary Iran's ideological conflict with the superpowers.

Nowhere in the world is that conflict as intense as in the Middle East—and here Iran's revolutionary interest in establishing its religiopolitical primacy in the region clashes with the vital interests of

the Soviet Union and the United States: with Soviet interests, because Iran abuts the Soviet southern borderlands as well as Soviet-
occupied Afghanistan, both of them areas inhabited by peoples who
share religious and cultural ties with Iranians; with American interests, because Iran abuts the entire eastern shore of the Gulf and dom-
inates the strategic Strait of Hormuz. This is, of course, a region on
which American NATO allies and Japan continue to depend for their
oil supplies, and where the Western world has a strategic interest in
containing the expansion of Soviet power and influence.

Between the two superpowers, Iran's conflict with the United
States has so far been the more intense, despite the evenhanded
sound of the slogan "neither East nor West." Directly, the revolutionary regime has destroyed all ties with the United States, while it has
maintained diplomatic, economic and commercial ties with the Soviet Union. Indirectly, the Khomeini government has persistently
challenged American strategic interests not only in the Gulf region
but also in the eastern Mediterranean, although it must be added that
in the Northern Tier it opposes mainly Soviet interests.

Nevertheless, it would be a mistake to characterize the Iranian
overall foreign-policy orientation as pro-Soviet. (The Soviets themselves say it is anti-Soviet.) As a rule, the Khomeini regime has resisted Soviet attempts to woo Iran and has opposed the "imperialist"
impulse of Soviet policies, despite the appearance of an early pro-
Soviet tilt. During the hostage crisis, the Khomeini regime tried to
counter the ill effects of Western economic and diplomatic sanctions
against Iran partly by establishing new economic and commercial
ties with Moscow. In doing so, it shrewdly exploited a Soviet desider-
atum. Moscow wanted to woo strategically important Iran, of course,
but was repelled by the Khomeini regime's militant brand of Islam,
which was objectionable to the Soviets not only on doctrinal grounds
but also as a threat to the Muslim-inhabited Soviet southern borderlands. After the settlement of the hostage dispute, however, the
Khomeini government stiffened its opposition to the Soviet Union, especially after Moscow resumed large-scale supplies of arms to Iraq in
the spring of 1982. It also abandoned its former expedient tolerance
of both the pro-Soviet Tudeh Communist party and the growing number of Soviet diplomatic personnel in Iran. It expelled eighteen Soviet
diplomats in 1983, demanded a further reduction of their number,
and arrested, jailed, and executed a number of Tudeh party members
on charges of espionage.

The Gulf

With or without the revolution, the Gulf would have continued to be a principal region of concern for Iranian foreign policymakers. The vital interests of revolutionary Iran in the Gulf region stem from the country's dominant geographic location, its historical perception of political primacy, and its cultural affinity with Shia Muslims and Iranian expatriates in neighboring countries—all, considerations as valid today as in the past. The reality of its economic dependence on the Gulf as the artery of the nation's oil and non-oil trade continues. But the drastic change from a basically pro-Western and anti-Soviet to a generally anti-Western and anti-Soviet orientation in world politics has dramatically altered the foreign policy of Iran in the area. Caught in the pangs of the revolution, even the shah's last Prime Minister, Shahpour Bakhtiar, realized the magnitude of popular dissatisfaction with the shah's Gulf policy. He declared that Iran would no longer play the role of the "policeman" in the region. His foreign minister, Karim Sanjabi, while conceding the centrality of the Gulf region in Iranian foreign policy, decried the kind of role that Iran had played in the area under the shah.

With the rise to power of Muslim radicals and the emergence of Iran's confrontational foreign policy, alarm bells began to ring throughout the Gulf region and as loudly in revolutionary Iraq as in conservative Saudi Arabia and the smaller sheikdoms. The new ideological drive to export the Islamic revolution, combined with Iran's old political ambitions and its cultural affinity with fellow Shia Muslims in other Gulf societies, plunged the revolutionary regime into an unprecedented discord with its neighbors. Before the fall of the Bazargan government, every Arab government had hoped for some kind of accommodation with the new revolutionary regime; afterwards, however, conflict and tension with Tehran came increasingly to characterize Arab-Iranian relations within the Gulf region. The underlying tension between Iran and Iraq finally led to war,[14] of course, while with the other Arab states the conflict characteristically took the form of a cold war.

By tearing up Iraq's 1975 agreement with Iran on September 17, and then escalating the longtime border skirmishes to "all-out war" (*harb al-shamilih*) by the bombing of ten Iranian airfields on September 22, 1980, Saddam Hussein started a war that he could not end. The Iraqi forces soon bogged down after their early thrust into

Iran's oil-rich province of Khuzistan. No stunning feat such as Sadat's spectacular Suez crossing in the 1973 October was in the cards for Saddam Hussein: the Iraqi forces failed to cross the Karun river, and were forced to lift their year-long siege of the oil refinery city of Abadan in September 1981. The success of Iranian arms then marked the beginning of the turn of the tide in the war against Iraq. It was followed by impressive Iranian offensives that began in March 1982 and culminated in the spectacular recovery of the port city of Khorramshahr on May 24. Hence, before the Israeli invasion of Lebanon (June 6, 1982) the bulk of Iraqi forces had been forced to leave Iranian territory.

By then, Iranian confidence in its capacity to inflict a decisive defeat on Iraq had soared. Khomeini warned that the Lebanon war was an American plot intended to divert Iranian attention from the "Iraqi-imposed" and American-backed war in the Gulf. The radical faction within Iranian policy circles apparently won the day over those who wished to limit military operations to Iran's borders. On July 13, 1982, therefore, the war was carried into Iraqi territory. Khomeini wanted to "deliver the Iraqi nation from this accursed party" (Ba'th Party) and from Saddam Hussein by means of a "final victory" (*fath-e naha'y*). The Iranian revolutionary leaders justified the Iranian counterinvasion in such terms as "hot pursuit of the aggressor" (*ta'qib-e mote javez*) and "strategic necessity" (*elzam-e stratigiky*). However, Iran's insistence on the overthrow of Saddam Hussein and the Ba'th party, coupled with its support for the dissident Iraqi religious leader, Hojatolislam Baqir al-Hakim, as the prospective leader of a pro-Iranian Islamic republic in Iraq, seemed to show Iran's real intentions. In the eyes of many Arab and Western observers, the Khomeini regime was and is intent on exporting its brand of Islamic revolution throughout the region by war as well as by subversion and other coercive means.

Whatever its intentions, Iran has certainly pursued an attritionist strategy in its war with Iraq. This strategy is premised largely on the notion that Iran's putative power will eventually prevail because of the "faith power" of the Iranian armed forces. In addition, the continued capacity of Iran to export its own oil (while obstructing Iraqi oil exports through the Gulf) and the domestic fragility of the Ba'thist regime are considered important factors. The revolutionary leaders have so far been able to pursue this strategy unflinchingly, despite large numbers of casualties, an ever-diminishing air power, and the repeated failure of offensives since July 1982. They have been able to sustain that strategy partly because of Iraq's inability to force Iran to the negotiating table, in spite of a variety of unscrupulous war tactics on Iraq's part: creating oil spills; using chemical weapons; attacking centers of civilian population, both before and after agreeing to desist from the practice by the terms of a United Nations-brokered moritorium on June 12, 1984; and attacking oil tankers within a fifty-mile war zone around Iran's Kharg Island oil terminal.

At sea, Iran's attritionist strategy has followed two tracks: a dogged defense of Kharg Island, and repeated threats to close the Strait of Hormuz to the export of all Gulf oil supplies. Ever since the start of the war, the Iraqi forces have targeted the Kharg oil terminal, but they have so far failed to knock out Iran's massive antiaircraft armory in and around the island. (Military incompetence, political restraint, or a combination of the two may explain the Iraqi failure.) The Iranian threat to close the Strait of Hormuz is not as dire as has sometimes been assumed. Hojatolislam Hashemi-Rafsanjani, the Majlis (parliament) speaker, said on October 14, 1983, that even if half of its oil exports were cut off, Iran would not find it in its interest to close the strait to the oil exports of all Gulf states. Since no such contingency has yet occurred, the threat has not been carried out— and even if such an eventuality should arise, it would not necessarily result in the closure of the strategic waterway. Iran might choose not to do so out of self-interest, or because of incompetence, or because of a combination of these considerations.

On land, Iran's attritionist strategy has so far focused on the strategic highway between Basra—the heavily Shia-inhabited Iraqi city in the south—and Baghdad. The Iranian offensive in February 1984 failed to reach the highway, but the Iranian forces captured parts of the artificial oil islands of Majnoon in Iraq, which sit atop seven billion barrels of oil. The resumption of Iraqi attacks on the Iranian population centers on March 4, 1985—in contravention of the June 12, 1984, agreement; the Iranian missile attacks on Iraqi cities in retaliation; and the consequent "war of cities" might have been intended by the Iraqis to goad Iran into its repeatedly promised final offensive, but this new Iraqi war tactic nearly backfired. At one point, the Iranian forces managed to advance to within striking distance of the Baghdad-Basra highway. The attempt by Iranian forces to cross the Tigris River, however, failed, as did the Iraqi efforts to cross the Karun river in the first year of the war. In fine, the Iraqi miscalculation in

invading Iran and the Iranian mistake in counterinvading Iraq have
made this a war of double blunder—and the costliest and bloodiest
war in contemporary Middle Eastern history.

Iran's conflict with the Gulf Arab states other than Iraq has taken
the form of a cold war. Tensions between Tehran and the various Arab
capitals have, of course, varied in intensity from country to country.
In the case of the United Arab Emirates (especially Dubai), relations
have been at least polite, if not exactly always cordial. But taking
Iran's relations with the GCC states as a whole, they have been generally militant since the fall of the Bazargan government, and especially since the outbreak of the Iran-Iraq war. The sources of conflict
between Iran and the individual Arab monarchies vary from one nation to another, depending on the configuration of a welter of factors,
including size, location, demographic composition, and historical
and economic relations as well as the divergent interests at stake.
But by and large, the conflict essentially reflects the ideological and
political differences between revolutionary Iran and the Gulf Arab
monarchies.

Iran's conflict with the Gulf Arab sheikdoms, however, has been
largely a function of the Iran-Iraq war. To be sure, with or without the
war the basic differences just mentioned would have strained Tehran's relations in the various Arab capitals, as was indeed the case before the war. In 1979, for example, a militant Iranian clergyman, Ayatollah Sadeq Ruhani, threatened the annexation of Bahrain if the
sheikdom failed to establish an Islamic government similar to Iran's.
In the same year, a clergyman related to Khomeini was expelled from
Kuwait because of political incitement. Nevertheless, the support by
the Arab monarchies of Saddam Hussein's war efforts against Iran has
fueled the fire of the conflict in a way that would have been otherwise
unimaginable. Fearful of the contagion of the Iranian revolution, the
Arab monarchies have dreaded the spread of the war to their own
countries. The fear of the spillover effects of both the revolution and
the war has therefore impelled the Arab leaders to side, in effect, with
Iraq in spite of their official neutrality.

Nevertheless, there is no evidence, to my knowledge, of any alliance between the Gulf monarchies and Iraq prior to the outbreak of
the war—Iranian claims to the contrary notwithstanding. No political understanding, such as that which existed between Sadat and
Faisal, or military axis (Sadat and Hafiz Assad), was formed between
the Gulf monarchies and Iraq in anticipation of the latter's invasion
of Iran. To be sure, there had been a flurry of diplomatic activity

within the Gulf Arab capitals, especially after the fall of the shah; however, the subsequent rapprochement fell somewhat short of an alliance, since it had been prompted not only by the eruption of the Iranian revolution but also by developments in the Arab-Israeli conflict. It had at first appeared that Egypt's signing of the Camp David accords in 1978 would lead to the strengthening of the so-called Eastern Front against Israel by the planned merger of Syria and Iraq. But as it turned out, the old Ba'thist feud between Baghdad and Damascus surfaced with a vengeance, and—after the Egyptians signed the peace treaty with Israel—the common Saudi/Iraqi resentment of Sadat's separate peace inclined them to closer cooperation in the Gulf. The Saudis in fact followed the Iraqi radical line in the second Baghdad conference, which imposed diplomatic and economic sanctions on Egypt in March 1979.

Far from amounting to an alliance, then, the wartime cooperation between Riyadh and certain of the other Arab capitals with Baghdad has been inhibited by an abiding suspicion of Iraq. Based on numerous conversations with Arab officials in the region, it is clear to me that the well-known distrust of Iraq as a subversive regime has persisted in spite of the fear of the spread of Islamic revolution and war. Furthermore, other factors have militated against full-fledged cooperation with Iraq. For example, the rivalry between Baghdad and Riyadh has continued, as has the territorial conflict between Kuwait and Iraq. Given the perception of revolutionary Iran as potentially the greater threat to the survival of the Gulf monarchies, however, they have cast their lot with Iraq under the present circumstances, while in fact their real attitude toward both revolutionary regimes is one of "a plague on both your houses."

This latent mistrust of Iraq on the part of the Gulf monarchies has been no source of comfort to Iran, however. For its part, Tehran has consistently tried to exploit this sentiment by emphasizing that Iraqi Ba'thists pose a common threat to all other Gulf nations, rather than only to Iran. The Iranian leadership has insisted that no real peace and security can ever be achieved in the region without the punishment of Saddam Hussein and the overthrow of the "accursed Ba'thist Party." What has angered the revolutionary leaders most of all, of course, is the continuous logistical and financial aid provided by the Gulf monarchies to the Iraqi regime—aid without which, Iran insists, Saddam Hussein could not possibly have been able to hang on to power and wage war as long as he has.

No matter how ambivalent the attitude of the GCC leaders toward

Saddam Hussein, for the moment at least the threat of revolutionary
Iran is considered greater than the threat of revolutionary Iraq—and
may be even more so once the war has ended. One of the best indicators of this attitude is the continuation of financial support for Iraq
in the face of the ever-diminishing incomes of the GCC states because
of decreasing oil revenues. But for the leaders of these countries, aid
to the Iraqi regime under the circumstances is a first line of defense
against the spread of the twin contagions of war and the revolution to
their countries.

Yet in spite of mounting concern with Iranian anti-establishment
policies, GCC leaders have striven to maintain some kind of a dialogue with revolutionary Iran. The best example of this attitude is the
way Riyadh handled the dogfight between Saudi and Iranian planes
on June 5, 1984, in the course of which an Iranian F-4 fighter plane
was downed by the Saudi F-15 jet fighters. To be sure, the Iranians
protested, claiming that their plane had been shot down over international waters—but that was all. The Saudis, too, downplayed the
whole crisis: they described it as an isolated incident, and expressed
the hope that it would not be repeated. The Iranian "under-response"
surprised most Western observers, but the Saudis were not so surprised: they had learned over the years, from the ritual of their annual dispute with Iran over the political agitation of Iranian pilgrims
in Saudi Arabia, that Iran's bark was fiercer than its bite. A number
of high-ranking Saudi officials told me that in spite of all ideological
and political differences with Iran, they have been able to manage
problems with Iranian officials on a pragmatic basis without too
much difficulty.

The Eastern Mediterranean

The foreign policy of revolutionary Iran in the eastern Mediterranean, as in the Gulf, essentially reflects its overall orientation
toward the superpowers. The general change from a pro-Western and
anti-Soviet to an anti-superpower orientation in world affairs has totally transformed Iran's prerevolutionary policies in the eastern Mediterranean. The shah's regime's alignments with Egypt and Israel
have been destroyed, while an axis with Syria has been formed. At the
same time, the nature and extent of Iranian involvement in Lebanon
have been transformed.

Once the Sadat government signed the peace treaty with Israel, the pressure of Muslim militants on the Bazargan government to terminate Iran's relations with Egypt mounted. The catalyst was the Baghdad foreign ministers conference at the end of March 1979. Given the pro-Palestinian stance of the nationalist as well as the Muslim fundamentalist and leftist forces, "the betrayal of the Palestinians" (to borrow Khomeini's words) by Egypt prompted the Iranian government to break diplomatic relations with Cairo on April 30, 1979, in line with the decision of the Arab foreign ministers to impose diplomatic sanctions on Egypt.[23]

Since then, Iran's revolutionary crusade against Egypt has been fueled by a variety of issues. Sadat's offer of political asylum to the fatally ill shah and his family infuriated the Muslim militants. Ayatollah Sadeq Khalkhali, the reputed "hanging judge" of Iran, for example, said that Sadat "would have to pay for his dirty act."[15] Another issue that angered the Khomeini regime was Sadat's supportive attitude toward the American rescue mission in April 1980. While most Arab leaders criticized the U.S. action (at least in public), Sadat not only refrained from doing so but also offered Egyptian logistical aid for the defense of the whole Gulf region.

The Khomeini regime's hostility toward the Egyptian government soared over the latter's change of attitude toward the Iraq-Iran war. Sadat at first characterized Saddam Hussein's Iraq as an aggressor, but by the time President Mubarak took power Egypt had fully sided with Iraq against Iran. The Mubarak regime has dispatched thousands of volunteers (soldiers) and one and a half million Egyptian workers (primarily farmers) to Iraq and sold Baghdad substantial amounts of arms, partly to checkmate Iran's bid for religiopolitical supremacy in the Middle East and partly in an effort to hasten the return of Egypt to the Arab and Muslim folds. And, as if the ideological and political conflict between Tehran and Cairo were not enough, the Mubarak regime's precipitous accusation against Iran during the summer of 1984 over the mysterious mining of the Suez Canal and the Red Sea added still more fuel to the fire.

From the perspective of the Khomeini regime, the Mubarak government shares the distinction of being an American lackey with the governments of "Shah Hussein" of Jordan and "Shah Hassan" of Morocco. As such, the revolutionary leaders have not only condemned all Egyptian initiatives for peace with Israel (as well as between Iraq and Iran), but have also denounced all efforts by Arab and Muslim states aimed at the return of Egypt to their fold. For all practical purposes, the Khomeini regime appears to be seeking to excommunicate Egypt by insisting that it is not, in President Khamene'i's words, "part of the community of Muslim and Arab nations."[16]

The Khomeini regime has more than destroyed the shah's alignment with Israel: it has vowed to destroy Israel itself by replacing it with a full-fledged Palestinian state, through armed struggle, and the "liberation of Jerusalem" is one of the fundamental principles of Iranian foreign policy. Viewing Israel as the "illegitimate offspring" of the "twin evils of Zionism and American imperialism," Tehran wages a campaign of implacable hostility toward Tel Aviv, despite the widely publicized Iranian purchase of Israeli arms.[26] This one-time-only, indirect $27-million purchase of military spare parts, including 250 retread tires for Iranian F-4 fighter planes, was most probably made without Khomeini's personal knowledge. I was told by reliable sources that Iran's purchase order was placed by phone from Isfahan early in the war, at a time when the central government's authority was threatened by revolutionary chaos. Despite rumors to the contrary, no such arms deal has been repeated, according to both American and Israeli sources. (Of course, Iran may well have subsequently bought Israeli-manufactured arms, as well as those made available by other major arms suppliers, on the international arms market.)

The revolutionary regime has proved to be "more Catholic than the pope" in its virulent hostility toward Israel: for example, even Syrian hardliners may accept the United Nations 242 and 338 resolutions, which Iran rejects along with such peace initiatives as the Fahad peace plan, the Reagan peace initiative, and the Arafat-Hussein agreement of February 11, 1985. The only way to resolve the Palestinian problem, the Iranian revolutionary leaders insist, is to use armed force, since Israel will never peacefully make any concessions to the Arabs generally or the Palestinians specifically. And the best way to wage a war of annihilation against Israel is for Iran, Syria, Libya, and Algeria to combine their military capabilities. The Arab armed struggle must be transformed into a general war by all Muslims against Israel, since Palestine is part of the "Islamic homeland."

The revolutionary destruction of the Tehran-Cairo and Tehran-Tel Aviv alignments has been paralleled by the formation of an axis between Tehran and Damascus. No doubt, Khomeini's and Hafiz Assad's common hatred of Saddam Hussein has contributed to the Iranian-Syrian alliance. But to leave the matter there would be too simplistic; other factors have been equally important. Syria's resentment of Washington is derived from the latter's special relationship with Tel Aviv, from the American engineering of the Sinai accords, from the signing of the Camp David agreements and the Egyptian-Israeli peace treaty, and from the official American attitude toward the Israeli annexation of the Golan Heights. As such, Syria's resentment coincided with the Iranian anti-American attitude as Syria and Iran forged an alliance in March 1982.

Besides the common dislike of Saddam Hussein, of Israel, and of the United States, however, the regimes of Ayatollah Khomeini and Hafiz Assad needed each other for different reasons. Hafiz Assad's regime had more than once been threatened by the Muslim Brethren—in July 1980, for example, when its supporters nearly succeeded in assassinating the Syrian president. From the Syrian perspective, therefore, an alignment with the religiously based regime in Iran could counter not only this internal threat but also the Syrian isolation in the Arab world. The Muslim Brotherhood was believed to be supported externally by Iraq, Jordan, Saudi Arabia, and certain Palestinian factions. From the Iranian perspective, an alignment with the ruling Alawite Shias in Syria could both mitigate Iran's international isolation after the hostage crisis and aid Iran's war efforts against Iraq as well. Consequently, the Khomeini regime hailed Hafiz Assad's brutal armed attack on the Muslim Brotherhood at Hama in February 1982, and signed an alliance with Damascus the following month.

Although in public Iran appeared to have signed only a couple of trade and oil agreements with Syria in March 1982, it was believed that in secret it had also negotiated an arms agreement with Damascus. The overall axis has redounded to Iran's advantage, especially in its war against Iraq. Besides receiving arms through and from Syria, it has benefited from the Syrian decision of April 10, 1982, to close the trans-Syrian pipeline to Iraqi oil exports. Given the Iranian destruction of the Iraqi oil exports through Gulf waters early in the war, the Syrian action has been a major blow to the Iraqi economy (and hence to its war efforts). As of this writing, no Saudi or any other Arab mediation effort struggling behind the scenes has resulted in the reversal of the Syrian decision. The Hafiz Assad regime has profited too handsomely from its alliance with Iran to prove susceptible to Arab persuasion in general or Saudi financial pressure in particular to lift its ban on the export of Iraqi oil. The Syrians have not only bought Iranian oil at reduced prices, but have also received shipments of oil completely free of charge. Furthermore, they have used some Iranian light crude to sweeten their own heavier, sulfur-laden oil, and to refine other Iranian crude in their own refineries at Homs and Banias for profitable sale in foreign markets.

Besides diplomatic and military gains, the Khomeini regime has benefited from its axis with Syria in yet another way: to project power and ideology into Lebanon. Unlike the Gulf, however, the eastern Mediterranean is not so accessible to the revolutionary regime. In addition to geographic considerations, the anti-Iranian regimes in Iraq and Jordan are the main obstacles. Given the Iraqi and Jordanian animosity toward the Khomeini regime, the Syrian axis has acted as the conduit for Iranian access to Lebanon. Syria's own presence there has also favored the Iranian involvement in Lebanese affairs, as long as it has served Syria in preserving its hegemonic interests in Lebanon against the encroachments of unfriendly powers.

Although the Iranian access to Lebanon through Syria is new, the Iranian interest in Lebanon is anything but. Before the Iranian revolution, the interest of the shah's regime in Lebanon reflected its basically pro-Western orientation. It supported the Chamoun government during the 1958 crisis, for example. (The pro-Western attitude of the Maronite-dominated Lebanese government and that of the shah coincided.) But for most Iranians, particularly the Shia clerics, it was the Shia community in Lebanon that was really important. The Lebanese Shia leader of Iranian origin, Imam Musa Sadr, complained to me as early as 1968 in Beirut about the social and economic grievances of the Shia community and predicted a Shia political movement similar to that of the Palestinians, especially in the wake of the 1967 Arab-Israeli war. He subsequently spearheaded what is now known as the Amal movement for the redress of the injustices suffered by the "dispossessed" Shias (*mahroomin*). The Iranian revolution, and especially the Israeli invasion, helped transform it into a revolutionary movement.

Nowhere in the eastern Mediterranean has the ideological and sociopolitical impact of the Iranian revolution been so explosive as in Lebanon. The populist, antiestablishment message of the Khomeini regime backed by the defiant example of the Shia state of Iran has generally inspired the Shia community in Lebanon; however, Iran's direct influence has been limited to the splinter extremist group known as the Islamic Amal. Over time, the Shia community had be-

come the single largest group within the multisectarian Lebanese society, but its social, economic, and political aspirations have not been
satisfied in spite of the illusion that the ten-year-old civil war might
result in eventually redressing the balance of internal forces in favor
of the Muslim majority. Of all the countries in the eastern Mediterranean, therefore, strife-torn Lebanon provided the most fertile soil for
a Shia revolutionary movement.

It was the Israeli invasion of Lebanon, however, that acted as the
radicalizing agent among the Shia community. The Israeli decision to
invade, I would argue, was rooted in a self-serving interpretation of
U.S. Secretary of State Alexander Haig's exaggerated view of the Soviet strategic threat to the region by Israeli Defense Minister Ariel
Sharon. Unless one understands the twofold nature of this blunder,
the current theories about the Israeli decision make little sense.
Whether one accepts the theory that Secretary Haig gave the green
light to Minister Sharon, or seeks to place the blame on Israeli militancy (because of the rise of New Zionism) or the ascendancy of the
Sephardic Jews in Israeli politics, two critical questions still remain:
First, why did the invasion not take place earlier? (Neither the New
Zionism nor Sephardic support of the Likud alignment was new to Israeli politics.) Second, why should the American secretary of state
have spoken in such a way that the Israeli defense minister could have
interpreted his comments as an American signal for the Israelis to invade Lebanon?

Secretary Haig's exaggerated notion of the Soviet threat stemmed
from the aftermath of the twin crises of the Iranian revolution and the
Soviet invasion of Afghanistan. That notion had underpinned his
well-known concept of strategic consensus—a concept that colored
his interpretation of regional events, including the Iraq-Iran war. As
late as May 10, 1982, when he called for expert advice on the Middle
East (including this author's), it was quite clear that the series of successful Iranian offensives since March had concerned the Reagan administration more than either the Arab-Israeli conflict or the Lebanese crisis: these two problems had obviously been put on the back
burner. He delivered the administration's only major policy statement on the Middle East on May 25, the day after the decisive Iranian
victory at Khorramshahr. With the memory of the collapse of the
shah's regime—the principal American security pillar in the Gulf region—still fresh in his mind, he and other officials of the Reagan Administration feared the potential threat of an Iranian victory to the

stability and security of Saudi Arabia and other friendly governments—a threat that could result in an even greater loss of American power and influence in the on-going competition with the Soviet Union.

Defense Minister Sharon must have believed that Secretary Haig's view of Israel's strategic value had soared in the aftermath of the Iranian revolution, the Soviet invasion of Afghanistan, and the Iranian military victory at Khorramshahr. Even before the victory the two like-minded leaders had forged an anti-Soviet "strategic understanding" (November 30, 1981). No wonder then that Sharon, only a couple of months later, unfurled his aggressive concept of a "safety valve" (January 1982), calling for the kind of military initiative that resulted in the invasion of Lebanon. How could an Israeli strategic foothold in Lebanon possibly displease Washington, particularly considering the mutual Israeli-American perception of Syria as a Soviet stooge? The green light was therefore seen as an antidote to the "red threat."

Khomeini depicted the invasion as an American plot intended to divert Iran's attention from the American-sponsored Iraqi war against Iran, but in effect he wanted to keep Iranian energies concentrated on his own war. Flushed with victory (and overconfidence) in the wake of their success at Khorramshahr, the militant Iranian leaders were threatening not only to carry the war into Iraqi territory, but also getting involved in a combat role with the Israelis in Lebanon. The day after the Israeli invasion, a high-ranking Iranian military and political delegation arrived in Damascus to plan, in the words of the commander of the *Pasdaran* (revolutionary guards), a *"jihad* (religious war) against the Zionist enemy." When United States contingents subsequently became involved in the multinational force, the Iranians could wage their ideological holy war against the "twin evils" of Zionism and "American imperialism" on Lebanese soil. Besides the support of the so-called Islamic Amal led by Hussein Musawi, a Lebanese of Iranian origin, the Iranian crusade in Lebanon was spearheaded by an estimated 1000 members of the revolutionary guards stationed in the Bekaa Valley town of Baalbek.

Beginning with the first bombing of the United States embassy on April 18, 1983, every major act of political violence in Lebanon, including the murderous car-bomb attacks on the United States and French military installations in Beirut on October 23, 1983, was blamed on Iran in one way or another. Although the Iranian officials vehemently denied the charges, they praised these acts as means of "resistance to imperialism" and hence, presumably, justifiable. In November 1983, Iran suffered its first and only major casualties at the hands of Israeli forces in Lebanon. In retaliation for a suicide truck-bomb attack on the Israeli military headquarters in Tyre, the Israelis mounted two air raids on Iranian barracks in Baalbek. When the bodies of twenty-three revolutionary guards arrived in Iran, the Iranian officials depicted the "martyrdom" as only the first one of its kind, a martyrdom that would eventually contribute, in the words of the Iranian Prime Minister Musavi, to "the Islamization of the struggle against Zionism and imperialism in the region."

The Northern Tier

The last, but by no means the least important, subregion of concern to Iran is the Northern Tier. In this, as in the Gulf and the eastern Mediterranean subregions of the Middle East, the policies of revolutionary Iran essentially reflect its overall orientation toward the superpowers. In this subregion, however, as opposed to the other two, it is concern with the Soviet Union rather than with the United States that shapes Iranian policies. To the historical Iranian antipathy toward Russia, the Iranian revolution has added the Islamic crusade against atheistic communism; and to the traditional Iranian fear of the Russian threat to Iran through its southern borderlands in the Caucasus and Central Asia, the Soviet invasion and occupation of Afghanistan have added the note of a Soviet threat from Iran's eastern border. "We are at war," Khomeini said on the occasion of the Iranian New Year (March 21, 1980), "with international communism no less than we are struggling against the global plunderers of the West.... Both superpowers are intent on destroying the oppressed nations, and it is our duty to defend those nations."[17]

Above all, of course, it is the defense of Iran itself against direct and indirect Soviet threats that concerns Khomeini in the Northern Tier. Besides the Soviet Union, Afghanistan and Iraq are the enemies of the Iranian revolution in this subregion. In such a context, friendship with neighboring Turkey and Pakistan is a geopolitical imperative—although other considerations also influence Iranian policy, of course. In contrast to the Arab Gulf states, Turkey and Pakistan are of greater interest to revolutionary Iran. They are, for example, relatively powerful neighbors, have republican forms of government, provide cheap overland transportation routes for Iranian exports, and—as oil-poor nations—have economies more complementary with Iran's. It is the combination of such realities that overshadows the influence of ideology in Iranian policy toward Turkey and Pakistan. These non-Arab neighbors have at least as extensive ties with the United States as have Iran's Arab neighbors; Turkey is even a NATO ally of the United States. When it comes to its relations with Turkey and Pakistan, however, Iran chooses not to insist on ideological purity.

All this is not to suggest that the Iranian relations with Ankara and Islamabad have never been strained, for in fact they have been. The Kurdish problem has been the single greatest irritant in Turko-Iranian relations. The Armenian attacks on the Turks in Iran, and Turkish criticism of Iranian treatment of Iraqi prisoners of war, have also ruffled feelings between Tehran and Ankara. Less seriously, rumors about counterrevolutionary activities against the Khomeini regime originating in eastern Turkey have annoyed the Iranians. Nor have the Pakistanis been completely spared the occasional wrath of Iranian revolutionaries. I was told by Pakistani officials in 1984 of the Iranian depiction of President Ziaul Haq as "an American dog" shortly after the fall of the shah's regime, and that Iranian propaganda in 1980 accused him of "antihuman ambitions" and playing games with the Islamic belief of the Pakistanis.[18] But no Iranian leader has ever used foul language against the Zia government. Khomeini himself set the friendly tone with Pakistan in the very first year of the revolution by stating categorically that "Pakistan and Iran are bound together by the unbreakable ties of religion, culture, and history." This dictum has not, of course, prevented the Iranian militants from trying to take advantage of the Shia-Sunni conflict in Pakistan, as in the Karachi incident of February 1983 when the followers of the two sects clashed; nor has it mitigated the Iranian differences with Pakistan over the settlement of the Afghan problem. Islamabad has sought a negotiated settlement through the United Nations, while Iran has opposed it; instead, it has advanced its own formula for the establishment in Afghanistan of a clerically dominated Islamic government.[19]

Although the imperative of geopolitics has continued to shape Iranian policies toward both Turkey and Pakistan since the Iranian revolution (just as it did during the shah's regime), the revolutionary regime has pursued a different strategy. The shah's regime had joined

Turkey and Pakistan in the pro-Western, anti-Soviet Baghdad Pact alliance, whereas the revolutionary regime withdrew from it on March 13, 1979, after consultations with Pakistani officials. Nevertheless, the Bazargan government not only declared its intention to "stand by other member countries of the Regional Cooperation Development (RCD) in continuing economic and social cooperation," but also invited all other neighbors of Iran to join hands in such cooperation since it could "contribute towards the achievement of regional peace and mutual international security."[20] Even the fall of the Bazargan government and its replacement by a generally confrontational foreign policy did not change Iran's pro-Pakistani and pro-Turkish attitudes. Although Bazargan's idea of extending the RCD membership to other Iranian neighbors was dropped, another old idea of the shah's days was revived by the revolutionary regime. By April 1982, the Iranian officials were suggesting the formation of an "Islamic common market" as a means of confronting "international imperialism."

The Pakistanis and the Turks have their own reasons to welcome friendly relations with Iran. Pakistan and Iran are in effect the confrontation states of the Northern Tier vis-à-vis Soviet-occupied Afghanistan; they share both the fear of Soviet penetration in Baluchistan and Sistan and the burden of the Afghan refugees (about 1 million in Iran and 3 million in Pakistan); and they mutually benefit from the legitimizing effects of the symbol of their Islamic republicanism. In Khomeini's words, "the simultaneous triumph of the Islamic ideology" in both countries makes their manifold ties "everlastingly immune to dissolution by adverse external or internal circumstance."[21] Although Pakistan denounced the taking of American hostages, it was also critical of the American rescue mission, always calling for the reduction of tensions between the two countries. In fact, during several visits to Pakistan, I was told by Pakistani officials that the United States has continued to be too critical of the Khomeini regime.

Turkish officials told me the same thing in 1984; they thought the Reagan administration should "cool it." Like the Pakistani officials, they consider Iran too important strategically to allow the current acrimony between Tehran and the United States to push it toward the Soviet Union, no matter how unpalatable the Khomeini regime. And the tolerant Turkish attitude toward Iran reflects more than mere geopolitics: it is also a function of the emergent Turkish orientation toward the Middle East. Far from damaging its relations with Iran, the Turkish military takeover in 1980 added a new impetus to the Turk-

ish interest in Iran, in spite of the ideological triumph of Kemalism
over Islamism as well as communism in Turkish politics. The Iranian
connection seems to be useful to the secularist Turks domestically,
since the Islamic consciousness has by no means disappeared among
the Turkish population since the military takeover. Furthermore,
just as the Pakistanis share with Iran a concern over the Baluchi
tribesmen, the Turks share a similar concern over the Kurds. The
Turks and Pakistanis also profit economically from a close relationship with the Iranians. In this connection, Turkish frustration with
paltry West European aid has made economic relations with Iran
even more attractive.

This brings me to the single most important instrument of Iranian policy toward both Pakistan and Turkey. Revolutionary Iran has
used its oil exports more resourcefully than did the shah's regime, to
expand economic and commercial relations with both neighboring
states. Iran has supplied Pakistan about 10,000 barrels of oil per
day—approximately ten percent of Pakistan's needs; in return, Pakistan has supplied Iran with rice, sugar, wheat, and other food imports. Beside its increasing reliance on Pakistan for such staples, Iran
has been keenly interested in overland transit through Pakistan as
both a means of reducing dependence on transit trade through the
Soviet Union and of acquiring access to world markets in case the war
with Iraq leads to the closure of the Strait of Hormuz.

On balance, Iran's economic and commercial intercourse with
Turkey has been more brisk than that with Pakistan. Not only has
Iran depended heavily on transit trade over Turkish territory, but its
own trade with Turkey has also grown over the years since the revolution (in spite of various ups and downs). During the Iranian year
that began on March 21, 1984, Iran became, in Prime Minister Musavi's words, "Turkey's foremost trade partner." In 1985, Turkey was Iran's largest trade partner in the Third World. In 1978 the trade between the two countries had amounted to only $22 million, while in
1984 it reached the $2.5 billion mark. In January 1985, Iran signed a
new trade and economic agreement with Turkey, aiming toward $3
billion worth of transactions in one year. As a result of this agreement,
Iran would export crude oil, oil products, and certain other goods to
Turkey, and in return would import metals, textiles, machinery, and
so forth. At the same time, the two countries signed another contract
according to which Iran's crude oil would be carried through pipelines to be constructed in Turkey to the Mediterranean coasts and the
Black Sea, and from there to world markets.

Increasing economic and commercial relations between Iran and Turkey and Iran and Pakistan were finally crowned by the revival of the RCD under the new name of Economic Cooperation Organization (ECO) on January 28, 1985. On this day the Supreme Council of Economic Cooperation between Iran, Pakistan and Turkey decided to set up two committees for infrastructure cooperation and educational and scientific cooperation in Ankara, and two committees for industrial/technical and agricultural cooperation in Islamabad.

The Iranian revolutionaries stressed that the new ECO, as opposed to the old RCD, would aim at reducing the influence of both superpowers in the Muslim countries of the region. The revolutionary rhetoric notwithstanding, it was clear from the context that the Iranians pressed for the formation of this new regional organization precisely for the same reason that they had developed bilateral economic and commercial ties with Turkey and Pakistan for years, in spite of revolutionary upheavals. The expansion of trade with these neighbors, the use of their territories for transit trade, and similar efforts were all aimed at reducing Iranian dependence on Soviet imports, markets, and transit routes. The projected export of Iranian natural gas by pipeline through Turkey and Greece to Europe, for example, is for all practical purposes a substitute for the second Iran natural gas trunkline (IGAT-2) through the Soviet Union. (This pipeline had been scheduled to open in 1981, but the Khomeini regime cancelled its construction in order to avoid any dependence on the Soviet Union.)

Conclusion

To conclude, the Middle Eastern policy of Iran during the first six years of the revolutionary regime has revealed both continuity and change. In spite of the revolutionary change from a monarchy to a republic, from an essentially secular and technocratic to a fundamentally religious and clerical power elite, and from a primarily Iranian to a predominantly Islamic ideology, the general goals of territorial integrity and political independence of Iran continue. Moreover, in spite of the ideological claim to an Islamic world order, the Middle East has continued to be the pivotal region of Iran's security concerns; similarly, the Gulf has remained the subregion where those concerns could be satisfied, the Iranians believe, only by the continuation of Iran's political primacy—especially at the Strait of Hormuz.

In spite of this continuity in the general goals of Iran's foreign policy and the particular concerns of its Middle Eastern policy, however, its overall orientation toward the superpowers and hence its regional alignments have undergone radical changes during the first six years of the revolutionary regime: an essentially pro-Western and anti-Soviet orientation has yielded to a generally antisuperpower outlook. As a result, both American strategic interests in the Gulf and the eastern Mediterranean and the Soviet presence in the Northern Tier through the occupation of Afghanistan have been attacked, while past alignments with Egypt and Israel have been destroyed and an alliance with Syria formed.

Yet these changes have not been written in stone: they, too, will no doubt change. In spite of the antisuperpower orientation of the Khomeini regime, its greater anti-Soviet thrust is already evident in the Northern Tier. In spite of all the revolutionary rhetoric about the differences between the old RCD and the new ECO, the same geopolitical realities have shaped them both. At the moment, these realities overshadow the ideological hostility of Iran toward the United States only in the Northern Tier, where the Soviets are too close for comfort. But in the long run, they will do so in the rest of the Middle East as well.

NOTES

1. See Rouhollah K. Ramazani, *The Foreign Policy of Iran, 1941–1973: A Study of Foreign Policy in Modernizing Nations* (Charlottesville: University Press of Virginia, 1975), pp. 70–86.

2. For details, see Ramazani, "Emerging Patterns of Regional Relations in Iranian Foreign Policy," *Orbis* XVIII, no. 4 (Winter 1975):1943–1969.

3. Ramazani, *The Persian Gulf: Iran's Role* (Charlottesville: University Press of Virginia, 1972), pp. 28–56.

4. See Ramazani, *The Persian Gulf and the Strait of Hormuz* (The Netherlands: Alphen aan den Rijn, 1979), pp. 55–80.

5. See Ramazani, "Iran and the Arab-Israeli Conflict," *The Middle East Journal*, Autumn 1978:413–428. On the question of the Iranian recognition of Israel, see also Uri Bialer, "The Iranian Connection in Israel's Foreign Policy—1948–1951," *The Middle East Journal*, Spring 1985:292–315.

6. See Ramazani, *The Northern Tier: Afghanistan, Iran and Turkey* (Princeton, N.J.: Van Nostrand, 1966).

7. See Ramazani, *The United States and Iran: The Patterns of Influence* (New York: Praeger, 1982), and "Who Lost America? The Case of Iran," *The Middle East Journal*, Winter 1982:5–21.

8. Mohandes Mehdi Bazargan, *Inqilab Dar Daw Harekat* (n.p. Chap, Naraqi, 1363), pp. 79–162.

9. My translation from the text of his declaration of 26 October 1964 as published in *Ettela'at* (reg. ed.) 26 October 1980.

10. Bazargan, *Inqilab*, pp. 104–105.

11. Ramazani, "Khumayni's Islam in Iran's Foreign Policy," in Adeed Dawisha, ed., *Islam in Foreign Policy* (Cambridge: Cambridge University Press, 1983).

12. Author's translation from the collection of Khomeini's speeches entitled *Sukhanraniha-ye Imam Khumayni Dar Shish Mah-Eye Avval-e 1359* (Tehran: 1459), p. 80.

13. For details, see "Iran's Islamic Revolution and the Persian Gulf," *Current History*, January 1985:5–8, 40–41.

14. Ramazani, "Iraq-Iran War: Underlying Conflicts," *Middle East Insight* 3, no. 5 (July/August 1984):8–11.

15. *New York Times*, 25 March 1980.

16. See Foreign Broadcast Information Service, *Daily Report, South Asia* 8, no. 172. (4 September 1984).

17. *Daw Peyam* (Tehran) Mujaheddin Inqilab-e Islamy, n.d., pp. 1–14.

18. Foreign Broadcast Information Service, *Daily Report, South Asia* (20 October 1980).

19. This formula was embodied in an Iranian proposal issued by the Iranian Ministry of Foreign Affairs in November 1981. Iranian leaders have been united in their condemnation of the Soviet invasion and occupation of Afghanistan. Khomeini himself has said "I vehemently condemn this savage occupation of Afghanistan." Given the war with Iraq, however, the Khomeini regime has been reluctant to press its case too hard against the Soviets in Afghanistan, although it houses about one and one-half million Afghan refugees, has given financial support to some Shia resistance groups, and supports anti-Soviet Afghan religious leaders.

20. *Pakistan Horizon* (First-Second Quarter, 1979), pp. 315–16.

21. Ibid.

6

Iraqi Policy
and the Impact of the Iran-Iraq War

William J. Olson*

The Foreign Policy System

THE IRAQI FOREIGN-POLICY SYSTEM is not an open book: the policy debates, positions of players within the community, and the thought processes behind policy are not matters of public knowledge. Thus, much of what one can say about the foreign-policy system of Iraq is based on extrapolation, on understanding the policy environment, on interpreting clues to behavior in verbal gestures and postures—and then matching these against what is known. As is true of other so-called democratic centralist regimes in which the inner workings of the party and government are not available for scrutiny, public conformity to the party line and the enforcement of unanimity in Iraq mean that little can be known for certain from the outside. Thus, the nature of the decision-making process in Iraq is largely what political scientists call a "black box."

Although it is clear that the current leader of Iraq, Saddam Husayn, and a coterie of trusted advisors are central to the process, the positions and opinions of the central participants are murky and the influences and information sources for decision-making are obscure. It is, therefore, virtually impossible to know with certainty why Iraqi policy-makers act the way they do—to know, for example, why they decided to begin the war with Iran. To undertake any analysis of Iraqi foreign-policy behavior, therefore, requires a framework

*The views expressed in this article are those of the author and do not necessarily reflect the official policy or position of the Department of Defense or the United States Government.

for understanding this behavior and an appreciation for the environment that influences it.

As with any nation-state, Iraq exists within a number of distinct, though overlapping and interpenetrating, foreign-policy environments. First is the historical environment: the circumstances of Iraq's creation; the accidents and incidents that have determined its extent, its demography, and to some degree its political character; and the influences that have shaped the minds of the nation and of its leaders. Second is the internal environment: the relationship among and between political and interest groups, religious elements, and ethnic subsocieties. Third is the local political-foreign relations system, which is divided into two subsets: relations with immediate non-Arab states (Iran and Turkey), and relations with immediate Arab states (Syria, Saudi Arabia, Jordan, Kuwait). Fourth is the regional environment, which is also divided into several subsets: relations with the Gulf states and relations with the Middle East as a whole, to include Israel, North Africa, and the Soviet Union as a regional power. Fifth is Iraq's relationship to the international system, and this too has several divisions: relations with the superpowers, relations with the developed world, and relations with the nonaligned states.

To these categories might also be added a sixth and a seventh dimension—the importance of oil and the ideological environment, respectively. Oil wealth has been a central factor in Iraq's emergence as a regional power, and has heavily influenced Iraqi behavior and capabilities. Ideology, too, has had a profound impact, primarily through indigenous and transnational ideas that have influenced decision-making or thought processes. This dimension would include the effects of nationalism as well as of pan-Arabism, anti-Zionism, antiimperialism, and, recently, Islamic revivalism.

These different environments or dimensions are not mutually exclusive—indeed, the dynamic interrelationships among these elements constitute an eighth dimension. An appreciation of Iraqi foreign policy must therefore begin with an understanding of the dynamics of these various elements.

The Historical Dimension

Iraq came into existence as a nation in 1919, largely as a result of British postwar Middle East policy. Arab nationalists had hoped to see a single, unified Arab state freed from the Ottoman Empire, but their feebleness and disunity were such that they could not prevent Britain and France from creating a series of local states, of which Iraq was one. The ethnic and religious complexity of the region also meant that Iraq began life with a variety of minorities and elite groups that could hardly be said to share a common vision of the nation-state. In addition, the creation of Iraq did not abolish all the old local and regional antagonisms; as a matter of fact, it fostered some new ones. Thus, Iraq came into existence with a limited self-identity, under foreign control, with a diverse population, and with the potential for rivalry both among its own internal groups and with other local states. Furthermore, like other Arab states Iraq retained a deep desire for Arab unity—for a super-Arab state that would re-create the Arab empire and usher in an age of power, prestige, and glory. This desire raised an implicit challenge to the legitimacy of any political system that maintained separation from this longed-for Arab national unity. In addition, even though Iraq eventually achieved full independence, foreign rule left a bitter resentment against outside interference in Iraqi affairs. This resentment helped to promote the revolution of 1958 against a monarchist regime seen as too closely linked to Britain, and it remains a key element in the Iraqi world view to this day.

Internal Environment

The complexity of Iraq's internal environment can only be outlined here. Until 1919, the region of Iraq was divided into several provinces under Ottoman rule; as such, what central authority there was to override parochial interests flowed from the Turkish political system, which created little in the way of Iraqi nationalism around which the disparate social and tribal elements could readily coalesce upon the arrival of independence. (Even the appeal of Arab nationalism was diffuse.) In addition, Iraq contains important minority groups that do not necessarily share the vision of unity and nationalism promoted by the political elite.

The three main ethnic and social elements in Iraq are the Kurds, the Sunni Arabs, and the Shia Arabs. The Kurds constitute the largest non-Arab minority, comprising about fifteen to twenty percent of the Iraqi population.[1] Divided among Syria, Turkey, Iran, and Iraq, the Kurds have for years sought their own state (or at least a degree of autonomy within existing states), and have continually waged armed struggles to achieve a measure of self-rule. In Iraq alone, the Kurds have waged an on-again, off-again war with the central government for more than fifty years, with a major effort occurring in the early to mid-1970s.[2] Apart from posing a domestic threat, the Kurds have been a magnet for external interference. The shah of Iran used the Kurds to influence Iraqi behavior in Iran's dispute over the Shatt al-Arab in the 1970s, as did the Israelis when they wished to divert Iraqi attention from the Arab-Israeli conflict; similarly, the Iranians and Syrians today aid various Kurdish elements in an effort to keep the Iraqi government pinned down with internal problems. In addition, Kurdish anti-regime activities in Turkey have resulted in several large Turkish military incursions into Iraq—with Iraqi approval—in recent years. Thus, the Kurds are not only a potent source of internal dissension but also the catalyst of foreign involvement in Iraqi affairs. Curiously, the reverse is also true: the Iraqis currently encourage revolt among Iran's Kurds. Indeed, the urge of Middle Eastern states to use the internal dynamics of political, ethnic, or religious differences in a neighboring country is a prime element in the regional foreign policy system, and precisely such meddling was a factor in the outbreak of the Iran-Iraq war.

Another major component of Iraq's population is the Arab Shia community, which comprises 50 to 55 percent of the total population and shares a religious affiliation with the majority of Iran's population. This means that the Sunni Arabs, who dominate political and social life, comprise only 30 to 35 percent of the total population— and this makes Iraq's ruling elite sensitive to the nuances of power distribution. The emergence of Khomeini's revolutionary Islam, which struck a responsive chord among Iraq's Shia community when it challenged the secularism of Iraq's leaders, made the Iraqi government nervous indeed. Khomeini's appeal to Iraqis to overthrow their Ba'athist leaders helped to accelerate that nervousness into open war. Although Iraq's Shias have shown little inclination to seek common cause with Iran, they nevertheless remain a potentially subversive element and a constant political constituency for Khomeini. This encourages Iran to meddle in Iraqi internal affairs, which in turn accentuates Iraqi sensitivity over such interference.

The last major social element in Iraq is the Sunni Arab community. This minority group is the dominant social and political element, although it is by no means a seamless, uniform group. (Nor are the other communities, for that matter.) Variations and distinctions according to class and orientation toward key social and political values—such as commitment to Ba'athism, Arab nationalism, or Islam—divide the Sunnis. In addition, the older pattern of relationships centered on family, community, or tribe still holds sway; for example, many of Iraq's key leaders today are either related to each other or come from the same general locale, the village of Takrit. In part, the circumstances of Iraqi-Ba'athist political development—of clandestine cells composed of close associates organized by region—helps to explain this fact, but family ties and shared regional affiliations remain important criteria for determining loyalty and hence status. What this suggests is an enclave structure within the political hierarchy, which—though it can produce unity of effort—can also lead to inflexibility and "group thinking."[3]

In addition to these three main communities, several other groups influence or affect foreign policy. Principal among these are the proponents of transnational ideologies, including the communists and the Ba'athists. The Iraqi Communist Party (ICP) is one of the oldest, best organized, and largest communist parties in the Middle East; it has been an actor of some importance in Iraqi politics, cooperating with the Ba'ath in several governments.[4] Although it has had limited influence in Iraq, the ICP has been a source of Soviet influence in the country and has challenged various Iraqi governments. Indeed, it was communist infiltration of the government and the military that led the Ba'athists to purge the ICP from the government in 1979, a development that helped further sour Iraqi-Soviet relations on the eve of the Iran-Iraq war.[5]

The key political element in Iraq is the Hizb al Baath al-Arabi al-Ishtiraki—the Arab Socialist Resurrection Party or the Ba'ath, founded in the 1940s in Damascus. Its ideology is secular, socialist, and strongly Arab nationalist. The Ba'ath initially played only a limited role in politics in Syria and Iraq until coups in both countries brought the Ba'ath to power in 1963 and 1968, respectively. Despite their shared origins, however, the respective wings of the party are bitter enemies, although today their enmity may be essentially a function of the personal rivalry of Saddam Husayn and Hafiz al-Asad—each of them a strong-minded leader who sees himself as the chief interpreter of Ba'athist/pan-Arab philosophy. Nevertheless, the existence of the two sister parties has led to numerous gestures of unity between the two countries, and opened up yet another avenue across the international border for the purpose of meddling in internal affairs.[6]

The Ba'ath in Iraq is a "democratic centralist" party, highly cen-

tralized and disciplined. Under Saddam Husayn, the party has made
a determined effort to expand its membership, which now numbers
about 1.5 million; in addition, since 1979, when Husayn assumed
control, it has made a serious effort to extend party control over every
facet of Iraq's political and social life.[7] This effort led to the purge of
the ICP and other elements that might challenge Ba'ath rule (and Husayn's position within the Ba'ath). The control of the party lies with
the Revolutionary Command Council (RCC), a nine-member group
currently dominated by Saddam Husayn.[8] The RCC largely deter-
mines Iraqi domestic and foreign policies, though the role of its various members in policy formation is not clear. Husayn's role is central, and his views predominate, but he must also consider the views
of Taha Yasin Ramadan, first deputy prime minister, a powerful figure
in internal politics. In addition, Foreign Minister Tariq Aziz has a substantial role in influencing policy, and Naim Haddad, who is speaker
of the national assembly, may also be an influential voice.

A final element with major impact on Iraqi society and policy is
the military. Although the Ba'ath has worked steadily to subordinate
the military to civilian control it was a military coup that overthrew
the monarchy in 1958, and the military has played a predominant
role in Iraqi affairs ever since. The Iran-Iraq war has, naturally, put a
new emphasis on the importance of the military, which may have far-
reaching political consequences.

The Local Environment

Iraq's relations with its neighbors are complex and contorted. As
mentioned earlier, many of the issues in Iraq's relations with its
neighbors result from historical circumstances—the heritage of
Iraq's experience as a new nation-state. The key issues revolve
around border disputes and ideological differences, aggravated by a
minority population (the Kurds) that straddles the boundaries of four
separate states and which continues to seek some form of autonomy.
The outstanding border dispute is with Iran, and this is to some extent an element in the current war. The primary ideological dispute is
with Syria, though Iraq's earlier antimonarchical, anticonservative
policies have also been a source of antagonism between Iraq and
Saudi Arabia, Kuwait (with which Iraq has a border dispute as well),
and Jordan.

Relations with these states have fluctuated between indifference and open hostility. With the exception of Turkey, with which Iraq has had fairly decent relations since the 1940s, Iraq since independence has had disputes varying in intensity from wars of words to direct military conflict with virtually all of its neighbors, regardless of the regime in power in Iraq. It is important to note, however, that not until the present war with Iran did Iraq resort to the use of major military force to resolve these disputes.

The Regional Environment

Initially, Iraq's major regional orientation was towards the Mediterranean area of the Middle East—partly because of early ties with Jordan and Syria, relationships deepened either by kinship or by shared Ba'athist ideology, and partly because the Mediterranean was Iraq's main oil outlet. In addition, Arab nationalism and anti-Zionism after World War II focused attention on the Levant; and the fact that Egypt under Gamel Abdul Nasser was the focus and inspiration of Arab nationalism also tended to divert Iraqi attention away from its other regional environment, the Gulf. The waning of Nasserism (Nasser was both a source of inspiration and a rival for Iraqi leaders), the growing importance of oil in Iraqi affairs, and the British withdrawal from the region after 1970 helped to focus Iraqi attention on the Gulf. Indeed, this shift has been the major postwar change in Iraqi interests, to some extent displacing or at least rivaling the Arab-Israeli dispute as the centerpiece of Iraqi regional foreign policy.

Iraq's principal involvement in Arab-Israeli issues, of course, grows out of the involvement most Arabs feel in Israel and what they perceive as its unwelcome presence in their midst. The Iraqis have also exploited this presence rhetorically and politically as an instrument to legitimize the rule of various governments and to promote Iraq's role as a leading Arab state. One can view the Egyptian-Iraqi war of words in the late 1950s and early 1960s equally as a rivalry for dominance in Arab affairs and as an attempt to deal with Israel.[9] Removed as it is from Israel's borders, Iraq has generally resorted to rhetorical flourishes designed for home and regional consumption more than to armed conflict.

Iraq's opposition to Israel is not purely rhetorical, however. Indeed, Iraq, although not a member of the Steadfastness Front, until very recently has been one of the more recalcitrant Arab states on the subject of Israel. Unlike other Arab states, for example, Iraq refused to accept United Nations Resolutions 242 and 338, and continues to refer to Israel as an illegal entity. Iraq was also one of the leaders of the movement to punish Egypt for Anwar Sadat's peace initiatives, and participated as well in the Tripoli Conference in 1977 that set the stage for the formation of the Steadfastness Front (composed of Syria, Algeria, Libya, the PDRY, and the PLO). (Iraq eventually refused to join—partly because it did not believe the front was radical enough and partly because it had not been allowed to play a more dominant role in its creation.) Iraq also continued its opposition to Egypt's peace with Israel by organizing the Baghdad conferences in November 1978 and March 1979 to coordinate an Arab response to the Egyptian peace effort.

This opposition, however, is only one element in Iraq's regional foreign policy.[10] Two other major elements have emerged in Iraq's regional policies: rivalry with Syria and efforts at rapprochement with the more conservative Arab states. The rivalry with Syria is both geopolitically and ideologically based, for the Syrians are a major rival of Iraq in the game of Arab leadership—a struggle exacerbated by the fact that Iraq and Syria share a Ba'athist/socialist ideology, and are as such also rivals for leadership of a significant political movement. Their rivalry has taken several forms, from interference in each other's internal affairs—each accuses the other of inciting and arming internal opposition—to more direct confrontation. Syria, for example, has used the fact that one of Iraq's major oil pipelines flows through Syria to pressure Iraq. In 1972, the Syrians unilaterally raised the transit fee for Iraqi oil, which Iraq had little choice but to pay; then, in 1976, Syria shut down the pipeline altogether, in an effort to extort yet more money. Also in the mid-1970s, Syria diverted Euphrates river water at a crucial period for Iraqi agriculture. Naturally, these actions embittered the relations between the two countries.

Various attempts at a rapprochement—over Camp David, for example—have failed. That enmity between the two states remains is currently illustrated by the fact that Syria has not only supported Iran in its war with Iraq but in 1982 once again shut down Iraqi oil exports through Syria, thus contributing to the force of Iran's economic war against Iraq. The pipeline remains closed, and efforts by the Saudis and the Soviets to work out a rapprochement between Syria and Iraq have failed. Iraq's policies toward other regional states, however, have fared better. In recent years, Iraq has made a number of gestures to enhance its status in the Arab world and beyond. Although using the Camp David agreements to capitalize on Egyptian isolation, Iraq tried to structure a position that left a bridge to Egypt so that it could eventually find a way back to the Arab fold. Iraq also began to court the conservative Arab states, particularly Saudi Arabia and Kuwait.[11] The Iraqis offered the Gulf states Iraqi protection against Iran in 1979, and in February 1980 Husayn announced an eight-point program for regional Arab solidarity.[12] The program called for a renunciation of armed force among Arab countries to resolve disputes, a call for joint resolution of disputes within the framework of Arab joint action, respect for mutual sovereignty and traditional integrity, and nonalignment.[13] Although these principles were similar to those in the Arab League charter, Iraq framed them as part of a diplomatic initiative designed to assert Iraqi leadership. (The themes from this pronouncement are also echoed in Iraq's current plan for ending the war with Iran.)

The moderation of the pronouncement also fit in well with Iraq's effort to woo the conservative Arab states, and in December 1980 Iraq carried this rapprochement further by signing an agreement with Saudi Arabia that resolved their decades-long border dispute.[14] Iraq also promoted a joint Arab development program at a meeting of the Arab Economic and Social Council (AESC) held in Amman in July 1980. Saddam Husayn tried to use the meeting to get the oil producers to agree on moderate pressure on the West to support Arab causes, and he developed an Arab development plan—sort of an Arab EEC—to promote an eventual pan-Arab federation. His attempts failed, largely because of Syrian opposition; however, Iraq revived elements of the program at the eleventh Arab summit in Amman in December 1980.[15] Saddam Husayn succeeded in getting the participants to agree to establish an Arab development fund that would make low-interest loans available to six underprivileged Arab states: Mauritania, Djubuti, Somalia, Sudan, and the two Yemens. This maneuver put Iraq in the position of benefactor and visible proponent of pan-Arabism. Through moderation, prudent use of the economic power of oil, and the championship of various Arab causes, Iraq endeavored to establish itself as the commanding Arab state.

The International Environment

Iraq's relations with the world at large are divided into several subsets: relations with the superpowers, with the developed world, and with the nonaligned states. By comparison, Iraq's relations with the superpowers are peculiar (as, to be sure, are relations between the superpowers and most smaller, regional states). This is true partly because the superpower-regional state relationship is generally also a part of the rivalry between the superpowers, and partly because the smaller state typically wants to use its relationship with a superpower—or to exploit the rivalry between the superpowers—either to enhance its own regional influence or to acquire sophisticated military equipment.

Iraq's principal superpower ally has been the Soviet Union. Although before the 1958 coup Iraq was deemed a pro-Western state, aligned with Great Britain and, to a lesser extent, the United States, the upsurge of Arab nationalism and the circumstances of Britain's loss of influence in the Middle East after the 1956 Suez fiasco meant that after the 1958 coup Iraq turned to the Soviets as its main source of support and arms. United States support of Israel, plus the local perception of the United States as the heir of imperialism in the region, helped to close the door on any close U.S.–Iraqi ties. Coninued U.S. support of Israel and later of Iran (seen as another prime threat by Iraq) reinforced this trend, and anti-Americanism remains a significant element in Iraqi rhetoric, although recently it has been somewhat muted.

The Iraqi relationship with the Soviet Union, however, has not been one of complete accord, either. The Iraqis want Soviet support and arms, but they have consistently resisted drawing too close to the USSR, and they have recently begun to diversify their arms suppliers. They have not permitted the Soviets to have the type of access to facilities in Iraq that they had in Egypt before July 1972 (or have in Syria today); despite a treaty of friendship signed in 1972, Iraq condemned the Soviet invasion of Afghanistan and purged the ICP when it appeared to threaten Ba'athist rule. The Iraqis have also tried to diversify their relations with the international community as a whole.

Although relations with the nonaligned world and with the developed community has been a fairly recent development, Iraq has maintained limited ties with Western Europe and Japan since the 1950s. This was even truer of Iraq's relations with the nonaligned world. For the most part, Iraq concentrated on regional and domestic issues until the expansion of its economy as a result of the oil price explosion in 1973. The subsequent rush to develop Iraq and to use the new-found influence that seemed to accrue to OPEC encouraged the Iraqis, along with many other oil producers, to take a more active international role. This included efforts to use the oil weapon to influence the foreign policies of Israel's supporters, and to expand economic and political ties with the nonaligned states. Oil wealth enabled Iraq to speak with a louder voice than its small population and limited military capacity would otherwise justify.

The Oil Environment

As with most other Middle Eastern oil states, foreign companies developed Iraq's oil fields and facilities and waged a bitter struggle with the central government over the methods of production, the details of payment, and—ultimately—over control of the resource itself. Iraq nationalized most potential oil-producing areas in 1968 and nationalized the producing fields and oil company assets in 1972[16]— a move that preceded the successful OPEC effort in 1973 to dramatically raise the price of oil and the Arab embargo during the 1973 Arab-Israeli war. Iraq's new-found wealth and oil independence were behind Iraq's ambitious internal-development programs and the effort to make Iraq a world actor. Iraq's gross national product rose from $2.5 billion in 1967 to $16 billion in 1976 and to almost $30 billion by 1980, largely as a result of the rise in oil prices and increased Iraqi oil production.[17] Oil production rose sharply after 1972, increasing by over 30 percent in 1973–1974 alone and reaching over 3.5 million barrels per day by 1980.[18] Similarly, the price of oil rose by over 1000 percent between 1972 and 1980: from $2.47 per barrel in 1972 to $30.60 per barrel in 1980.[19] This dramatic increase in price and production enabled Iraq, like most oil producers, to launch ambitious development programs. In addition, it fueled a new foreign policy, or at least gave wider scope to latent elements already present in Iraqi policy.

Oil revenues enabled Iraq to enlarge its military dramatically, to finance a diversification of foreign economic suppliers, and to assume a prominent role in the nonaligned movement. Oil monies also gave Iraq some leverage in dealing with the Arab-Israeli issue, with Iraq resorting to its oil weapon to try to force European powers to reduce or break off relations with Israel and to pressure the United States to change its policies.[20] Iraq has also tried to use its oil to influence the policies of France, Britain, West Germany, Japan, and other states, either to gain special concessions or to bring change in their policies towards Iraq.[21] Iraq has also extended aid and assistance to certain Third World states, as a means of recycling oil monies and extending Iraqi influence, and it supported OPEC in its effort to maintain prices and protect the bargaining power of the cartel. Thus, oil has been a major element in Iraq's emergence as a regional power and, together with its increased military power, forms the basis of its international influence, also.

The Ideological Environment

Of all the elements in the Middle East environment, the interplay of ideological influences has been one of the most complex, volatile, and difficult to grasp. That people are moved—often, moved passionately and violently—by ideas is clear, but the specific motivations of their reactions are more difficult to grasp. A number of key ideologies in the Middle East have influenced many individual, group, and state actors, including such ideas as Arab nationalism, Zionism, socialism or communism, and Islam. Such ideas have transcended mere national frontiers to mobilize or inspire people to acts both creative and destructive. They have brought people together and have driven them apart ... made governments and countries, and unmade them.

Iraq's particular environment includes four ideologies: Arab nationalism, Ba'athist socialism, communism, and Islam. A great deal has been written on all of these issues, so it is not necessary to dwell on their importance here; nevertheless, it is essential to remember that these ideological reference points are crucial to understanding Iraq's foreign-policy environment.

The newest ideology among those just mentioned is Iraqi nationalism. As with many Third World states that were artificial creations rather than natural coalitions, Iraq has had serious problems of national identity and political legitimacy. Iraqis have for years struggled with themselves and others to define their idea of themselves and of a government they can cheerfully follow. Early notions of Iraqi nationalism were not, therefore, precise concepts that evoked immediate support from all segments of the population. On the contrary, until fairly recently Iraqi nationalism was largely the product of national elites that encouraged or enforced their own particular vision of Iraq on the general population; the primary reference point was Arab nationalism or the appeal of parochial interests. But, as Fouad Ajami has eloquently noted, the appeal of Arab nationalism has been eclipsed by emerging local references.[22] Moreover, for Iraq the war with Iran has been a flame that has tempered a new, more general sense of "Iraqiness." Regardless of its future strength or direction, the emergence of Iraqiness will surely be a major force in shaping the future Iraqi world view and consequent policies.

These elements form the background for Iraqi foreign policy. Further, the influence of these factors shapes both the nature of Iraq's environment and the minds of its leaders, and limits or enhances Iraq's scope for action. It is within these contexts that foreign-policy decisions are made and must be understood.

Iraq's Foreign Policy Goals

Despite political upheaval, several major political coups, and abrupt changes in government, Iraqi foreign policy has been remarkably consistent since independence.[23] The most important elements in this policy have been promotion of Iraq's independence and integrity, the search for an outside guarantor of that independence, the effort to develop a sense of identity, and efforts toward Arab unity—with, of course, a prominent role for Iraq in that unity.[24] The principal policy changes have been shifts in the demonology of opponents, the perception of the changing nature of the threat to independence, changing attitudes toward political allies, and the impact of oil on the level of foreign-policy activity. In addition, Iraq has recently managed to control its internal social matrix and, with the revenues from oil, has thus had both more energy and more money to devote to a more active role in international affairs. Saddam Husayn, a dynamic figure, has spearheaded this more active role and, like the late shah of Iran, has visions of turning his state into a serious world actor.

Today, the principal Iraqi foreign-policy goals can be summarized as follows:

Maintenance of political independence and integrity
Development of Arab unity
Maintenance of friendly relations with regional states

Promotion of nonaligned issues
Promotion of internal development
Promotion of productive relations with the developed world
Development of cordial relations with the superpowers
Promotion of anti-Zionism
Promotion of the Arafat wing of the PLO
Establishment of Iraq as a major Arab power
Exclusion of outside (superpower) influence in regional affairs.[25]

In addition, of course, the central element in current Iraqi foreign policy is the search for a resolution to the war with Iran. Indeed, the main Iraqi preoccupation for the last six years has been the threat from Iran and the issues and problems arising from the war. To put it even more forcefully, of all the issues Iraq has had to deal with since the Egyptian-Israeli peace and the Israeli invasion of Lebanon, the Iranian revolution and subsequent war have predominated. Although Iraq continues to pursue the goals outlined above, virtually all of Iraq's foreign-policy initiatives and efforts necessarily revolve around the war. Thus, we must take a close look at the war if we are to understand recent Iraqi policy, since the consequences of the war and the way it finally ends will determine major elements of Iraq's future policies.

The War

Iran and Iraq have always been uneasy neighbors. Rather than trace the long history of border disputes; of ethnic, religious, and cultural antagonisms; and of a tangled politico-ideological rivalry, suffice it to say that there have been a number of clashes between the two states since Iraq's independence in the 1930s. As for the present war, it grew out of a number of distinct issues: a border dispute, geopolitical rivalry, the ideological threat from Iran, and the coincidence of political dislocations in Iran with a new Iraqi strength that seemed to recommend quick gains for Iraq if it moved boldly.

The principal element in the border dispute was control of the Shatt al-Arab—the vital waterway that not only forms part of the border between the two countries, but is also significant to both as a channel for their oil exports. The Shatt is of particular importance to

Iraq because of that country's limited coastline—less than fifty miles—and consequent vulnerability to blockade. In addition, both Iran's and Iraq's major oil refineries are located inland from the Gulf, with the Shatt as the logical transportation artery. The accidents of nature that placed both oil and water in this conjunction, and the vagaries of history that put two states in opposition to one another at this juncture, practically foreordained a confrontation. The main issue in the dispute over the Shatt revolved around whether the border would be on the eastern bank, with the entire watercourse falling in Iraqi territory, or would follow the so-called Thalweg principle of placing the boundary down the middle of the deepest channel, thus providing joint control. It was resolved for a time in 1975 when Iran pressured Iraq into accepting the Thalweg principle (with the Iraqi Kurds providing part of the leverage).

This agreement worked reasonably well until the fall of the shah in 1979. And even after his fall, Iraq sought to establish friendly relations with the Islamic republic and did not move to abrogate the 1975 agreement—a fact that tends to refute some analysts who have argued that the present war is largely about borders.[26]

Two key factors helped to rekindle the rivalry between the two states after Khomeini's return from exile. First was the Iranian revolution, which converted Iran into the epicenter of a potentially charismatic wave of regional Islamic revivalism that threatened Iraq's secular leadership. This development had two aspects: the potential appeal of Khomeini's Shia philosophy for Iraq's large Shia population, and the political challenge to the survival of other regimes with which Iraq had begun to develop closer ties. The revolution also rekindled a fervent Iranian nationalism (linked to an Islamic internationalism) that challenged Arab nationalism and the validity of existing frontiers. Khomeini challenged the existing order both in Iraq and in the Gulf, and the Iraqis saw themselves as the appropriate force to preserve that order—thereby not only ending the threat to themselves but also earning the recognition and respect of the other Gulf states for Iraq's role in that preservation.

This brings us to the second major element in the rekindling of the Iran-Iraq rivalry: geopolitical conflict. Under the shah, Iran had become the dominant Gulf power. Iran's extensive littoral, stretching the length of the Gulf and beyond, and the shah's vigorous military buildup had combined to make Iran a major regional force. However, the Iraqis also saw themselves as a major regional power, and were therefore rivals with Iran for regional dominance. The collapse of the shah and the consequent confusion in Iran seemed to undermine Iran's power and give Iraq the ideal opportunity to assert its regional influence.

Still, Iraq did not immediately attack the Islamic Republic: the initial Iraqi response to the neighboring revolution was a cautious friendliness. Only when it became clear that Khomeini was implacably hostile did Iraq become increasingly belligerent, thus exacerbating the cycle of racial invective, religious slurs, political name-calling, and eventual border clashes that would escalate into war. And although one can only speculate on Iraqi motives for ultimately taking the unprecedented step of launching a major military offensive, Saddam Husayn clearly expected the war to be quick and decisive. Either he expected the shock of the invasion to topple the apparently feeble revolutionary government, or he anticipated significant internal support for Iraq in Iran. This could come either from the Arab Iranian population in Khuzistan—the important southern province invaded by Iraq—or from fifth-column elements: ex-shah supporters driven underground, military officers, and the like. These dissident elements in Iran would rally to the Iraqi forces and either destroy Khomeini or force him to negotiate. Such, at least, may have been the hope.

It is also possible that the Iraqi leadership, familiar with the pattern of short wars that characterized the Arab-Israeli conflict, may have believed that after Iraq made a few significant territorial gains the international community—principally, the superpowers—would intervene to impose a truce and force a settlement. In any event, Iraq attacked, hoping to end what it perceived as a serious potential threat to its independence and integrity (as well as to Ba'athist rule), and to humble Iran to the point that Iraq could build its regional power position unchallenged, at least for a time, by a powerful neighbor.

Saddam Husayn clearly continues to see Iraq as the Arab bulwark against the Iranian menace. In a July 1983 speech he noted that

> Had it not been for Iraq's steadfastness in the face of the Iranian designs for expansion, the entire Arab East would have collapsed, including the Arabian Peninsula and the Gulf, and would have been transformed into small states, dominated by big power and local forces.[27]

Implicit in this remark and many others by Husayn and other prominent Iraqi leaders are two important themes in Iraq's current world view: namely, that Iraq is the key Arab state defending the true Arab cause and that the enemy—Iran—is both local and linked to international forces. This is a heroic vision, and Iraq's leaders, aware that they are fighting for survival, have exploited it both internally and externally to legitimize their past decisions and their future rule.

In examining Iraq's policy in responding to Iran and coping with the war, it is useful to return to the framework of the foreign-policy environment outlined above and to trace the evolution of Iraq's recent policy by looking at several key elements—principally, at the internal, the regional, and the international environments.

The Internal Environment

The Iraqi leadership has responded to the war internally by continuing to hammer home the themes of Iraqi greatness, steadfastness, historic mission, and independent power. Its aim is to generate internal support for the regime and to encourage Iraqi nationalism. When propaganda fails, as in the case of political dissidence or subversion, the government has moved swiftly and ruthlessly, particularly in the case of the Shia community. Those leaders of the Shia community who might have posed a threat to the regime—principally, Ayatollah al-Sadi, members of the al-Hakim family, and the supporters of the clandestine Shia al-Dawa party—have been purged. Correspondingly, the government has devoted considerable attention to economic activity in Shia areas as a means of coopting dissidents. Since large numbers of Shias are in the military, the government is concerned to both control and placate this important minority. Fortunately for the Iraqi regime, the Shias have shown only minimal interest in Khomeini's appeal.[28] Although the Iranians support a member of the al-Hakim family, Baqir al-Hakim, and a Shia-Iraqi government-in-exile built around the so-called Supreme Assembly of the Islamic Revolution of Iraq, this group has made little progress in its efforts to subvert the Ba'ath.

The Kurds, too, have profited little from the central government's preoccupation with the war. The Iranians have supported Kurdish elements in Iraq—principally the Barzani brothers, sons of Mustafa al-Barzani, the leader of the major 1970s Kurdish revolt supported by the shah. This effort has not been very successful, however, especially as compared to Iraqi support of Iran's Kurds in their bid for autonomy. This is true largely because of the rivalry that exists among the major groups of Iraq's Kurds. The Syrian-supported Patriotic Union of Kurdistan (PUK) led by Jalal al-Talabani is a bitter rival of the Barzanis, and this enmity has served to split Kurdish loyalties. In addition, Iraq's military capabilities have grown significantly since 1975; despite the manpower demands of the war, Iraq is able to deploy sizable units in the Kurdish areas. A measure of Iraqi power can be seen in the country's ability to protect the major oil installations and the vital pipelines through Turkey, all of which are in Kurdish areas. The intervention of Turkish forces into Iraq (albeit with tacit Iraqi approval) to punish transborder Kurdish activities indicates, however, that Iraq cannot exercise unquestioned authority in the rugged border regions of northern Iraq—at least not while engaged in a full-scale war.

Despite an increase in the number of Kurdish attacks after 1980; the support to Talabani from Syria; and efforts at unity among various Iraqi opposition forces, including the PUK, the ICP, and others, all efforts to topple Saddam Husayn or otherwise effect major internal changes has been ineffectual.[29] The Ba'ath have exploited rivalries among the Kurds and other opposition groups to keep them divided, and they have used the carrot-and-stick approach to intimidate opponents and woo potential supporters. The government has pursued negotiations with Talabani (so far unsuccessfully) in an effort to end his opposition, and it has played on the autonomy plan and the creation of a Kurdish legislative assembly and other programs dating from the end of the Kurdish revolt in the 1970s to win the support of the Kurds, most of whom seem to favor a semiautonomous status within Iraq.[30]

The Ba'ath has also taken steps to broaden its internal appeal. As noted earlier, the party has taken steps to increase its membership; also, the expansion of the military due to the threat of invasion from Iran has enabled the leadership to play on the strings of Iraqi nationalism. The government has also expanded the Popular Army (PA), a militia force formed in 1970 and commanded by Taha Yasin Ramadhan, a powerful member of the RCC. The PA is a paramilitary force designed to inculcate Ba'athist values and Iraqi nationalism in a broader segment of the population. It can be used as a militia to counter coup attempts by the regular military (as its intensive training in combat techniques in urban terrain suggests), or as a training body and reserve unit for the military. Today, the PA numbers over 400,000 men, up from only 75,000 at its inception, and is established throughout the country as a force for molding government support.[31] It has also been used on the battlefield.

In addition, Saddam Husayn has delivered on a long-standing Ba'athist promise to establish a national assembly. First elected in 1980, elections for its second term were held in October 1984. Although the assembly has limited authority, it gives a measure of popular input into the government and, perhaps more important, gives the leadership an important platform from which to drive home key aspects of Ba'ath doctrine. Although it remains largely a rubber-stamp body for the leadership—indeed, the speaker of the assembly is a member of the RCC—the institution offers a chance to broaden the Ba'ath's political base, and to provide Saddam Husayn a new base for displaying his leadership.

Iraq has also worked to increase its stature as a leader of the Arab world. This is an important rhetorical effort that reflects general Iraqi sentiment and, as such, is important psychologically in developing Iraqi nationalism and legitimizing the regime. The theme of Iraqi leadership of the Arab world finds repeated expression in both the thrust of Iraqi foreign policy and in statements obviously intended for domestic consumption; under Saddam Husayn, however, this policy has found its most ambitious expression internally, to bolster the regime.

As noted earlier, the war itself stems in part from Iraqi recognition of an opportunity to render Iran impotent, after which Iraq could bask in the sunshine of victory to the immense enhancement of its regional standing. Of course, Iranian subversion in Iraq was also a prime factor in convincing the Iraqi regime to launch the war. The other prime consideration was the convergence of Iran's revolutionary threat in the region and Iraq's regional ambitions.

The Regional Environment

The main thrust of Iraqi policy in the region since 1982 is three-fold: containing and isolating Iran, ending the war, and surviving. From the perspective of this book, it is important to recall a major coincidence in the Iran-Iraq war. In March 1982, the Iranians launched a series of offensives that drove the Iraqis ignominiously from their occupying position in Iran. By late May, the Iranians had recaptured Khurramshahr (the only major Iranian city to have fallen to the Iraqis) and captured tens of thousands of Iraqi soldiers and tons of equipment. On June 10, in an effort to marshal Islamic solidarity against Israel following the Israeli invasion of Lebanon, Saddam Husayn ordered a complete and unilateral Iraqi withdrawal from Iran (except for a few minor areas), and offered Iran a ceasefire and a negotiated end to the war through binding arbitration. At the same time, Husayn offered safe passage through Iraq to Iranian troops marching against Israel. At the time, the Iraqi army seemed to be in complete disarray, the Iraqi economy was in shambles, and the imminent collapse of the country under a renewed Iranian offensive seemed inevitable, so it seemed obvious to many observers that Saddam Husayn's offer was more an effort to extricate Iraq from the war than a move to forge a Muslim coalition against Israel. Not unexpectedly, therefore, the Iranians—who were preparing an offensive calculated to deliver a final blow to Iraq—ridiculed Saddam Husayn's offer, and declared that their road to Jerusalem lay through Baghdad—over Saddam Husayn's dead body. Its efforts at ending the war having failed, Iraq countered by trying to link Iran and Israel in a plot against Iraq and the Arab nation. This remains an important rhetorical theme to this day.[32]

Iraq, of course, had already developed the theme that the Iranian revolution was a foreign implantation—a plot hatched jointly by imperialism and Zionism to destroy Arab unity, with Iraq the bulwark against the threat. After the Israeli invasion of Lebanon, the Iraqis embellished this theme to include Libya and Syria in this unholy alliance. Thus, even as they denounced the Israeli invasion the Iraqis tried to exploit it in their struggle with Iran. In an interview with Le Monde in August 1982, for example, Tariq Aziz, a leading member of the Ba'ath, declared: "Israeli expansion and Persian hegemony are the same battle."[33] Similarly, in the same month an Iraqi broadcast to Azeri-speaking Iranians took up the theme:

> Developments over the past three years indicate that the Khomeini clique is a most evil force which carries out the plans drawn up by international imperialism and Zionism for the Middle East, and which causes discord, instability and agitation in the region.[34]

The broadcast also linked the Syrians to the plot.
The Iraqis, of course, felt justified in these claims because of the coincidence of a number of factors. It must be remembered that in June 1981 Israeli warplanes bombed Iraq's nuclear power project; Iraq reacted by denouncing Israel and linking the raid to the war with Iran. Thus, in Iraqi minds, there was already a clear connection between the two enemies. Then, in June 1982, before the Israelis invaded Lebanon, Ariel Sharon publicly declared that Israel was supplying Iran with arms. Although this was perhaps an element in an Israeli disinformation campaign, the Iraqis seized on it for its propaganda value, declaring that

> the arms cooperation between the Tehran and Tel Aviv regimes against the Iraqi land, people and army commits every Arab to review his stand, regardless of the justification he had in the past, and to support Iraq and its just battle against this evil alliance because it is not directed against Iraq alone but also against the whole Arab nation.[35]

Similarly, Syrian and Libyan support for Iran further confirmed the Iraqi belief in a conspiracy. Not only were the Syrians providing Iran with arms and spare parts, but in April 1982, after making a deal with Iran for oil, Syria closed down Iraq's oil pipeline through the country, further tightening the economic vise on Iraq. The Iraqis see such actions as un-Arab and treasonous: "When one speaks about the regime in Syria," noted Taha Yasin Ramadhan, "and considers it an Arab regime, it is difficult to attribute to this regime the minimum Arab qualities or attributes." He went on to note that in 800 years of Arab disunity the Arab nation "has never known such treason and support for the enemy as the Syrian rulers have shown."[36]

Iraq has also accused the Syrians of aiding the Israeli seige of Beirut. To the Iraqi government, Syria and to a lesser degree Iran and Libya are not only implicated in the Israeli invasion of Lebanon, but are also part of a larger plot to eliminate Iraq as the champion of genuine Arab causes. The validity of this charge aside, it is a useful propaganda tool that Iraq uses both to discredit its principal enemies and to promote Iraqi leadership of the Arab cause. For even though Iraq is somewhat hamstrung by the war, its leaders still have an eye on larger goals—goals that were, after all, part of the rationale for starting the war in the first place.

The comparatively low-key Iraqi response to Israel's invasion of Lebanon deserves particular attention, as does Iraq's open support of PLO leader Yasser Arafat and his efforts to reach a settlement for a Palestinian state. Iraq has been one of the most intransigent Arab states in opposing Israel's existence. Thus, the fact that Iraq should spend more time denouncing Syria than Israel in the context of the critical regional situation is noteworthy. Even more remarkable, however, are the moderate statements that Iraqi leaders have recently made about Israel. Particularly interesting were remarks made by Saddam Husayn in a lengthy interview with U.S. Congressman Stephen Solarz in late 1982. Husayn's views on Israel came after a *tour d'horizon* with Solarz on the range of regional problems and on the state of U.S.–Iraqi relations. Even making due allowances for hyperbole and for Husayn's obvious effort to influence a U.S. congressman (and through him, U.S. public opinion), his statements on Israel are still significant. Saddam Husayn hedged his remarks with the normal rhetoric, but after carefully reiterating Iraq's unwavering support for any program worked out by Arafat to resolve the Palestinian question—a significant departure in itself—he went on to remark as follows:

> I tell you frankly that there is not a single Arab official now who believes in the possibility of removing Israel.... On the other hand, there is not a single Arab who believes in the possibility of coexisting with an expansionist, aggressive entity.[37]

Reinforcing this point, he noted that "there is not a single Arab official who considers his policy the so-called destruction of Israel and its obliteration from existence." More rhetoric, perhaps, for words are cheap, of course, and their use can be wholly cynical; still, one must note the difference in attitude they signify. These remarks are close to a tacit recognition of Israel, and the words are given greater meaning by certain Iraqi actions that follow.

The Iraqi support for the Arafat wing of the PLO has already been noted. Only a few years earlier, however, the Iraqis and Arafat were taking pot shots at one another, both rhetorical and real.[38] (Abu Nidal was employed by Iraq at one point to assassinate key PLO leaders.) This animus was directly related to the rise or fall of Syrian influence within the PLO, so that in reality the PLO-Iraqi feud was a continuation of Syrian-Iraqi animosity by other means. Thus, Arafat's sharp break with Syria was ample grounds for an Iraqi-PLO rapprochement. Iraqi support for Arafat goes even further, however. Over the past four years, that support has become increasingly less quali-fied—a fact partially explained by Iraq's need to win broad Arab sup-port for the struggle with Iran. Jordanian support for Iraq coupled with the present close ties between King Husayn and Arafat rein-forces this connection, to the point that Iraq has indicated its support for any solution that Arafat or the PLO and Jordan are able to effect—even direct negotiations with Israel, if that is at last deemed neces-sary. Iraq has expressed its belief that a PLO-Jordanian joint state is impracticable, but Iraq does not oppose such an arrangement. Iraq has come out in support of the Fez program and is improving its ties with Egypt, despite Camp David—further evidence of its moderating stance. So, there are signs of change in Iraq's position. The influence of the war and Iraq's need to establish the broadest base of interna-tional support possible are obvious considerations here, but, for the present, interesting possibilities for recent Jordanian-PLO peace ini-tiatives exist.

The Iraqis have not ignored the situation in Lebanon. They rec-ognize that they have only limited influence in Lebanon, and so have encouraged an international settlement. The Iraqis denounced the Is-raeli invasion, demanded the expulsion of Israel from the United Na-tions after the Sabra and Shatilla massacre, and called upon the ma-jor powers to stop the fighting and to suggest a lasting and just settlement. The Iraqis called upon Israel to withdraw and to recog-nize the PLO and the need to establish a Palestinian state, and called on *all* foreign forces to withdraw from Lebanon. The Iraqis have also declared their support for an independent Lebanon, urging the inter-nal parties to resolve their differences and the external parties to quit meddling.[39]

In a most frank and revealing commentary, Naim Haddad, a lead-ing Ba'athist and the speaker of the popular assembly, noted, however, that the problems in Lebanon are complex:

> If we were to look back at the situation [in Lebanon] with hindsight and tried to diagnose it scientifically and objectively, we would find that everyone is responsible.... This applies to the Lebanese people themselves because of the internal bloody conflicts, the criminal activities in Lebanon by many Arab countries [read: Syria and Libya], and the international interference by quarters seeking to have a foothold in Lebanon with the aim of disrupting the unity of that fraternal country.[40]

Haddad went on to note that no Arab state had fulfilled its declared task in regard to Lebanon. The Syrians, of course, he held particularly to blame, quite apart from the Iraqi propaganda effort to link Iran, Syria, and Israel in a generally anti-Arab and specifically anti-Iraqi conspiracy. As discussed earlier, the motive behind this effort is clear, for the Iraqis are hard-pressed by the war with Iran and resentful of Syrian efforts to benefit from Iraq's problems. Deeper, however, is the continuing Iraqi desire to become the leading state of the Arab world. Syria's actions in Lebanon and its relations with Iran, are but the raw materials Iraq uses to weave a tapestry depicting itself as the savior of the Arabs—the vigilant defender against threats from without and treachery from within.

Iraq's desire to lead the Arab world was clearly demonstrated well before the war with Iran; as a matter of fact, to some degree the war with Iran grew from it. Saddam Husayn has been tireless in his efforts to establish better ties with the conservative Arab states, particularly Saudi Arabia, and Iraqi diplomatic efforts before the war endeavored to exploit Iraq's oil wealth to establish an economic development program for the Arab world behind Iraq's leadership. Iraq also led the effort to isolate Egypt as punishment for Egypt's peace with Israel, thereby to enhance Iraq's overall position, again supported by Iraq's "bridge building" to Saudi Arabia. Saddam Husayn has clearly had strong pan-Arab ambitions from the beginning—ambitions wholly in keeping with Iraqi and Arab tradition.

The war, however, has compromised this effort significantly. The war has seriously distracted Iraq, undermined its economy, and distorted its development programs; it has also made Iraq dependent on other Arab nations, particularly the conservative states. The wisdom behind Iraqi efforts to promote rapprochement with Jordan, Saudi Arabia, Kuwait, and other Gulf states is clearly illustrated by the support Iraq has received during the war: figures on direct loans, for example, range anywhere from $25 billion to $60 billion over the five years of the war. In addition, the conservative Arab states have provided transit rights for goods (including vital military equipment), helped the Iraqis fulfill their oil contracts, and lent considerable diplomatic support. The Saudis, in particular, are actively helping the Iraqis to circumvent Iran's oil blockade.

Iraq's oil export routes through the Gulf have been closed since the war began in 1980, and Iraq's main pipeline through Syria has been closed since the spring of 1982. This has left Iraq dependent on the single, limited-capacity pipeline through Turkey—and on Arab

charity. Since 1983, however, there has been considerable activity to
provide Iraq with alternate routes, with plans for oil pipelines through
Jordan and Saudi Arabia and an expanded route through Turkey. The
Jordanian route has fallen through in part, it appears, since the Israelis refuse to guarantee not to attack it. The Turkish and Saudi projects, however, are well under way. Iraq received a $500-million line of
credit from Italy, and approval from Saudi Arabia to immediately
construct an oil line to link up with the Saudi's trans-Arabian pipeline and eventually to construct an Iraqi pipeline across Saudi Arabia
to the Red Sea with a capacity of almost one million barrels of oil per
day.[41]

The Iraqis have also indicated that they may attempt to export
through the Gulf despite the war,[42] which may require both rebuilding
damaged oil terminals at the head of the Gulf and putting pressure on
Kuwait for access to or control of the islands of Bubiyan and Warbak.
This effort, however, depends upon Iraq's ability to break Iran's
blockade or on Iran's tacit acceptance.

In any event, the support Iraq has received from the conservative
states has been crucial to its survival during the war. This support has
enabled the Iraqis to finance their war effort, and, more intangibly, to
claim a degree of legitimacy in Arab affairs for internal consumption
(thereby in turn enforcing the legitimacy of the regime). The long-
term impact of this aid, however, is unclear. If Iraq lives up to the ob-
ligations incurred, it is likely to mean a continuingly moderate Iraqi
foreign policy. Saddam Husayn or his successor, however, may not feel
compelled to live within the implied constraints of the aid. And, apart
from issuing charges of colossal ingratitude and threats to close the
oil pipeline through Saudi Arabia, the conservative states could do
little to stop Iraq from repudiating its debts and pursuing a more aggressive Gulf policy, such as demanding possession of the Kuwaiti islands of Bubiyan and Warbah. Iraq benefits from the fact that the
threat of an Iranian victory is a strong incentive for the conservative
states to continue their support, regardless of any misgivings they
may have about Iraq's reliability; Iraq retains a certain freedom of
movement, therefore, despite its need for support. No one can say
with certainty what will happen when Iraq is freed of the Iranian
threat and no longer needs this support. Although Iraqi prewar diplomacy indicated a moderate approach, the influence of the war and
particularly how it is eventually resolved may have an unpredictable
impact on future Iraqi actions.

The far-reaching effect of the war on Iraqi policy is highlighted further by a review of Iraq's relations with Egypt. Iraq, of course, not only broke off diplomatic relations with Egypt over Camp David, but was also instrumental in coordinating a comprehensive Arab response calculated to punish Egypt. At the outbreak of the Iran-Iraq war, then, Iraqi-Egyptian relations were at a low ebb. Interestingly enough, though, Iraqi diplomacy did not completely close the door on Egypt. The essence of the campaign was to isolate Egypt as a warning to anyone else who might be considering joining the Camp David process, but to leave Egypt the option to return by repudiating Camp David. Along with some other Arab states, the Iraqis singled out Anwar Sadat as the villain. The real thrust of the policy was to isolate and discredit him, depicting Camp David as his folly, and thus undermine the peace initiative. But Egypt did not repudiate Camp David, and by the time of Sadat's death in October 1981 Iraq was locked in its struggle with Iran and needed all friends it could get. The state was therefore set for change, and since October 1981 there has been a steady improvement in Iraqi-Egyptian relations, with Egypt providing Iraq with valuable direct and indirect support. Directly, the Egyptians have helped to supply Iraq—at cost—with critical Soviet replacement parts and equipment, a source admittedly more important in 1981 than today, given the warming of Iraqi-Soviet relations. Indirectly, the Egyptians have provided agricultural and other laborers to man vital segments of Iraq's economy and free Iraqis to fight at the front. Clearly, Egypt hopes to parley this warmer relationship into a ticket to return to the Arab fold with its Camp David credentials intact.

To date, the Egyptians have not succeeded in this, but the Egyptian-Iraqi relationship has steadily improved. There have been a number of high-level exchange visits, crowned by the March 1985 visit of Egyptian president Hosni Mubarak to Baghdad at the height of a fresh Iranian offensive. In addition, Iraqi official announcements have increasingly noted Egypt's important contributions to Iraq, as well as Egypt's vital role in Arab affairs. Cairo appears to be moving gradually toward reestablishing diplomatic relations, a move that would see Egypt able to escape its isolation without compromising its Camp David commitments. The Iraqis have even hinted at an unconditional return, with Saddam Husayn remarking in April 1983 that

we must give him [Mubarak] a chance to extract Egypt from its legacy [Sadat] and liberate it from its shackles [Camp David].... We must not link Egypt's return to the Arabs to conditions that Egypt will not be able to fulfill.[43]

But a reluctance to readmit an Egypt still marked with Camp David remains. In November 1983, Naim Haddad noted that Iraq favored Egypt's return, seeing the recall of Egypt's ambassador to Israel (over Lebanon) and similar moves toward nonalignment as positive steps. This is similar to Iraq's position all along: Saddam Husayn noted in November 1984 that there would be no unilateral restoration of relations, and that he favored an Arab League approval.[44] Thus, the road to reestablished relations could be a very long and tortuous one. Iraq is not ready to move yet, since it does not want to be among the first (now that Jordan has established diplomatic relations with Egypt) Arab states to embrace Egypt openly.

The course of the war is likely to be crucial in the timing of any change. If the war continues, as is likely, the move to restore Egyptian-Iraqi relations is likely to move forward. A sudden end to the war, however—even one that left Iraq with a status quo ante—could very well see a delay, for the pressure would then be off and Iraq's opposition to the Camp David process could once again take precedence over its need for an Egyptian rapprochement.

The International Environment

Iraqi foreign policy on the international scene has focused on winning support for Iraq in the war, isolating Iran (and putting pressure on it to negotiate), keeping alive Iraq's role in the nonaligned movement, and diversifying its economy and sources of arms. The most dramatic international event was the reestablishment of U.S.–Iraqi relations after a chill of almost twenty years. Severed after the 1967 Arab-Israeli war, there had been a steady improvement in relations; however, it was the Iran-Iraq war that accelerated the process.

The process of resuming relations was slow and deliberate. In the decade before the Iran-Iraq war, the U.S. Interest Section in the Belgian Embassy had grown steadily, as had the small but healthy U.S.–Iraqi trade relationship. Trade with Iraq had grown from around $25 million in 1972 to $700 million by 1980,[45] and this growth was reflected in the burgeoning of the U.S. permanent mission in Iraq. The Carter Administration revealed its inclinations when it began to explore the resumption of diplomatic relations and agreed to the transfer or sale to Iraq of several jets and marine engines in 1979. A storm of protest in Congress over this resumption of official trade (and trade of a military character, at that) with a state still regarded as a supporter of international terrorism forced the Carter Administration to backtrack, but the direction of drift was clear.[46]

The fall of the shah and (particularly) the Iran-Iraq war accelerated the process, especially after Iraq withdrew from Iran in the summer of 1982. With Iraqi armed forces in disarray, the country's economy stagnating, and Iran poised for an invasion, the specter of an Iraqi collapse that would see a victorious Iran and a triumphant Islamic fundamentalism in Baghdad loomed on the horizon. Although the United States continued its policy of official neutrality in the war (a position both Iran and Iraq called a cover for the support of its enemy), the United Stated did lend its efforts to alleviating Iraq's economic difficulties. These difficulties arose from the fact that Iraq had tried to prosecute the war while maintaining an ambitious internal development program at the same time. Iran's blockade, joined by Syria in April 1982, increasingly undermined this effort, and by late 1982 Iraq's economic situation was serious. Iraq could not meet payments on its foreign loans, its foreign exchange reserves were virtually depleted (from a prewar high of more than $30 billion), and the country was having difficulty raising money to meet its operating costs. Support from its Arab allies helped to tide Iraq over the worst of these problems, and Iraq's principal trading partners, notably France and Japan, agreed to reschedule loan payments. The United States supported these efforts, arranged for Iraq to receive assistance in buying $600 million in agricultural products in the United States, and supported Iraq's efforts to raise money in Europe.[47] While perhaps not significant in themselves, when these gestures by the United States were added to the good offices of Iraq's other trading partners and friends, the country was able to weather an economic crisis while its armed forces successfully weathered the military one.

The movement toward improving U.S.–Iraqi relations received further encouragement when the Reagan administration succeeded in removing Iraq from the list of terrorist sponsors in October 1983.[48] The administration continued to work to open more avenues to Iraq. In December 1983, Donald Rumsfeld, President Reagan's special Middle East envoy, delivered a personal message to Saddam Husayn, who responded cordially. This was the follow-up of an earlier meeting be-

tween Secretary of State George Shultz and Iraqi Foreign Minister
Tariq Aziz at the United Nations. The two statesmen discussed the resumption of relations, agreeing to pursue the issue after the 1984 U.S.
elections.

Iraq did not rush into a resumption of relations, however. Saddam
Husayn declared in 1979 that the resumption depended upon Iraq
seeing a benefit in restoring ties, but he did not suggest a timetable.[49]
The war created more favorable circumstances, however, and Saddam Husayn indicated in January 1983 that he was interested in resuming relations, but not in such a way as to suggest that Iraq was
doing so out of necessity—a situation that could have been exploited
by Iran or Syria.[50] Consequently, Iraq's economic and military situation had to improve before Saddam Husayn had the maneuvering
room to restore ties; in the meantime relations continued to improve,
and the United States supported international efforts to find the funding for pipelines through Jordan, Turkey, and Saudi Arabia that would
permit Iraq to export the oil necessary to alleviate the country's financial difficulties. (The United States also dropped its efforts to prevent France from supplying arms to Iraq.)

Resumption of relations, however, was not without its problems.
Throughout the period before the resumption of relations in November 1984, the Iraqis indicated their objections to untempered U.S.
support for Israel, especially in Lebanon—although they sent mixed
signals on the Reagan plan and supported the Fez plan. The United
States, for its part, was not wholly pleased with Iraq, either, especially
over the latter's use of chemical weapons in its war with Iran. Despite
these problems, however, the momentum to restore relations accelerated, culminating with the exchange of ambassadors in November
1984. Clearly, this was no match made in heaven, but it indicated the
pragmatic trend in Iraqi foreign policy, and the war obviously encouraged both sides to resume ties. The fate of these relations after the end
of the war is unclear, of course. But if Iraq continues to pursue its
pragmatic approach, and to cultivate relations with Jordan and Saudi
Arabia, the prospects for a healthy if less than ardent U.S.–Iraqi relationship seem good.

Iraqi relations with the other superpower, the Soviet Union, are
more complex. The Soviet-Iraqi relationship, affirmed by a Treaty of
Friendship in 1972, is one of the oldest in the Middle East for the Soviets. The Soviet Union has also been Iraq's major supplier of arms.
This relationship has not been without its problems, however, and the

emergence of Saddam Husayn and the fall of the shah marked the beginning of a troubled period. Iraq under Saddam Husayn pursued a more openly nonaligned policy than previously, one indication being its search for alternative sources of major military equipment. In addition, Saddam Husayn launched a vigorous campaign against the Iraqi communist party and executed much of its leadership, a move that strained Soviet-Iraqi relations. Iraq had never allowed the Soviets to get too close; and with Iraq's new vigor under Saddam Husayn, the distance between the states grew. Capitalizing on its booming oil income, Iraq sought advanced Western technological assistance in all fields, thereby lessening its economic ties to Moscow. Iraq began buying sophisticated military equipment from France and elsewhere, a move that may have been encouraged by the Soviets' seeming reluctance to supply Iraq with the latest equipment.[51]

Conversely, the fall of the shah encouraged the Soviets to explore more dynamic relations with the anti-U.S. Khomeini regime. The Soviets would have preferred to maintain cordial relations with both states, but Iran seemed the more promising partner—especially since it appeared to offer the opportunity to exploit regional anti-Americanism and thus further undermine the U.S. presence. Moreover, relations with Iraq continued to deteriorate as the Iraqis roundly condemned the Soviet invasion of Afghanistan in December 1979, and encouraged the Saudi effort to try to reduce Soviet influence in North and South Yemen.[52] Saddam Husayn went further and accused the Soviets of "salami" tactics—that is, of trying slowly to encircle the oil states with Soviet clients—and denounced Soviet activities in Syria and Ethiopia while supporting Somalia and the Eritrean resistance.[53] The Iraqi invasion of Iran further undermined relations.

The Soviets, trying to build bridges to Iran and to expand on the anti-American sentiments in the region, did not appreciate Iraq's unilateral move. The Soviets declared their neutrality in the war and called on both parties to negotiate, though the tone of Soviet broadcasts favored Iran and indirectly condemned Iraq. Further, the Soviets pursued neutrality with a vengeance, cutting Iraq off from Soviet arms—the worst effects of which action were obviated by Iraq's imposing stockpile of equipment and by its program to diversify arms suppliers. The Soviet cutoff, nevertheless, angered the Iraqis and may have pinched subsequent Iraqi military efforts. Iraqi-Soviet ties remained strained until late 1981 when a thaw set in.

As the war progressed, the Soviets began to appreciate that Iran's "Neither East Nor West" policy precluded any close relationship. The USSR paused to reevaluate the benefits of close ties with Iran at the risk of damaging relations with the Arab world. The Iranian invasion of Iraq in June 1982 confirmed this trend in Soviet thinking: the Soviets resumed major arms shipments to Iraq in the fall of 1982, and exchange visits and economic agreements have proliferated ever since. The Iraqis, however, are not likely to forget Soviet neutrality—much as Pakistan is unlikely to forget the attitude of the United States during the 1971 Indo-Pakistani war. Nevertheless, the Soviets remain Iraq's major arms supplier, and for this reason alone the Iraqis are interested in maintaining cordial relations with the Soviet Union.

The Iraqis have not limited their international relationships to the superpowers, however. As noted earlier, the Iraqis had developed extensive international ties before the Iran-Iraq war, and the war has only reinforced for Iraq the need for such ties. The Soviet decision to cut off arms supplies to Iraq, for example, vividly illustrated for the Iraqis the benefits of diversified sources of supply. The Iraqis have continued an aggressive arms-purchasing program, concluding deals with a number of states, including France, Brazil, and China. In addition, the Iraqis have tried to use their diplomatic ties to interdict arms supplies to Iran as one means of forcing an end to the war. They have also tried in a number of ways to link the international community to efforts to end the war.

The most pointed of these efforts has been the so-called tanker war. The Iraqis launched this offensive in August 1982 after the Iranians drove Iraq from Iran and threatened Iraq with invasion and economic ruin. Frustrated on the battlefield and faced with the prospect of a protracted war, the Iraqis began to consider strategies that would both break the stalemate and force the international community to take a more active interest in the war. The essence of the program was to threaten to interdict shipping to Iran's main port at Bandar Khomeini and to the principal oil terminal on Kharg Island. Although the Iraqis lacked the means to carry out this threat, they nevertheless declared an exclusion zone in the upper Gulf, warning shippers to stay out of Iranian waters. The Iraqi objective was twofold: to impose an economic blockade on Iran, and to threaten to attack international shipping so as to put pressure on the international community to take a more active interest in settling the war.

At first this program failed to excite much interest. However, the

Iraqis used their arms relationship with France to steadily improve their military capabilities to attack shipping, and they skillfully exploited the international attention focused on anti-ship missiles generated by the Falklands war to heighten anxiety about the vulnerability of shipping in the Gulf. The delivery to Iraq of French Exocet missiles and Super Etendard aircraft thus neatly combined both military and psychological elements. Increased Iraqi attacks on shipping since early 1984 accentuated the effect, and the Iraqis could take some encouragement from the fact that the international community did indeed increase its efforts to mediate an end to the war. So far, the effort has produced minimal results as far as settling the conflict, but Iraq has been able to isolate Iran diplomatically, capitalizing on a mixture of skillful diplomacy and Iranian intransigence to portray Iran as the principal threat to regional and international harmony.

Iraq has taken advantage of virtually every forum to portray itself as reasonable and ready for peace, and to point to Iran's overweening ambitions as the major stumbling block. The main features of Iraq's peace proposals are very moderate. In the fall of 1983, for example, Tariq Aziz indicated that Iraq would accept earlier Iranian demands for an international arbitration committee to examine the causes of the war and assess responsibility and recompense for losses.[54] In December 1983, Saddam Husayn declared that Iraq was prepared to enter into negotiations with no preconditions, dropping one of Iraq's original war aims: a settlement of the Shatt dispute in Iraq's favor. Husayn defined three essentials for peace: respect for frontiers, respect for independence and integrity, and respect for internal security.[55] These are the essential elements of Iraq's proposals, and they bear a remarkable resemblance to any number of similar Iraqi pronouncements since 1978.

Iraq has accepted all United Nations resolutions calling for an end to the war; has sought the intercession of the Islamic Conference Organization, the Gulf Cooperation Council, the Arab League, and the Non-Aligned Movement; and has welcomed the mediation efforts of such individual countries as Algeria and Japan. While these efforts are sincere, they are also part of a strategy designed to enhance Iraq's status and isolate Iran—and overall, this program has worked. One example of the success of the program has been Iraq's ability to weather the adverse publicity over the use of chemical weapons. Although Iranian intransigence and a growing international numbness in the face of a seemingly endless war contribute to the lack of response, Iraq has developed an overt policy that has managed to keep international attention focused on Iran's stubbornness. Iranian determination to continue the war has meant, however, that the Iraqis have failed to achieve their primary objective: forcing Iran to negotiate. In addition, the Iraqis have suffered at least one major setback.

The key diplomatic failure for Iraq came with the cancellation of the meeting of the nonaligned states scheduled for September 1983 in Baghdad. The Iraqis put a great deal of emphasis on their role in the nonaligned movement, and hosting the 1983 meeting meant that Iraq would have assumed the chairmanship of the movement. The Iranians, too, realized its importance for Iraq, and they threatened to disrupt the meeting—by force if necessary. In the end, the nonaligned states decided not to meet in Baghdad, delaying the meeting and eventually holding it in India. Despite this reversal, however, Iraq's international posture has steadily improved, and in the face of the negative effects of the war on oil exports and the economy, the Iraqis have managed to maintain an active trade effort with the support of other Arab states. Iraq's potential oil export capabilities have also influenced a number of states to support Iraq with both continued financial assistance and sophisticated weapons.

The question remains, however, as to what direction the war will take and how Iraq will cope with it. Although Iraq weathered the difficulties of 1982–83, there are still problems ahead, and the way the war progresses and ultimately ends will, of course, have a profound impact on future Iraqi foreign policy.

Prospects

The Iran-Iraq war can take four major directions. It can continue, with various alarms and diversions; it can wind down to a settlement, de facto or de jure; it can produce an Iranian victory; or it can finish with an Iraqi victory. Each outcome has its own significant implications.

A continuation of the war without significant change seems likely for the foreseeable future. Neither Iran nor Iraq currently has the inherent capability to overthrow the other, and the strategy of attrition that seems to be the current approach is not apt to produce sudden changes. The timing of a victory based on a strategy of wearing an opponent down rests on such imponderables of the enemy's public morale and institutional fortitude—variables that are as difficult to control as to assess. Attrition has the added disadvantage of placing one's own society in a waiting game, which can undermine one's own system as much as the enemy's. Such a strategy also produces frustrations and the potential for escalation as the parties search for new approaches to break the stalemate. Iraq's resort to, variously, the tanker offensive, the use of gas, and the use of long-range rockets are three examples of Iraqi actions that moved the war onto the strategic level and increased the potential for further escalation.

If Iraq's tanker offensive, for example, succeeds in putting greater economic pressure on Iran, the Khomeini government may feel compelled to retaliate against those Gulf states known to support Iraq, however incidentally. This could mean a program of subversion or terrorism or, as the Iranians demonstrated earlier in the war, of direct air assaults on regional oil facilities. Conversely, if Iraq feels sufficiently threatened it could begin long-range missile attacks on Tehran, perhaps with gas weapons, or launch a more effective air campaign against Kharg Island. In any case, the war could easily escalate.

The war could also conceivably end with one or the other state as victor. An Iranian victory, for example, could proceed from a collapse in Baghdad that sapped Iraq of the will to fight. Such a development could see Iraq fragment, and the Iranians occupying part or all of the country. The prospect of victorious Iranian forces in Iraq, with the impetus victory would give the Ayatollah's revolution, is a disquieting prospect. It would certainly mean years of internal turmoil in Iraq and the creation of a radical Islamic state inside the Arab world. The permutations are disturbing.

Conversely, Iraq could win the war. This is not likely to be the result of direct military effort, but rather as a result of Iran's internal collapse, either through war-weariness or the political confusion that might follow the death of Khomeini, say. This result would leave Iraq intact, but it would mean political chaos on the Iranian plateau. Civil war in Iran could easily see Soviet indirect involvement to support a pro-communist party; such a development could easily occasion a counter-U.S. involvement to forestall a Soviet victory, a development that could lead to a direct U.S.–Soviet confrontation. Even if this did not develop, the spillover effect of turmoil in Iran would disturb the peace and security of the Gulf. Thus, neither an Iranian nor an Iraqi victory presents a very reassuring picture for the future.

The best outcome would be a negotiated settlement that restored the status quo ante; but even this settlement would not restore the pre-Khomeini relative stability in the region. Iran's revolutionary zeal is an unavoidable reality for the foreseeable future, and it cannot be other than disruptive. In addition, Iraq's ambition to be a leading regional power will continue to clash with Iran's dynamism. Geopolitical and ideological rivalry between these two states, then, will continue to be a major factor in Gulf politics.

Iraq's future foreign policy will likely focus on recovering its share of the oil market, expanding its international ties, and perhaps using its influence to settle old scores with Syria and Libya. Domestic politics in Iraq immediately after the war are likely to revolve around the need for reconstruction and the issue of responsibility for the war. This latter concern could spark an internal power struggle, the outcome of which would have much to say about the future of Iraqi foreign policy. The main tenets of foreign policy are likely to follow the goals outlined earlier, but whether the pursuit will be moderate or radical only the future can tell.

NOTES

1. William Hazen, "Minorities in Revolt: The Kurds of Iran, Iraq, Syria and Turkey," in *The Political Role of Minority Groups in the Middle East,* ed. R. D. McLaurin (New York: Praeger, 1980), p. 52; and David Long and John Hearty, "Republic of Iraq," in *The Government and Politics of the Middle East and North Africa,* ed. David Long and Bernard Reich (Boulder, Colo.: Westview Press, 1980), p. 118.

2. Abbas Kelidar, "Iraq: The Search for Stability," *Conflict Studies, No. 9* (July 1975); and Edmund Ghareeb, *The Kurdish Question in Iraq* (Syracuse, N.Y.: Syracuse University Press, 1981).

3. This idea is explored by William Staudenmeier in "Defense Planning in Iraq: An Alternative Perspective," in *Defense Planning in Less-Industrialized States,* ed. Stephanie Neuman (Lexington, Mass.: Lexington Books, 1984), p. 55.

4. See Christine Helms, *Iraq: The Eastern Flank of the Arab World* (Washington, D.C.: Brookings Institute, 1984), pp. 73–82; R. D. McLaurin et al., *Middle East Foreign Policy: Issues and Processes* (New York: Praeger, 1982), pp. 105–108; and Kelidar, "Iraq."

5. Ibid. See also Robert O. Freedman, "Soviet Policy Toward Ba'athist Iraq: 1968–1979" in *The Soviet Union in the Third World: Successes and Failures,* ed. Robert H. Donaldson (Boulder, Colo.: Westview, 1981), pp. 161–91.

6. On the Ba'ath, see Helms, *Iraq,* pp. 59–131; and Reeva Simon, "Iraq," in *World Encyclopedia of Political Systems and Parties,* vol. I, ed. George Dalvey (New York: Facts on File, 1983), pp. 493–500.

7. See Simon, "Iraq," p. 496; Majid Khadduri, *Socialist Iraq: A Study in Iraqi Politics Since 1968* (Washington, D.C.: Middle East Institute, 1978), pp. 123ff; John Devlin, *The Ba'ath Party* (Stanford Calif.: Hoover Institute Press, 1976); Helms, *Iraq;* and Ofra Bengio, "Iraq," in *Middle East Contemporary Survey III: 1977–1978,* edited by Colin Legum (New York: Holmes and Meier, 1980), pp. 559–81.

8. See Daniel Dishon and Bruce Maddy-Weitzman, "Inter-Arab Affairs," in *Middle East Contemporary Survey IV: 1979–1980,* ed. Colin Legum (New York: Holmes and Meier, 1981), pp. 169–225; Amazia Baram, "Saddam Hussain: A Political Profile," *The Jerusalem Quarterly* 17 (Fall 1980), pp. 115–44; and Elaine Sciolino, "The Big Brother: Iraq under Saddam Husayn," *New York Times Magazine,* 3 February 1983, pp. 16ff.

9. See Malcolm Kerr, *The Arab Cold War* (New York: Oxford University Press, 1971).

10. See Dishon and Maddy-Weitzman, "Inter-Arab Affairs."

11. David Tinnin, "Iraq and the New Arab Alliance," *Fortune* 3 (November 1980), pp. 44–46; and Stephen Kashkett, "Iraq and the Pursuit of Nonalignment," *Orbis* 26 (Summer 1982), pp. 447–94.

12. Baram, "Saddam Hussain," p. 142.

13. *Foreign Broadcast Information Service: The Middle East and Africa* (hereafter *FBIS:ME* V (1 July 1982):E-21. For a discussion of the eight-point program, see Adeed Dawisha, "Invoking the Spirit of Arabism: Islam in the Foreign Policy of Saddam's Iraq," in *Islam in Foreign Policy,* ed. Adeed Dawisha (New York: Cambridge University Press, 1983), pp. 117–22.

14. *Facts on File,* 31 December 1981, p. 995E1.

15. David Shirreff, "Arab Summit: Saddam Husayn Short Circuits Economic Strategy," *Middle East Economic Digest (MEED)* 5 (December 1980):3ff; and Baram, "Saddam Husayn," p. 142.

16. Paul Stevens, "Iraqi Oil Policy: 1961–1976," in *Iraq: The Contemporary State,* ed. Tim Niblock (New York: St. Martin's Press, 1982), p. 179; Khadduri, *Socialist Iraq,* pp. 123ff; and Edith Penrose and E. F. Penrose, *Iraq: International Relations and National Development* (Boulder, Colo.: Westview Press, 1978), pp. 405–417.

17. Jed Snyder, "The Road to Osiraq: Baghdad's Quest for the Bomb?" *Middle East Journal* 37 (August 1983):556.

18. Dishon and Maddy-Weitzman, "Inter-Arab Affairs," p. 528.

19. *Basic Petroleum Data Book,* vol. 5 (January 1985), section VI, table 14 (Washington, D.C.: American Petroleum Institute, 1985).

20. *Middle East* 70 (August 1980):53–55.

21. Claudia Wright, "Iraq—New Power in the Middle East," *Foreign Affairs* 58 (Winter 1979–1980):257–77.

22. Fouad Ajami, "The End of Pan Arabism," *Foreign Affairs* 57 (Winter 1978–1979):355–73; and Nabeel Khourfy, "The Pragmatic Trend in Inter-Arab Politics," *Middle East Journal* 36 (Summer 1982):374–88.

23. Khadduri, *Socialist Iraq,* pp. 142–43; and Tim Niblock, "Iraqi Polities towards the Arab States of the Gulf, 1958–1981," in *Iraq: The Contemporary Society* (New York: St. Martin's Press, 1982), pp. 125ff.

24. Niblock, "Iraqi Politics," p. 125ff.

25. See R. D. McLaurin et al., "Iraqi Foreign Policymaking," in *Middle East Foreign Policy: Issues and Processes* (New York: Praeger, 1982), pp. 131–94. See also "A Conversation with Dr. Saddam Hammadi, Iraq's Foreign Policy," AEI Study #352, Washington, D.C. 1981; and "Interview with Tariq Aziz," *Arab-American Affairs* 10 (Fall 1984):71–78.

26. See in particular Daniel Pipes, "A Border Adrift: Origins of the Conflict," in *The Iran-Iraq War: New Weapons, Old Conflicts*, eds. Shirin Tahir-Kheli and Shaheen Ayubi (New York: Praeger, 1983), pp. 3–26. For details of the border dispute, see Husain al Baharna, *The Arab Gulf States: Their Legal and Political Status and Their International Problems* (Beirut: Librairie du Liban, 1975); J. M. Abdulghani, *Iraq and Iran: The years of Crisis* (Baltimore, Maryland: Johns Hopkins Press, 1984); Tareq Ismael, *Iraq and Iran: Roots of Conflict* (Syracuse: Syracuse University Press, 1982); Lenore Martin, *The Unstable Gulf* (Lexington, Mass.: Lexington Books, 1984); S. H. Amin, "The Iran-Iraq Conflict: Legal Implications," *International and Comparative Law Quarterly* 31 (January 1982):167–88; Robert Tomasek, "The Resolution of Major Controversies between Iran and Iraq," *World Affairs* 139 (Winter 1976–1977):206–230; and Alan Day, ed., *Border and Territorial Disputes* (Detroit: Gale Research Company, 1982), pp. 214–18.

27. Speech, Baghdad Radio, Voice of the Masses, *FBIS:ME* V (18 July 1983):E-5.

28. See Helms, *Iraq*, pp. 25–30; and Hanna Batatu, "Iraq's Underground Shi'a Movements: Characteristics, Causes and Prospects," *Middle East Journal* 35 (Autumn 1981):578–94.

29. See Thomas Mullen, "Will Saddam Outlast the Iran-Iraq War," *Middle East Insight* 3 (1984):33–34.

30. McLaurin et al., *Foreign Policy*, pp. 95–105; and Hazen, "Minorities."

31. Helms, *Iraq*, pp. 99–100.

32. Baghdad Radio, *FBIS:ME* V (14 June 1982):E-2.

33. *Le Monde* (Paris), *FBIS:ME* V (18 August 1982):E-1.

34. Baghdad International Service in Azeri, *FBIS:ME* V (17 August 1982):E-2.

35. Baghdad Radio, *FBIS:ME* V (1 June 1982):E-4.

36. *Akhbar al-Khali* (Manama, Bahrayn), *FBIS:ME* V (15 June 1982):E-1.

37. Baghdad Radio, August 1982, *FBIS:ME* V (4 January 1983):E-8–9.

38. Interestingly, Saddam Husayn was an early supporter of Iraqi-PLO ties; thus, efforts to improve relations with Arafat since he came to power represent both a continuation of Husayn's ideas and further indication of his pragmatic bent. See R. D. McLaurin et al., *Foreign Policy*, p. 128.

39. Paris Radio, Monte Carlo, *FBIS:ME* V (7 October 1983):E-1.

40. Baghdad Radio, *FBIS:ME* V (3 June 1982):E-2.

41. *Middle East Economic Digest,* 18 January 1985, p. 20, and 4 January 1985, pp. 10–11; and *Quarterly Economic Review of Iraq, 1983–1985.*

42. Manama (Bahrayn), *FBIS:ME* V (2 December 1983):E-1.

43. *Kuna* (Kuwait), *FBIS:ME* V (28 April 1983):E-2.

44. For an Egyptian perspective, see p. 336 of this volume.

45. *Middle East Economic Digest,* 30 December 1984:18.

46. *New York Times,* 6 August 1979, and ibid., 28 September 1979.

47. *Middle East Economic Digest,* 3 November 1984:32–33.

48. *Washington Post,* 8 October 1983, p. A-25.

49. Wright, "Iraq," p. 258.

50. Solarz-Husayn interview, *FBIS:ME* (4 January 1983):E-1.

51. See Adeed Dawisha, "The Soviet Union in the Arab World: The Limits to Superpower Influence," in *The Soviet Union in the Arab World,* eds. Adeed Dawisha and Karen Dawisha (New York: Holmes and Meier, 1982), pp. 16–17; Karen Dawisha, "Soviet Decision-Making in the Middle East: The 1973 October War and the 1980 Gulf War," *International Affairs* 57 (Winter 1980–1981):49.

52. Various works have explored the decline in Soviet-Iraqi ties. See Caludia Wright, "Iraq—New Power," cited above. Wright has even gone so far as to suggest that one motive in Iraq's invasion of Iran may have been an effort to establish a more stable regime in Iran as a bulwark to the Soviets: "Behind Iraq's Bold Move," *New York Times Magazine,* 26 October 1980, p. 43; Adeed Dawisha, "Iraq: The West's Opportunity," *Foreign Policy* 41 (Winter 1980–1981): 134–53; and Marvin Feuerwerger, "Iraq: An Opportunity for the West?" *Middle East Review* (Fall/Winter 1981–1982), pp. 26–30, which takes a skeptical view. See also Oles Smolansky, "The Kremlin and the Iraqi Ba'ath, 1968–1982: An Influence Relationship," *Middle East Review* 15 (Spring/Summer 1983):62–67; Freedman, "Soviet Policy," pp. 161–91; *Newsweek,* 30 July 1979, pp. 49–50; and Karen Dawisha, "The USSR in the Middle East: Superpower in Decline?" *Foreign Affairs* 61 (Winter 1982–1983):438–52.

53. Steven Kashkett, "Iraq and the Pursuit of Nonalignment," *Orbis* 26 (Summer 1982):489.

54. Baghdad Radio, Voice of the Masses, *FBIS:ME* V (3 October 1983):E-1–4.

55. Saddam Husayn interview, *Al-Ahram, Cairo, FBIS:ME* V, (5 December 1983):E-4.

III

The Political Dynamics of the Core Area

7

Jordanian Policy: The Politics of Limitation and Constraint

Aaron David Miller *

Introduction

MORE THAN THREE YEARS after Israeli forces moved into Lebanon, Jordan's King Hussein is still dealing with the consequences of the June 1982 invasion. The Israeli operation—an ambitious effort to crush the PLO and to create a new political order in Lebanon—generated risks and opportunities in the Arab-Israeli arena that were too important for Hussein to ignore. On one hand, the Lebanon war appeared to feed Shia and Palestinian radicalism, strengthen Syria, and reduce the prospects for a negotiated settlement; on the other, the invasion seemed to force Yasser Arafat's truncated PLO into closer cooperation with Jordan, strengthen the Israeli Labor party at the expense of the Likud, and open new opportunities for negotiations under American auspices. Above all of these immediate consequences, however, hung Hussein's worst-case vision of the future: that the invasion—in conjunction with Israel's de facto annexation of the West Bank—would lead to an even more radical PLO, which would look to Jordan and its Palestinian majority as the obvious next base for continuing the struggle against Israel.

It was this Palestinian dilemma that preoccupied Hussein's attention in the three years following the Israeli invasion. Other concerns—Jordanian security, economic development, relations with the United States—were also of critical importance of course. But it

* The views expressed in this article are those of the author and do not necessarily reflect the views of the Department of State or the United States Government.

was the king's Palestinian diplomacy and his search for the Arab and
international backing required to support it that emerged as the major theme in the period under review. This policy was pursued fitfully,
with an acute concern for Jordan's security but often without coherent tactics. Nonetheless, the strategic goal was clear: to position Hussein to move into negotiations with Israel over the West Bank should
the opportunity for serious movement arise.

Hussein's Palestinian diplomacy, then, provides the focus of this
essay. During the period 1982 to 1985, this diplomacy fell into three
stages. The first, extending from the Israeli invasion to the collapse of
the first Hussein-Arafat negotiations in April 1983, witnessed Jordan's initial efforts to exploit Arafat's weakness and American involvement in an effort to explore prospects for negotiations with Israel. The second stage, from April 1983 to the spring of 1984, was a
period of retrenchment as the PLO's internal problems and U.S. involvement in Lebanon made progress on the peace process impossible. Finally, the third period—from the fall of 1984 to the spring of
1985—saw Hussein's reengagement and his partial success in gaining American and Palestinian support for negotiations. The essay
concludes with an assessment of Hussein's diplomacy in the aftermath of his May 1985 visit to the United States.

The Legacy of the Past

It would be very misleading to suggest that the risks and opportunities Jordan confronted in the wake of the Lebanon war occurred
in a vacuum. Indeed, Jordan's efforts to deal with the post-1982 Lebanon environment must be seen in the context of three decades of
Hashemite domestic and foreign policy. Two elemental but critical
themes immediately stand out from a review of these early years:
first, Jordan has operated under powerful domestic and external constraints that flow from its military weakness, economic dependence,
and large Palestinian population; second, these factors have limited
Hussein's options in the Arab-Israeli arena and have combined to
produce a cautious leader with a finely tuned sense of the relationship
between Jordan's national interests and the limited resources at his
disposal to achieve them.

Nonetheless, this cautiousness and reserve have conflicted with
a traditional Hashemite desire to play a major role in the Arab world,

including the Arab-Israeli arena. This ambition, which can be traced back to Hussein's great grandfather Sharif Hussein, is interwoven with the Hashemites' own sense of importance and historic responsibility as direct descendents of the prophet Muhammed and standard-bearer of Arab nationalism. Indeed, the irony of the Hashemite predicament is that for reasons of ideology and self-interest Jordan has regional ambitions but lacks the political and military power to carry them out. For Abdullah, and particularly for his grandson Hussein, this dilemma has been most clearly reflected in Jordan's relationship with the Palestinian issue and the West Bank—a source of prestige as well as vulnerability for both Hashemite kings.

Before examining Hussein's relationship with this issue in the three years that followed the Israeli invasion of Lebanon, however, we must briefly examine the traditional constraints under which Jordan has operated. Jordan's position in the Middle East and its role in the Arab-Israel conflict flow from its location and its demography—factors that are difficult if not impossible for any nation to alter. Both where Jordan is and what it has become cut to the core of the challenges confronting the Hashemite kingdom and limit Jordan's options in the region. Three basic challenges confront the Hashemites: a Palestinian majority, economic dependence, and the struggle for political legitimacy and security in a hostile regional environment. All have combined to shape Hashemite domestic and foreign policies since the emirate of Transjordan was created in 1922—although these challenges have been most formidable in the three decades since Hussein ascended the throne.

The presence of more than a million Palestinians within the Hashemite kingdom (constituting some 60 percent of the total population) poses enormous political and economic challenges both to Jordan's identity as a nation and to its future stability. The refugee flows in the wake of the 1948 and 1967 Arab-Israeli wars added almost 700,000 Palestinians to the East Bank's already sizeable Palestinian population. The contrasts between the Palestinians and Jordanians were striking. To a basically conservative and rural Jordanian population were added hundreds of thousands of urbanized and better educated Palestinians with a higher standard of living and a vibrant political consciousness. Moreover, the estimated quarter of a million refugees who crossed the Jordan River in the aftermath of the 1967 war were less well-established than their predecessors and more susceptible to the nationalist feelings of the Palestinian fedayeen. It is from this group that the majority of poorer Palestinians who currently inhabit the shantytowns and refugee camps of Amman are drawn.

Although there were tensions between native East Bankers and Palestinians well before 1967, the war and resulting popularity of the PLO (between 1967 and 1970 based primarily in Jordan) accelerated the conflict between them. Militarily, the confrontation reached its peak in the events of Black September 1970–1971, in which Hussein violently crushed the fedayeen challenge to his authority and drove Palestinian fighters out of Jordan. Politically, however, the Palestinian national movement would present an equally formidable challenge. Not only did the PLO emerge as an alternative source of loyalty and identity for many Palestinians on the East Bank, but it complicated Hussein's plans to assert his influence on the West Bank, which was now under Israeli control. In 1974, the Arab summit at Rabat designated the PLO as the sole legitimate representative of the Palestinian people, thus depriving Hussein of his right to represent the Palestinians in any future negotiations over the West Bank.

Jordan's Palestinian dilemma affected its domestic and foreign policies in important ways. Although the 1948 refugees assimilated remarkably well into the Jordanian economic and social system, there were inevitable tensions. Although the Palestinians came to dominate most sectors of the Jordanian economy, they were not represented proportionately in the political system. Jordanians controlled the army and security services, and often regarded the Palestinians as second-class citizens and potential troublemakers. Moreover, there was the complex question of identity. Were the refugees Palestinians attached to Palestine who simply happened to live in Jordan—or "Jordanized" Palestinians with a new, primary loyalty to the Hashemites? After all, they carried Jordanian passports and were able to live and work where they pleased. But did they *feel* like Jordanians? And what was their role in the political system of a country dominated by a Hashemite king and a handful of prominent Bedouin tribes and Jordanian families? Finally, were their loyalties tied to Palestine and the PLO or to a charismatic, well-intentioned, but ultimately patronizing King?

These questions became even more acute as the nature of Jordanian society began to change. As one of the pillars of Hashemite authority—the bond between the king and the tribes—began to weaken as the Bedouin played a progressively less important role in

Jordan, the need to redefine a new sense of political community based on a Jordanian national identity became more apparent. What role would an insecure and alienated Palestinian majority, whose loyalties were also tugged at by the Palestinian national movement, play in such a process? While the passion for stability of an entrenched Palestinian community should not be underestimated, it is not an inexhaustible resource. And in the future, Palestinians will want to play a greater political role in Jordan, whether or not the West Bank issue is resolved. Indeed, the feeling among the vast majority of Jordan's million-plus Palestinians that they are not full-fledged participants in the political system may well constitute the single greatest challenge to the stability of the Hashemite kingdom.

The presence of a Palestinian majority in Jordan acts as both an incentive and a constraint for Hussein in his role as participant in the Arab-Israeli arena. On one hand, the king—mindful of the long-term consequences that a potentially hostile and irredentist Palestinian majority pose for the security and survival of the Hashemite kingdom—calculates that Jordan must play the key role in managing Palestinian national aspirations. For Hussein, this means finding a territorial solution to the Palestinian problem that both satisfies these aspirations and guarantees Jordanian security. Thus, Hussein looks to the return of the West Bank in close association with Jordan as a way to manage both the security and political problems inherent in a Palestinian homeland. Hussein is under no illusion that a West Bank entity would solve the problem of a Palestinian majority on the East Bank. But he reasons that the creation of a Palestinian homeland closely aligned with Jordan would help to defuse Palestinian nationalist irredentist ambitions, stem the influx of West Bank residents to Jordan, and help to satisfy the psychological needs of East Bank Palestinians who feel shut out of the Jordanian political system and who still maintain their identity as Palestinians.

At the same time, however, the presence of an East Bank Palestinian majority and the tension between Jordan and the Palestinian national movement acts as a serious constraint on Hussein's ability to pursue these objectives. For example, after the Rabat decision of 1974 Hussein was forced to work through the PLO rather than around it. Jordan could not move diplomatically without coordination with Arafat—a development that linked Hussein's West Bank diplomacy to the vagaries of inter-Palestinian and Arab world politics. Also, Hussein's East Bank Palestinian constituency, however docile and assimilated, had to be assuaged. These Palestinians, already suspicious of Hashemite ambitions, could emerge as a potential force of opposition should Hussein try to cut the PLO out or compromise on the question of Palestinian national rights. Both of these factors limit Hussein's room to maneuver, therefore—not only in the Arab world but also in any future negotiations with Israel. Indeed, at a time when Hussein needs maximum flexibility to deal successfully with the Israelis, he has to contend with these Palestinian and Arab constraints.

The second factor that limits Jordan's options results from its geography, and to some extent from its political isolation within the Arab world. For almost two decades following the creation of the Emirate of Transjordan in 1922, the Hashemites were relatively immune from the volatile world of inter-Arab politics. As others have pointed out, Jordan, much like the Gulf sheikhdoms, existed as a traditional desert emirate attending to its own economic problems and dealing as best it could with border invasions from rival tribes. Moreover, unlike such other Arab states as Iraq, Syria, and Egypt, the process of Jordan's transition from European influence to its own independence was much less traumatic. As a consequence, in the admittedly hypocritical and contradictory world of Arab ideology, the Jordanians were never fully accepted as a progressive nationalist force with proper "anti-imperialist" credentials. That is to say, Jordan's Arab nationalist credentials were products not of the struggle for independence but of an earlier period associated with the British-backed Arab revolt against the Turks. Indeed, the close and positive association with Britain implicit in the very establishment of Transjordan reinforced a sense of isolation and left the Hashemites open to the criticism of their Arab neighbors. The fact that the Hashemites were a monarchy transplanted from Saudi Arabia to an area in which they had no indigenous roots only increased their vulnerability.

Jordan's political isolation was heightened further during the 1940s and 1950s. Abdullah's own ambitions, in part stimulated by his desire to play a larger role on the Arab stage, brought him into bitter conflict with Egypt, Syria, and Saudi Arabia. His vision of a Hashemite-centered greater Syria and his annexation of the West Bank in 1950 left him vulnerable to the charge that he sought to exploit inter-Arab rivalries and the Arab and Palestinian defeat suffered at the hands of the Zionists and "Western imperialists" in the 1948 war to benefit purely Jordanian interests. The presence of the British-financed, trained, and led Arab Legion; the subsidy from London; and

Hussein's close ties to Britain (and later to the United States) further removed Jordan from the ranks of the more "progressive" and radical Arab nationalists. True, Jordan tried to adopt a more nationalist posture in the months preceding and following the 1956 Suez crisis; but tensions with Nasser's Egypt and with Syria continued in the wake of the attempted officer coup against Hussein in April 1957, and for the next ten years some of the most vitriolic anti-Hashemite rhetoric emanated from Cairo and Damascus.

Israel's crushing military defeat of Jordan, Syria, and Egypt during the 1967 war paradoxically brought Jordan into a closer relationship with Egypt and even with Syria. Despite the climate of rapidly shifting alliances within the Arab world, the war and subsequent loss of Jordanian territory created a bond that helped Hussein to normalize his relations within the Arab world. Moreover, the king has moved to ensure that Jordan remained within the Arab consensus on key issues. Nonetheless, the Hashemites' traditional sense of isolation and vulnerability continues: sandwiched between militarily superior Israel, Syria, and Iraq and a Saudi Arabia that has been both a traditional Hashemite rival and a patronizing benefactor, Jordan has been forced to proceed cautiously as it balances its own interests against those of its neighbors. Jordan's pragmatic approach to Israel since 1967, its traditional alignment with the West, and the fact that it is one of the few remaining monarchies in the region has at times made balancing Hashemite and Arab interests a difficult proposition, and it must be conceded that Hussein has succeeded to a remarkable degree. But the price has been a cautious and conservative approach to Arab-Israeli issues that severely limits Jordan's flexibility within the Arab world and its dealings with Israel. Unlike Egypt, Jordan possesses neither the advantages of geography nor the political and military power to defy the Arab and Palestinian consensus on such key issues as peace with Israel.

Jordan's physical security has been the paramount Hashemite concern since the days of Abdullah. Not only do the Jordanians perceive a threat from Israel, but from their Arab neighbors as well. Twice in the past decade and a half, Syria has used military pressure against Jordan to achieve political objectives. The Jordanian army is well-trained and proficient, but it is small and incapable of deterring any determined attack from Syria, let alone Israel. Moreover, in recent years, the Jordanians have been forced to deal with the unconventional threat of assassination and internal sabotage at home and abroad. No matter how proficient the security services have become, they cannot hermetically seal the borders. The murder of exiled West Bank mayor Fahd Qawasmeh in December 1984 in broad daylight in a residential area of Amman indicates how vulnerable Jordan remains to this kind of threat. These acts, and the constant threat of conventional Syrian military pressure, raise fears in the minds of many East Bank Jordanians that Hussein's peace process diplomacy carries serious risks. Such factors also force the king to keep that diplomacy well within the parameters set by his Arab allies and Palestinian supporters.

Indeed, the most powerful constraint under which Jordan operates is not the military threat from Syria but its lack of support within the Arab world. This dilemma—how to further Hashemite interests within the parameters set by more powerful and influential Arab states—has been one of the Hashemites' greatest challenges. Jordan operates in a volatile environment of shifting rivalries and alliances, where commitments to Arabism, Arab independence, and Palestinian rights remain the hallmarks of influence and prestige. Given the Hashemites' traditional rivalries with almost every other Arab state (and Jordan's mixed record on the Palestinian issue), Hussein's foreign policy, particularly on Arab-Israeli issues, must be reconciled within the prevailing Arab consensus—although the king has periodically taken issue with the principle of consensus decision-making. The practical consequences for the peace process are not difficult to divine. For its own protection Jordan must seek broad Arab support, PLO backing, and international cover for negotiations with Israel. Even more problematic, Jordan seeks assurances that the advantages of participation in negotiations will be worth the risks—a negotiating style that demands a reasonably clear picture of the final vision of a settlement before negotiations begin. All of this severely limits how far and how fast Hussein can move in his relations with Israel.

The third and final constraint derives from Jordan's economic dependence. Given Jordan's limited natural resources (phosphates and potash) and its meager industrial base, the country's economic growth and development amount to a major success story. The Jordanians have diversified their economy, become the world's third largest producer of phosphates, and kept inflation and unemployment at low levels. Between 1975 and 1980, Jordan's economy grew at a remarkable annual real rate of 9 percent, although world recession and the drop in phosphate prices and in Arab subsidies have depressed growth over the past four years.[1]

Nonetheless, the Jordanian economy has historically suffered from a structural dependence and balance-of-payments problem that make it highly vulnerable to the support of others. This economic dependence is inevitably linked to political factors within the Arab world and invariably influences Jordan's own decision-making on Arab-Israeli issues; further, it binds Hussein's strategy on negotiations with Israel to the Arab consensus. Jordan is highly dependent on Arab petrodollars as well as on remittances from Jordanians employed in Saudi Arabia and the Gulf—factors that make Saudi support essential to Jordan's political and economic well-being. In 1982 alone, Jordan received between 800 million and one billion dollars in subsidies from Arab donors. In 1983 and 1984 however, these subsidies dropped substantially as a result of the economic slowdown in the Gulf and falling oil prices.[2] Worker remittances from the estimated 300,000 Jordanians and Palestinians working in the Persian Gulf also declined in 1985.

Thus, the relationship between Arab grant aid and Jordan's economic welfare is clear. Hussein cannot afford to take his Saudi-Gulf connection for granted, let alone risk a further decrease in or even cutoff of aid by taking bold action on peace-process issues. Jordan's trade deficit and the prospect of rising unemployment triggered by population growth and constriction in local job opportunities suggest serious economic problems in the years ahead. Unless Hussein can develop non-Arab sources of assistance, he will remain dependent on regional allies who may not support his desire to move ahead into negotiations with Israel. Increased economic aid from the United States—which quadrupled in fiscal 1985 and 1986—is a possibility, but a viable one only if Hussein commits himself fully to negotiations with Israel. These economic factors will remain major considerations as Jordan assesses the risks and opportunities for movement in the peace process in the months ahead.

New Risks and Opportunities: June 1982 to April 1983

Israel's June 1982 invasion of Lebanon and the events that unfolded over the next year seemed to highlight both the risks and opportunities for Hussein in the Arab-Israeli arena. The Jordanians harshly condemned the invasion as an example of Israeli aggression and expansionism, but other concerns were lurking not far below the surface. The invasion and the crushing defeat of the PLO combined with Likud's policy of de facto annexation of the West Bank seemed to foreshadow a more radicalized PLO under a Syrian leadership actively committed to undermining the Hashemite kingdom. After all, the Jordanians believed that the chief architect of the invasion, Israeli Defense Minister Ariel Sharon, was committed to solving Israel's Palestinian problem at Jordanian expense by driving Palestinians across the river and forcing them to create their own state on the East Bank. Referring to the long-term danger that the invasion posed for Jordan, Hussein informed French television audiences in August 1982 that "they [the Israelis] are now working to achieve this factor in the occupied territories by forcing many Arabs to leave the area and settle Israelis in their place."[3] In a nationwide address a month later, the king was even more direct: "I repeat my firm belief that we in this Arab land will be a target, if not the first target, for Israel's aggression after Lebanon."[4]

Paradoxically, however, the events of June 1982 also presented potential opportunities for Jordan, although they seem not to have been immediately apparent to the king. First, the Israeli invasion and expulsion of the PLO from Beirut weakened Arafat and brought to the surface his long-standing tensions with Syria. The combination of a PLO without an independent base and a rift between Arafat and Assad that went deeper than any previous confrontation held out the possibility of increasing Jordan's leverage over the PLO and its dependence on Amman. Moreover, despite his deep suspicions of the king's motives, Arafat might begin to see the Jordanian option as his only realistic course in the wake of the invasion.

Second, the Israeli invasion resulted in a renewed direct American involvement in the Arab-Israeli conflict and the formulation of a U.S. diplomatic initiative that addressed the Palestinian issue. Not only did the American initiative, outlined in President Reagan's September 1982 address, accord Jordan the central role in the future of the West Bank, but it seemed to coincide closely with Hussein's own vision of a West Bank entity closely associated with Jordan. Moreover, the initiative seemed to indicate that the Americans were prepared to actively engage in an effort to resolve the Arab-Israeli dispute—a key Jordanian requirement for a successful peace process. In fact, the king interpreted the Reagan initiative as an effort to move beyond the Camp David approach. Hussein was further encouraged when the Arab summit that convened in Fez, Morocco, in early September did not directly condemn the American initiative. Thus, the invasion appeared to give Hussein new opportunities to involve both the PLO and the Americans in his concept of a solution to the Palestinian problem. Throughout the fall of 1982, Hussein began to explore the prospects of establishing a closer relationship with the PLO that would give Jordan a position of primacy in any future negotiations. "Perhaps it is time to begin a dialogue and work with the PLO," Hussein noted in mid-September, "to formulate a concept and picture of the relationship that can be established between the Palestinian entity and the Jordanian entity in the form of a federation."[5] What was important at this stage of the process were not the details of the ultimate relationship between Jordan and a Palestinian entity, but rather a determination of whether the post-Lebanon environment had produced a sufficient change in the PLO's position to warrant closer cooperation. The presence of a million Palestinians in Jordan, Hussein's access to the West Bank, the loss of independence in Lebanon, and American recognition of Hussein's centrality in negotiations were important incentives for Arafat to cooperate with Jordan. At the same time, however, disincentives were pulling the PLO in the opposite direction. Still reeling from the effects of the Israeli invasion, Arafat was trying to hold the PLO together and maintain his relations with Syria. Long suspicious of his ties with Hussein, Assad and the PLO's independent as well as Syrian-controlled groups were determined to block any new rapprochement. And for his part Arafat, unsure of his tactics or strategy in the wake of the invasion, was not yet prepared to risk a major initiative with Hussein.

On the surface, however, it appeared that Jordanian-PLO ties were improving. In October 1982, Arafat paid his first visit to Amman since the Israeli invasion. The subsequent talks with Hussein were short on substance, although the atmosphere surrounding the visit was very positive. On the eve of the visit, Hussein pardoned more than 700 Palestinians jailed since 1970 for security-related offenses.[6] The official rhetoric and press speculation talked of the "special relationship" between Jordan and the PLO and the importance of "joint action." Arafat loyalist Khalid al-Hassan expressed support for the idea of a Palestinian-Jordanian "confederation," while PLO spokesman Mahmud Labadi stated that the PLO was "inclined" toward such a confederation after a Palestinian state had been formed.[7] Two weeks after leaving Amman, Arafat was reported to have endorsed the principle of confederation.[8]

While the questions basic to any PLO-Jordanian relationship—

who would represent the Palestinians in future negotiations; what they would be negotiating for—were left unresolved, it appeared that both Arafat and Hussein had a stake in promoting the image of closer cooperation. Indeed, on the eve of Hussein's December visit to Washington it seemed as if the relationship had progressed to a more formal stage. Reports that a joint PLO-Jordanian delegation had been created began circulating as a higher Jordanian-Palestinian joint committee formed in November issued a formal statement agreeing "to move together politically on all levels based on a commitment to the Fez summit resolution...."[9] While the coordination was partly designed to convince the Americans that Hussein had made progress in his Palestinian diplomacy, it may also have reflected Arafat's own efforts to prepare the ground for a new relationship with Jordan. Referring to his recent discussions with Hussein, Arafat informed the Egyptian press that he and Hussein had reached agreement on a "confederal link" subject to approval by the Palestine National Council (PNC).[10] Reports emanating from Washington in the wake of the Hussein visit to the effect that the United States and Jordan were looking for ways to deal with the issue of Palestinian representation in the context of the Reagan initiative only heightened speculation about a Jordanian-PLO deal.[11]

By early 1983 the focus of Arab-Israeli peace-process diplomacy centered almost exclusively on the emerging Jordanian-PLO relationship. Arafat's two visits to Amman in January and February suggested that the Jordanians were beginning to press Arafat for an agreement that would formalize the relationship and position Hussein for negotiations with Israel. All that was needed, it seemed, was the PNC's approval of this new relationship; attention therefore focused on the upcoming PNC session set for mid-February.

Nevertheless, it should have been clear that the regional environment was not conducive to a PLO-Jordanian deal, let alone to negotiations with Israel. The United States was engaged in an effort to facilitate the withdrawal of Israeli and Syrian forces from Lebanon, thereby making its peace-process strategy hostage to both Assad and Begin—the last people who wanted to see it succeed. The Syrians, having been humiliated by the Israelis in Lebanon, were being resupplied by the Soviets and increasing their own leverage over the Lebanese central government and Palestinian forces in the Bekaa Valley. Finally, whatever Arafat maintained publicly, he was in no position to push a new line with the Jordanians: not only were the Syrians and other constituent PLO groups against the Jordanian option as conceived by Hussein, but many in Arafat's own Fatah organization opposed it. In a closed-door session of Fatah's Revolutionary Council held in January, Said Musa Muragha (Abu Musa), later military leader of the Fatah dissidents, bitterly attacked Arafat's political strategy and the concept of cooperation with Jordan.[12]

As might have been expected, the results of the sixteenth session of the PNC that convened in Algiers in mid-February included no clearcut verdict on Arafat's Jordanian option. It cannot, however, be described as an outright failure from the Jordanian perspective. The key resolution pertaining to Jordan was ambiguous, to be sure;[13] yet it did formally incorporate in a PNC resolution the principle of a confederation with Jordan. Nonetheless, the PNC attacked the Reagan initiative on the grounds that the PLO was not included as the sole legitimate representative of the Palestinians and that the Palestinians could not establish an independent state. At a time when the unity and independence of the PLO were still Arafat's primary concerns, the Jordanians might have calculated that he was in no position to develop a new relationship with Hussein that compromised traditional PLO goals. Still, the sixteenth PNC session set a useful precedent with Arafat's own efforts to develop a constituency for a new relationship with Jordan.

What the PNC session did not do, as Hussein was soon to discover, was to authorize Arafat to make concrete deals with the king that eroded traditional PLO positions on "authorization" and the final status of a settlement. Nonetheless, the Jordanians appeared to believe that Arafat could not only be brought around to their conception of a negotiating process, but that he could also bring the PLO along with him. By the end of February it seemed clear that the Jordanians were setting the stage for a campaign designed to press Arafat for concessions. Foreign Minister Marwan al-Qasim informed the Saudi press that, while PLO participation in negotiations would be the "ideal solution," in the event this could not be achieved a negotiating delegation should include other representatives expressing the wishes of the Palestinian people.[14] While Hussein had no intention of actually moving to cut the PLO out, the impression the Jordanians hoped to leave with Arafat was unmistakable. Attention was thus focused on Arafat's April visit to Amman.

The details of the Hussein-Arafat conversations leading to the collapse of the negotiations are not clear. Certainly, the fact that Arafat arrived by car from Damascus was not particularly encouraging, suggesting as it did that he was still very much in the shadow of Syria. Nonetheless, intensive discussions between March 31 and April 6 apparently produced a draft agreement. The agreement, although amorphous and vague and therefore not viable as any sort of negotiating initiative with Israel, was reported to include at least two major concessions on Arafat's part: no specific reference to an independent Palestinian state before confederation with Jordan, and no explicit reference to the PLO's exclusive right to negotiate for the Palestinians.[15] In effect, Arafat was reported to have made it possible for Jordan and the non-PLO Palestinians to negotiate together with Israel. Presumably, the Jordanians planned to use this PLO authorization to enter into talks with Israel in the context of the Reagan initiative.

All of this Jordanian-PLO maneuvering, however, proved academic. Pleading the need for consultation with his PLO colleagues Arafat flew off to Kuwait, where the draft accord was repudiated and later amended by the PLO's executive committee and Fatah's central committee to reflect a hardline position. Hussein, exasperated by Arafat's equivocation and embarrassed by the failure of this round of his Palestinian diplomacy, appeared ready to withdraw from the field. On April 10, the Jordanian Cabinet issued a strongly worded statement that, while it respected the PLO's decision not to cooperate, "we leave it to the PLO and to the Palestinian people to choose ways and means for the salvation of themselves and their land."[16] Moreover, the king was reportedly losing patience with the Americans as well. Citing the U.S. inability either to halt Israeli settlement activity or to get Israel out of Lebanon, Hussein intimated that there was little chance of progress in the peace process.[17] "If the United States is unable to force Israel to withdraw from Lebanon . . . how can the United States affect Israel on the issues of the West Bank, Gaza, and the Golan?" Hussein asked.[18]

Retrenchment: April 1983–September 1984

In the wake of the abortive Arafat-Hussein agreement, several things became clear to the Jordanians—realizations that would have important consequences for their future tactics on the peace process. Since the Israeli invasion, Hussein's approach to the Arab-Israeli conflict hinged on two sets of relationships. First, Hussein had set out to convince the United States that that country must engage in the peace process in a way that was supportive of Jordan's conception of both process and substance; and second, the king calculated that he had to work out a new relationship with the PLO in order to garner the necessary Palestinian support for negotiations. Once this was achieved, he believed, it would be easier to get broader Arab support for an initiative. While the Israeli invasion had coincidentally pushed both Arafat and the Americans in his direction, Hussein had not yet achieved the coordination and cooperation he believed necessary to accomplish his objectives.

For the next year and a half, Hussein basically adopted a wait-and-see policy as the situation in Lebanon preoccupied the attention of both the United States and the PLO, complicating the king's efforts to get them involved in the peace process on his terms. Moreover, for the next year Syria, already fundamentally opposed to Jordan's diplomacy, exercised enormous influence over the PLO and was able to successfully oppose Israeli and American efforts to broker a Lebanese settlement. Syrian prestige and credibility rose proportionately, raising Jordanian concerns that Assad would be able to increase his influence over broader peace-process issues as well. Indeed, it was only after the United States and the PLO were able to disengage from the Lebanese morass that Hussein was able to get his diplomatic initiative back on track.

With the outbreak of the Fatah mutiny in the summer of 1983 (and Syria's efforts to exploit Arafat's troubles to undermine him politically and militarily), there was little Jordan could do but to watch from the sidelines, issue statements supporting Palestinian independence, and blast Syrian interference in the PLO's affairs.[19] The Jordanians doubtless saw opportunities in the Syrian campaign against Arafat: the more dissension between Arafat and Assad, and the more strain on the relationship between Fatah's moderates and radicals, the fewer options Arafat would have and the more leverage Jordan would possess. The danger in this scenario, of course, was that the PLO might fall completely under Syrian control, in which case it would be stripped of any credibility as a negotiating partner. While a discredited Arafat opened up new possibilities for undermining the Rabat decision of 1974, it also raised the risk that there would be no credible Palestinian partner with which to garner Arab support. Indeed, while the thought of moving into talks with Israel in partnership with well-heeled West Bankers must have been a tempting one for

Hussein, he recognized that such a unilateral approach would never gain the Arab support on which Jordan depended. Thus, the king probably hoped for an outcome in which Arafat would be badly weakened but not entirely discredited.

Syria's decision to expel Arafat from Damascus and later to push his forces from the Bekaa Valley and finally from Tripoli seemed to be quickly closing his Syrian and Lebanese options. There was little Hussein could do to exploit these developments, however. The open rebellion within Fatah and Arafat's rift with the Syrian-backed PLO groups plunged Arafat into internal Palestinian matters that would take months to sort out. Moreover, by the fall the United States was involved in a political and military effort to support the Lebanese central government, an involvement that brought the Americans into direct confrontation with Syria and its Lebanese allies. No one, then—least of all Arafat and the Americans—had West Bank issues on their minds. In September, when asked about prospects for resuming a dialogue with Arafat, Hussein replied: "At the moment there are so many other problems that are occupying the thoughts of all in the area—Lebanon is really the focal point."[20] With the United States involved militarily in Lebanon, it was futile to try and convince Washington to focus on other issues. And much to Hussein's dismay, Syria was waging a successful campaign in Lebanon to frustrate American objectives and undermine U.S. credibility.

Nonetheless, by the end of 1983 it appeared as if the confrontation between Syria and Arafat was coming to a head and that the PLO might be able to free itself from Syrian influence. The Jordanians sensed that the Syrian-backed effort to drive Arafat from Lebanon might be a watershed in PLO-Syrian relations that might make a future accommodation extremely difficult. While the Jordanian press hammered home the theme that any resumption of the Arafat-Hussein dialogue might now have to be on Jordanian terms, the king was much more forthcoming. The door to dialogue with the PLO is still open, Hussein commented in November, and "we cannot close it."[21] On the eve of Arafat's departure from Tripoli in December, Hussein informed an American television audience that the PLO leader's death would not help the peace process.[22] Indeed, after Arafat had departed Lebanon, the *Jordan Times* noted that it was in the context of "keeping all options alive for a lasting joint Jordanian-Palestinian partnership that Arafat's expected visit to Jordan in the post-Tripoli era, will be most productive and promising."[23]

Reengagement: January 1984–June 1985

Arafat's second forced exit from Lebanon in as many years opened new possibilities for Hussein's relationship with the PLO. The circumstances under which Arafat departed Tripoli—under military pressure from Syrian-backed PLO groups—appeared to widen the already sizable gap between Fatah and Assad. Even more encouraging was Arafat's surprise meeting in late December with Egyptian president Mubarak. Not only was the reconciliation certain to antagonize Assad, but it raised Hussein's hopes that a new Egyptian-Jordanian-PLO alignment might be formed to pursue a more pragmatic political line. Such an axis, although the Jordanians were careful not to use such terms, might also counter Syria and further moderate Arafat's own thinking. Foreshadowing his own decision to restore full diplomatic ties with Egypt within a year, Hussein informed the BBC in January 1984 that it was "inevitable" that Jordan would be the first Arab state to welcome Egypt back into the Arab fold.[24]

Hussein was under no illusions that Arafat's Tripoli departure could be exploited easily, and he continued to move cautiously within the Arab consensus established at the Fez summit. At the same time, the Jordanians continued to hammer home the importance of an international conference and supported fully the PLO's independent role in any settlement. Moreover, in the wake of the formation of a new government under Prime Minister Ahmed Obeidat, there was increasing speculation that Jordan would improve relations with Syria.[25] Nonetheless, the king continued to send signals that he was interested in laying the groundwork for a possible move into negotiations. In January 1984, he reconvened the Jordanian lower house of parliament in a move that had clear foreign policy implications. The recall of parliament and need to elect new West Bank representatives—the first since Jordan had lost the territory in 1967—theoretically would make it easier for Hussein to proceed with legitimate Palestinian representation should he want to move into negotiations with Israel. Moreover, as part of his government reorganization Hussein brought two of his ministers—Foreign Minister Marwan al-Qasim and Minister of Information Adnan Abu Odeh—into the palace as advisors on peace-process issues.

Whatever Hussein's intentions with regard to negotiations over the future of the West Bank, he was in no position to make any unilateral moves. In an effort to counter criticism that the recall of parliament was somehow designed to cut the PLO out of the picture, the Jordanians did their best to leave the impression that the PLO was still very much in the process. Court Minister Abu Odeh went out of his way in a January interview to stress that the recall of parliament was not intended to infringe on the Rabat decisions of 1974.[26] And, in an interview with the BBC a week later, Hussein noted that Jordan intended to proceed in a manner that represented no "threat to the PLO."[27] Moreover, the king must have calculated that the time was not yet ripe for an initiative: the PLO's house was still in disarray, the United States was bogged down in Lebanon, and U.S.–Jordanian relations were still not as sound as the king would have liked. Indeed, in a blistering March 1984 interview with the *New York Times,* Hussein—bitter over his perception that Washington was disregarding Jordanian interests on a range of issues from Israeli settlement activity to arms sales—blasted the United States.[28]

For the next six months the Jordanians appeared to be biding their time. With Israeli elections scheduled in July and U.S. presidential elections set for November, Hussein doubtless calculated that there would be little activity. For its part, the PLO appeared no closer to resolving its internal differences; in fact, the PLO accord reached in Aden in June seemed to suggest that Arafat still put organizational unity above a viable joint approach with Hussein on the peace process. Thus, the Jordanians watched and waited, keeping all of their options open. Hussein continued to push for an international conference, and maintained his ties to Moscow: within a three-month period, both the Jordanian prime minister and the chief of staff visited the Soviet Union, the latter in connection with an arms deal. There were also rumors of a Hussein visit to Moscow.[29]

Thus, the period between the Israeli elections in July and the American presidential elections in November would have seemed like a most unusual time for any Jordanian activity on the peace process. The Jordanians interpreted the results of the Israeli elections—a virtual deadlock between Labor and Likud—as further evidence that Israel was not prepared to deal with the West Bank issue. Nonetheless, during these five months Hussein initiated a number of important steps that would help to lay the groundwork for possible talks with the Israelis about matters in the Palestinian and Arab arenas. It is unlikely that Hussein had a detailed diplomatic strategy; rather, the king seemed to be operating from a number of general principles designed to exploit possible opportunities as they arose. Hussein's initiative centered on creating Arab support and a new relationship with Arafat as a prelude to convincing the United States to become more actively engaged in Middle East diplomacy—on Jordan's terms. Only then, if circumstances were favorable, did Hussein probably contemplate negotiations with Israel. While Hussein's initiative was uncharacteristically bold for him, it was still gradualist and cautious, and designed to expose Jordan to the fewest possible risks. Indeed, throughout the next year, Hussein would continue to proceed carefully, to keep all his options open and burn no bridges behind him against the time he found it necessary to retreat.

Jordan's decision to restore formal diplomatic ties with Egypt in September was the first indication that Hussein was contemplating a more forward-leaning approach to Arab-Israeli issues. The move, of course, had its rationale in an Arab context, and had been under consideration for months. Indeed, the Jordanian press hammered home the theme that Jordan was engaged in an effort to draw Mubarak away from Camp David "so that the transient alienation will not turn into a permanent fact to be exploited solely by our enemy."[30] Nonetheless, the fact that Jordan ws the first Arab state to restore relations with Egypt (the only Arab country to have a peace treaty with Israel) could not be ignored. Hussein, the most likely participant in the next round of Arab-Israeli negotiations, was sending clear signals to both Israel and the United States that he was strongly committed to a negotiated settlement and was willing to take limited risks to support this principle. Arafat, always concerned about possible Jordanian peace-process maneuverings and interested in both the risks and opportunities inherent in a Hussein-Mubarak reconciliation, showed up in Amman the day after the Jordanian announcement.[31]

The fact that Arafat had come to Amman to discuss Hussein's Egyptian diplomacy was not as striking as the increasing speculation that the PLO might hold the next council session of the PNC in Amman.[32] By the fall, the issue of where and when to convene the session had become a test case of Arafat's leadership and a tug of war between the PLO Chairman and Assad. In an effort to undermine Arafat's authority, the Syrians had played upon the split within the PLO and the PFLP's and DFLP's disaffection. Although the Aden accord had set September 15 as a date for convening the PNC, the Syrians had successfully blocked plans for the session. Algerian and South Yemeni mediation failed to broker an agreement as Arafat searched for a venue: the Algerians would not confront Damascus or take responsibility for splitting the PLO; Arafat did not want to alienate the Iranians by convening in Baghdad; and holding the meeting in Cairo was certain to cause a major row within Fatah. Unless Arafat could find a way to convene the session, however, Assad would have effectively paralyzed the PLO's institutions and undermined Arafat's independence and authority.

The possibility of convening the seventeenth session of the PNC in Amman had apparently been under discussion for some time. The Jordanians were not entirely enthusiastic about the idea, although Hussein doubtless saw an opportunity to present himself as the patron of the PLO, preserving its "independence" while increasing Jordanian leverage over Arafat. In fact, the issue of Palestinian independent decision-making—a codeword for avoiding Syrian domination—was an important component of Hussein's initiative. "Let them decide. Let the Palestinians decide for themselves. Let them not be a tool in the hands of certain regimes," Jordanian Foreign Minister Taher al-Masri noted.[33] By late October Hussein was reported to have offered the PLO an invitation to convene the meeting in Amman if the Palestinians requested it.[34]

Hussein's decision to host the PNC in Amman and Arafat's willingness to allow it to convene there in November ushered in a new stage in the evolving relationship between Jordan and the PLO. It is important to point out that the Amman session did not represent a fundamental convergence of interests between the two men, but rather a tactical coincidence of objectives. For Arafat, pursued by Syria and its Palestinian allies, convening a successful PNC had become a test of his own authority and leadership. Reaffirming the independence of the PLO and demonstrating the functioning of its institutions would send a message to Israel and to Syria that the Palestinian movement was still resilient and credible enough to muster a consensus in Arafat's favor. While Arafat had other purposes in mind, including demonstrating that he had a Jordanian option and buoying the hopes of the West Bankers, he did not necessarily intend that the PNC session would be the first step in a major rapprochement with Jordan. Indeed, Arafat doubtless calculated that he could use the Amman venue for his own purposes without subordinating the PLO's interests to Hussein.

Hussein's perspective, although colored by much of the same kind of tactical maneuvering, was very different. For the king, convening the PNC in Amman—a development that made many East

Bankers nervous, incidentally—was the first step in a campaign to work out a new relationship with Arafat that would permit Jordan to play the lead role in any future negotiations with Israel. Hussein had calculated, based on the abortive April 1983 agreement, that trying to get "authorization" from Arafat to have Jordan negotiate on behalf of the PLO, let alone trying to end-run the organization, was unfeasible. While the king was unsure as to just how and when the PLO could be brought into the process, he believed that he would have to involve Arafat in order to share the responsibility for entry into any negotiations and for any concessions at the bargaining table. Moreover, by hosting the PNC Hussein hoped to achieve two other important objectives: first, the king doubtless recognized that an Amman PNC would reduce the already slim chances for a reconciliation between Arafat and Assad or a rapprochement with more hardline PLO groups; second, the Amman venue gave the Jordanians an opportunity to take their message directly to a West Bank constituency that could be expected to follow the PNC session with acute interest. Thus, in the presence of the PLO's supreme authority—the PNC— the king was given an opportunity to hammer home the message that negotiations with Israel had to be based on Resolution 242 and on the principle of territory in exchange for peace. Implicit in this message, which the king believed to be the only realistic basis for negotiations, was a choice for the Palestinians. Having sketched out the benefits of cooperation with Jordan, Hussein noted in his speech before the PNC: "However, if you believe that the PLO can proceed alone, we will tell you to go ahead, with God's blessing."[35]

Although the resolutions passed by the PNC went no further than the Algiers resolutions of a year earlier, in the months that followed the Amman meeting the results of Hussein's strategy appeared to be paying off. To be sure, there was increasing terrorism against Jordanian interests—most dramatically, the murder of PLO executive committee member Fahd Qawasmeh in Amman in December—as well as an increase in anti-Jordanian rhetoric from Damascus. Nonetheless, with the conclusion of the Arafat-Hussein framework agreement on February 11, 1985, it was clear that PLO-Jordanian relations had reached a new stage. Like the convening of the PNC itself, the February 11 accord represented a coincidence of interests between Arafat and Hussein, although this time on a more formal level. The agreement, although vaguely worded on the key issues of Palestinian representation and the final status of a settlement, represented a

loosely defined framework within which Arafat and Hussein could begin to develop a joint approach to future negotiations with Israel. The
accord, therefore, clearly had more to do with Jordanian-Palestinian
relations than it did with negotiating with Israel; in fact, it had never
been intended to provide a detailed strategy for negotiations. Nonetheless, it did have significant implications for the Arab-Israeli peace
process.

For Hussein, the February 11 accord was designed to formalize
his relationship with Arafat on a pragmatic basis that would placate
his Palestinian and Arab constituencies without alienating the United
States. The American audience was particularly important in this regard. The accord was intended to establish Jordanian primacy on two
key issues: who would represent the Palestinians in negotiations, and
what they would be negotiating for—all without undermining Arafat's credibility. Indeed, the Jordanians had no intention of cutting
Arafat out or even negotiating by proxy; rather, they appeared determined to bring Arafat in by transforming the PLO into an acceptable
interlocutor, first for the United States and ultimately for Israel. While
the accord did not explicitly refer to U.N. resolutions 242 and 338,
the king stressed that Arafat's acceptance of the principles of land for
peace was an implicit endorsement of the concept contained in 242
and thus a sign of his moderation. With proper inducement (most
likely from the United States), Hussein doubtless believed that Arafat
could be persuaded to move toward the American position on negotiations. The fact that the accord stressed the importance of an international conference and the need to bring the PLO to the negotiating
table—positions both Israel and the United States opposed—were
problems that the king hoped could be resolved along the way.

Perhaps the accord's most significant accomplishment from the
king's perspective (as well as the one that the United States seemed
most intrigued by) was what it did *not* say on the issue of the future
Palestinian entity. The king believed that the absence of a reference
to an independent state—one of the PLO's core positions—represented a fundamental shift in Arafat's thinking. The Palestinians, to
be sure, were to exercise their right to self-determination through a
confederation that "is intended to be established between two states
of Jordan and Palestine."[36] While the PLO continued to assert that the
accord did not compromise its right to independence, the Jordanians
had a different position. The future relationship between Jordan and
the Palestinian "state" was to resemble not so much a confederation

of two equal entities but a federation where foreign policy and defense would be tightly controlled in Amman. Indeed, what the king envisioned was, with minor variations, the plan outlined in the United Arab Federation Plan he had espoused a decade and a half earlier.

For the next several months, the Jordanians worked to consolidate support in Palestinian circles for the February accord, to fend off Syrian criticism, to broaden Arab support, and to attract American interest. Despite some back-pedaling by the PLO, Arafat succeeded in developing support for the principles of closer cooperation with the king, although serious doubts about the accord remained. The key to Jordan's partial success with Arafat seems to have stemmed from the decision in Amman not to push him too far too soon—a lesson Hussein had learned from the April 1983 episode. Similarly, rather than deal only with Arafat, the Jordanians tried to influence Fatah as a whole.

The Jordanians had much less success in the Arab world, however; in fact, with the exception of Egypt, Jordan failed to get an enthusiastic endorsement of its initiatives from a single Arab state. Iraq offered cautious endorsement, as did the Algerians, but the Saudis would not openly confront the Syrians over the king's diplomacy. Consequently, Hussein faced the difficult problem of turning a bilateral accord with Arafat into an agreement broadly endorsed within the Arab world. Fear of increased polarization, Syrian retaliation, and Israel's rejection, plus the equivocal U.S. response, made the key Arab states reluctant to support Hussein's initiative without first testing the waters.

How to handle the Syrians was another matter. In the wake of the PNC meeting in Amman and the February 11 accord, the Syrians launched a torrent of virulent rhetoric. "This conspiracy goes far beyond the Palestinian framework and falls within the framework of the big Camp David conspiracy against the Arab nation," commented the Syrian newspaper *Tishrin* in mid-February.[37] In March, a Palestine National Salvation Front composed of most of the PLO's constituent groups was formed in Damascus to oppose Arafat's policies. Over the next several months terrorist attacks commonly associated with pro-Syrian groups were launched against Jordanian interests in Europe.

In an effort to counter Syrian opposition and insulate himself against accusations that Jordan planned to cut a separate deal with the Israelis under U.S. auspices, Hussein continued to insist on an international conference that would offer Syria a seat at the negotiations. This was not a new idea, of course, but emphasizing it now and trying to persuade the United States (and the Soviet Union) to accept it was a ploy designed to protect Jordan's Arab flank. Whether Hussein was committed to convening a full-fledged international conference or merely sought an international umbrella to cover his entry into the negotiating process is not clear. One thing is certain, however: the king was not prepared to negotiate with the Israelis alone, without broad Arab and international backing. An international conference, then, was a way to compensate for the Arab support he did not yet have.

Hussein's decision in April 1985 to replace Prime Minister Obeidate with Zaid Rifai, a boyhood friend and close confidant, also indicated that the king was holding open the option of improved ties with Assad. Rifai ws reputed to have excellent contacts in Damascus, and was known to favor close relations with Syria. While no dramatic improvement in relations with Syria was anticipated (and none ensued) in the wake of the Rifai appointment, Hussein had clearly positioned himself for such an eventuality in the event the peace process collapsed further down the road. Nonetheless, it was difficult to see how an Assad-Hussein rapprochement could occur as long as the king continued to actively push his initiative with Arafat.

In the wake of Hussein's visit to Washington in late May 1985, it was still unclear in which direction Hussein intended to move, or what the fate of the king's Palestinian diplomacy would be. To date, Hussein's public acceptance of U.N. resolutions 242 and 338 on behalf of the PLO and his ambiguous statement on nonbelligerency with Israel have not provided the catalyst to move the peace process forward significantly. While Hussein's diplomatic initiatives have attracted considerable interest in Washington and pushed the Reagan administration to consider the sale of sophisticated military equipment to Jordan, they have failed to make a dramatic impression on Israel or to move the process along toward direct negotiations. Hussein's insistence on bringing the PLO into the process, or at minimum into a dialogue with the United States, combined with his need for an international conference have not been well received by a Labor-led National Unity government in Israel that would like to explore possibilities of negotiations with Jordan. Nor is the idea of a meeting between the United States and a joint Jordanian-Palestinian delegation attractive to an Israel fearful of "pre-negotiations" as well as of any U.S.-PLO dialogue.

Although it is clear that Hussein is committed to the principle of negotiations with Israel on the future of the West Bank and would like to see progress made in the future, he has not survived for thirty years by taking giant leaps in the dark. While Hussein's initiatives between 1982 and 1985 have been uncharacteristically assertive, they have been incremental and deliberate, leaving Jordan's options intact. Unless Hussein can find solutions to the two major problems blocking the road to direct negotiations—Palestinian representation and international support—he is unlikely to risk any solo initiatives. Even then, the Jordanians would be reluctant to commit themselves to open-ended negotiations with Israel until they had some assurance as to the outcome.

Despite all of these problems, however, the king probably believes there is still hope for progress. Indeed, a combination of circumstances—a humbled Arafat; a Labor-led Israeli government committed in principle to the idea of some territorial compromise; an American two-term president who has attached his name to a diplomatic initiative that accords Jordan the central role; and an October 1986 deadline when the Likud takes over the Prime Minister's office—have combined to produce a sense of urgency and to create environment with real opportunities for movement. Whether this mix of factors can actually lead to negotiations, however, may come to depend on Hussein and his willingness to take risks for a peace process whose outcome cannot be guaranteed. Whatever direction the king moves, however, one thing is certain: Hussein will continue to respect the limits and constraints that have kept him from negotiations with Israel but at the same time have helped him stay on the throne for so long.

NOTES

1. For an analysis of Jordan's economic growth and foreign economic dependence see Adam M. Garfinkle, "Jordanian Foreign Policy," *Current History*, January 1984, pp. 22–23.

2. Ibid.

3. Amman Domestic Service, 7 August 1982, *Foreign Broadcast Information Service, Daily Report—Middle East & Africa* (hereafter cited as *FBIS/MEA*), 12 August 1982:F2–5.

4. Ibid., 20 September 1982, *FBIS/MEA,* 21 September 1985:F1–7.

5. Ibid., 21 September 1982, *FBIS/MEA,* 21 September 1982:F1–7.

6. Ibid., 6 October 1982, *FBIS/MEA,* 7 October 1982:F-1.

7. Middle East South Asia Review, 12 October 1982, *FBIS/MEA,* 12 October 1982.

8. Radio Monte Carlo, 28 October 1982, *FBIS/MEA,* 28 October 1982:A-2.

9. Amman Domestic Service, 14 December 1982, *FBIS/MEA,* 15 December 1982:F-1.

10. MENA (Cairo), 29 December 1982, *FBIS/MEA,* 30 December 1982:A1–3.

11. *New York Times,* 24 December 1982, pp. 1, A-4.

12. Eric Rouleau, "The Future of the PLO," *Foreign Affairs,* Fall 1983:142–43.

13. Voice of Palestine (Algiers), 22 February 1983, *FBIS/MEA,* 24 February 1983:A-15.

14. 'Ukaz (Jidda), 15 February 1983, *FBIS/MEA,* 28 February 1983:F-1.

15. Rouleau, "Future of the PLO," pp. 151–52.

16. Amman Domestic Service, 10 April 1983, *FBIS/MEA,* 11 April 1983:F1–4.

17. *New York Times,* 12 April 1983, p. A-1.

18. Amman Domestic Service, 30 April 1983, *FBIS/MEA,* 2 May 1983:F1–5.

19. Ibid., Press Review, 7 June 1983, *FBIS/MEA,* 8 June 1983:F-2.

20. Ibid., 19 September 1983, *FBIS/MEA*:F-1.

21. *Le Monde* (Paris), 15 November 1983, *FBIS/MEA,* 16 November 1983:F-1.

22. Amman Television Service, 11 December 1983, *FBIS/MEA,* 13 December 1983:F-1.

23. *Jordan Times* (Amman), 22–23 December 1983, *FBIS/MEA,* 23 December 1983.

24. Ibid., 25 January 1984, *FBIS/MEA,* 26 January 1985:F-4.

25. *ar-Ray al-Amm* (Kuwait), 12 January 1984, *FBIS/MEA,* 16 January 1984: F-3.

26. QNA (Doha), 14 January 1984, *FBIS/MEA,* 16 January 1984:F-3.

27. BBC Television Network, 23 January 1984, *FBIS/MEA,* 24 January 1984: F-1.

28. *New York Times,* 15 March 1984, p. 1.

29. AFP (Paris), 15 September 1984, *FBIS/MEA,* 17 September 1984:F-1. See also Amman Domestic Service, 7 August 1984, *FBIS/MEA,* 8 August 1984:F-1.

30. Amman Television Service, 25 September 1984, *FBIS/MEA,* 25 September 1984:F-1.

31. Petra-JNA (Amman), 26 September 1984, *FBIS/MEA,* 2 September 1984: F-3.

32. Amman Domestic Service, 27 September 1984, *FBIS/MEA,* 27 September 1984:F-4.

33. *al-Hawadith* (London), 30 October 1984, *FBIS/MEA,* 31 October 1984:F-1– F-5.

34. *al-Dustur* (Amman), 30 October 1984, *FBIS/MEA,* 31 October 1984:F-1– F-5.

35. Amman Domestic Service, 22 November 1984, *FBIS/MEA,* 25 November 1984:A-13–A-18.

36. Ibid., 23 February 1985, *FBIS/MEA,* 25 February 1985:F-1.

37. SANA (Damascus), 13 February 1985, *FBIS/MEA,* 13 February 1985:H-1.

8

Palestinian Politics
after the Exodus from Beirut

Rashid Khalidi

I

THE RIVER OF EVENTS flows especially swiftly in the Middle East—or perhaps it only seems that way to those whose unenviable fate it is to analyze them. In the three years since 1982, Israel drove the PLO out of its long-established base in Lebanon, that organization was profoundly divided over fundamental questions of policy, and its mainstream wing came to an historic accommodation with Jordan. These are only the main outlines of a complex and often contradictory sequence of developments that includes many subplots of critical importance, including the continuing Palestinian role in Lebanon, the ambiguous nature of bilateral PLO relationships with such Arab powers as Egypt, Syria, and Jordan, and the shifting tide of public opinion in the various sectors of the Palestinian polity, whether inside Palestine or in the diaspora.

In an attempt to impose order on these events, this essay confines itself to dealing with the evolution of Palestinian politics in the aftermath of the 1982 war, with its focus on the policy developed by the PLO in the wake of that conflict. It begins with a look back at the alignment of forces within the movement on the eve of the war, continues with a brief review of the PLO's political stance before and during that conflict, and then assesses developments in the Palestinian arena since the war. Special attention will be paid to the split within Fatah; the shift of the mainstream PLO to a greater dependence on its constituency in Palestinian communities in the occupied territories, Jordan, and the Gulf; and the orientation of the policy followed by Yasser Arafat and the PLO leadership after the November 1984 Amman meeting of the Palestine National Council (PNC), including the February 1985 accord with Jordan.

II

On the eve of the 1982 war, the PLO's strategy had reached a dead end. Summed up in the metaphor of a gun in one hand and an olive branch in the other (which Yasser Arafat had used before the U.N. General Assembly in 1974), neither of these two components was functioning especially well. In practice, the gun had come to be confined to a growing semiregular military presence in south Lebanon in a basically defensive posture, and with increasingly poor relations with its primarily Shi'ite environment.[1] The olive branch referred to a diplomatic approach which, though it had scored gains, had still failed to affect the central balance between the PLO and Israel.

The pretense that PLO military forces had an offensive orientation was progressively undermined beginning in the mid-1970s. Among the landmarks in this process were the PLO pledge to the Lebanese government to cease offensive operations from Lebanon (made first in 1975 and repeated several times afterwards), and the ceasefire established under United Nations auspices in the wake of the 1978 Israeli invasion of south Lebanon. This self-prohibition was reiterated following another ceasefire in the wake of the five-month round of fighting initiated by the Begin government in March 1979. Yet another ceasefire was negotiated by U.S. envoy Philip Habib, the Saudis, and the U.N. in July 1981 after Israeli attacks on Lebanon led to cross-border exchanges of unprecedented ferocity. Palestinian attacks on Israel from areas other than Lebanon did continue sporadically throughout the pre-1982 period, as did resistance activity under occupation. But the former were often carried out by non-PLO or even anti-PLO formations, some of them acting under the inspiration of Arab regimes, while the latter was frequently either spontaneous or organized by autonomous groupings in the occupied territories. Moreover, all of these activities had at best a nuisance value in terms of their impact on Israel.

More significant, while at the same time considerably more vulnerable, was the PLO's military presence in south Lebanon. As was demonstrated during the nine days of cross-border fighting in 1981, the PLO had developed a certain capacity for sustained combat in-

volving artillery and rocket units as well as a competent logistical service to back them up, and had shown it could inflict meaningful losses
on Israel. Though by this point it did so only in response to Israeli-
initiated actions, by 1981 the PLO had revealed the kernel of a deterrent capability that was worrisome to Israeli planners. This was
unquestionably one of the most important immediate factors in precipitating the Israeli decision to invade Lebanon and uproot the
PLO.[2]

But the PLO military presence served other purposes than deterring Israel and defending the Palestinians against its attacks. It performed similar functions vis-à-vis the PLO's other rivals, such as
Syria and the Phalangist-dominated Lebanese militia. In addition, it
was a vital component—together with the PLO's large and growing
civilian infrastructure in Lebanon[3]—in another aspect of PLO strategy. This was diplomacy and information—the olive branch of Arafat's metaphor. This semiregular military identity gave weight and
substance to a PLO presence in fragmented Lebanon that served as a
sort of counter on the regional chessboard, and gave the PLO a measure of standing and importance in the game.

In effect, the PLO's strategy was a static one, for it had neither the
military power to coerce its opponents in Israel and the United States
to change their positions nor a diplomatic posture attractive enough
to lure them to the negotiating table. It was thus a strategy with a very
small stick and a tiny carrot. Moreover, in practice it rested almost
entirely on the PLO's presence in Lebanon. This presence was ex-
ceedingly vulnerable not only militarily but also politically in the face
of Israeli and Phalangist claims that the PLO was exploiting Lebanon
and exposing it to the full force of Israeli vengeance without Lebanon
(or indeed the Palestinians themselves) having the slightest hope of
gaining anything as a result of the costly exercise. Not surprisingly,
such propaganda had a deadly cumulative effect on Lebanese public
opinion. Ultimately, in any case, the PLO presence was not strong
enough to stand up to the kind of assault that Israel finally mounted
against it.

PLO leaders, knowing that they were vulnerable, increasingly
avoided certain kinds of overt provocation of Israel;[4] but they also
seem to have believed that Israel could not sustain the lengthy, costly
operation that, in their judgment, would be necessary to uproot the
PLO. In the short run, of course, they were terribly wrong, as was
demonstrated in the course of three bloody months during the sum-

mer of 1982. But three years after the events, it can be seen that in a certain sense they were right, and that the Begin government went beyond the limits of what the Israeli polity was prepared to tolerate. It was the great misfortune of the PLO, and indeed also of Lebanon, Israel, and the entire region, that Israel's leaders were able to do what they did notwithstanding this fact.

III

The constellation of forces within the PLO before the 1982 war, and its political posture, must be briefly reviewed if postwar developments are to make sense. This is especially important since the principal postwar divisions were present in embryo before the war, as were the positions of both the PLO mainstream and the opposition.

It has not been fully appreciated by most observers how radical a break with prior policies the PLO made beginning in 1974. In that year, the Palestine National Council (PNC) adopted resolutions calling for the establishment of a Palestinian entity alongside Israel. This was initially hedged around with so many conditions and phrased so opaquely that it could easily have been misunderstood by the uninitiated. But it was expressed with increasing clarity as time went on: for example, the term *national authority* of the 1974 text was replaced by the word *state* at the twelfth PNC in 1977, and a few more key changes were made in order to clarify the meaning of resolutions passed in the years that followed.[5]

If there were any doubt as to how fundamental a change this represented in comparison to the pre-1974 PLO position of calling for a secular democratic state in all of mandatory Palestine, it was necessary only to look at the intense inter-Palestinian debates of 1972–75 over this issue, or at how seriously the opposition, grouped after 1974 in the so-called Rejection Front, took this departure. Extreme rejectionist elements, allied in the mid-1970s with Iraq, went so far as to assassinate a number of PLO envoys abroad, accusing them of espousing "capitulationist" views which, in their eyes, involved both direct recognition of Israel and acceptance of a bi-state solution in Palestine.

The rejectionists were not entirely incorrect, of course, as interviews and statements by PLO leaders revealed over the years. Reluctant to accept the full implications of their stand, these leaders shied away from seeming to favor outright recognition of Israel as well as from the acceptance of Security Council resolution 242 (on the grounds it did not deal with the Palestine question per se). But by the time of the 1982 war, the PLO was fully committed to a negotiated peaceful solution of the crisis on a bi-state basis. And during the course of the war, it formalized this position by supporting a Franco-Egyptian draft resolution of June 1982 that proposed a simultaneous solution of the Lebanese crisis and the Arab-Israeli conflict.[6]

Drafted in close consultation with the PLO, this resolution would have accepted Security Council resolution 242, together with certain other United Nations resolutions more favorable to the Palestinians, as the basis of a Middle East peace settlement. It explicitly stressed the principle of peace in exchange for land, which is at the heart of resolution 242. At the same time, it added a call for the establishment of a Palestinian state and, finally, proposed a mechanism for the negotiation of the dispute between the Palestinians, the Israelis, and other parties under United Nations auspices. While stubborn U.S. opposition killed this initiative, preventing it from even being tabled in the Security Council, it was nevertheless an index of how far the PLO had come by 1982.

Just as interesting as the details of this proposal is the fact that by 1982 the opposition within the PLO to the idea of a Palestinian state existing next to Israel as the result of a peaceful settlement process had dwindled radically. The rejection front had in practice ceased to have any real meaning early in the 1975–76 Lebanese war, as pressing practical considerations brought all PLO groups close together against the common enemy. Even after that phase of the Lebanese conflict had ended, principled Palestinian opposition to the mainstream PLO line did not revive with anything like the force it had had before 1975. By 1978, the Popular Front for the Liberation of Palestine (PFLP), the only rejectionist group of any weight or substance (or with any popular support), had rejoined the PLO executive committee, and had reluctantly accepted the idea of a Palestinian state in the West Bank and Gaza Strip.[7]

Although there was enormous skepticism, even among avid supporters of the idea of such a Palestinian state, as to the likelihood of such a settlement coming about, it is remarkable how little opposition there was in principle to the idea within the ranks of the PLO on the eve of the 1982 war. Indeed, the primary objection to it was that it was impractical and hard to realize given the unfavorable balance of forces between the Palestinians and Israel.

There were cleavages within the Palestinian polity, however—

many of them important for an understanding of the post-1982 splits. The most significant, if perhaps the least visible, were within the core group of the PLO, Fatah. Many of these antedated the 1975–76 war, dating from the period of intense debate within the PLO over the idea of a West Bank/Gaza Strip state. Others went back to 1976 disputes over wartime strategy and policy toward Syria, while still others were related to the course which should be taken by the PLO in Lebanon. Their common denominator was that they pitted a somewhat more radical group, including many senior military officers and political cadres like Colonel Abu Musa (Sa'id Musa Maragha) and Colonel Abu Khalid al-'Amleh, against the traditional core leadership of Fatah.[8] Although most outsiders barely perceived the differences between the two sides on the eve of the 1982 war, they were significant enough to provide the foundations for the split within Fatah which ensued in mid-1983.

IV

The 1982 war had several important direct consequences for postwar PLO policy. These included the need to develop an alternative strategy after the collapse of the previous one (which had been based on the existence of a politico-military presence in Lebanon), and the need for a reassessment of the PLO's Arab alignments. It was generally felt among Palestinians after the defeat of 1982 that Lebanon as a "front" against Israel was hereafter closed to independent Palestinian action, and that this necessitated either finding a new front (perceived as unlikely) or developing an entirely new approach. There was some dissent from this way of posing the problem, with the Fatah dissidents arguing that Lebanon was still a viable arena for PLO action and with many Palestinians committed to the belief that resistance activity in the occupied territories could take up the slack. Nevertheless, this philosophy underlay mainstream PLO thinking and its search for a new approach.

As to the PLO's Arab alignments, the 1982 war left all Palestinians with an intense feeling of bitterness about the feeble effort of their Arab "brethren" during three months of Israeli assaults on Lebanon. This feeling was perhaps most intense with respect to Syria, notwithstanding the fact that Syria was the only Arab state whose forces fought in Lebanon (albeit for only two weeks of the ten-week war).

The sense that Syria had let down the PLO, had failed to take seriously the signs of an impending Israeli invasion, had reacted weakly when that invasion came, and was to some extent pleased at the blow suffered by the PLO; was current among Palestinians in the months after the war. (This fact helps to explain Arafat's insistence on avoiding Damascus after his evacuation from Beirut, and the simmering tension between the PLO and Syria in the months that followed.)

There was not much better feeling for the other Arab states, all of which were condemned as having been supine in the face of the Israeli attack and as having failed to exert the pressure on the United States that might have led to a more favorable outcome of the war. Paradoxically, one Arab state that came off relatively well in terms of Palestinian perceptions of its wartime performance was Egypt. To be sure, the post-Sadat leadership was still stigmatized by its separate settlement with Israel, which in Palestinian eyes was the sine qua non of the aggressive Likud policy in Lebanon since 1978; but Egypt's cosponsorship of the Franco-Egyptian draft resolution in 1982 was generally accepted as marking a clear departure from the Palestinian part of the Camp David formula.[9] Similarly, Egypt's refusal to change its position on the terms of the evacuation from Beirut (in striking contrast to the Saudis and Syrians, who accepted the Habib formula with what in Palestinian eyes was indecent alacrity), was also much appreciated.[10]

These were some of the factors, then, which precipitated the confusing series of moves and countermoves within the Palestinian polity in the period following the evacuation from Beirut. According to the Fatah opposition, which split from the leadership in mid-1983, Arafat and his closest colleagues were basically committed to a new approach even before the 1982 war. Described in Palestinian political parlance as the "Jordanian option," this involved a shift from the Lebanese theater to the Jordanian one. It had numerous implications, of course, including dependence on a Palestinian constituency in the occupied territories, Jordan, and the Gulf (rather than one in Lebanon and Syria); a willingness to alienate the Ba'ath regime in Damascus; and a reorientation away from armed struggle and toward a diplomatic approach. The defeat in Lebanon, they argued, simply provided PLO leaders with a welcome opportunity to follow through on these long-desired revisions of policy.

This argument oversimplifies the attitudes of the members of the core PLO leadership, and obscures in particular key differences be-

tween individual members of the Fatah central committee. While
some leaders, such as Abu Jihad (Khalil al-Wazir) and Abu Sa'id
(Khaled al-Hassan), were very much inclined to explore the Jordanian option, others, such as Abu Iyyad (Salah Khalaf) and Abu Lutf
(Faruq al-Qaddoumi), were more skeptical (and more concerned to
preserve links with Syria). All were restrained in their enthusiasm for
such an option by the knowledge that it would meet with intense opposition from Fatah, in other PLO groups, and from Syria. The Fatah
leadership was undoubtedly aware of the cohesiveness of the group
identified with Abu Musa that formed the core of the Fatah opposition;[11] they also knew that this group had links with leaders of other
more radical PLO groups, and was in contact with the Syrian leadership.

Before 1982, and indeed for many months afterwards, an appreciation of these facts served to restrain the Fatah leadership in its
drift toward a new orientation. But with the Fatah mutiny of the
spring of 1983, and the rapid and overt alignment of Syria and its subordinate groups within the PLO with the Fatah dissidents, all such
constraints on the freedom of action of the core Fatah leaders who
dominated the PLO gradually disappeared.

In principle, the Jordanian option dated back to well before 1985.
By the decision of the March 1979 meeting in Baghdad of Arab foreign
and finance ministers, Jordan and the PLO were given joint responsibility for supervising the distribution of Arab League funds to support the people and institutions of the occupied territories. A Palestinian-Jordanian joint committee was set up, and successfully
carried out this function in spite of the obstacles erected by the Israeli
occupation authorities. The Palestinian side of this joint committee
was headed by Abu Jihad, who thus came to have something of a base
in Jordan and a stake in good relations with the Jordanian regime. Because of the unexceptionable purpose of the joint committee—supporting the well-being of the Palestinian population under occupation—until 1982 the Fatah opposition and other critics of the
Jordanian option were limited in what they could say against this approach, although they remained strongly dissatisfied with it.

Politically more significant than the joint committee was a key
resolution of the sixteenth PNC held in Algiers in February 1983. For
the first time, the council called for a Palestinian-Jordanian confederation as the framework within which Palestinian self-determination
in the West Bank and Gaza Strip was to be exercised.[12] This was a ma-

jor if unheralded new departure for the PLO, which had hitherto called for a completely independent Palestinian state with no reference to any special relationship with Jordan. Surprisingly enough, in spite of some opposition at the Algiers meeting—notably from factions aligned with Syria—it was passed by the PNC with the approval of most of the PLO's constituent groups. This resolution was to be the foundation for the similar resolution passed by the seventeenth PNC held in Amman eighteen months later. In exchange for the approval of the concept of a confederation with Jordan, however, Arafat was obliged to make concessions on language dealing with the Reagan plan (which was termed an unsuitable basis for a Middle East settlement), on ties with Egypt, and on contacts with the Israelis.

Before the policy switch to overt espousal of the Jordanian option could be regarded as complete, however, two more important events must be discussed. The first was the PLO's expulsion from north Lebanon by Syria and its Palestinian proxies in December 1983. The second was the failure of repeated attempts over the months which followed to reconcile the Fatah leadership with some of the other groups in the PLO, notably the PFLP and the Democratic Front for the Liberation of Palestine (DFLP). By the fall of 1984 it had become clear that, in spite of the accords reached at Aden and Algiers with these groups, no meaningful agreement was possible. In consequence, the Fatah leadership finally decided to hold the long-delayed seventeenth meeting of the PNC in Amman in November 1984. A few months later, the Arafat-Hussein accord of February 1985 was reached, formalizing the PLO's new approach.

V

A full analysis of the two episodes that were necessary prerequisites for the Amman PNC—the Tripoli incidents and the Aden-Algiers accords—would be both lengthy and tedious. Both involved a complex set of motivations on the part of all of the various protagonists, and both went through numerous stages over a period of many months. Nevertheless, it is necessary at least to underline the role each played in paving the way for the overt shift in PLO policy represented in the Amman PNC and the Hussein-Arafat accord that followed.

The dramatic expulsion of Yasser Arafat and the PLO forces under his command from Tripoli in December 1983 was the culmination of a process which had begun in the spring and summer of that year. At that time dissident Fatah forces, backed by their pro-Syrian Palestinian allies and strongly supported by Syria, had gradually narrowed the zone of operations and freedom of action of the forces loyal to the Fatah leadership in the Bekaa Valley and north Lebanon. But while the desultory fighting in the Bekaa and the slow spread of the area controlled by the Fatah rebels under Colonel Abu Musa and Colonel Abu Khalid al-'Amleh were closely watched by Palestinians everywhere, they had nothing like the dramatic impact of the Tripoli incidents.

There are many reasons for this, but two of them are of paramount importance: first, the fighting at Tripoli involved the city itself and two adjacent Palestinian camps, Nahr al-Bared and Baddawi, which suffered heavy artillery bombardment; and second, the controversial figure of Arafat himself was involved in the fighting, the negotiations, and the eventual evacuation. The siege and bombardment of Tripoli and the camps played a major role in turning Palestinian and Arab public opinion against the Fatah rebels and their Syrian backers. The departure of Arafat and his forces from Tripoli by sea after a lengthy battle, little more than a year after they had been forced to leave Beirut by the Israelis in superficially similar circumstances, reinforced this effect, which was magnified by the fact that the PLO leader had already been expelled once by the Syrian authorities—from Damascus in June 1983.

Critics have pointed to Arafat's return to Tripoli in the late fall of 1983, and his insistence on having a "last stand" there against the Syrians and their allies, as a cynical maneuver designed to force his opponents into attacking him.[13] In the same way, it is argued, Arafat in effect provoked the Syrians with statements and actions in the months preceding his June 1983 expulsion from Syria: ostentatiously refusing to come to Damascus after leaving Beirut, constantly downplaying if not actually denigrating the role of Syria during the 1982 war, and generally declining to give the Syrian regime the deference it considered its due from PLO leaders.

There may be some truth to these accusations; certainly, Arafat was unwise in his treatment of the Syrians. For however unshakable their intention to remove him from leadership of the PLO may have been—and this has always been the conviction of Arafat and many other PLO leaders—there seems to have been little point either in provoking them gratuitously or in providing them with specious pretexts for actions they were going to take in any case. On the other hand, it is hard to see what else Arafat and his colleagues were expected to do in the face of the overt Syrian backing of the Fatah dissidents. Moreover, there can be little doubt that once the dissidents were firmly identified in the public mind with Syria, they lost all their legitimacy and most of their credibility. There was thus a certain oblique logic to Arafat's accusations of Syrian complicity in the Fatah mutiny from an early stage, although such behavior certainly exacerbated relations with Syria in the days before he was forcibly put on a plane by a junior Syrian officer at Damascus airport. Similarly, the action of the dissidents, backed by Syrian artillery, in shelling Tripoli, was the best propaganda Arafat could have wished for.

Riding on a wave of Palestinian popular sympathy in the occupied territories; in the Tripoli camps, where rebel leaders were manhandled by furious residents; and even in the Palestinian camps in Damascus, where posters of Arafat could be seen in shops, homes, and offices, the Palestinian leader made a surprising move upon his departure by sea from Tripoli. He stopped in Egypt—his first visit there since Sadat announced before a 1977 National Assembly session attended by Arafat that he, Sadat, was willing to go to Jerusalem. In Cairo, the PLO leader met with Egyptian President Hosni Mubarak.

Although this action may have cost Arafat some of his new-won sympathy in Palestinian public opinion (which still regarded the Egyptian regime as beyond the pale), it was yet based on a certain logic. Egypt had been supportive in 1982, and had been even more so in 1983 during the Tripoli fighting when it sent supplies to Arafat and helped to protect his withdrawal from northern Lebanon. Strategically, moreover, this move made ample sense in terms of the diplomatic situation the PLO found itself in. After its defeat in northern Lebanon, at a time when it was confronted with implacable Syrian hostility, and the PLO was unable to depend on the Saudis, who were as always supremely responsive to the mood of Damascus; or on Baghdad, which had impaled itself on the sharp point of Iranian power by its foolish decision to go to war; or on Moscow, which as always was unwilling to take any step which fundamentally jeopardized its relations with Damascus, however much it may have sympathized with Arafat's predicament. In such circumstances, a tilt toward Egypt made sense—especially in view of the fact that it was highly compatible with the Jordanian option, which depended to a great extent on achieving a change in the American point of view. But at the same

time, it was difficult for many Palestinians to accept a meeting with
an Egyptian leader whose regime was still tied to Israel by a peace
treaty, however cold that peace may have become after the invasion
of Lebanon. This point was to be a central obstacle to the Fatah leadership's efforts to bring together the main PLO groups behind a development of the idea of confederation with Jordan, first put forward
at the Algiers PNC.

The effort to negotiate a formula for a new PLO strategy to be unveiled at the seventeenth session of the PNC that would be acceptable
to the PFLP, the DFLP, and the Palestinian Communist Party (grouped
together in what was called the Democratic Alliance) continued for
the better part of ten months. At the outset, the effort was hampered
by the outcry over Arafat's visit to Egypt, which the PFLP violently
opposed and about which even some members of the Fatah Central
Committee had grave reservations. At a later stage, after extensive
mediation by the Algerian and South Yemeni governments and a
number of Arab communist parties, an agreement was reached in
Aden and later further elaborated in Algiers.[14] This agreement would
have provided for a more collective PLO leadership, and some reduction in the power of the chairman of the executive committee through
the creation of new offices of vice-chairmen and of a permanent sec-
retariat for the executive committee. It would also have given the PLO
central council executive functions in addition to its consultative
ones, limited PLO contacts with Egypt until the latter had moved further away from the Camp David approach, and laid the basis for a rapprochement with Damascus. Most important to Fatah, the accords
set September 15, 1984, as the deadline for a meeting of the PNC, at
which it was virtually certain that Arafat and his colleagues would
have a majority.

There was much recrimination afterwards about responsibility
for the failure to implement these accords. In the end many factors
were responsible. However, more than anything else, it was Syrian
pressure on Algeria—the preferred venue for the PNC meeting and a
key mediator—and on the PFLP, which seems to have realized that
Fatah got the better of the deal at Aden and Algiers, that led to the
breakdown.[15] In an apparent reaction to the failure, Arafat and his Fatah central committee colleagues called for a meeting of the PNC in
Amman. To be sure, this is perhaps what Arafat and some of his allies
had wanted all along. But in the event, he had the support of the core
Fatah leadership, which had been eager for a reconciliation with the

Democratic Alliance—and he could sincerely claim that he had tried all possible avenues toward securing an agreement with the other PLO factions.

VI

What was important at Amman was not the resolutions, which differed little from those approved in Algiers;[16] the differences lay in the venue, the participants, and the absentees. The venue was important because it marked the first time since 1970 that a PNC meeting was held in the Jordanian capital. For many delegates and observers, it was their first visit there since that time. Not surprisingly, detailed security arrangements had to be worked out to allow for the presence of PLO cadres whose entry into Jordan would otherwise have been prohibited for political reasons, or who were under sentence by Jordanian courts.

The venue was also important because of the symbolism involved in holding a PNC in Amman in the face of desperate Syrian attempts to abort the meeting. These efforts went so far as the issuance of veiled threats by the Syrian president during a visit to Algeria in late August 1983. In effect, the PLO and the Jordanians were defying Damascus by holding the meeting not only against Syrian wishes but in Amman—a daring undertaking indeed in view of the accretion of Syrian power in the wake of the U.S.-Israeli debacle in Lebanon.

Finally, and most significantly, the venue was important since it meant that the PLO had made a strategic decision to follow the course of the Jordanian option after years of deliberation and intense internal debate. And the implication was that this time, unlike April 1983 when Yasser Arafat and King Hussein had made an abortive attempt to come to an agreement, such a line of policy would first be submitted to the PNC, the largest and most representative Palestinian political forum, to receive the sanction of popular legitimacy. And all of this was being done, furthermore, in the country that contained the largest concentration of Palestinians outside of Palestine itself, and which was physically the closest state to the occupied West Bank.

The nature of both the participants and absentees was also important, for a number of reasons. The latter included not only the Syrian-line factions, including the Fatah rebels, grouped together in the so-called National Alliance. More important, the absentees included

the groups of the Democratic Alliance, which were negotiating with
the Fatah leadership until the very eve of the PNC session, and whose
most prominent leaders, Dr. George Habash and Naef Hawatmeh, flew
to Moscow while it was in session. The failed negotiations resulted in
recrimination between partners in the Democratic Alliance, with the
DFLP accusing the PFLP of partial responsibility for the nonimple-
mentation of the Aden-Algiers accords, and the PFLP for its part laying the blame on the Fatah leadership.[17] Several DFLP and Palestinian
Communist party PNC delegates were in Amman and indeed participated in the council's opening session, but most withdrew before the
quorum was taken.

It was over the issue of the quorum that perhaps the most significant and dramatic event of the seventeenth PNC took place. There
had been great tension over the question of whether a quorum of two-
thirds of all eligible members would be assembled, and thus whether
the seventeenth session would take place in Amman at all and have
the requisite legitimacy. In the event, in spite of the absence of pro-
Syrian and Democratic Alliance delegates as well as a large number of
independents, a quorum was narrowly achieved. There were complaints later from opposition groups as to the manner in which this
was done, and some of the PLO leadership's maneuvers were probably
questionable (while others simply constituted debatable parliamentary practice). But there can be little doubt that the overwhelming
majority of the members of the PNC were there, some of them in spite
of determined Syrian attempts to prevent their appearance.

Even more significant was the telecasting of almost the entire
PNC proceedings live on Jordanian television for the better part of the
eight days the council was in session. Consequently, the proceedings
were seen not only throughout Jordan, but also and more important
throughout virtually all of Israel, and the occupied West Bank and
Gaza Strip whose Palestinian population was extremely interested in
the proceedings. The PLO leadership was thus presented with an un-
paralleled opportunity to reach out to the Palestinian people, including—significantly—those key segments of the Palestinian population that the leadership envisioned as the core of its constituency for
its new approach along the lines of the Jordanian option: the populace of the occupied territories and Jordan.

Viewers in these areas had a chance to watch PLO leaders they
had previously only read about in the unfriendly Jordanian and Israeli press, or perhaps seen fleetingly on the television news. Now

they appeared for days on end, debating, making speeches, taking part in parliamentary maneuvers, and otherwise showing themselves as familiar and quite human politicians engaged in an exercise permitted neither in the occupied territories nor in Jordan itself: the free and open debate of major political issues. The impact was enormous, and provoked the Syrians and the Palestinian opposition to attempt to match the Jordanian TV spectacle with Damascus television broadcasts of press conferences, speeches, and responses to points being made by speakers in Amman. It was unrivaled political theater, and the end effect almost certainly reinforced the impression Arafat and his colleagues wanted to give: that they were the true leaders of the Palestinian people.

In addition to who was or was not at the seventeenth PNC and where it was held, what was said there was important, too. The resolutions themselves, differed little from those of earlier councils, largely due to the need to avoid the appearance of any sharp heretical break with the past that could be exploited by the Syrians and the opposition. (Hence the call for the continuation of a policy of "armed struggle.")[18] But in addition to the resolutions, the participants in the seventeenth PNC expressed themselves in a number of other ways, including debate on the floor, procedural maneuvers at various stages of the proceedings, and formal speeches.[19]

Perhaps the strongest impression that emerges from all of these forms of expression is that the PNC constituted more than simply an endorsement of the leadership of Yasser Arafat and the core group in the Fatah central committee that led the PLO in the face of challenges to their authority from within and without the Palestinian polity. For the PNC session certainly was an endorsement, with the 268 delegates and hundreds of observers enthusiastically responding to what was said about Palestinian decision-making independent of "external" (read: Syrian) influence, applauding vigorously the speeches made by members of the large Egyptian delegation,[20] and rejecting Arafat's resignation of the post of chairman of the PLO executive committee. But in addition, what was said and what was not said also revealed the nature of the popular constraints on Arafat and the PLO leadership. Clearly sounded in much of the speech-making and debate (and implicit in much of the rest) was the theme that the PLO and its leadership represented the Palestinian people, but only so long as they continued to discharge this responsibility themselves. No support was expressed either directly or indirectly for the idea of the PLO delegating its authority to other parties, such as Jordan, in the context of negotiations.

Moreover, there was a clear insistence that a final regional settlement must include a separate, independent Palestinian political entity on the West Bank and Gaza Strip within the context of the envisioned confederation between a Palestinian state and Jordan. Speakers and other participants at the PNC laid much more stress on these two points than on such procedural matters as the issues of Security Council resolution 242 or the form and context of the negotiations for a settlement. These considerations were not ignored: it was simply that the others were considered of the utmost importance and received the most attention. And while this was a healthy democratic expression of what is undoubtedly the overwhelming feeling of Palestinians, it did serve to constrain what the PLO leadership could do with the mandate it received in Amman.

In the end, the PNC marked a step forward for the PLO in at least two ways. First, in spite of the new division it introduced into Palestinian ranks, it signified the emergence of a willingness to abandon the principle of consensus and unanimity in favor of that of majority rule. In practice, this meant a move away from the immobility of the past, when a minority could paralyze action by refusing to give its consent to a given proposition or initiative. The Fatah leadership was in effect saying that it considered the factions closely aligned with Damascus in the National Alliance as beneath notice, and that while the support of the Democratic Alliance was desirable it was not worth the price of freezing all Palestinian political and institutional activity until their wishes had been satisfied. This was a momentous step, as Arafat and the Fatah leadership for the first time in more than a decade abandoned the coalition tactics that had so hampered any decisive response to certain events while at the same time providing only a modicum of Palestinian unanimity. Although places were left vacant for the absent groups on the executive committee, it was made abundantly clear the PLO could and would manage without them if necessary.

The second advance was the new focus by the PLO on the wishes and aspirations of the population of the occupied territories. While it is wrong to suggest that these had been totally ignored in the past by the Palestinian national movement in exile, it was certainly true that the Palestinians in the diaspora were now both better represented and better able to express their desires in PLO forums. These problems could not be corrected in their entirety in Amman, for PNC delegates from the West Bank and Gaza Strip—who most probably would have overwhelmingly supported Arafat's line—were forbidden to participate by the occupation authorities (as indeed they had been in all previous PNCs). But the Amman PNC certainly came closer to expressing a broad spectrum of Palestinian views than had most previous sessions.

The main reason for this was political. For the Jordanian option, with its necessary concomitant of cooperation with the Hashemite regime, was naturally unattractive to those Palestinians living far away from occupied Palestine. Many of these had bitter memories of Amman; others had few or no links with Jordan, and as a result could not appreciate the importance of such links to West Bankers and Gazans. But the situation was different for the Palestinians in the occupied territories: they realized, albeit unenthusiastically in some cases, that their main objective—ending the occupation— would be difficult to achieve without some degree of formal cooperation with Jordan. This was due in part to Israeli and U.S. insistence on a Jordanian role, and in part to the practical necessity of links between two Palestinian populations separated only by a narrow river.

Thus, while nearly all Palestinians had negative feelings about the Hashemites (just as they did about the Syrian Ba'ath regime), those in the occupied territories conceded that, due to Jordan's control of entry and exit from the West Bank, and the presence of over a million of their relatives in Jordan, some links with Jordan were inevitable even for a fully independent West Bank and Gaza Strip Palestinian state. The problem of ending the occupation was also a more pressing and immediate problem for them than for Palestinians in the Gulf and other distant parts of the diaspora.

VII

This same sensitivity to the differing needs and outlooks of the two elements of the PLO's constituency—those under Israeli occupation and those in the diaspora—marked the organization's behavior during the process of negotiation of the Hussein-Arafat agreement of February 11, 1985. The accord, which provided for a common PLO-Jordanian negotiating position and a joint delegation at the projected international conference to resolve the Middle East crisis, also affirmed the principle of a Palestinian-Jordanian federation involving two sovereign states as the hoped-for outcome of such a negotiation.[21] Further, it attempted to leap over the procedural hurdle involving resolution 242 by stressing the principle of land for peace that formed the central focus of that resolution, while affirming that the two sides accepted *all* U.N. resolutions—that is, both 242 and others more favorable to the Palestinian position.

There was a long process of internal Palestinian debate over the accord, which was announced during King Fahd's visit to Washington. As usual, contradictory statements were reported, and the customary confusion erupted.[22] But when the smoke cleared, it became apparent that the PLO and Jordan had agreed to something along the lines set down above, and that this accord was durable enough to withstand such confusion and disagreements, at least for a period of several months. It also withstood intense Syrian and Palestinian opposition pressure, expressed in the murder of deported Hebron Mayor Fahd al-Qawasmeh soon after his election to the PLO executive committee and in the formation of a Palestinian "National Salvation Front" by opposition groups in Damascus.[23]

Little can be said at this stage about the results of the approach adopted by the Amman PNC and represented in the Hussein-Arafat accord. In view of the U.S. and Israeli reactions, which ranged from indifference to hostility, and the state of disarray in the Arab world (characterized by strong Syrian opposition and little enthusiastic support elsewhere), it seems doubtful whether this approach can produce any results. Nevertheless, there are some clear indicators of Palestinian feeling about this question, including demonstrations of support for Arafat in the refugee camps in Lebanon and the elections to the Bir Zeit University student council and the Jerusalem Electric Company workers' union directorate, in both of which Arafat supporters won clear victories.[24] These and other signs indicate that a majority of Palestinians favor the Jordanian option.

Even among its supporters, however, there is profound skepticism concerning the possibility of the accord producing any substantive results. Most Palestinians would seem to be supportive of the mainstream PLO leadership, and willing to give them the chance to bring the approach they have chosen to fruition; however, this is not an uncritical support. There was intense criticism at the Amman PNC of past failings of the PLO, and there is similar criticism in the camps in Lebanon today—some of it even bluntly conveyed in the PLO's central organ, *Filastin al-Thawra,* in interviews and reportage from Palestinian camps in Beirut and South Lebanon.[25]

In the words of Abu Lutf, implicitly responding to such criticism, "Neither I, Abu Ammar, Abu Iyyad nor anyone else are without error."[26] What is politically important is that among Palestinians in general, although this generation of leaders is seen to have made many errors there is yet perceived to be no serious alternative to these men, who have, after all, constituted the core leadership of the Palestinian national movement for nearly twenty years.

NOTES

1. For more on the predicament of the PLO in Lebanon before 1982, see R. Khalidi, *Under Siege: PLO Decisionmaking during the 1982 War* (New York: Columbia University Press, 1986), ch. 1.

2. Ibid. See also Ze'ev Schiff and Ehud Ya'ari, *Israel's Lebanon War* (New York: Simon and Schuster, 1984), pp. 35–38, where the PLO is described as having "scored an impressive military achievement" in July 1981 that deeply disturbed Israeli decision-makers.

3. See Cheryl Rubenberg, *The PLO: Its Institutional Infrastructure* (Belmont, Mass.: Institute for Arab Studies, 1983); and R. Khalidi, "The Palestinians in Lebanon: The Social Repercussions of Israel's Invasion," *Middle East Journal* 38, no. 2 (Spring 1984):255–58.

4. Schiff and Ya'ari, *Israel's Lebanon War,* pp. 81–94, provides many details of the PLO's circumspection in this regard.

5. The relevant texts for the first through thirteenth PNC sessions are in Rashid Hamid, *Munadhamat al-tahrir al-filistiniyya* [The Palestine Liberation Organization] (Beirut: Palestine Research Center, 1977). English translations of PNC resolutions from the fourth session in 1967 through the fifteenth in 1981 can be found in the annual *International Documents on Palestine,* published by the Institute for Palestine Studies from 1970–1983. For an informed discussion of this subject, see Helena Cobban, *The Palestinian Liberation Organization: People, Power and Politics* (Cambridge: Cambridge University Press, 1984), pp. 10–18.

6. The text of this draft can be found in the *Revue d'Etudes Palestiniennes,* no. 5 (Autumn 1982), p. 145.

7. This process paralleled a decline in the influence of the PFLP and its leader, Dr. George Habash, throughout the 1970s. In the words of Cobban, *Palestinian Liberation Organization,* by the early 1980s Habash appeared to be "a respected elder stateman under the patronage of the Fatah bosses" (p. 15). Several years later, such a description no longer seems accurate.

8. Both men were former Jordanian Army officers who had come over to the PLO at the height of the 1970 fighting in Amman. They had been the main field commanders during the 1975–76 war, the former in the Sidon area and the latter in the Upper Metn. Popular with their men, both were eased out of senior commands after 1976. They and many other former Jordanian Army officers opposed the "Jordanian option" and the idea of a West Bank/Gaza Strip Palestinian state, although their opposition to the latter had waned somewhat by 1982.

9. This was stated explicitly to PLO envoys at the U.N. by senior Egyptian diplomats during the discussions over the Franco-Egyptian draft resolution at the height of the 1982 war. Khalidi, *Under Siege*, p. 149 n.42.

10. Ibid.

11. This group's importance within Fatah was shown during the movement's fourth Congress in 1980 when it was instrumental in the election of two new central committee members, Majid Abu Sharar (killed in Rome in 1981) and Qadri (Samih Abu Kweik), currently a leader of the Fatah dissidents. After several years without holding a major command, Col. Abu Musa was appointed deputy director of PLO operations in 1980—a move that could have been meant to appease him.

12. The resolutions of the sixteenth PNC are reproduced in Cobban, *Palestinian Liberation Organization*, pp. 264–66.

13. For an example of this critical attitude, see the hostile questioning of Abu Iyyad on this point by 'Adel Ilyas of the Kuwaiti paper *al-Qabas*, in *Foreign Broadcast Information Service, Daily Report—Middle East & Africa* (hereafter cited as *FBIS/MEA*), 8 May 1985:A-3.

14. The Aden-Algiers accords were hammered out after a lengthy series of meetings in the two capitals, culminating in a draft initialed by Fatah and the groups of the Democratic Alliance in late June 1984, followed on July 13 by the "final" agreement; see *FBIS/MEA*, 28 June 1985:A-1–A-2 and 29 June 1985:A-1. There was a series of further meetings between the two sides in Algiers for implementation of the accords in the months that followed, but these proved fruitless.

15. At the end of August 1983, Syrian President Hafiz al-Assad made the first trip outside of his country since his recent illness, visiting Libya and Algeria. According to PLO and Algerian sources, Assad put strong pressure on Algerian president Chadli ben Jedid to retract his offer to host the PNC in Algiers. (Personal interviews, Tunis, 29 August 1984.)

16. For the political statement and resolutions of the seventeenth PNC, see *FBIS/MEA*, 30 November 1984:A-1–A-3 and 3 December 1984:A-2–A-6.

17. As a result, the DFLP froze its participation in its joint command with the PFLP. It laid "primary responsibility" for the situation on the National Alliance, adding that "the PFLP did not take the positive stand required by the critical circumstances" by evading its commitment to the Aden-Algiers provision concerning the deadline for the holding of the PNC (*FBIS/MEA*, 21 November 1985:A-4). Habash blamed the crisis on "Arafat and his Central Committee" (ibid.). The DFLP later affirmed the legitimacy of the Amman PNC (*FBIS/MEA*, 25 November 1985:A-2).

18. The desire to avoid exacerbating relations with Syria was manifest throughout the PNC meeting, in spite of the sharp rhetoric heard on the floor and the presence of members of the Syrian opposition (one of whose leaders, Jasim 'Alwan, was allowed to speak to the council). An example of this desire, on the first day of substantive debates, was the rejection of a motion to discuss the actions of some of the dissident PLO

leaders. If this had been allowed, it would have opened the floodgates for attacks on Syria, and set the tone of the entire session.

19. The flavor of debate and maneuvering on the floor is best conveyed by some of the reports of such foreign correspondents as Eric Rouleau (*Le Monde*, 23 November 1985:1–2; 25–26 November 1984:20), and by the Amman press—especially *al-Ra'i* and *The Jordan Times*.

20. The Egyptian delegation of 160, the largest at Amman, included representatives of the government, the National Assembly, all political parties, unions and professional bodies, and popular groupings. While the speech of the head of the Egyptian delegation, the Deputy Speaker of the Egyptian National Assembly, Mahmud Dabbur, was well received, the most enthusiastic reception went to that of the head of the Egyptian lawyers guild, a prominent opponent of the Sadat regime, who received several standing ovations.

21. The text of the Hussein-Arafat agreement was supposed to have been kept secret, and was therefore never formally released. Nevertheless, different versions of it were leaked to the press. For one such version, see *The Washington Post*, 13 February 1985, pp. A-1, A-17. Two weeks after the meeting, a Jordanian minister released a text (*FBIS/MEA*, 25 February 1985). For a "Palestinian version," see *FBIS/MEA*, 26 February 1985:A-5.

22. The confusion was provoked by the PLO leadership's old habit of airing their differences in public. See, for example, Radio Monte Carlo interviews with Abu Lutf and Abu Iyyad, *FBIS/MEA*, 14 February 1985:A-1–A-2; 15 February 1985:A-1; and 28 February 1985:A-2–A-4.

23. This grouping was formed in late March 1985, but its impact was diluted by the long delay in its formation and by the refusal to join of a number of PLO independents, as well as both the DFLP and the Palestinian Communist party. The latter opposed Arafat's moves, but apparently wanted to avoid formalizing the split with him. For the Front's program, see *FBIS/MEA*, 26 March 1985:A-7.

24. The election results are reported in *FBIS Middle East and Africa*, 23 January 1985:I-8. Demonstrations of support, such as banners in the streets of camps and pictures of Arafat in homes and offices, can be followed in reportages with pictures in the PLO central organ, *Filastin al-Thawra*; e.g., no. 550, March 23, 1985, "Mukhayyamat Sur: 'La ya khalti, Abu 'Ammar ma qassar'" (The Tyre Camps: 'No auntie, Abu 'Ammar did not let us down'), pp. 10–13, no. 551, March 30, 1985, "*Filastin al-Thawra* fi Burj al-Barajneh: Nahnu ma' 'Arafat liannana ma' al-qarar al-mustaqil" (*Filastin al-Thawra* in Burj al-Barajneh: We are with 'Arafat because we are with the independent decision), pp. 14–19.

25. See, for example, *Filastin al-Thawra*, no. 547, 2 March 1985, "'Ain al-Hilweh yukhaib amal al-a'da'" ['Ain al-Hilwah disappoints the hopes of enemies], pp. 31–33; ibid., no. 548, 9 March 1985, "*Filastin al-Thwara* fi mukhayyamay 'Ain al-Hilweh wal-Miye wa-Miye" [*Filastin al-Thawra* in 'Ain al-Hilweh and Miye wa-Miye camps], pp. 14–21; and ibid., no. 549, 16 March 1985, "Yawm al-mar'a fi mukhayyam Shatila" [Women's day in Shatila camp], pp. 14–15.

26. *FBIS/MEA*, 1 May 1985:A-3. For a detailed self-criticism of the PLO's actions in Lebanon before the 1982 war, its military strategy, and other subjects, see 'Adel Ilyas' interview with Abu Iyyad cited in note 13 above.

9

Israel Since the Lebanon War

David Pollock

T HE THREE YEARS between the Israeli invasion of Lebanon in June 1982 and the withdrawal of the last major remaining Israeli combat units from that country in June 1985 represent a convenient if somewhat arbitrary specimen of Israeli foreign policy in operation. It is convenient, because those years appear to encompass the beginning and end of a dramatic military and political adventure. But the time frame is also artificial, because the issues that produced the war in Lebanon are still unresolved, and because other, even more basic issues temporarily eclipsed by the Lebanese drama have since returned to the fore. In any case, the period is especially interesting because it offers an unusually vivid demonstration of the links between Israeli foreign and domestic policy.

This chapter will attempt to put the entire controversial period in perspective. In order to do so, it will look first at the background of Israeli foreign policy before the war in Lebanon, next at Israeli policy during and just after that war, and then at the development of some of the other major issues that simultaneously confronted the Jewish state. This will be followed by a brief concluding analysis of the underlying trends in Israeli policy revealed during the above episodes, and of the country's foreign-policy prospects in the light of the preceding discussion.

The general argument is that, for all the sound and fury of the Lebanese war itself and of its various apologists and critics, Israel's international position today is very little different from what it was before the war began. In this connection, two difficulties must be acknowledged at the outset. One is the intensely partisan (and therefore selective, if not overtly biased) nature of much of the reportage about Israeli policy in general and about its policy toward Lebanon in particular—reportage that provides the raw material for the analysis presented here. This is a problem not just of critical evaluation of sources, but also of inherently uncertain judgments about events that have yet to run their course, answers to hypothetical questions about what might have been, and expert opinion in matters where the experts themselves disagree. The only solution to this problem is a combination of emotional detachment and factual detail, plus a healthy dose of humility in undertaking the analyst's task.

The other, more substantive difficulty is the almost irresistible temptation for outside analysts to impose artificial order on actual disarray. In other words, there is a tendency to reason backwards, from the observable behavior of a government to some coherent, long-term strategy, when in fact the policies of the Israeli (or any other) government are often improvised and perhaps not fully rational responses to changing internal pressures and external events. On this issue, the argument developed here is that the truth, as is so often the case in the Middle East, lies somewhere in between. On Lebanon, the Israeli government started out with a grand strategy and ended up pursuing ever more ad hoc and reactive policies; but on other fundamental international issues, conventional wisdom to the contrary notwithstanding, Israel managed to maintain a fairly consistent policy—if only one of standing still.

Background of Israeli Policy

In one sense, the background of Israel's foreign policy over the past three years lies in the domestic political shifts that in 1977 elected Menachem Begin and the Likud Party to power in Jerusalem for the first time and returned them to office in 1981.[1] In another, deeper sense, however, the remote background of Israel's recent policies must be sought in the legacy of the entire decade after the previous Arab-Israeli war, in 1973. That war began the process of Israeli withdrawal from territory captured in 1967 in return for progress toward peace with Egypt—the one front where the two governments in question were equally willing to make that exchange.

On the other fronts there was, as Israel viewed the situation, both much less geographical room for maneuver and much greater internal political pressure against territorial concessions. The policies of Israel's potential interlocutors on those other fronts were likewise prob-

lematic: Syria was in no hurry to make peace with Israel, even in exchange for the Golan Heights, while Jordan's interest in negotiating
the return of the occupied West Bank was complicated by the role of
the PLO, anointed by Arab consensus at the 1974 Rabat summit as
the "sole legitimate representative of the Palestinian people" but rejected by Israel. The result was prolonged stalemate on the northern
and eastern fronts, even as the peace process with Israel's Egyptian
neighbor to the south proceeded fitfully to its conclusion.

In this sense, Begin's first electoral triumph marked a shift in emphasis and degree (but not in kind) from Israel's basic policy in the
aftermath of the October War. Israel now displayed a willingness, in
response to Sadat's sensational trip to Jerusalem, to return the entire
Sinai peninsula in exchange for fullfledged peace with Egypt—and a
categorical insistence on retaining Israeli control over the entire West
Bank, henceforth officially referred to by the Biblical appellation of
Judea and Samaria.

Almost immediately after his election, Begin made a ceremonial
visit to a Jewish settlement in that area, and soon afterward the new
Likud government formally authorized three existing colonies there.
These early moves were largely symbolic, but statements by various
officials, including then Minister of Agriculture Ariel Sharon, suggested that many more such settlements were in the offing.[2] Even so,
American-Israeli consultations on the Palestinian issue continued,
and in October 1977 the Israeli government actually agreed to the inclusion of some "non-PLO" Palestinians in a unified Arab delegation
to a Geneva conference aimed at negotiating a comprehensive Arab-
Israel peace.[3] That project was quickly derailed, however, by Sadat's
unprecedented initiative the following month, which shifted negotiations onto a bilateral (soon a triangular: American-Israeli-Egyptian)
track. To the Israelis, Sadat's visit was doubly welcome: it offered
long-awaited symbols of recognition and acceptance, and it also
promised Israel a tactical advantage in negotiating strictly bilateral
issues. In fact, Jerusalem had for some time been enamored of precisely the prospect that both Cairo and Washington had initially
sought to avoid: a separate peace with Egypt.

Sadat himself, both in his speech to the Knesset and afterward,
rejected this notion—although he might have been satisfied with a
specific agreement on the recovery of Egyptian territory alone, provided that it was accompanied by an acceptable declaration of general principles on other matters. Israel, for its part, sought to entice

him away from even this commitment with an offer to restore Cairo's sovereignty over all of Sinai. Indeed, a secret offer of this kind had quite probably been tabled in advance of the Egyptian president's arrival in the Israeli capital.[4] This would explain several still quite mysterious aspects of this important episode: why Israel conceded the Sinai virtually at the very start of negotiations; why those negotiations broke down temporarily when that offer was later qualified; and, most important of all, why Sadat took the risk of going to Jerusalem in the first place.

As for the other disputed territories, Israel offered the Palestinians in the West Bank and Gaza only "self-rule" under continued Israeli occupation. When Sadat demurred, American emissaries kept the two sides in contact while attempting to elicit an Israeli commitment in principle to withdraw from at least some part of the West Bank. The central question throughout the year of difficult negotiations that followed the euphoria of Sadat's first visit to Israel thus became the connection (if any) between the fate of Sinai and that of other occupied lands. Progress was excruciatingly slow. At first, the Israeli government would not admit that the requirement of Israeli withdrawal mentioned in U.N. resolution 242 of 1967 even applied to the West Bank at all. Later, in response to pleas from Washington, the cabinet agreed to discuss "the nature of relations between the parties," the issue of sovereignty, and perhaps even the possibility of "territorial compromise" on the West Bank, but only after a five-year period during which Israeli control would be maintained. Meanwhile, on a practical level, the policy of creating or authorizing new Jewish settlements there remained in effect. One new settlement, at Shiloh, was launched during this time on the pretext of an archeological expedition.[5]

After nearly a year of such tedious maneuvers, President Carter decided that only an intensive, summit-level effort would suffice to secure an Egyptian-Israeli accord. At Camp David, in ten days of uninterrupted negotiations, two agreements popularly named after the well-known presidential retreat emerged: one on a bilateral peace treaty, the other on Palestinian "autonomy" as a transition toward a comprehensive peace.[6] In the former instance, Egypt essentially had its way on the territorial question, recovering the entire Sinai peninsula with no encumbrances save a few demilitarized zones and one tiny disputed enclave, at Taba, which was left in Israeli hands pending agreement on its ultimate disposition—an agreement, significantly, that continues to elude the two parties nearly seven years later. The price for all this was peace—that is, diplomatic and economic "normalization" with Israel, to be phased in as Israel's withdrawal from Sinai proceeded over a period of three years. But Israel had its way, after an additional six months of haggling that included a last-minute diplomatic shuttle by Carter himself, on the issue of "linkage" between the two Camp David accords. On March 26, 1979, Israel and Egypt signed a peace treaty whose terms fell far short of the kind of linkage to the Palestinian problem that Cairo had demanded—especially after an Arab summit at Baghdad resolved to ostracize Egypt for its separate peace with Israel, and after the Islamic revolution in Iran. Any explicit link with a more comprehensive Mideast peace was confined to the preamble of the treaty, which was declared binding "regardless of the action or inaction of any other party."[7]

The other Camp David accord, on Palestinian autonomy, offered only limited Israeli concessions beyond Begin's original "self-rule" proposal. Israel now accepted, for example, language that recognized the "legitimate rights of the Palestinian people," and agreed to "redeploy" some of its occupation troops. But on many critical issues, this accord was riddled with troublesome ambiguities. For example, nothing definite was said about the future of Jerusalem, the fate of Jewish settlements, and the physical resources or final political status of the West Bank and Gaza. Autonomy, whatever it might be taken to mean, was to last only for five years, after which Israel, Egypt, Jordan, and the local Palestinians would all have to agree on further steps—that "all" embodying, in effect, an Israeli veto over future political arrangements.

All this ambiguity proved to be autonomy's undoing. The ink was hardly dry on this Camp David accord before it appeared that Israel's consistently narrow interpretation of its provisions combined with Arab refusal to participate in an autonomy scheme would turn the entire painstakingly negotiated document into a dead letter. Indeed, American-Egyptian-Israeli talks aimed at implementing it proceeded for another couple of years, but at a glacial pace. Months of meetings were required just to come up with an agenda, and then to review widely divergent Egyptian and Israeli versions of autonomy. American-Israeli controversy focused on two major omissions from the list of issues agreed upon at Camp David: the future of Israel's physical presence on the West Bank, and the future political role (if any) of the PLO. As to the former, the Begin government contended that neither

the text of the agreement nor any unwritten understandings prohibited expansion of Jewish settlements (which in fact continued to
grow). In July 1980, this issue of "creeping annexation" was further
clouded when the Knesset passed a bill proclaiming all of Jerusalem,
including the former Jordanian sector, to be Israel's "eternal and undivided capital."[8]

On the question of Palestinian representation in peace negotiations or in a transitional "self-governing authority," a typical dispute
erupted in mid-1979 when U.S. diplomats began sounding out PLO
reaction to an "updated" version of resolution 242. As part of those
consultations, U.N. Ambassador Andrew Young met privately with
the PLO's chief representative in New York. Israeli complaints that
the meeting violated a 1975 U.S. commitment, coupled with Young's
own belated and confusing explanations, resulted in his dismissal—
and there the matter was dropped.[9] By the end of 1980, it was clear
that little progress was likely even on such procedural matters, let
alone on more concrete questions of the meaning and limits of Palestinian autonomy.

Thus, one key element of Israeli foreign policy—the maintenance of an unshakeable, if somewhat uneasy, hold on the West
Bank—outlived the peace with Egypt; it was destined, as we shall
soon see, to outlive the war in Lebanon as well. Indeed, the separate
peace and the three-year calendar of Israel's phased withdrawal from
Sinai contributed to the deferral of serious pressures emanating from
either Cairo or Washington for additional concessions from Jerusalem. The peace with Egypt itself, the second basic element of Israel's
strategy, was preserved, despite considerable apprehension on both
sides. In a curious way, the assassination of Sadat in October 1981
made observance of the treaty's terms even more imperative, if the
peace was to last at all. Israel's evacuation of Sinai thus proceeded on
schedule to completion in April 1982, notwithstanding large-scale
protests at the last major Israeli settlement of Yamit.

As for the third element in Israel's long-term strategy—its close
American connection—it too remained intact. American-Israeli relations in 1981, the first year of the Reagan administration, had their
minor ups and downs.[10] The year began with an American focus on
"strategic consensus" with Israel, only to end with mutual recrimi-
nations (and even a short-lived embargo on combat aircraft deliveries) after Israel's bombing of Baghdad's nuclear reactor, its battle
against the AWACs sale to Saudi Arabia, and its annexation of the Go-

lan Heights. (Ironically, the last move was probably designed partly to make it easier, in Begin's domestic political setting, to evacuate Yamit.) But the dialogue between Washington and Jerusalem regarding the stalled Arab-Israeli peace process and other regional issues remained generally low-key and low-level, as domestic political and economic matters took precedence in both capitals. Not until mid-1982, therefore, did a new crisis, in a previously marginal area, threaten to disrupt the back-burner status of the unresolved Arab-Israeli issues. This was, of course, the Israeli invasion of Lebanon launched on June 6, 1982.

Genesis of the War in Lebanon

Throughout the preceding seven years, Israel had stayed largely on the sidelines of the Lebanese civil war. Jerusalem did establish some links with Maronite militias, both on the border and around Beirut, as early as 1976;[11] but the Labor government then in power acquiesced in Syria's intervention in Lebanon that year, under an arrangement (informally dubbed the "Red Line") that kept Syrian forces far from the Israeli frontier and Syrian missiles out of the country altogether. One result of that arrangement, however, was that the PLO kept the relatively free rein it had acquired in south Lebanon. As a consequence, over the next few years a succession of new Israeli governments adopted an increasingly activist policy of reprisal—"preemptive" and eventually "preventive" assaults on Palestinian positions north of the border.

On March 11, 1978, PLO commandos launched off the Lebanese coast hijacked an Israeli bus, killing 32 passengers—the highest such toll ever. Three days later, in "Operation Litani," Israel sent three armored brigades into Lebanon in order to clear the area of PLO units and establish a security belt between the frontier and the Litani River. The U.N. Security Council, actively supported on this occasion by the United States, demanded an Israeli withdrawal. Jerusalem complied by mid-June, and a new U.N. Interim Force in Lebanon (UNIFIL) peacekeeping presence was sent in. In the immediate border zone, however, Israel turned over its positions not to UNIFIL but to a friendly, mostly Christian Lebanese militia commanded by Major Saad Haddad.[12]

The following two years were comparatively tranquil; but, by early 1981, the Lebanese cauldron had begun to boil again. One factor behind this switch was a change in Jerusalem's domestic political scene. That is not to say that the new series of incidents was exclusively "made in Israel"; indeed, it would be misleading to draw a simplistic distinction between, say, a "bellicose" Likud and a "pacifist" Labor approach to Lebanese affairs, especially since much also depended on the course of external events. Nevertheless, there was a distinct escalation, both in rhetoric about Lebanon and in real Israeli military operations in that country, under the first and especially under the second Likud government, elected in June 1981. An increasingly hawkish internal constellation faced a new external challenge, in the form of greater PLO ability and willingness to attack Israeli border settlements at long range.

The consequences of these shifts were quickly apparent in a series of military incidents and frenetic "crisis-management" efforts in Lebanon all through the first half of 1981. In April, Syrian and Israeli activity in that country suddenly assumed alarming proportions, with Israeli air strikes to relieve an abortive Christian offensive at Zahle, Syrian anti-aircraft missile deployments that jeopardized the tacit Red Line understanding, and threats of war from both sides. The following month, Philip Habib was summoned back from retirement for a round of shuttle diplomacy that succeeded in convincing Israel (temporarily, as it turned out) to exercise restraint but failed to budge the Syrian missiles. In July, Begin—personally outraged by Israel's first civilian deaths from PLO rockets in about two years and committed by campaign pledges to keep hostile fire from Israel's northern towns—ordered a bombing raid on suspected PLO lodgings in Beirut. By mid-August, after another round of Habib's mediation, Jerusalem reluctantly accepted an American proposal for a "cessation of hostilities across the Lebanese border," though without mentioning the PLO nemesis by name.[13]

Behind the scenes, however, Israeli plans for a cross-border military operation continued. Those plans were affected by other events inside Lebanon at around this time—in particular, the rise of a relatively cohesive Maronite leadership under Bashir Gemayel, with whose forces Israel's military and Mossad intelligence agency kept in increasingly close contact.[14] By early 1982, the invasion strategy formulated in Jerusalem had acquired correspondingly ambitious objectives: not merely the elimination of the guerrilla threat from the border, but the eradication of all PLO and even Syrian influence from

Lebanon; the installation there of a friendly Gemayel government; and, ultimately and indirectly, the consolidation of Israeli control over the other occupied territories. This agenda was thinly disguised by billing the invasion as Operation Peace for Galilee, thus emphasizing only Israel's desire for a forty-kilometer "security zone" along its northern frontier.[15]

That the war was designed to achieve such grandiose objectives should not obscure the importance to Israel of its more modest aim: to get rid of the limited but troublesome security threat of PLO military concentrations in south Lebanon, now capable of reaching, literally, over the heads of U.N. peacekeeping forces or local militias and into Israel. True, there had been no casualties on that front during the year or so between the ceasefire mediated by Habib in August 1981 and the onset of Israel's invasion. True, too, the immediate pretext for that invasion was an attempt on the life of Israel's ambassador in London carried out by a renegade PLO faction, and a renewal of PLO shelling provoked by Israel's own air raids. But regardless of such details, the potential for a resumption of PLO nuisance raids and rocket barrages remained a real issue—and this in an area where, in view of the Lebanese government's inability to police its own territory, the conventional military deterrence effective on other fronts might not apply. Moreover, the political price of continued quiet on the northern front—some form of Israeli recognition, however reluctant and indirect, of the PLO—threatened to escalate beyond the limits acceptable to Jerusalem.

The 1982 War

The Lebanon war and its aftermath were the top priorities of Israeli foreign policy during the entire period under consideration. The actual large-scale fighting, beginning in June 1982, lasted only three months, but the withdrawal of Israel's forces from Lebanon dragged on for another three years. During that time, Jerusalem strove to pursue a series of increasingly modest (and somewhat contradictory) objectives in Lebanon: to salvage some broad political gains from the costly military effort; to protect the security of Israel's northern border, for whose sake the war had ostensibly been launched; and, finally, to minimize the human and political burden that the occupation of Lebanon imposed on Israeli society.

Once Israel crossed the border, the war went through two major stages.[16] The first was a series of rapid thrusts that overran PLO strongholds in the southern part of the country and brought Israeli troops, after some brief but intense ground and air battles against Syrian forces and some unexpectedly tough Palestinian resistance near Beirut, to the outskirts of the Lebanese capital. During this phase, Israel's forces generally distinguished themselves, from a purely military standpoint, with some of the same successful tactics they had employed in past wars: lightning advances that bypassed and then isolated fortified enemy positions; insurance of local superiority in numbers and firepower; and impressive technical and human performance against hostile aircraft and sophisticated air-defense installations. But Israel did not cut off the PLO guerrillas' retreat immediately or fully—perhaps in the vain expectation that the allied Lebanese forces would engage them, or perhaps as part of an elaborate but confused "salami tactic" intended to disguise the expansion of the war beyond the vaunted forty-kilometer security zone along the border. Thus the operation left the main PLO fighting units holed up in the Lebanese capital.

This time, though, Israel was determined not to repeat the mistake of Operation Litani, when PLO guerrillas were driven out of the border zone only to return in greater strength once the Israelis withdrew. Moreover, the continued presence of PLO and allied forces threatened the broader Israeli objective of transforming the military—and thereby also the political—situation inside Beirut and, by extension, in the country as a whole. The largely Maronite Lebanese forces, according to Israel's original conception, were supposed to do the job of taking over the Lebanese capital, but they did not. The Israelis, for their part, were reluctant to take on the daunting task of street-by-street fighting that would be required to capture the hostile sections of the city. So, after some hesitation and internal debate, the Israeli high command settled on an alternative strategy, which initiated a new stage in the war.

This second stage involved a protracted and bloody two-month siege of Beirut, during which Israeli naval, air, and artillery bombardments, along with intermittent cutoffs of essential supplies, kept up the pressure on the PLO to evacuate the city. As the siege dragged on, public signs of impatience with Israel's conduct mounted in both Jerusalem and Washington. Eventually, however, a combination of continued Israeli military pressure and American mediation yielded an agreement under which more than 10,000 PLO troops left Beirut and dispersed to other Arab countries, and the organization's headquarters were transferred to Tunis. The last "official" PLO contingents were thus gone from Beirut by September.[17]

Israel therefore achieved one of its objectives, albeit in a much slower and sloppier fashion than anticipated. But events during the wartime summer of 1982 revealed three weaknesses in Israel's strategy that would come to haunt its policy in Lebanon over the next three years: a sensitivity to casualties that constrained Israeli military options, an absence of consensus on Lebanon on Israel's home front, and a temporarily troubled relationship with the United States on this and certain other issues. Quite apart from American objections to specific aspects of Israel's operations in Lebanon, a new Arab-Israeli peace plan unveiled by President Reagan in early September made clear that Washington opposed a central, if largely unspoken, premise of the entire campaign: that the destruction of the PLO would pave the way for a new era of untroubled Israeli occupation of the West Bank. Instead, the Reagan Plan, timed to coincide with a new Arab summit convened in Morocco at Fez, urged Palestinian self-government in association with Jordan—implicitly excluding the now prostrate PLO from the peace process, to be sure, but explicitly disavowing Israel's claims on West Bank territory. Not surprisingly, the Israeli government immediately rejected this notion.[18]

For the time being, however, other factors intervened to bury Reagan's proposal, as all eyes turned to another upsurge of violence in Lebanon. In this connection, a further and more immediately damaging weakness in Israel's strategy came to light when Bashir Gemayel, the newly elected president of Lebanon, was assassinated in mid-September. As noted above, the Israeli invasion had been designed, in part, to facilitate the rise to power of this militant Maronite leader, whose shared opposition to Palestinian and Syrian influence in Lebanon was expected to preserve a close working relationship with Israel. But neither the Israelis nor anyone else proved capable of providing enough security in Beirut to consolidate a friendly new regime in power. Amin Gemayel was quickly chosen to take his late brother's place as president, but he possessed neither the personal following nor the disposition to coordinate political strategy with Israel that had been characteristic of his predecessor. The revenge massacre in the Sabra and Shatilla refugee camps that followed Bashir's assassination provided additional evidence that Maronite militias could not be counted as loyal and disciplined allies of the Jewish state.

The bare outlines of Israeli complicity in that episode can be pieced together from journalistic reportage; from official documents, including the published excerpts of a report issued by a special Israeli investigatory body, popularly named the Kahan Commission; and from subsequent testimony in the libel suit brought by Sharon against *Time* magazine.[19] Israeli troops, who had returned to the outskirts of Beirut to "restore order" after Gemayel's assassination, allowed allied Christian units into the camps (ostensibly, in order to flush out hidden PLO guerrillas and arms caches) and provided them with logistical support as they proceeded to murder hundreds of civilian inhabitants. While there is no evidence that Israel planned this brutal operation in advance, there is every indication that neither the Israeli units on the scene nor the higher authorities in Jerusalem did anything to stop it for about two days, even after they had good reason to suspect that a massacre of some sort was under way. In seeking to understand the motives behind Israeli policy in this episode, one important but often overlooked factor was probably the desire to "activate" the hitherto disappointing Maronite alliance in something like combat conditions—even though, according to the Kahan Commission, the initial decision to allow the Lebanese units into the camps was made on the spot and at a relatively low level. The most important effect of this sorry chain of events, as far as Israel was concerned, was that it brought to a boil the domestic debate about the war that had been simmering since the early days of Israel's invasion.

Domestic Developments, 1982–1985

Before turning to the domestic repercussions of the Lebanese war, a bit of the background of Israel's recent internal political evolution is required. The 1977 election that ended the era of rule by Israel's Labor party, which had dominated the country's coalition governments during the entire post-independence generation, had marked a watershed in Israeli political history; ever since, Israel has had not only an active democratic system but a fiercely competitive one as well. Likud's coming to power was at first viewed as something of a fluke, since it was only by virtue of heavy voter defections from Labor to a third, middle-of-the-road/domestic-issue-oriented, reformist party called the Democratic Movement for Change (DMC;

often known by its Hebrew acronym "Dash") that Likud gained its plurality in the Knesset and thus its opportunity to head a coalition. But the first Likud government, confounding both the pundits and the public-opinion polls, maintained a majority in the Knesset for a full term of four years, establishing itself thereby as a viable alternative to Labor-led coalitions. It did so, moreover, despite incessant factional squabbling and occasional defections by erstwhile political allies.[20] Likud's success reflected a number of factors, both immediate and structural: the charismatic appeal of Menachem Begin; the staleness and internal disarray of Labor, now cast in an unaccustomed opposition role; the accumulated momentum of nationalist impulses regarding the West Bank; and, most important of all, the increased demographic weight and political coming-of-age of Israel's Sephardi Jewish majority, who voted disproportionately for Likud largely as a protest against their longstanding second-class socioeconomic status under the Labor "establishment."[21]

By 1981, however, the developing foreign policy stalemate and, especially, the country's deteriorating economy had cut sharply into Likud's apparent electoral appeal. DMC strength had dwindled, in the wake of factional fighting and lackluster performance in the ruling coalition, to almost nothing; its successor, the Shinui ("Change") party, won just two seats in the election that year. The new contest was therefore primarily (and directly) between Labor and Likud. Not surprisingly, under these circumstances, it proved to be a bitter and very close electoral battle, marred by an unusual degree of ethnic (Sephardi-Ashkenazi) polarization and invective. The Sephardi Jews turned out more heavily than ever, by a two-to-one majority, for Likud; the Ashkenazim cast their ballots in exactly the reverse proportion. It was this ethnic divide, more than any other single factor, that gave Likud a repeat, razor-thin plurality of forty-eight Knesset seats as against Labor's forty-seven, and made Begin prime minister of Israel for the second time.[22]

Other issues also played a part in Begin's come-from-behind triumph. Most conspicuous was some last-minute economic pump-priming organized by Likud Finance Minister Yoram Aridor, which was evidently electorally effective. (It was also disastrously expensive: the national shopping spree that followed Aridor's well-timed relaxation of controls contributed to an inflationary spiral that, over the next four years, moved Israel's annual price-increase index even higher into the triple-digit range.) Foreign policy issues were also relevant; Begin derived some domestic political benefit from a variety of new militant gestures directed against assorted targets ranging from Lebanon to Germany, whose prime minister was accused of past Nazi loyalties in a well-publicized and well-timed flap. Also among these measures was Israel's precision bombing attack on a nuclear reactor outside Baghdad; elections were due on the last day of June, very soon (suspiciously so, some of Begin's harsher critics charged) after the Israeli raid.

But such incidents were a consequence as well as a cause of Israeli domestic political changes. During the six months preceding the 1981 election, Begin himself had held the defense portfolio and delegated most of that responsibility to the atypically hawkish chief of staff, Rafael ("Raful") Eitan. And during the campaign itself, Begin's moves in foreign policy were clearly calculated with an eye to electoral advantage. The more cautious counsel of Moshe Dayan or Ezer Weizman was missing from the Israeli government coalition. Then, in the Likud government that was returned to office, the new defense minister was Ariel Sharon, who was justly reputed to be more aggressively inclined. It was Sharon, of course, who spearheaded Israel's plunge into Lebanon, unwittingly precipitating important developments on the Israeli domestic political scene.

Throughout the summer of 1982, the question of government control over and public support for the war became increasingly controversial. It appears, so far as the evidence can be reconstructed from unofficial but generally reliable sources, that the cabinet as a whole did not have adequate advance information regarding some of the important decisions about the scope and objectives of Israel's military operations—decisions made by Sharon and Eitan and presented to the civilian leadership as if required by military necessity, or as faits accomplis. Even Begin is reported to have remarked sardonically that he, at least, was always informed about the latest Israeli moves in Lebanon—"sometimes before the fact, and sometimes after."[23]

At first, the Cabinet went along—meekly, in some individual cases; enthusiastically, in others—with Sharon's designs. But later, as the siege of Beirut dragged on, a few voices of dissent were heard, particularly from ministers of Likud's Liberal faction and the National Religious Party, about certain Israeli actions—including, for example, the fierce bombardment of the city ordered without formal government authorization on August 12. The same reactions, by and large, characterized the leaders of the Labor party opposition, who supported the initial invasion but in some cases expressed second thoughts thereafter. Despite these vocal misgivings, the pattern of communications failures—or, as some charged, of deliberate deception and withholding of information—at high levels persisted well into September. The subsequent report by the Kahan Commission disclosed that local military commanders did not always report to the government, and that such senior ministers as Begin and Shamir who _ did become privy to details of the unfolding atrocity at Sabra and Shatilla did not bother to share the information with their colleagues.

Outside the government, in the streets and even on the front lines, there were other instances of wartime opposition to Israel's policy. Perhaps the most celebrated such case was that of Eli Geva, a young commander who resigned his commission rather than carry out the order to besiege Beirut. Behind the scenes, a number of senior officers also reportedly questioned some of Sharon's directives. There is no evidence, though, that such unusual but still isolated incidents had a significant impact on either military operations or overall policy. Moreover, despite these well-publicized examples of dissent, popular and mainstream political support at least for the broad outlines of government policy declined only slightly during the long siege of the Lebanese capital.[24] It did seem, after all, that Israel had succeeded in its aims of driving out the PLO, defeating the Syrians, and installing a new and friendlier regime in Beirut. The immediate domestic political repercussions of Israel's war in Lebanon were thus marginal, until the dramatic chain of events in Beirut in September exposed both the practical flaws in Israel's political calculations and the human cost of its military presence in Lebanon.

The catalyst behind this shift was the massacre at Sabra and Shatilla, which generated a storm of criticism and protest both in Israel and abroad. Objectively, the nature and number of the victims at Sabra and Shatilla represented but a minute fraction of the general indiscriminate carnage in Lebanon, but the subjective impact of this latest massacre was profound. In Israel, a massive protest demonstration on September 25, 1982, demanding a commission of inquiry, brought out nearly 400,000 participants, over ten percent of the country's entire Jewish population. The commission's report, made public the following February, accused Sharon of "indirect responsibility" for the killing in the camps. A new wave of demonstrations, including one in which a dovish activist was killed by a grenade, compelled him to resign the defense portfolio, although he retained ministerial status. (Sharon was replaced by fellow Likud hardliner Moshe Arens.) Eitan, likewise charged with dereliction of duty, was permitted to serve out his term until April, when he was succeeded as chief of staff by the apolitical Moshe Levy. Both new appointees quickly moved to reevaluate Israel's options in Lebanon, responding in part to popular crosspressures to cut Israel's losses there without sacrificing the short-term border security advantages that had accrued from the war.[25]

Just as the immediate domestic turmoil triggered by Lebanese issues finally seemed to be subsiding, a new political bombshell exploded in Jerusalem. In late August 1983, an exhausted and depressed Begin, apparently deeply affected both by the unraveling of Israel's wartime policy and by the deaths in quick succession of his wife and of long-time political confidant Simcha Erlich of Likud's Liberal faction, abruptly announced his resignation as prime minister. He was quickly succeeded by a compromise candidate, Likud stalwart and foreign minister Yitzhak Shamir, but the country was immediately engulfed in an economic crisis sparked by the collapse of bank shares on the Tel Aviv exchange. In these inauspicious circumstances, Shamir—lacking Begin's personal authority and saddled with internal party rivals like Sharon and Deputy Prime Minister David Levy—struggled mightily to hold the coalition together. He succeeded for only about six months, when his government lost a vote of confidence in the Knesset and was compelled to call new elections, scheduled for July 1984. As usual, the immediate causes of the government's fall were a combination of controversy over relatively inconsequential domestic issues and shifting political ambitions on the part of both the major opposition party and several minor coalition partners.

Despite the closeness of the contest and the potentially explosive quality of the issues at stake, the 1984 electoral campaign proved to be considerably more orderly and tranquil—some would say, almost surrealistically so—than the previous one, three years before. Once again, it was internal (particularly, in this instance, economic) rather than external issues that dominated the debate: Labor accused Likud of mismanagement that had brought the country to the brink of ruin, and the latter replied with charges that Labor was still insensitive to the plight of Israel's poorer (and disproportionately Sephardi) social strata. Insofar as foreign policy was concerned, Likud campaigned under a slogan implying that it alone was genuinely in the "national camp," emphasizing its traditional militance and commitment to "Eretz Yisrael" (the Land of Israel, occupied territories included). Labor, by contrast, argued for a territorial compromise with Jordan that would somehow manage to maintain Jewish settlements in place, establish the Jordan River as Israel's "security border," and keep Greater Jerusalem under Israeli sovereignty. Even this much flexibility was deliberately downplayed, as part of a futile effort to appeal to the ever larger Israeli floating vote with presumably diverse foreign policy orientations. When the returns were tallied, Labor had just barely edged out Likud, with forty-four Knesset deputies returned on the former's ticket as against forty-one for the latter.[26]

The remaining seats in Israel's 120-member parliament were split among an assortment of small parties at opposite ends of Israel's political spectrum. As a result of this polarized partisan lineup, neither Labor nor Likud alone could put together a coalition with a workable governing majority. Internal party pressures on Peres and Shamir, both of whom faced potentially serious challengers for their respective party leadership positions, compounded the uncertainty, and eventually helped convince both politicians to consider a unique solution to the domestic political deadlock.

In mid-September 1984, after protracted negotiations, Labor and Likud signed an unprecedented agreement to share power (and political patronage, including ministerial portfolios in a larger-than-ever Cabinet) equally in a National Unity government. An "inner Cabinet" of ten ministers, five from each major party's bloc of members and allies, was formally set up in order to help manage this unwieldy government structure. Labor's Peres became Israel's new prime minister, with his immediate predecessor, Likud's Shamir, scheduled to take over the reins again in two years' time. On substantive policy issues, the coalition agreement tried to paper over the differences separating these strange bedfellows. On the divisive West Bank issue, for example, the agreement attempted to have it both ways, calling both for peace talks with Jordan and for continued Jewish settlement in Judea and Samaria, albeit at a slower pace. As for territorial concessions there, the new government committed itself to hold another election in the event that peace negotiations ever reached that decisive stage—a promise reminiscent of the similarly constraining one made, for broadly similar reasons of internal coalition politics, by Labor's Yitzhak Rabin (now defense minister) when he succeeded

Golda Meir as prime minister back in 1974. On the equally divisive religious question, both major parties essentially agreed to maintain the famous though rather ill-defined Israeli status quo, mollifying the newly fragmented bloc of Orthodox splinter parties with an assortment of high-level positions. In the short term, however, the new team in Jerusalem was preoccupied with efforts to extricate Israel from its economic crisis and from Lebanon, not with any of these arguably more fundamental issues.

Aside from Labor and Likud, the political party configuration that emerged from the 1984 election may be briefly sketched as follows: The new Yahad ("Together") party led by former Likud defense minister Ezer Weizman, which won three Knesset mandates, offered a vague overall program including an apparent preference for some form of Palestinian autonomy. Shinui, which also elected three deputies, was another centrist splinter party whose program was slightly more dovish. Both these centrist parties joined the National Unity coalition, each one gaining one Cabinet post.

In the religious camp, the most notable result of 1984 was a further fragmentation of party representation for an essentially unchanged overall electoral base of about ten percent of Israel's population. The National Religious Party lost another two seats; with a mere four Knesset deputies left, it was now on a par with a brand-new Sephardi religious party called Shas (an acronym for Sephardi Torah Guardians). The latter began as a breakaway faction from the ultra-orthodox Agudat Yisrael party, which accordingly lost half of its previous four Knesset seats. All of these parties could be considered, with some unavoidable oversimplification, as more concerned with rather narrowly defined domestic issues, particularly the special interests of their constituents, than with foreign policy.[27] After some last-minute bargaining over patronage, all three eventually joined the governing coalition. The only holdouts in this respect among the religous parties were the new Morasha ("Heritage") party, with two seats, which combined orthodoxy with militant nationalism; and the one Knesset deputy who remained of Tami, a North African ethno-religious party whose strength was largely spent after a promising start in 1981.

The others who remained in opposition were a diverse group indeed. On one end of the spectrum, they included six deputies of the leftist-dovish Mapam faction that broke away from Labor because it had agreed to include Sharon in the Cabinet, and four (including one other Labor defector) from the reformist-dovish Citizens' Rights

Movement headed by the outspoken feminist, Shulamit Aloni. Also in the dovish camp were two small parties elected almost entirely by Israeli Arab voters: the (nominally communist) Democratic Front, also known as Rakah, with four members in the new Knesset as in the previous one; and the Progressive List, which garnered two mandates in its electoral debut. Both parties featured an even Arab/Jewish split in their respective rosters of Knesset deputies; however, behind this facade, both are universally viewed as nationalist protest vehicles for about half of Israel's growing Arab minority.

At the opposite end of the opposition spectrum were the ultranationalist Tehiya ("Revival") party, which gained two new seats for a total of five; and, perhaps most conspicuously of all, the Kach ("Thus!") party led by erstwhile American rabbi Meir Kahane, which passed the 20,000-odd vote threshold needed to elect one deputy to parliament for the first time. Kahane explicitly advocated the eventual expulsion of Israel's Arab citizens and of West Bank Palestinians on the grounds that democracy and Zionism were mutually exclusive, since the former required a "truly" Jewish state. The provocative nature of this appeal, along with Kahane's own talent for attracting publicity, brought him an enormous and—at least at first—disproportionate share of attention both in and outside Israel.[28] Subsequent polls showed that his appeal among Jewish youth and in predominantly working-class Sephardi development towns and neighborhoods was continuing to grow to the point that an election held in mid-1985 might have produced a fivefold or even greater increase in Kach's representation in the Knesset. Yet much of this support seemed to come at the expense of Likud, and the major parties began to cooperate in efforts (including legislation against "racism") to contain Kahane's political fortunes and reverse a sense of antidemocratic drift in Israeli politics as a whole. As a result, Kahanism is likely to remain no more than an irritant from an Israeli government standpoint, rather than a serious challenge to the established political order.[29]

In this connection, one other internal political development during this period deserves brief mention: the greater visibility of organized but extraparliamentary pressure groups active on opposite sides of Israel's domestic debate on foreign policy. On the hawkish side is Gush Emunim (Bloc of the Faithful), founded in 1974 but especially active under the Likud governments, which has developed an extensive network of settlements and affiliated institutions on the

West Bank; an indeterminate but probably substantial number of other supporters, including influential political personalities in and out of government; and a considerable base of popular sympathy as well. Any domestic showdown over West Bank issues would almost certainly involve this group, which could probably mobilize thousands of highly motivated, well-organized, and possibly even armed adherents—many times the number that had to be evacuated, not without force, from Israel's last settlements in Sinai.

On the dovish side is Peace Now, a more amorphous but also fairly large group founded in 1978, which advocates a freeze on further West Bank settlement in order to get negotiations started. This group has been able to organize mass demonstrations on a few occasions: during the early Sadat-era negotiations; after the Sabra and Shatilla massacre and Kahan Commission investigation; and finally on a smaller scale, after the exposure of Jewish terrorism on the West Bank in 1984. But Peace Now has had little effect on settlement policy or on overall Israeli policy toward the West Bank. In fact, despite the increased importance of such pressure groups on either side of Israel's foreign-policy divide, the policy process has largely reverted to the established partisan political channels. Another indicator along these lines are the shifting fortunes of Gush Emunim: When the (Likud) government in power was in broad sympathy with that group's position, it appeared to enjoy great influence; since then, however, it has been considerably less effective.

More broadly (while still harder to quantify), the perception of many seasoned observers of the country's political scene was that ethnic and foreign policy tensions had lately eased, at least superficially, even as tensions between religious and secular groups (perhaps most notably in Jerusalem) were on the rise. Such frictions, when combined with the economic troubles and external pressures afflicting Israeli society, engendered an overall air of national malaise. Simple solutions continued to elude the established politicians; charismatic mainstream leaders were conspicuously absent. Nevertheless, it must be emphasized that everyday life kept a large measure of normalcy. Except for a continuing trickle of emigration—and a morale-building rescue of more than 10,000 Ethiopian Jews—most Israelis, regardless of partisan or other affiliation, continued to go about their personal business more or less as usual, with little sense either of noble determination or of grim persistence.[30]

In the realm of high politics, the only major initiatives launched by the government from late 1984 through 1985 consisted of a series of emergency economic austerity measures: package deals of wage and price freezes negotiated with the giant Histadrut labor federation/conglomerate, currency devaluations, budget and subsidy cuts, tax increases, and the like. By late 1985, such measures had at least begun the painful process of reversing Israel's ingrained inclination to live beyond its means, but at the price of a perceptible decline in national living standards.[31] Meanwhile, the greatly increased personal popularity of Peres, the continued factionalism and jockeying for position inside Likud, and the bargaining leverage of small coalition partners on divisive domestic issues all suggested uncertain prospects for the survival of the current National Unity government beyond the scheduled rotation of prime ministers in late 1986. Over against such disruptive factors, however, must be set the time-tested ability of Israeli politicians to hang on to power, and more fundamentally, their widely shared commitment to maintain the country's democratic political order essentially unchanged— including, rather paradoxically, its fractifying electoral system of pure proportional representation. The experience of the past three years, indeed, has confirmed the basic pattern of Israeli politics since 1977: a close but indecisive contest for support between the two major parties; a consequently disproportionate weight for smaller, "swing" parties; and a volatile public mood divided over ethnic and religious as well as foreign-policy issues (and increasingly preoccupied with economic problems). It was in this developing climate of internal political polarization and unease, with new personalities if not new ideologies at the helm, that Israel had to confront the legacy of its Lebanese adventure.

Israel's Postwar Predicament

In the sobering circumstances that developed after Bashir Gemayel's assassination, a beleaguered Israeli government tried to salvage what it could in the way of political advantage from the war in Lebanon. The Israelis offered Amin Gemayel the prospect of their withdrawal from Lebanese soil in exchange for favorable security arrangements and some degree of recognition, hoping for a new peace treaty or at least something of a similar kind. Israel was under increasing pressure to pull its forces back anyway, for a number of reasons: to improve their logistical position, minimize the continuing drain of casualties, reduce friction with the new multinational (American, British, French, and Italian) peacekeeping forces and with the diverse local militias in Lebanon—and, by no means least, to demonstrate progress and justify the war effort at home. The situation was complicated by the internal political turmoil in both Israel and Lebanon. After several months of inconclusive negotiations, a mediation effort by the new U.S. secretary of state, George Shultz, produced an Israeli-Lebanese agreement signed on May 17, 1983.[32] Although it fell considerably short of a formal peace treaty, it did provide—in exchange for Israeli withdrawal—important elements of "normalization" between the two countries: economic links, joint security patrols, political liaison offices in each other's capitals, and so on. However, an accompanying private understanding with the United States stipulated that the withdrawal of Israeli forces would be contingent upon a parallel withdrawal of Syrian forces from Lebanon—a stipulation that led some observers to wonder whether the agreement so laboriously negotiated might be stillborn.

It was not long, in fact, before the May 1983 Lebanese-Israeli accord proved to be fatally flawed because of two related factors: the abject weakness of Amin Gemayel's regime, and the resurgence of Syrian military power and political influence in Lebanese affairs. A few analysts have since argued that timing was the critical problem—that had the agreement been concluded sooner, a weakened Syria might have gone along, which would in turn have strengthened the moderates in Lebanon's society and government. But it is hard to imagine why, even in the aftermath of military defeat, Assad would have agreed to reward Israel's invasion in this manner, or how the reassertion of centrifugal and radical tendencies inside Lebanon could have been prevented. The Israelis, at any rate, were soon skeptical about the value of the piece of paper they had signed in May; this was reflected in their decision to effect a unilateral partial withdrawal in September, leaving the strategic Chouf region open to the skirmishes of rival local irregulars. The Israeli move was made, ironically, in the face of American entreaties not to substitute a partial for a complete Israeli pullout.

It is not easy to fathom the calculations of Israeli policymakers during this turbulent time. Some have speculated that they continued to pursue Sharon's grand strategy by other means, deliberately stalling the Lebanese negotiations in order to avoid addressing the

West Bank issues raised in Reagan's peace plan. But the American government did not in fact pursue its own proposal with any great vigor, and most Arab governments rejected the Reagan plan almost as quickly as did Israel. Moreover, it is too Machiavellian to suppose that the Israelis were engaged just then in some cunning tactic of playing for time—not because they are constitutionally incapable of such tactics, but because of the rapid turnover in Israel's Cabinet, the uncertain shifts underway inside Lebanon itself, and the natural inclination of decision-makers everywhere to focus on the most immediate crisis. Indeed, there is another, more convincing explanation for the evolution of Israel's early postwar policy on Lebanon: a gradual downward reassessment of what was realistically possible there. This was coupled with the gathering strength of domestic pressure to show some results, or at least to lessen the pain of partial failure.

By September 1983, the Israeli government appeared to have done just that: it had an agreement with Lebanon, and it had pulled some Israeli troops back out of harm's way. But these achievements were soon overshadowed by new domestic difficulties in Jerusalem. In Beirut, the ability of the central government to exercise any authority, let alone implement its accord with Israel, was more and more in doubt. The security situation continued to deteriorate, as demonstrated most dramatically by the car-bombing of the U.S. Marine barracks in October. By February 1984, as Muslim forces overran new sections of the city, American troops were withdrawn, and the following month the Gemayel government formally abrogated the agreement it had signed with Israel and ratified less than a year before. And in south Lebanon, a new guerrilla resistance spearheaded by local Shi'a groups was beginning to exact a mounting toll of casualties among Israeli troops in their new, supposedly safer positions. Indeed, of the more than 600 Israeli military deaths in Lebanon, more than half occurred not in the war itself but in the three years of increasingly harrowing occupation duty that followed.

Faced with these challenges, Israeli policy now developed in a rather confused and dilatory manner—a policy whose timetable reflected domestic politics and short-term reactions to events on the ground more than any coherent long-term plan. The latest political contortions in Beirut no longer had much effect in Jerusalem, which was distracted by government crises of its own. Barely a month after the final collapse of the Lebanese-Israeli agreement, it will be recalled, Shamir's government had been forced to call new elections. In the electoral campaign that followed, both Labor and Likud promised, with minor variations, to "bring the boys home." By September 1984, when the extraordinary National Unity government headed by Peres was finally patched together, a continuing trickle of Israeli casualties had kept Lebanon on the national agenda. Lebanese-Israeli military talks at the border town of Naqourah, convened in an effort to establish a procedure and terms for a final Israeli evacuation, meandered on to no avail, and in January 1985 the cabinet voted by a solid majority to proceed with another unilateral withdrawal.[33]

This phase, bringing Israel's forces back across the border, was essentially completed by June 1985; and the nightmare of a "North Bank" under indefinite Israeli occupation against violent resistance faded. The only Israelis who remained behind were a few hundred agents, nicknamed the "Mercedes army," attached as advisers to Israel's latest proxy militia in the border zone: the South Lebanon army of some 1,500 soldiers commanded by Major Antoine Lahad. The Israeli military redeployment was accompanied by an attempt to improvise a suitably new political strategy for Lebanon, aimed at cultivating links with different groups in that country instead of relying solely on the ill-fated Maronite alliance.[34]

The key to the success or failure of this strategy may well be Israel's relationship with the Shi'as, the dominant group in south Lebanon and the largest single community in the country as a whole. By late 1985, battles for three Palestinian refugee camps around Beirut suggested that hostility between the PLO and Amal, by far the strongest Shi'a organization, remained intense. The Israeli government, for its part, was signaling its desire to reach an understanding with Shi'a forces—for example, by releasing hundreds of prisoners taken in south Lebanon—hoping to cement a common interest in keeping armed Palestinian units out of the border zone. The prospects for such an understanding were clouded, though, by the legacy of bitterness and terrorism spawned by Israel's lengthy occupation, by the Islamic dimension of local resistance, by the fragmentation of Shi'a authority in Lebanon, and by Israel's continuing connection with the Christian-led South Lebanon Army.

Thus, as the third anniversary of Israel's latest war passed, it appeared that the effort had succeeded in uprooting the PLO but had failed to bring about a clearcut transformation of the situation on Israel's northern border (not to mention Beirut) in a direction favorable to Israeli objectives in the region. The question of the Lebanese war's overall impact on Israel's policy is a complex one, however. In the military sphere, Israel did achieve its minimum objectives, although at considerable cost. Significantly, no major tactical or organizational innovations have been introduced in Israel's defense establishment as a consequence of its experience in Lebanon—and this notwithstanding the unique success of the Shi'a guerrillas in accelerating the Israeli evacuation. As for the elusive but important factor of morale, official postwar measurements of such things as troop attitudes and volunteer rates for special combat assignments have been reassuring. Other, independent observers are significantly less sanguine.[35]

In foreign-policy terms, the postwar situation bears an uncanny (though naturally incomplete) resemblance to the status quo ante— not just in Lebanon but in the wider Arab-Israeli arena as well. It is indicative that those Israelis who most vocally castigate the war as tragically misguided do so mainly on the grounds that it was unnecessary or futile, not because it fundamentally threatened their country's international position. Among Israel's outside sympathizers, conversely, even some of those who most eloquently defend the war explicitly leave open the question of whether the limited military gains were worth the price of more than 650 casualties and the addition of several billion dollars to Israel's already crushing defense burden.[36] Within this framework of ambiguous or inconclusive results, the major implications of the war were its indirect or intangible ones—a period of political polarization and demoralization inside Israel, and on the Arab side a realignment of Palestinian politics (to be discussed below). For Israel, finally, perhaps the most crucial outcome of the war was something else that it failed to bring about: a serious strain in Israel's vital network of relations with the United States.

American-Israeli Relations

Of all the elements in Israel's foreign policy, none is more complicated or more important than its relationship with the United States. It has become a truism (that is nonetheless true for that) that Israel depends to a considerable—even critical—extent on American diplomatic, military, and especially economic support. In the last connection alone, direct U.S. aid accounted for more than 10% of Israel's annual GNP during the period under consideration—and the figure

will climb even higher due to the emergency commitment of an extra
$1.5 billion for 1985–86 necessitated by Israel's dangerously low lev-
els of hard-currency reserves.[37] But this dependency has not been
and probably cannot be easily translated into overt influence, since
the American-Israeli relationship most nearly resembles a web of mutual concerns in which strategy, domestic politics, and myriad other
interests are all entangled.[38] That relationship underwent some typical strains after 1982, but emerged—again typically—essentially intact and even reinforced. A key element of Israel's overall strategy has
thus remained in place, regardless of the vicissitudes of its involvement in Lebanon over the past three years.

In seeking to cement its ties to Washington, Israel confronts the
obvious obstacle of policy differences over specific issues and, more
generally, of countervailing American interests in the Arab world.
The Reagan administration that has been in power over this entire
period has been basically well-disposed toward Israel, but conten-
tious bilateral issues have nevertheless arisen. The tension between
these two aspects of American-Israeli relations has produced an al-
ternating series of understandings and minunderstandings, all within
the parameters of the enduring "special relationship." Compounding
the complexity has been the usual chorus of somewhat different
voices within the American foreign-policy machinery dealing with Israel, which now has an unusual twist: the U.S. secretary of defense is
viewed in Jerusalem as less sympathetic than either of his successive
counterparts at the department of state, while the president and a
string of national security advisors are seen to have adopted, for the
most part, an uncharacteristically low profile on Arab-Israeli affairs.

A new element entered the picture in early 1982, when Sharon's
plans for Lebanon were added to the private agenda of American-
Israeli consultations. Whether or not, in the course of those consultations, the U.S. government (in the person of Secretary of State Alexander Haig) gave Israel a green light to invade Lebanon remains a
subject of intense but inconclusive debate.[39] What seems most likely
is that Haig indicated tacit approval for something like a reprise of
Operation Litani—that is, a rapid and temporary Israeli incursion
designed to wipe out the PLO military infrastructure in south Lebanon—but not for the sort of massive, drawn-out, and far-reaching
military operation that the Israelis eventually mounted. From Israel's
point of view, however, even that much American understanding
would have been an improvement over the attitude most often
adopted on this issue by the previous administration in Washington.

In the event, though, as Israel's campaign in Lebanon went beyond the limits apparently endorsed by Haig, a series of tense mo-
ments in American-Israeli relations ensued. A warning from the
United States helped produce a Syrian-Israeli ceasefire after a few
days of fighting in early June, demonstrating once again the special
American sensitivity to Soviet concerns in Mideast crisis situations.
Later, in early August, the sharply negative publicity surrounding the
siege of Beirut proved embarrassing to Washington. A couple of tele-
phone calls from Reagan to Begin ended some of Israel's most concentrated artillery and air assaults against the city, while the perennial
U.S. mediator, Philip Habib, put the finishing touches on the PLO
evacuation agreement.

Similar pressures, including another partial suspension of arms
deliveries, accompanied the negotiation of the May 1983 Lebanese-
Israeli accord.[40] In one sense, though, the continuing focus on Lebanon relieved Israel of the burden of objection to the broader Reagan
peace plan—a reversal, interestingly enough, of the prewar situation,
when the Carter administration's concern over the fate of Egyptian-
Israeli relations had muted its objections to some of Israel's earlier operations in Lebanon.[41] And by the end of 1983, as Washington discov-
ered that it shared with Jerusalem common interests, common enemies, and common frustrations in Lebanon, the dispute between the
two capitals had greatly softened. The following year brought election
season in both countries, along with the usual respite from controversial initiatives in Arab-Israeli affairs. In the Israeli case, moreover,
domestic political and economic fragility actually continued to shield
the government further from any of the notions occasionally enter-
tained in Washington about pressure on sensitive foreign policy matters. Public support for Israel in the United States fluctuated with
events, but the overall trend remained consistently and heavily in
sympathy with the Israeli as against the Arab side. As of mid-1985, to
take one indirect but revealing barometer of American domestic support, Israel could still count on more than two-thirds of the U.S. Senate opposing the sale of sophisticated weapons to Jordan. On top of all
these factors, U.S. policymakers evidently felt so badly burned by
Lebanon that they were loath to take on another painful and quite
possibly thankless Mideast peacemaking mission that might put
American-Israeli relations to the test again.[42]

Under the circumstances, the emphasis naturally reverted to the
understanding—indeed, the virtual alliance—between the two parties. The renewed warmth in American-Israeli ties was symbolized by

the revival in late 1983 of a formal "strategic understanding," which had been announced and then held in abeyance two years earlier. On a more concrete level, it was manifest in expanded cooperation on such things as bilateral free trade, weapons development, intelligence exchanges, international broadcasting, and—probably—even coordinated activity in certain specialized areas as far afield as Central America.

In retrospect, the 1982–1985 period confirms three basic long-term patterns of American-Israeli relations. First, quite apart from the crucial American domestic political factor, those relations are marked by a mixture of convergent and divergent attitudes and interests. Second, the divergences tend to come to the fore, briefly but decisively, during wartime crises—especially when there is concern in Washington about possible Soviet intervention and the U.S. president therefore gets personally involved. Third, once such crises are over, it is the convergence of interests that again typically predominates, as both governments take care to avoid a major falling out over those issues that still divide them. Thus, the vital asset (from Israel's perspective) of a close American connection emerged from the Lebanese imbroglio unimpaired and even reinforced. The sole area of lingering potential contention—and one that started to surface anew once both countries were gone from Lebanon—was the stalemated peace process that called into question another perceived vital Israeli asset: the West Bank.

The Peace Process and the West Bank

In conventional post-Camp David diplomatic parlance, the "peace process" has to do primarily with the Palestinian question—particularly the prospects for some form of Palestinian self-government, and even more particularly the fate of the Palestinian Arabs on the West Bank. (Gaza, which is much smaller, less populous, and less politically active, has usually been neglected.) Israeli policy toward that territory can usefully be divided, borrowing a distinction from the early Zionist political lexicon, into practical and political spheres. The former concerns actual Jewish settlement and control "on the ground"; the latter, the diplomatic aspects of that control.

In the practical sphere, relations between the Israeli government and the native West Bank population have remained troubled. A 1981 attempt to encourage a pliant Arab leadership in the form of village leagues under a civilian Israeli administration was largely abandoned after an upsurge of local resistance in the spring of the following year. Instead, a number of outspokenly nationalist elected or appointed municipal officials were ousted in favor of Israeli military governors. In the last two years, concern about violent opposition has mounted because of several factors directly or indirectly related to the situation in Lebanon: the inspiration of successful Shi'a guerrilla activity; the strain the Lebanese invasion imposed on Israeli intelligence resources; the transfer of some PLO operations to Jordan, just across the river from the West Bank; and the temptations aroused by Israel's agreement to prisoner exchanges that included large numbers of convicted Arab terrorists in November 1983 and again in May 1985. A serious short-term challenge to Israeli control is unlikely, however, because of a combination of countervailing factors. These include the relative affluence of the West Bank and its intimate economic ties to Israel; its isolation from nearby sanctuaries or staging areas for guerrilla activity; the depth of Israel's counterintelligence penetration of its society; the fact that the intense, even suicidal religious fervor characteristic of some other predominantly Muslim populations is all but unknown; and, not least, the much greater Israeli determination to hang on to the territory.

In this environment, Israel's use of such preventive and punitive measures as censorship, school closings, and—infrequently—the demolition of houses, detentions, and deportations have sufficed to keep trouble within tolerable limits and will most likely remain effective. Even so, sporadic demonstrations and murders of Jewish settlers or travelers have continued to plague the occupation authorities.[43] The past few years have also witnessed the emergence, in response, of Jewish vigilantes and underground "counterterrorist" cells among the West Bank settlers. A handful of such extremists were apprehended in 1984, and most were tried, convicted, and sentenced to prison terms in a controversial proceeding the following year. Nevertheless, a resolution of the underlying problems is remote; the odds are, rather, that the cycle of low-level violence on the West Bank will sputter on, but to no decisive effect.

More to the point is another, somewhat surprising recent trend: the pace of Jewish settlement on the West Bank has declined since 1982. The major expansion took place before the Lebanon war, when the number of settlers outside greater Jerusalem more than tripled

(from about 5,000 to about 16,000) under the first Likud government, from 1977 through 1980, and more than doubled again in
1981–82. Since then, growth has been slower in both absolute and
relative terms—and this despite ambitious plans and a new policy of
encouraging the rise of Jewish suburbs and satellite towns in the vicinity of major Israeli cities across the 1967 Green Line, made attractive by an assortment of government subsidies and other incentives.
Estimates vary, but a reasonable guess is that no more than 12,000–
15,000 new settlers have moved to the West Bank over the past three
years. Fiscal pressures on Israel's government have been largely responsible for this retrenchment, but the Labor party's relative lack of
enthusiasm for the entire project has also been a factor since the National Unity government was established in late 1984. The coalition
agreement specified a mere half-dozen new settlements for immediate construction, and even some of these have been delayed. In August 1985, Labor's Yitzhak Rabin (now the defense minister) took the
hitherto rare step of evicting a symbolic contingent of unauthorized
settlers from the southern West Bank town of Hebron.[44]

Nevertheless, the simple passage of time has begun to erase or at
least to obscure the old Green Line; by 1986, Israel will have controlled the West Bank for as long as Jordan did before the Six Day War.
During this time, the Israelis have managed to erect an imposing ar-
ray of settlements, complete with high-rise housing projects, a network of new roads, and local government councils, scattered throughout the length and breadth of the West Bank. Moreover, according to
Meron Benvenisti's carefully researched account, as of mid-1985 Israeli government and quasi-government authorities had managed to
acquire formal title (through purchase, demarcation for security purposes, and expropriation of unoccupied land) to a slim majority of the
entire area. This formidable physical presence has led some analysts
to conclude that the practical and political aspects of Israeli control
over the West Bank have imperceptibly merged; Israel's occupation,
in this view, is today almost a fait accompli, and as such irreversible.

In fact, however, from a purely demographic perspective, Jewish
settlers are still only a tiny minority on the West Bank—some 42,000
as against 750,000 Arabs. Moreover, the pace of Arab emigration
from the territory has slackened dramatically in recent years. Furthermore, more than half the settlers could conceivably be accom-
modated in Israel with only a minor modification of the boundaries
of 1967. The remainder, along with the structure of economic inter-

dependence and the infrastructure (water, power, transport, and the like) of West Bank connections with Israel that have grown up since that year, might theoretically be maintained in place under some alternative arrangement. The fact of Israeli occupation, then, is indeed difficult—but not literally impossible—to reverse. It could be ended, or at least altered, by an admittedly unlikely combination of changes in Israeli domestic politics and in the international arena.

In that arena (moving on from the practical to the political sphere), several of Sharon's statements suggest that the struggle to keep the West Bank and the war in Lebanon were connected, at least in his own mind and in the minds of some of his colleagues, in an indirect but important way. By crushing the PLO and thus depriving the Palestinians of a symbolic focus of resistance, Israel hoped to compel West Bank Arabs (and others) to accommodate themselves to permanent Israeli control over that land.[45] Though Israel fell far short of that objective, the Lebanese imbroglio did help postpone any serious international consideration of the West Bank issue for nearly three years. In this sense, peace with Egypt and war in Lebanon were of a piece in helping to consolidate Israeli control over the West Bank. It took a new situation on the Arab side (and a new government in Israel) to redirect attention to diplomacy aimed at loosening Israel's grip on the territory.

In the interim, the Israeli government had no trouble rejecting peace plans proposed both by President Reagan and by the second Arab summit at Fez in September 1982, whose most salient common thread was a call for Israel to relinquish the West Bank. The collapse of the first attempt at dialogue between King Hussein of Jordan and Yasser Arafat of the PLO in April 1983 pushed the whole issue further into the background; and, over the next eighteen months, all interested parties to the Arab-Israeli dispute reverted to their preoccupation with Lebanon. By the autumn of 1984, however, several new developments had combined to resuscitate talk of a "Jordanian option" for the West Bank.[46] These developments included the election of Shimon Peres, whose party advocated territorial compromise and whose new coalition pledged to seek negotiations with Jordan, as prime minister of Israel; the restoration of Jordanian-Egyptian diplomatic relations and resumption of summit-level consultations; and, most important of all, Hussein's renewed call, delivered at an unprecedented Palestine National Council meeting in Amman, for a joint Jordanian-PLO diplomatic initiative. Thus, almost exactly a decade after the Rabat summit where the Jordanian monarch had reluctantly ceded the right to represent the Palestinians to the PLO, he publicly reasserted his own claim to the Israeli-occupied West Bank.

The PLO, the other partner in this Arab diplomatic minuet, was now more receptive to Hussein's invitation. The reason was fairly obvious. An unintended byproduct of Israel's defeat of the PLO in Lebanon was a Syrian-supported split in the organization, sparked by a mutiny against Arafat led by one of his erstwhile commanders, Abu Musa. By the end of 1983, the PLO dissidents and their Syrian allies had forcibly ousted Arafat and his loyalists from their last remaining foothold in Lebanon, around Tripoli. For the redoubtable PLO leader, the price of maintaining his own position intact and independent of Damascus was a move toward Amman, if necessary even at the expense of previous policies. Thus, the PNC resolved to reopen the dialogue with Hussein, and to refer his proposal for a joint diplomatic approach to its executive committee. PLO spokesmen even began to talk of a Jordanian-Palestinian confederation in West Bank territory to be negotiated out from under Israeli control.[47] One might go so far as to say that, if the PLO was suddenly a prospective partner to a putative Jordanian option for Arab-Israeli peacemaking, Sharon had only himself to blame.

As for the new Israeli government, one might have expected some interest in this option as well; the Labor half, at least, of the National Unity coalition advocated a more flexible line on the West Bank, and Israel's chronic economic crisis compromised its ability to continue to colonize the area. Nevertheless, public reaction to the PNC meeting, both in the press and in the government, was generally indifferent at best.[48] The explanation for this goes beyond bargaining tactics, domestic political sensitivities, or substantive differences over territorial issues—all of which were important enough. Another obstacle was precisely the Israeli government's preoccupation with economic issues: the same financial pinch that had slowed West Bank settlement also relegated that whole issue to a public-policy back burner. Israel's quagmire in Lebanon had the same effect.

However, there was another, more immediate reason for Israeli reticence: Hussein was offering not a Jordanian but a joint Jordanian-PLO option. Even among those Israelis who profess, as does the Labor party, that the West Bank is negotiable, precious few would agree to negotiate it with the PLO. Opposition to that prospect is deeply rooted in a mixture of emotional and practical considerations. Therefore, so long as Hussein insisted on including the PLO, any Israeli government was almost certain to deflect his proposals.

In February 1985, Hussein announced agreement with Arafat on a joint diplomatic strategy, though there was still no explicit and unequivocal PLO endorsement of peace negotiations with Israel. The Reagan administration, too, continued to explore (though not at the highest levels) the possibility of negotiations with a combined delegation of Jordanian and PLO-approved representatives—a revival, after many diplomatic detours, of something approaching the formula that Israel's first Likud government had reluctantly (and but briefly) accepted back in 1977. But the current Israeli government, ever wary of indirect negotiations, of the PLO, and of the long-dreaded domestic and diplomatic showdown over the West Bank, objected to the nature of the proposed Palestinian delegation.[49] Behind such procedural wrangles, of course, lay a conflict of much greater substance: the kind of compromise, if any, that might still be possible on the West Bank.

On this issue, the Israeli government and public opinion alike remained deeply divided. In the former arena, the close election of 1984 produced (as in the previous election of 1981) a fragmented parliament in which both proponents and opponents of the "not one inch" school on territorial questions could claim substantial followings. Likud lost seven seats in the Knesset, but ultranationalists of various stripes (represented by the Tehiya, Morasha, and Kach parties) gained a total of five; the net difference was thus negligible. Within the ruling coalition, Likud of course remained staunchly opposed to any territorial concessions on the West Bank. Indeed, it extracted, as part of the price for joining the National Unity government, a promise of new national elections in the event that issue should ever be put to the test—a clause that greatly lessened the odds that it ever would.

The divided unity government was thus practically paralyzed on West Bank issues. Coalition crises loomed even over such relatively minor matters as cabinet-level visits to Cairo, arbitration of the Taba dispute, and the approval of a prisoner exchange. In the realm of public opinion, contradictory tendencies could be discerned over the three years since the Lebanese war: greater strength for the far right ultranationalists, but along with that a generally moderate drift in public sentiment as a whole. As of late 1984, for instance, a bare majority in several Israeli public opinion samplings was willing to contemplate some West Bank territorial concessions in exchange for peace, while a similar majority opposed continued unrestricted settlement there.[50]

But as usual, these numbers do not tell the whole story. For there exists a fluid yet very sizable segment of Israeli society, including a minority of hard-core militants, that remains opposed to any concessions on the West Bank to anyone under any circumstances. It is the existence of this "veto group" that, in great measure, has led some liberal Israelis of late to lament the emergence of militarist, mystical, and even racist tendencies in their society.[51] The fact is, however, that even those Israelis who are not ideologically committed to keeping the West Bank have no sure answers to either the security or the internal political problems posed by the prospect of withdrawal. As a result, it would probably take a dramatic move on the Arab side—perhaps something on the order of the surprises Sadat came up with in 1973 or 1977—plus a sustained, high-level diplomatic follow-up by the United States to produce any substantial shift in the Israeli position.

Regional and Global Environment

If Israel could afford the luxury of an optional war, even an inconclusive one, during this period, it was partly because its larger position in the region was more secure than had been the case on many occasions in the past. This reflected not just the defection of Egypt from the ranks of Arab confrontation states but other elements as well. The opportunities and constraints affecting Israel's foreign policy must be understood against the background of this regional environment, discussed elsewhere in this volume in detail. Suffice it to say here that two bitter enemies of Israel, one old and one new, were engaged against a different foe: Syria and, especially, Iran were preoccupied with hostility toward Iraq, the Arab state sandwiched between them.

A full-scale war between Iraq and Iran had erupted in September 1980, nearly two years before the Israeli invasion of Lebanon—and it was still underway more than three years afterward. At first, according to credible unofficial reports, Israel actually continued to sell a modest variety of weapons and spare parts to the new revolutionary government in Tehran. Later, Jerusalem reacted with uncharacteristic "benign neglect" to the improvement both of Baghdad's supply pipeline (literally and figuratively!) through Jordan, and of Iraqi-American diplomatic ties. But Israel had little more to do than look on, with barely disguised satisfaction, as these two potential foes battled each other.

There was, however, one troubling aspect, from Israel's standpoint, of Iran's regional role during these years: its instigation—or, at a minimum, inspiration—of a variety of militantly anti-Israel fundamentalist Shi'a groups in Lebanon, probably including Islamic Amal and Hezbollah. Still, those alarmists who proclaimed that Israel had acquired, metaphorically speaking, a hostile border with Iran vastly exaggerated the importance of this factor.

Syria, meanwhile, was also embroiled in a war of words (and worse) against Jordan, which had (as noted) enticed part of the PLO into contemplating peace talks with Israel. Such inter-Arab rivalries did nothing to advance Israel's quest for recognition, but they did serve as added insurance against an Arab war coalition on the eastern front. The "second circle" of Arab states was likewise distracted—in this case, by problems of internal security; by the Gulf war; and even by an unaccustomed financial squeeze occasioned by the international oil glut. True, Syria was quietly proceeding with an impressive military buildup that appeared aimed, both in rhetoric and in fact, at matching Israel's armed might all alone; but it was doubtful that Damascus could succeed in this endeavor in the foreseeable future. As so often before, divisions within the Arab camp did much to keep the Arab-Israeli dispute in a twilight zone of "no peace, no war."

In this connection, special mention must be made of the separate Egyptian-Israeli peace. Some observers have rather casually blamed this "betrayal" by Cairo for Israel's ability to strike at Lebanon with impunity. But it is not clear what Egypt could have done about that issue in any event; and it is worth noting that the Lebanon invasion took place after Israel's final withdrawal from Sinai—just when Jerusalem (and Washington) had greater reason to wonder whether the Egyptians, having recovered all their lost territory, might be more disposed to risk a reaction. Conversely, the previous Israeli invasion of Lebanon had occurred in early 1978, after Sadat's visit but before the successful conclusion of the Camp David and final peace treaty negotiations.

One would be hard-pressed, given this chronology, to argue that it was the actual treaty that somehow gave Israel the go-ahead in Lebanon. One might, however, make a plausible case that the Israelis, in planning their invasions, correctly calculated that, peace or no peace, Cairo was no more capable than any other Arab government of anything beyond symbolic protests. After all, Sadat had sought a deal with Israel precisely because his country was weak, committed to its American connection, and no longer willing to sacrifice immediate national objectives for the sake of a pan-Arab leadership role.

As for bilateral Egyptian-Israeli relations during this period, the record is decidedly mixed.[52] On the one hand, many Israelis were dismayed that normalization not only did not progress but actually regressed after the Lebanese war (although not nearly as many accepted some responsibility for this state of affairs). Attacks in the Egyptian media intensified; many cultural and commercial contacts were frozen; and Cairo's ambassador was recalled from Tel Aviv in the wake of the Sabra and Shatilla massacres. For the next three years, Egypt insisted that his return depended on a complete Israeli withdrawal from Lebanon, a satisfactory resolution of the Taba dispute, and—sometimes—on progress toward a comprehensive Arab-Israeli settlement as well. On the other hand, oil sales, formal diplomatic relations, and quiet on the southern front all continued. Indeed, Egyptian-Israeli peace survived several significant challenges during this time: the assassination of Sadat, the broader Islamic onslaught, the final return of Sinai, the war in Lebanon, and the entrenched stalemate on the Palestinian problem.

For Israel, peace with Egypt provided not just the tangible benefit of partial relief from the country's security burden, but also the intangible yet important benefit of partial acceptance in the Arab world. Once the National Unity government took office in Jerusalem, there was a slight thaw in the frustrating "cold peace" with Cairo. In the best of circumstances, this might have triggered a dynamic wherein the two capitals could reciprocate each other's moves, trading diplomatic flexibility for a further warming of bilateral ties. It might have been so, were it not for the fact that the issues involved were so intractable, the Israelis so hopelessly divided, and Egyptian leverage on all parties so limited.

While Israel's relations with its immediate neighbors and with Washington continued to overshadow all other issues, economic and to a lesser extent political and even psychological imperatives also continued to drive the Jewish state to cultivate as wide a range of outside connections as possible. In this wider context, Israel remained largely isolated in the United Nations and other international forums, with as little concrete effect as before. The country's relations with Western Europe, important primarily for economic reasons, were generally stable, except for occasional minor squabbles over the peacekeeping forces in Lebanon and the like. Elsewhere, there was actually a slight improvement in Israel's diplomatic position and economic/security relations with several countries in Asia and Latin America toward the end of the period. The trend was noticeable even in Black Africa, despite the fact that Jerusalem maintained significant diplomatic, economic, and probably also military links with the increasingly hard-pressed South African white minority regime.[53]

The period also witnessed several meetings at a relatively high level between Israeli and Soviet representatives, at which the former professed their interest in a renewal of the diplomatic relations that had been severed in 1967. But Israel had been drawn toward ever more explicit association with Washington's anti-Soviet regional strategy, while the Soviet Union remained publicly committed to a "peace process' that included Syria and the PLO in roles no Israeli government could accept. As a result, no major changes in the mutually wary relationship between Moscow and Jerusalem appeared on the horizon. Finally, Israel scored one interesting symbolic success in the airlift of over 10,000 black Jews from Ethiopia, mostly via the Sudan, during 1984–1985. None of these peripheral issues, though was likely to have a major effect on Israel's future foreign policy, whose prospects our next, concluding section will explore.

Conclusion: Post-Lebanon Trends and Prospects

Looking back over the turbulent record of Israeli internal and external affairs since the war in Lebanon, one can see how, broadly speaking, the interaction between foreign and domestic affairs, and between grand strategy and improvised tactics in the latter arena, has shaped Israeli policy. Israel's policy in Lebanon was intimately connected with the careers of individual policymakers and the course of Israeli domestic politics as a whole; that connection helps explain the nature both of Israel's original grand strategy there and of its subsequent retrenchment to an essentially reactive approach. But the main lines of Israel's long-term strategy—alignment with the United States and peace with Egypt, despite the deadlock on other fronts—have been much more loosely linked with Israel's internal turmoil, or, for that matter, with Lebanon. As a result, that strategy has survived largely intact.

Since 1982, indeed, the logic of Israel's geopolitical position has reasserted itself. The country is incapable, as the war in Lebanon suggested, of reordering the political map of the region on its own; indeed, it remains dependent, to some indeterminate but undoubtedly important and ever-increasing extent, on the political goodwill and economic largesse of its superpower patron. At the same time, notwithstanding all the problems of the last few years, Israel has retained a good measure of both internal stability and strategic superiority (especially in view of the changes in Egypt's capabilities and intentions) over any likely combination of outside challengers. It has also retained a substantial capacity for independent action—or stubborn inaction, as the case may be. On the perennial issue of the occupied territories, for example, Jerusalem is still militarily capable of holding on, and probably politically incapable of letting go. In short, Israel's basic security posture has been remarkably unaffected by its drawn-out involvement in Lebanon, and remarkably resistant to change from within.

To be sure, halfway through the 1980s, Israel faces chronic economic problems that may, if unchecked, eventually have a real adverse effect on its political cohesion and defense posture alike— whether in the area of manpower, of morale, of equipment, or of truly inhibiting dependence on American assistance. For the foreseeable future, though, Israel appears quite capable of muddling through this crisis. Moreover, insofar as economic factors affect the regional equation, the evidence so far suggests that the Arab side has also missed the boat in the last decade: it has failed to translate the post-1973 and post-1980 oil bonanzas into usable political or military power. Indeed, by aggravating internal and inter-Arab tensions, the oil boom may well have boomeranged on its inheritors; in any event, it is now fast fading altogether.

Over the past four years, Israelis have been disappointed in both peace (with Egypt) and war (in Lebanon). They have attempted an ambitious strategy, aimed at altering the regional political constellation, and failed; and they have yet to come up with a coherent replacement strategy. The reasons for this, as the preceding discussion has shown, have much to do with the country's delicate domestic balance and with the significant regional and global constraints on its foreign policy—and also with the relative acceptability of an uneasy but manageable status quo.

The prospects for a major alteration of that status quo are, as with everything else in the Middle East, unlikely but uncertain. In the short term, Israel can simply sit still; indeed, the marriage of convenience between Labor and Likud inclines the government to eschew major (and inevitably divisive) initiatives, either for peace or war. The scheduled transfer of leadership from Peres to Shamir in late 1986 offers some prospect of movement, before or after the event, but even that is no guarantee. If the ruling coalition were to split over West Bank issues, the moderates might still manage to keep a majority in the Knesset; some of Likud's nominal allies would probably prefer to stay in power, and much of today's moderate opposition might join. Israeli society would be sharply divided, even though there are probably a fair number of Likud supporters, especially among the Sephardim, who are not categorically committed to Greater Israel.[54] But any Israeli government would need a compelling reason to confront the large, doctrinaire, and entrenched militant bloc on this matter.

In the medium term, a great deal will depend, as the analysis above suggests, on the interaction of Israeli and American policy—specifically, on how much leeway each affords the other in avoiding or in confronting, after nearly two decades, the issue of the occupied territories on which the two governments have theoretically been at odds many times since 1967. The issue will soon be complicated by domestic politics on both sides: the rotation of prime ministers (or time-consuming and unpredictable government shuffles or new elections) in Israel, and the next congressional (and, before too long, presidential) elections in the United States. Next to such factors, shifts in internal or regional political alignments on the Arab side pale by comparison; certainly, a more substantial and improbable change in the Arab constellation would be required to provoke an American-Israeli diplomatic showdown. Short of that, the odds of a major change in Israel's foreign policy, even in the medium term, are not very high. The cold peace with Egypt has confirmed for many Israelis, even those predisposed toward relatively moderate positions, that foolproof safeguards or guarantees are simply not available, and that the recompense for risky concessions remains almost as elusive as ever.

Finally, in the long term, the Arab-Jewish demographic issue inside Israel and the occupied territories may well become a more explosive one than it has been over the past generation. It will probably stay under control, if at increasing cost. But sooner or later, the unsettled regional conflict is likely to erupt in another major war. The precedent of peace with Egypt, the tortuous evolution of a more moderate Arab consensus, and Israel's own chastened attitude in the aftermath of its intervention in Lebanon combine to offer some hope of averting this gloomy scenario.

Yet even a settlement of the Arab-Israeli dispute, given the enduring animosities and shifting fortunes and ambitions of all sides, may be inherently unstable. Altogether, the experience of the last few years suggests that Israel's foreign policy will remain geared, for both internal and external reasons, toward short-term crises, medium-term security, and long-term uncertainty—in other words, to the uncomfortable but not unmanageable situation that has been the country's fate so far.

NOTES

1. On these issues see, inter alia, Robert O. Freedman, ed., *Israel in the Begin Era* (New York: Praeger, 1982).

2. See *New York Times,* 3 September 1977.

3. On this episode, see especially Raymond Cohen, "Israel and the Soviet-American Statement of October 1, 1977: The Limits of Patron-Client Influence," *Orbis 22, no. 3 (Fall 1978):613–33.*

4. *See Jeune Afrique,* No. 904 (3 March 1978); Sidney Zion and Uri Dan, "The Untold Story of the Middle East Talks," *New York Times Magazine,* 21 January 1979, pp. 20ff; and *New York Times,* 26 August and 27 November 1977.

5. *Ha'aretz,* 14–17 August 1978; and *Jerusalem Post,* Weekly International Edition (hereafter *Jerusalem Post*), 18 April and 25 July 1978.

6. Text in U.S. Congress, House of Representatives, Committee on Foreign Affairs, *The Search for Peace in the Middle East: Documents and Statements 1967–1979* (hereafter *Documents*), Committee Print (Washington, D.C.: U.S. Government Printing Office, 1980), pp. 20–29.

7. See *ibid.* for text of the treaty and accompanying letters.

8. *Jerusalem Post,* 6–12 July 1980; U.S. Congress, House of Representatives, Committee on Foreign Affairs, *Status of the Middle East Peace Talks Regarding the West Bank and Gaza,* Hearings Before the Subcommittee on Europe and the Middle East, 96th Congress, 1st Session, 23 October 1979. Also see *Jewish Week* (Washington, D.C.), 3–9 April, 31 August–6 September, and 23–29 October 1980.

9. *Documents,* pp. 322–324; *Washington Star,* 15 and 16 August 1979; and *Washington Post,* 24 September and 17 October 1979.

10. A more extensive discussion of these issues can be found in David Pollock, *The Politics of Pressure: American Arms and Israeli Policy Since the Six Day War* (Westport, Conn.: Greenwood Press, 1982), ch. 7.

11. In a 1979 interview with the author, Yitzhak Rabin, who was Prime Minister of Israel from 1974 to 1977, went so far as to state that Israel's links with friendly forces just across the Lebanese frontier during that period were actually "minor" by comparison with the emerging relationship between the Jewish state and the Maronite militias further to the north.

12. See the excellent summary of this episode in Norman F. Howard, "Lebanon's Clouded Future," *Current History*, January 1979:23ff. In a 1979 interview with the author, Mordechai Gur, who was Israeli Chief of Staff during Operation Litani, confirmed that Israel's concern about Carter administration reactions to its use of American-made weapons in Lebanon—and more broadly, about the entire vital arms pipeline from Washington—was an important constraint on Israeli policy in Lebanon during this period.

13. See, inter alia, *Jerusalem Post*, 17–23 May, 26 July–1 August, and 16–22 August 1981; and *New York Times*, 24 April and 23 July 1981.

14. On this period, see the valuable summary analysis in Itamar Rabinovich, *The War for Lebanon, 1970–1983* (Ithaca, N.Y.: Cornell University Press, 1984), ch. 4.

15. The best discussion of Israeli planning is in Ze'ev Schiff and Ehud Ya'ari, *Israel's Lebanon War*, tr. Ina Friedman (New York: Simon and Schuster, 1984).

16. A useful though occasionally biased or inaccurate overview of the military aspects of the war can be found in Richard A. Gabriel, *Operation Peace for Galilee: The Israeli-PLO War in Lebanon* (New York: Hill and Wang, 1984). Other perspectives are provided in a number of articles in recent issues of the *Journal of Palestine Studies*. An interesting if partisan brief analysis of the political utility of Israel's siege tactics is in Sara Averick, "Pressure and Progress: Israel and West Beirut," *Near East Report* 26, no. 33 (13 August 1982):162–63.

17. See, inter alia, Rabinovich, *War for Lebanon*, ch. 5.

18. For text of the Israeli Cabinet communiqué rejecting the Reagan plan, see *Journal of Palestine Studies* 12, no. 2 (Winter 1983):211–12.

19. Text of the Final Report of the Kahan Commission may be found in Itamar Rabinovich and Jehuda Reinharz, eds., *Israel in the Middle East: Documents and Readings on Society, Politics, and Foreign Policy, 1948–Present* (New York: Oxford University Press, 1984), pp. 348–56. Among the numerous accounts of this incident, see especially Schiff and Ya'ari, *Israel's Lebanon War*, and also Schiff's shorter piece, "Who Decided, Who Informed," *New Outlook*, October 1982, pp. 19–22.

20. These aspects of Israeli domestic politics during this time are analyzed at length in David Pollock, "Likud in Power: Divided We Stand," in Freedman, *Israel in Begin Era*, p. 21.

21. On domestic issues during this period, see, in addition to the works already cited, Alan Dowty, "Israel: From Ideology to Reality," in Alvin Z. Rubinstein, ed., *The Arab-Israeli Conflict: Perspectives* (New York: Praeger, 1984, pp. 107–44, esp. pp. 130–42; Don Peretz, "Israeli Policy," in Robert O. Freedman, ed., *The Middle East Since Camp David* (Boulder, Colorado: Westview Press, 1984; Asher Arian, *Politics in Israel: The Second Generation* (London: Chatham House, 1985); and Charles Liebman and Eliezer Don-Yehiya, *Religion and Politics in Israel* (Bloomington: Indiana University Press, 1984).

22. See Asher Arian, "Elections 1981: Competitiveness and Polarization," *Jerusalem Quarterly*, no. 21 (Fall 1981):3–27.

23. For details on these developments, see especially Schiff and Ya'ari, *Israel's Lebanon War*; and Dan Horowitz, "Israel's War in Lebanon: New Patterns of Strategic Thinking and Civilian-Military Relations," in the exceptionally valuable compendium edited by Moshe Lissak, *Israeli Society and Its Defense Establishment* (Jerusalem: Biblio Distributors of Israel Universities Press, 1984), pp. 83–101. An important "corrective" argument, one that has been taken into account here, is presented in Avner Yaniv and Robert J. Lieber, "Personal Whim or Strategic Imperative? The Israeli Invasion of Lebanon," *International Security* 8, no. 2 (Fall 1983):117–42.

24. A good summary of wartime domestic trends is in Yael Yishai, "Dissent in Israel: Opinions on the Lebanon War," *Middle East Review* 168, no. 2 (Winter 1983/84:38–44.

25. See, for example, Ehud Ya'ari, "Israel's Dilemma in Lebanon," *Middle East Insight* 3, no. 4 (April/May 1984):18–23.

26. In analyzing the 1984 election, the author has benefited from a review of primary campaign materials collected in December of that year by Hanna Herzog and Charles Berlin of the Judaica Department, Widener Library, Harvard University. See also, inter alia, Don Peretz and Sammy Smooha, "Israel's Eleventh Knesset Election," *Middle East Journal* 39, no. 1 (Winter 1985):86–104.

27. An excellent analysis of the ebb and flow of interest in foreign policy on the part of the National Religious Party, the long-time electoral leader in the religious camp, is in Stuart Reiser, *The Politics of Leverage: The National Religious Party of Israel and Its Influence on Foreign Policy*, Harvard Middle East Papers, Modern Series, No. 2 (Cambridge, Mass.: Harvard University Center for Middle Eastern Studies, 1984).

28. The preceding analysis of party strength and positions and of coalition formation is based largely on the author's interviews and discussions in Israel in September 1984.

29. The "Kahane phenomenon" has been extensively analyzed and debated in the Israeli press, both Hebrew and English: See, for example, *Jerusalem Post,* various weekly editions in August and September 1985.

30. The foregoing is based on the author's discussions with a variety of participants in and observers of Israeli life and politics scene throughout the summer of 1985. A contrary but unconvincing impression is conveyed by Ze'ev Schiff, usually an astute commentator but perhaps a bit too removed from the Israeli scene at the time, in "The Specter of Civil War in Israel," *Middle East Journal* 39, no. 2 (Spring 1985):231–45.

31. On the economic package deals, see the extensive Israeli reportage translated in *Foreign Broadcast Information Service, Daily Report: Middle East and Africa* (Washington, D.C.), various issues in November 1984 and April 1985. Other relevant issues are treated in detail in recent issues of the monthly *Israel Economist* (Jerusalem). For a sense of the most recent developments, see "Record inflation is all part of plan" (sic!), *Jerusalem Post,* 24 August 1985. A good outline of some of the underlying problems is Ibrahim M. Oweiss, "The Israeli Economy and Its Military Liability," *American-Arab Affairs,* no. 8 (Spring 1984):31–40.

32. The text of the agreement is in *Journal of Palestine Studies* 12, no. 4 (Summer 1983):91–101.

33. See *Davar,* 17 January 1985, and *Yediot Aharonot,* 22 and 24 January 1985.

34. A useful overview of the evolution of Israeli policy on Lebanese issues may be found in Ze'ev Schiff, "Lebanon: Motivations and Interests in Israel's Policy," *Middle East Journal* 38, no. 2 (Spring 1984):220–27.

35. For different views of this and related questions, see various articles and research notes in recent issues of the valuable *Jerusalem Quarterly* and David K. Shipler, "Israel: Voices of Moral Anguish," *New York Times Magazine*, 27 February 1983.

36. See Elliot A. Cohen, "'Peace for Galilee': Success or Failure?" *Commentary* 78, no. 5 (November 1984):24–30; and Charles Krauthammer, "Who Won Lebanon?" *New Republic*, 24 June 1985:15–16.

37. For solid, week-by-week accounts of the urgent American-Israeli economic consultations throughout 1984 and 1985, see the reportage of Wolf Blitzer in *Jerusalem Post* (various issues during this period). A good analytical treatment of this important topic, however, is not yet available.

38. For an exhaustive analysis of one key aspect of this relationship over the period 1967–1981, see my *Politics of Pressure*, supra.

39. Ze'ev Schiff, in the works cited above and elsewhere, has advocated the "green light" thesis; other authors cited above dispute that contention. Haig's own memoir predictably skirts the issue, and no one else, to my knowledge, has presented conclusive evidence or argument.

40. On these points I am following the line of argument convincingly offered by William B. Quandt in a presentation to the Harvard University Center for International Affairs Mideast Colloquium, Cambridge, Mass., October 1984.

41. Information based on author's interviews with U.S. policymakers in the National Security Council and Department of State, Washington, D.C., July 1979.

42. See *Washington Post,* 12 September 1985, and *New York Times,* 13 September 1985.

43. For an account of recent incidents of this sort and official and unofficial reactions to them, see "Army acts to prevent terror; Rabin warns vigilantes not to take law into their hands," *Jerusalem Post,* 14 September 1985.

44. For useful reports on the West Bank settlement program, see especially Meron Benvenisti, *The West Bank Data Project: A Survey of Israel's Policies* (Washington, D.C.: American Enterprise Institute for Public Policy Research, 1984); Ann M. Lesch, "Israeli Settlement in the West Bank: Mortgaging the Future," *Journal of South Asian and Middle Eastern Studies* 7, no. 1 (Fall 1983):3–23; and Peter Demant, "Israeli Settlement Policy Today," *MERIP Reports,* July/August 1983, pp. 3–13. All three sources are better on fact than on analysis, and the gloomy conclusions of the first two authors are in part disputed here.

45. This interpretation is perhaps most forcefully argued in Shmuel Sandler and Hillel Frisch, *Israel, the Palestinians, and the West Bank* (Lexington, Mass.: Lexington Books, 1984), ch. 7.

46. This conjuncture is analyzed in more detail, particularly from an Arab perspective, in my article "Jordan: Option or Optical Illusion?" *Middle East Insight,* March/April 1985, pp. 19–26, from which some of the material that follows is adapted.

47. See the interview (in Arabic) with PLO leader Nabil Sha'ath in *Al-Sharq Al-Awsat,* 27 December 1984, p. 8.

48. See reportage and editorial comment in *Ma'ariv,* 25 and 26 November 1984; *Ha'aretz,* 25 and 30 November 1984; and *Jerusalem Post,* 6 December 1984.

49. "Fears in Israel over U.S. policy on PLO," *Jerusalem Post,* 14 September 1985.

50. A provocative yet serious analysis of recent trends is to be found in Gloria Falk, "Israeli Public Opinion: Looking Toward a Palestinian Solution," *Middle East Journal* 39, no. 3 (Summer 1985):247–69.

51. An incomparably poignant, even poetic personal tour of Israel's contemporary political landscape along these lines is Amos Oz, *In the Land of Israel,* tr. Marie Goldberg-Bartura (New York: Harcourt Brace Jovanovich, 1983).

52. A reasonably recent survey is in Joel Beinin, "The Cold Peace," *MERIP Reports,* January 1985:3–9.

53. This point was made by Naomi Chazan, one of Israel's leading academic specialists on Africa, in a presentation at the Africa Colloquium, Center for International Affairs, Harvard University, Cambridge, October 1984.

54. Some interesting theories about the alleged hawkishness of Israel's Sephardim are presented in Ofira Seliktar, "Ethnic Stratification and Foreign Policy in Israel: The Attitudes of Oriental Jews towards the Arabs and the Arab-Israeli Conflict," *Middle East Journal* 38, no. 1 (Winter 1984):34–50. An eloquent rebuttal that calls Seliktar's basic assumption of Sephardi hawkishness into question is Daniel Meron, "Sephardi Foreign Policy Attitudes and Their Significance to the West Bank Issue," unpublished paper, Harvard University, January 1985.

10

Syrian Policy in the Aftermath of the Israeli Invasion of Lebanon

John F. Devlin

T HE ISRAELI INVASION of Lebanon in June 1982 set in train events that have altered Syrian relations with all the principal elements operating in geographic Syria, an area consisting of the present Syrian Arab Republic, Lebanon, Jordan, Israel, and the Israeli-occupied West Bank and Gaza. Those elements—the major Lebanese factions, the Palestine Liberation Organization (PLO) and its constituent parts, Jordan, Israel, the superpowers, and certain less influential actors—are all discussed below with reference to Syria. So also are certain developments relating to Iraq and Iran that have affected Syrian policy and actions. Although the chief issues are treated separately, there is a high degree of interaction among them all.

Domestic Affairs

In the months preceding the invasion, the Ba'ath regime had ruthlessly crushed an uprising of the Islamic Front in Hamah. Dealing extensive damage to the city (Syria's third largest) and inflicting thousands of casualties, government troops succeeded in breaking the back of a campaign of violence that the Islamic movement had begun six years earlier. Although the Muslim Brotherhood, the Front, and a number of secular political organizations formed a National Alliance for the Salvation of Syria in March 1982, there has been little anti-regime activity since.[1] Indeed, there have been reports that the movement has been further weakened since Hamah by internal divisions stemming from long-standing differences among members of the Brotherhood concerning the utility of armed struggle—differences that were exacerbated by its failure.

The centralized, authoritarian system of rule developed by Hafiz
al-Assad to suit his personal style has remained intact and effective
up to the present.[2] A government with an authoritarian cast has long
been the norm in Syrian political life, although there was a brief and
not very successful experiment with elections and parliaments in the
early years of Syrian independence. The person of the ruler is all-im-
portant, however, and Syrians had a sharp reminder in 1984 that
Hafiz al-Assad, for all his fifteen years in power, was mortal and that
his indefinite continuance in office was far from assured.[3]

President Assad was forced to stop working on November 13,
1983, due to a heart attack. Unable to perform the duties of his office
for several weeks, he began to make limited appearances in early December, returned to his office on January 28, 1984, and gradually resumed a full workload. (Like so many leaders, he is a workaholic.)
During his incapacity, a half-dozen of his principal lieutenants ran the
country.[4] The military establishment, which he has controlled
through a patron-client pyramid, remained loyal to him. However, his
brother Rifa'at—then in command of the *Saraya al-Difa'* (defense
companies), a large, heavily armed, very well-paid organization that
was personally loyal to him—had ambitions of his own.

In late February 1984, a somewhat bizarre series of events began.
Large numbers of pictures of Rifa'at al-Assad were plastered on walls
in Damascus one night and were promptly removed the next day. In
short order, Damascenes were experiencing a situation not seen since
Hafiz al-Assad seized power through threat of force in his "corrective
movement" of November 1970. Armed units loyal to Rifa'at were facing other armed units from the presidential guard commanded by Adnan Makhluf, from the special forces commanded by Ali Haydar, and
the Third Division commanded by Shafiq Fayyad. (All three are Ala-
wis, as are many of the senior military officers.) President Assad's
first move to defuse this crisis was to appoint three vice-presidents on
March 11. Rifa'at was one; Abd al-Halim Khaddam, long-time foreign
minister, was the second; and Zuhayr Mushariqah, number two in the
Ba'ath party hierarchy, the third.[5] This move did not affect the military establishment, which is the most important prop of Assad's regime; nor did it end the confrontations of armed bodies, though there
was no fighting of any consequence.

President Assad could not risk an open feud with his brother:
family solidarity is too important to Syrians. But Rifa'at's initiativ.
put at risk the stability of the regime, for many of the president's sup-

porters were loyal to him personally. Moreover, Rifa'at, though he had been a tower of strength in internal security matters, had gained a reputation for corruption and high living, and was attempting to build a personal following in the Ba'ath party. At the end of May, President Assad sent Rifa'at, Fayyad, and Haydar on a mission to the USSR. This was apparently ceremonial, for there seems to have been no particular reason for it (nor any apparent results). The other officers returned fairly soon, but Rifa'at went to Europe and stayed there until November.

When Rifa'at al-Assad returned to Syria he did so as vice-president for national security matters, so designated by presidential decree of November 10, 1984.[6] In midsummer, however, at least half of the personnel of the defense companies was put under ministry of defense command. Despite his current title, Rifa'at does not appear to have operational control or command authority over the civilian intelligence apparatus (*mukhabarat*), the Deuxieme Bureau (G-2), or the special forces, and only indirect—though probably effective—control of the much reduced defense companies. Three of his supporters, including the minister of interior and the head of the national security office, lost their positions on the regional command of the Ba'ath party at its January 1985 congress.[7] By contrast, there have been no significant changes in the military establishment. Minister of Defense Mustafa Talas, Chief of Staff Hikmat Shihabi, Deputy Chief of Staff Ali Aslan, the only full generals in the Syrian armed forces, remain in the posts they have held for years, as do most divisional commanders.

There are two schools of thought as to the meaning of Rifa'at's adventures and current position. One is that President Assad is cautiously restoring Rifa'at to his former prominence. The other theory, and to my mind a much more likely one, is that the president is seeking to avoid public disgrace and a family feud, but is nevertheless determined to keep his brother on the sidelines where he has less opportunity to harm the regime through excess. He may still be useful to the president, however, especially in external matters, since he has close personal ties to both Saudi crown prince Abdallah and former president Franjiyah of Lebanon.

Three events that took place in early 1985 show the extent to which Syria is running normally. First, in January, the Ba'ath party held its eighth regional congress, which brought together eight-hundred party delegates for a discussion of reports and the selection of a new party command. The newly chosen command has five new members, three of whom replaced supporters of Rifa'at who were downgraded to lesser party status and the others replacing a man who had died and one who is terminally ill. Second, the new command nominated Hafiz al-Assad for a third seven-year term as president; the nomination was approved, as the constitution requires, by the people's assembly and ratified by 99.9 percent of the voters in a referendum. (He began his term March 12.) Third, Prime Minister Abd al-Ra'uf Kism formed a new cabinet. Many of the ministers were technicians with qualifications appropriate for the ministries they head, which are in any case administrative rather than policy-making organizations. Ba'ath party members dominate the cabinet with twenty-two out of thirty-six posts, including the ministries of defense and interior and the deputy premierships for defense, services, and economic affairs.[8]

External Affairs

The guiding principles of Syria's external policy, as practiced under Ba'ath party rule, may be summarized as follows:

1. Syria must be "an actor in the Middle East scene, rather than a stage on which others tried to play roles."[9]

2. The Fertile Crescent is the area of primary Syrian concern. Ottoman or geographic Syria—the area stretching from the modern Syrian-Turkish border to Aqaba, and from the Mediterranean to the desert—is Syria's special sphere of interest in which other states intrude only at the risk of Syrian hostility.

3. Pan-Arabism is not an important contemporary Syrian interest.

4. The support of another major Arab state is critical if Syria is to make lasting gains in geographic Syria.

5. Exclusive reliance on one of the two superpowers is not in Syria's best interests.

The first two principles are readily discernible from an appraisal of Syrian conduct since the mid-1960s.[10] Although Syrian leaders do not formulate their external policy philosophy in these words, I believe that the first two principles and the last would be considered accurate by Syrian leaders. Such is not the case with the third and fourth points, however. Official Ba'ath ideology remains pan-Arab; for example, President Assad ended a recent speech by referring to the historic Ba'ath goals of Arab unity, freedom, and socialism;[11] and the Ba'ath party has a nominal pan-Arab structure. In practice, however, that structure outside Syria is limited to party units of Lebanese, Palestinians, Jordanians, and Iraqis in roughly that order of size. Even so, Syrian state interests are the driving force in Damascus's relations with Fertile Crescent states.

The fourth proposition is less immediately apparent. Evidence in support of it lies in Damascus's successes of the early to mid-1970s, when relations with Egypt were strong. It will be discussed in more detail below.

Guidance for the policy and actions of the Ba'ath regime flows from these propositions. It must resist Israel, especially the latter's efforts at expansion whether on the ground (as in the Golan) or by manipulation of local elements, as in Lebanon. It must try to limit or channel the influence that other regional states can bring to bear in Lebanon, in Jordan, and among the Palestinians. It must oppose Iraqi ambitions for a pliant Ba'ath regime in Damascus and, conversely, try to weaken the regime in Baghdad.

The analysis that follows treats Syrian interests and activities in the light of these propositions and their implications.

Lebanon

The strife-torn little state lying immediately to its west has occupied much of Syria's attention as well as much of the resources it allots to external matters. In June 1982 Lebanon had for six years effectively been divided into several major—and many minor—autonomous pieces. The major pieces were the Syrian-occupied area in the north and east; the PLO-dominated area in the south; the Maronite heartland controlled by Bashir Gemayel's Lebanese Forces; the enclave along the southern border run by the late Sa'ad Haddad (with Israeli support and direction); and former president Franjiyah's fiefdom in the hills east of Tripoli. The events of 1982 rearranged the boundaries of these regions, eliminating that of the PLO, and brought new forces to the fore, notably in the Shi'a community. Events did not, however, change the underlying pattern of a virtually powerless central government presiding over, but scarcely able to influence, its several constituent pieces.

The war itself has been extensively reported, but a brief review is in order. The Begin administration, whose Lebanese policy was in the

hands of Defense Minister Ariel Sharon, had been waiting for months
for an excuse to strike the PLO, destroy its military power, and
weaken if not eliminate its influence in the West Bank. It also hoped
to make Bashir Gemayel president of a friendly Lebanon.[12] Israeli
forces drove to the outskirts of Beirut, pushed Syrian ground forces
north beyond the Beirut-Damascus highway, destroyed Syrian missile sites, and shot down some eighty-five Syrian aircraft. When PLO
forces left Beirut at the end of August 1982, Israel controlled the
south, Syria the northern part of the Bekaa Valley and the region
around Tripoli, and Gemayel the Maronite heartland.

The Syrians had been beaten and, moreover, had failed to manage
the situation in Lebanon so as to prevent Israeli forces from advanc-
ing to positions from which they could now threaten Damascus from
the west. However, Assad was not disposed to abandon a field of such
crucial importance to Syria. He first turned to the USSR for equipment to make up the severe losses which had left Syria vulnerable,
especially in air defense, just as Egypt had done during the 1969–
1970 war of attrition. Early in 1983, the Soviets deployed surface-to-
air missile systems at two sites. Manned by Soviet troops, the systems
gave protection to much of Syria and covered Lebanese and some of
Israel's airspace as well.

In regard to Lebanon, from the beginning Syria objected to equat-
ing the presence of its forces, which had been invited by the Lebanese
government, with the Israeli "aggressors."[13] The Syrians also began to
talk more and more about the unacceptability of Israeli gains in Lebanon as a result of what Damascus termed aggression. The Syrians
also made it clear that they intended to leave after the Israelis did.[14]
After weeks of wrangling over venue and agenda, the U.S.–sponsored
Lebanese-Israeli talks began on December 28, 1982. A month later,
Foreign Minister Khaddam stated: "We reiterate Syria's rejection of
the Israeli terms. We reject any terms imposed on Lebanon if these
terms harm its security, future, unity, interests, and sovereignty; or if
these terms harm Syria's security and interests."[15] Damascus rejected the terms of the agreement that was worked out when Lebanese Foreign Minister Elie Salem presented them in early May before
the formal signing.[16]

The Lebanese-Israeli agreement of May 17, 1983, marked a new
stage. The Lebanese government signed it basically because President Amin Gemayel believed that the United States would stand behind his government in its attempt to assert authority over the coun-

try. Given Gemayel's weak position—with the Lebanese Forces loyal to the memory of his dead brother rather than to him, and under extreme pressure from powerful figures within the Maronite community—he needed external support to have any hope of achieving that goal. Although Gemayel was correct in his expectations of U.S. support, the Reagan administration dealt with the Lebanese situation under the shadow of a fundamental perceptual error: it treated the Gemayel regime as the legitimate and rightful government, rather than recognizing it for what it was—just one among several actors on the Lebanese stage. Certainly, Gemayel conducted himself much more as a Maronite leader than as president of all Lebanese. In any event, both Gemayel and the Americans were wrong in believing that any amount of support and force would enable the majority of the Maronite community to dominate Lebanon against the desires of the Shi'as, Druze, Sunnis, and other Maronites.

Damascus was the logical—indeed the only—place for these actors to turn for assistance. The Druze, under Walid Jumblatt, entered into hostilities early in 1983 with units of the Lebanese forces that Israel had allowed into the mixed Druze-Maronite area of the Chouf after the summer of 1982.[17] When the Israelis pulled out of the Chouf at the beginning of September 1983, the scale of hostilities grew. Jumblatt's Druze had plenty of support from Syria, while the Lebanese Forces and Maronite units of the Lebanese army got active help from the United States. On September 19, guns from U.S. warships fired in support of Lebanese troops under attack at Suq al-Gharb.[18] Guns and aircraft were used on a number of other occasions, and two carrier aircraft were shot down late in the year. The Marines, originally sent in as peacekeepers, ended up as targets; 240 died in a single bombing on October 23, 1983. The United States withdrew its land forces on February 26, 1984, and its naval vessels left Lebanese waters a few weeks later.

Amin Gemayel is, if nothing else, a realist. A week after the U.S. Marines pulled out, Lebanon abrogated the May 17, 1983, agreement with Israel. He went to Damascus in early April 1984 for three days of talks with Hafiz al-Assad. In the succeeding year, he made substantial accommodations to the reality that Damascus—having helped push the United States out, driven Yasser Arafat from Tripoli, and encouraged Shi'a forces to exert pressure on the Israelis—was the dominant force in his country. In accepting Syrian predominance, however, Gemayel was out of tune with opinion in the bulk of the Maronite community. As of this writing, that majority has given no indication that it is willing to accept the slightest reduction in its status. (The Lebanese Forces turned against Gemayel in March 1985, choosing as their leader Samir Ja'ja'.)[19]

Efforts of the Lebanese Forces to exert control over areas outside the Maronite heartland have failed. It was a contingent commanded by Ja'ja' that lost to the Druze in the Chouf in the fall of 1983. Later, Ja'ja' sent troops loyal to him into the group of Christian villages east of Sidon when the Israelis pulled out of that area in February 1985. They were unable to hold the area, and on their withdrawal in late April, most of the villagers fled from their homes. In both cases, significantly, the Lebanese Forces' troops were drawn from the Maronite heartland, not from the population of the areas in which the fighting took place. Whether the Ja'ja' effort in the Sidon area was undertaken in the belief that Christian forces could hold the half-dozen villages, or whether it was a somewhat devious way to force these Christian villagers to seek new homes in the Israeli-controlled border strip or the Maronite heartland, is unclear.[20] The Lebanese Forces have not proved effective fighters, and their leaders appear to believe that even a small piece of Lebanon under absolute Christian control is preferable to even a slight reduction in their traditional privileged status.

By late spring, the ineffectiveness of Ja'ja' 's tactics had redounded against him. He was replaced in May after only two months in command of the Lebanese Forces. His successor, Elie Hobeika, has indicated that a measure of cooperation—or at least nonconfrontation—with Syria is required by the realities of the Lebanese situation.

In the bloody disarray that marks the Lebanese scene today lies the foundation for Lebanon's future. Reconstruction of the Lebanese state created during the French mandate is not possible. The future almost certainly lies in a form of cantonization along sectarian lines, although the boundaries of the major cantons (Maronite, Druze, Shi'a); the role and status of the smaller communities (Orthodox, Armenian, even Sunni Muslim);[21] as well as how to treat "mixed" areas are knotty problems, many of which may well prove insoluble.[22] Based on the evidence of the events of the first six months of 1985, fighting, forced population movements, and similar events will have an effect on the boundaries of future cantons. There is also every indication that within the Shi'a community, which is clearly the largest

one in the country and which has jettisoned its traditional leadership, the competition among prospective leaders will be intense.
Amal leadership is under challenge from men who seek an Islamic
state, and there is an influential, traditional religious structure to be
heard from as well.

In southern Lebanon, Syria watched as the local Shi'a population, antagonized by prolonged Israeli occupation, pressured the Israelis to withdraw. Frequent attacks took many Israeli lives in 1984
and early 1985, the worst being a car bomb on March 10, 1985. Reports of attacks have diminished sharply, especially after the Israelis
pulled out of the Shi'a villages between Tyre and Nabatiyah in April.
Whether this is because the Shi'a forces in the south are essentially
local residents who are content once their immediate surroundings
are free; whether they were distracted by the need at that time to fight
Ja'ja' 's forces; or whether some other reason or combination of reasons is operating is unclear. Syria, for its part, has made it clear that
its forces are not going to move into areas that the Israelis evacuate.
When Israelis pulled out of the Jabal Baruk and Jazzine areas, units
of the Lebanese First Brigade moved into the area.[23] Israeli defense
minister Rabin has opined that Syria "will refrain from doing things
that will bring about direct military confrontation" with Israel.[24] In
effect, there seems to be tacit agreement between the two sides to
avoid direct conflict.

The problems facing Hafiz al-Assad in trying to wield influence in
Lebanon are formidable. Each of the major actors is eager for Syrian
help, but only in support of its own cause. The determination of the
Shi'a community not to allow armed Palestinian formations back into
south Lebanon had led to Amal attacks on the three main Palestinian
centers south of Beirut.[25] Amal forces have been opposed not only by
pro-Arafat elements there, but also by troops of Abu Musa who, with
Syrian backing, led the revolt against Arafat. The Druze, who joined
Amal in defeating a Sunni militia in West Beirut early in 1985, have
allowed Palestinians in Druze areas to shell Amal forces. President
Gemayel had lengthy talks with Assad in late May; he would like to get
the Syrians more directly involved.[26] Assad appears to want to wait
until the Lebanese leaders themselves start making the compromises, especially in the allocation of power by religious group (which
would be required to construct even a minimally functioning governmental system), before committing himself more deeply in Lebanon.

The Palestinian Factor

The forced departure of Palestinian fighters from Beirut at the end of August 1982 effectively took away from the Palestinian guerrilla organizations the possibility of conducting further significant military activity against Israel. Most of those evacuated from Beirut went to Syria, where they were placed under the same strict control that Palestinians had endured in that country since Assad came to power. The PLO leadership, on leaving Lebanon, took up a peripatetic life, moving from one Arab capital to another. This development sharply reduced Syria's influence on the PLO. For years, that organization had relied on Damascus; indeed, much of the military equipment stockpiled and used by the Palestinian forces in Lebanon had reached them through Syria. With the scattering of Palestinian forces to locations far from any potential battlefield with Israel, Syrian leverage slackened. Similarly, Yasser Arafat, as an individual leader, was no longer dependent on Syria. On his part, and on that of Palestinians broadly, there was deep anger at Syria for agreeing to a separate ceasefire on June 9, 1982. Arafat and Assad did not meet again until May 1983, eight months after the Palestinian forces left Beirut.

That Assad and Arafat have not gotten along well over the years is well known; however, the differences between the two are not merely personal. The Syrian regime wanted to keep a tight rein on the PLO organization, for an uncontrolled PLO was a potential menace to Syrian policy. "Control of the PLO has been, since 1970, a primary objective of Syria's regional strategy. Jordan ... envisage[s] a similar role for the PLO.... One key issue thus was whether the PLO would be an appendage to Syria or to Jordan."[27] Assad had sent Syrian forces into Lebanon in 1976 on the side of the Maronites in part to prevent the Palestinians from expanding their already extensive state-within-a-state. Then, after their expulsion from Beirut in 1982, Arafat and the majority of the Fatah leadership sought the maximum freedom of maneuver. Whether Assad planned to provoke a showdown with Arafat after their meeting in May 1983 is a matter of speculation; he may well have judged that the latter was vulnerable. What is certain is that Arafat gave Assad an opportunity to support and perhaps even to instigate an anti-Arafat movement within Palestinian ranks.

In late May of 1983, Arafat appointed several officers loyal to him to commands over PLO forces in Syrian-held areas of the Bekaa Valley in Lebanon. Two of these men had disgraced themselves by fleeing when Israel attacked PLO positions in Lebanon in June 1982.[28] For Arafat, however, the overriding concern was to have trusted subordinates in positions to deal with groups that were opposed to him and which were already active in the area. The appointments were taken as an insult by other Palestinians, both in the Bekaa and elsewhere. (In Damascus, anti-Arafat factions were allowed to seize food and weapons storehouses.)[29] Within a week intra-Palestinian fighting broke out in the Bekaa and continued through June; after a three-week hiatus, it broke out again. Arafat's loyalists were defeated, driven from the Bekaa and forced to regroup around Tripoli in north Lebanon. Arafat himself was expelled from Syria "for his continued slanders against Syria and its sacrifices"; the government ordered "him not to continue coming to its territory."[30] After extensive travel, Arafat arrived in Tripoli in October, while his opponents claimed that they had won the first round.

The PLO dissidents were not about to leave the situation at that, however; in November, they attacked Arafat and his loyal troops again with thinly disguised Syrian help. The ensuing fighting resulted in heavy casualties, as Arafat's forces lost first one and then the second of two Palestinian refugee camps in the Tripoli region. Penned inside the city, Arafat continued to resist until, with 4,000 adherents, he left under escort of French warships on December 20, 1983. Arafat had lost again. In addition, the bulk of armed Palestinians remained in Syrian-controlled Lebanon or in Syria.[31]

The next phase of the Palestinian saga revealed both the extent of the Syrian capacity to affect PLO affairs and its limits. The rebels within Fatah joined with three other groups—the Ba'athist-dominated Saiqah, Ahmad Jibril's Popular Front for the Liberation of Palestine-General Command, and the small Popular Struggle Front—in a National Alliance committed to armed struggle. (So far, the Syrians have carefully kept them away from Israel and Israeli-occupied Lebanon.) A coalition of three other groups known as the Democratic Alliance, whose most prominent members are George Habash (Popular Front for the Liberation of Palestine) and Naef Hawatmah (Democratic Front for the Liberation of Palestine), is dedicated to preserving the unity of the Palestinian movement. The Democratic Alliance, with the assistance of the governments of South Yemen and Algeria, worked out a formula for a Palestinian national council meeting to be held in Algiers, a meeting "which would have reinstated Arafat [as PLO Chairman] with pan-Palestinian legitimacy."[32] This was more than Assad was prepared to tolerate, however, and he made a special trip to Algeria in August to persuade President Chadli Ben Jedid not to allow it to take place. The Algerian leader could not go back on an agreement, but he did qualify his position by postulating, that if one signatory of the Aden formula refused, the meeting would be off. When George Habash's PFLP backed out, primarily due to Syrian pressure,[33] Algeria was "off the hook."

Faced with this development, Arafat convened the PNC meeting in Amman from November 22–29, 1984. Although Syrian pressure easily kept those Palestinian organizations grouped in the National and Democratic Alliances away, a quorum of the PNC nevertheless attended. This was possible because the Palestinian groups subject to Syrian suasion were small, often with only modest personal followings.) Arafat followed up his tactical victory in being able to convene and successfully carry through the PNC meeting by reaching agreement with King Hussein on an approach to the Arab-Israeli conflict. The February 11, 1985, agreement between them stops short of recognizing Israel's right to exist or of endorsing U.N. Security Council resolution 242 (1967), but it does accept the principle of land for peace and the formation of a joint Jordanian-Palestinian delegation as a mechanism for talks with the United States and Israel. Syria's reaction has been verbally abusive. Also, under Damascus's prodding, all the Palestinian groups in the two alliances, save only Hawatmah's DFLP, have joined in an anti-Arafat Palestinian National Salvation Front.

The vast change in the Palestinians' situation and in Syria's relations with them springs directly from the Israeli invasion of Lebanon. Deprived of the freedom of action that they had enjoyed in Lebanon and of the pretensions to preparation for a war of liberation, a majority of Palestinian leaders have recognized that another avenue of approach is needed. Given the realities of Israeli politics, of U.S. policy, and of Egyptian attitudes, a link with Jordan is perhaps the only option open to that majority and its constituency. Hussein wants to reassert control over the West Bank or as much of it as can be retrieved from the Israelis. Arafat knows this, and his maneuvering within the bounds of his agreement with Hussein is designed to get him as much operating room as possible during the preliminaries, during any negotiations that may occur, and in the event of an agreement with Israel.

Syria has its own agenda, including a felt need to control the Palestinian political mechanisms. In this it is no different than Egypt or

Jordan.[34] Damascus does not face an isolated Amman in the contest for influence among the Palestinians, however. Jordan has strong ties with Iraq and with Egypt, and the three present a formidable obstacle to Syrian aspirations—not only with respect to the Palestinians, but for hegemony in its immediate neighborhood. Any partial arrangement involving the West Bank that is achieved through Jordanian participation cannot satisfy Syrian regional aspirations. Damascus therefore espouses a maximalist position, and will attempt to spoil the prospect of any agreement involving Jordan and Arafat. In this, of course, it is in accord with the view of the Palestinian National Salvation Front.

In 1984 and 1985, Assad watched Israel withdraw its forces from Lebanon, having failed to achieve any of the political and strategic aims it sought except the destruction of the PLO infrastructure there. From Assad's point of view, there was little profit from harassing them during this process. He had not sought war in 1982;[35] and there is every reason to believe that a tacit agreement of the sort that was in effect from 1976 to 1981 will govern Syrian-Israeli military relations in the postwithdrawal period. Israeli Defense Minister Rabin believes that Syria "will refrain from doing things that will bring about direct military confrontation."[36]

The situation in the southern quarter of Lebanon is one which, from the available evidence, Syria lacks the capability to control. True, it has ties to various elements in the Shi'a community, notably Amal and the militant Islamic groups; however, much of the anti-Israeli activity is loosely organized, conducted by shadowy, ad hoc groups. Assad may well feel it is better for Damascus to stay aloof in this new and constantly changing situation while elements in the Shi'a community strive to establish their positions both among themselves and with other elements of the population of south Lebanon. Israel's policy of maintaining control of a border strip through Antoine Lahad's puppet militia and through village defense forces with Israeli mentors carries the constant potential of incidents with the Shi'as, who have taken strong stands both against any return of armed Palestinians to the south and against an Israeli security zone. However, if events unfold in such a way that Israel conducts military operations in south Lebanon, Syrian forces would not be near the area of operations.

Massively resupplied by the USSR since their losses in 1982, Syrian leaders regularly refer to their goal of "strategic parity" with Israel. Crude numbers of tanks, guns, and planes are only one measure in the military equation. Historically, Syria has had insufficient trained manpower to use all the armaments in its inventory. The qualitative advantage therefore remains with Israel in most, if not all, areas; this is demonstrably the case in air warfare, electronics, and intelligence. Rabin expressed full confidence in Israel's capability vis-à-vis Syria, noting that the Syrians "can miscalculate but it would be a grave mistake on their part."[37]

Iraq and Iran

The Israeli invasion of Lebanon coincided with the concluding phase of an Iranian offensive that caused Iraq to withdraw its forces to defensive lines along the international border. Two months earlier Syria had closed the border with Iraq, shut the pipeline that had been carrying about 300,000 barrels of Iraqi crude oil a day to the Mediterranean for export, and entered into broad economic and political relations with Iran. These ties have persisted, despite some strains over Syrian nonpayment or long-delayed payment for Iranian oil, despite the fundamentally different ideologies the two countries espouse, and despite the great reduction in financial support to Syria on the part of the Gulf oil states.[38] Only in mid-1985, when Lebanese Shi'a militia were fighting Palestinians for control of the refugee camps near Beirut, has Iran differed publicly with Syria, opposing Syrian-backed Amal's "campaign to disarm the Palestinians in Lebanon."[39]

The reasons for Syrian-Iraqi differences are many. Some go back for years; indeed, since World War II relations between Syria and Iraq have been generally poor. Fundamentally, Syria's geopolitical ambitions run counter to those of Iraq, which wants assured access to the Mediterranean. For a country whose rulers aspire to Arab leadership, Iraq is poorly situated: access to the world, both for normal communications and for the export of oil, lies either through the Gulf and Strait of Hormuz or across other countries. By comparison, Syria lies athwart the most direct route to the Mediterranean.

The Iraqi oil-export pipeline was shut for half a year in 1956–57 by Syria due to the Suez war; for half a year in 1966–67 (again by Syria, in a dispute over transit fees); from 1976 through 1979 at Iraqi initiative (high transit fees had encouraged the Iraqis to build alternative outlets for a fairly low volume of exports); and from 1982 to date. The last closure hit Iraq quite hard, reducing oil exports (which had been cut deeply by the war) by some forty percent. The institutionalized animosity between the Assad regime and Saddam Hussein of Iraq—each of whom heads a party that considers itself the sole legitimate descendant of the Ba'ath party founded in 1947—is strong.[40]

The current phase of Syrian-Iraqi hostility dates to the failure of an attempt to unify the two countries and their respective parties in 1978–1979. Immediately after the Camp David agreements, the two sides began to explore the possibilities of unification. Some practical consequences ensued—for example, transit trade through Syria to the Gulf and the opening of the oil pipeline. The latter was particularly useful to Iraq, which at that time was picking up some of the market Iran was losing due to the domestic turmoil attendant on the shah's overthrow. The two sides were, however, unable to agree on any positive steps toward unifying either party or government. In early July 1979, Saddam Hussein replaced Iraqi president and party head Ahmad Bakr, ostensibly on grounds of the latter's ill health. Shortly after assuming power, Saddam indirectly accused Damascus of sponsoring a group plotting a coup; Damascus, for its part, blamed Saddam for sabotaging the unity process. Bitter enmity has persisted since. When the Iraq-Iran war broke out, Syria, already on good terms with the Khomeini regime, gave it first verbal and then increasing material support. In January 1983 it joined Iran and Libya in publicly calling for the downfall of Saddam Hussein.[41]

The level of Syrian animosity toward Iraq has remained about constant since the spring of 1982. However, Iraq's standing in the region has grown while Syria's has not. Iranian military pressure on Iraq has contributed to a realignment of certain Arab states that has had adverse consequences for Syria. Iraq, needing help in the face of Iranian attacks, changed its attitude toward Egypt, for example. Baghdad, which had taken the lead in condemning Camp David and the Egyptian-Israeli Peace Treaty, was a positive force for reintegrating Egypt into the Islamic Conference Organization in 1984. It has taken every step toward normalization but that of restoring diplomatic relations, and it has been a factor in emboldening Jordan to take that bold step. In sum, the Baghdad-Amman-Cairo axis has become a potent barrier to Syria's regional ambitions.

Although Syria maintains respectable relations with the all of larger Arab states except Egypt and Iraq, it is closest to PDRY, Algeria, and Libya. In regard to the latter, Damascus seems to treat its connection with Libya as one might tolerate an eccentric—but occasionally generous—relative, rather than as one of real harmony and mutual benefit. (A unity program proclaimed between the two in October 1980 remains moribund.) Ties with Saudi Arabia are fairly good, but Syria takes Saudi advice only when it coincides with existing Syrian positions. Saudi heir-apparent Abdallah is regularly welcomed to Damascus, where he enjoys a close relationship with Assad's brother, Rifa'at—a circumstance that no doubt worked in Rifa'at's favor in the 1984 family dispute.

None of the Arab states that have strong interests in Lebanon and a concomitant record of involvement in that country's affairs shares a policy or outlook with Syria. Iraq is, as noted, a bitter enemy. Jordan views any strengthening of the Syrian position in Lebanon as increasing pressure on itself, while Hussein and Assad are fighting to control the Palestinians. As for Saudi Arabia, that country seems to strive to maintain good relations with Arab states generally and tries not to side with any one in contests for influence. Even Libya, under Kaddafi's idiosyncratic rule, from time to time takes steps that run counter to Syrian policy in geographic Syria. The lack of strong support from even one influential Arab state has hampered Syrian effectiveness in Lebanon.

While dramatic changes in inter-Arab relations are not unusual, there seems little likelihood of one in the immediate future for Syria and Iraq: their intense mutual animosity and incompatible regional aims are divisive, and new causes of friction may lie ahead. Iraq lies downstream on the Euphrates River and intends to use its water; so do the upstream riparians, Syria and Turkey, neither of which has yet displayed any interest in a formal arrangement for sharing of the available water.

Curiously, however, in some ways each country acts as if it assumes that the bitter hostility of recent years will in time be ameliorated. This is noticeable in the economic infrastructure of the two countries. Syria, for example, has in the past fifteen years enlarged and improved its rail system. One part of this is a line from Dayr al-Zur to the Iraqi border at Abu Kemal, scheduled to go into service in 1987. The Iraqis, for their part, are completing a rail line to the border there; the link should also be ready for use in 1987.[42] In addition, the Iraqis are building a four-lane highway that will meet the Syrian road net in the north when it is completed. A similar situation prevails in the relationship between Syria and Jordan where, despite political differences, commercial and transportation ties continue to prosper modestly.[43]

The Superpowers

The events of the past three years have not fundamentally changed Syrian relations with the United States and the USSR. The former finds Syria an impediment to its preferred course of dealing with discrete portions of the Arab-Israeli issue, while from the Syrian perspective the U.S. approach to the region is not conducive to the Syrian aim of dominant influence in its immediate neighborhood. Syria favors an approach involving all interested parties—both superpowers and the appropriate Arab states—which would compensate for its position of relative weakness.

The USSR's desire to have good relations with individual Arab states and to use those relations to advance its program of opposing the United States in the area is adversely affected by disputes among the Arab states. Relatively isolated among its Arab neighbors, Syria maintains close ties with the USSR, which the latter values. Consequently, Moscow has been forced to make choices in cases where it would rather have remained equally friendly to two parties;—for example, in the Assad-Arafat dispute. Also, the USSR sees the United States growing closer to Syria's enemy, Iraq with which the Soviets were once closely associated. At the same time, it is without significant influence on Syria's ally, the Khomeini regime in Iran.

The U.S. sponsorship of Lebanese-Israeli negotiations leading to the May 17 agreement and its support of Amin Gemayel made it a partner for a time of one of the Lebanese factions. In so doing, the United States moved away from being a power broker and slid into a position in which it was ranged against factions supported by Syria. United States forces on several occasions fired at Syrian positions, while two U.S. aircraft were shot down by Syrian batteries. (The French also attacked Syrian-held areas.) Although they were given much publicity, these actions remained small-scale. The big confrontation was one of will and determination, and Damascus had the pleasure of seeing the United States pull its forces out and virtually wash its hands of the Lebanese affair early in 1984.[44]

United States support for a Jordanian-Palestinian dialogue with

Israel as a means to approach the impasse—often referred to as the "Jordanian solution"—runs contrary to what Syria perceives as its interests. (Conversely, should the United States have chosen to rely primarily on Syria, Jordan and its associates would have judged such a move to be against *their* interests.) Syria reads the Jordanian solution as aimed at excluding it from the role it wants in the Levant. Hence, the Assad regime has resisted and will continue to resist this process by any means at its disposal, including the promotion of splits and dissension within the PLO and strongarm tactics against its opponents. Its aim is to demonstrate that it is too large and powerful in the region to be successfully ignored. It has been encouraged by the setback it helped inflict on the United States in Lebanon, and by the forced withdrawal of Israeli military units from Lebanon without Israel having achieved any of the political Lebanese gains that the Begin administration had hoped for (other than the ouster of the PLO).

Developments over the past three years have allowed the Soviets to strengthen their position in Syria. The way in which this occurred illustrates both the extent of the Soviet advances and the limitations on their capacity to achieve their objectives in the area. The USSR moved rapidly to replace extensive Syrian material losses incurred in the June fighting, a process which was essentially completed by October.[45] According to the Syrians, the value of these military goods amounted to several billion dollars.[46] The flow of Soviet arms continued over the next two years, raising equipment levels far above what Syria had possessed in June 1982. Syrian appreciation for Soviet assistance was expressed in areas not of primary concern to Damascus. For example, Syria joined the USSR and other Socialist states in opposing the U.N. General Assembly resolution calling for the withdrawal of Soviet forces from Afghanistan.[47]

More dramatic was the agreement that was apparently reached during Foreign Minister Khaddam's December 1982 visit to Moscow, whereby the Soviets agreed to deploy two air-defense complexes with SA-5 missiles in Syria. The installations were manned by, guarded by, and under the control of Soviet troops. The missiles' range extended over Lebanese and much of the Israeli air space as well as Mediterranean waters. As had been the case with the air-defense forces that the Soviets had deployed in Egypt during the war of attrition, these missiles warned the Israeli air force against trying to range through Syrian air space, and also offered protection to important Syrian popu-

lation centers in the event of hostilities. They were also a signal to the
world in general that the USSR would defend Syria in certain circumstances. The Soviet ambassador in Beirut said: "These defensive missiles are for the country's sovereignty and their existence is apt [sic]
to deter those who are lying in wait for Syria...." He clearly excluded
Lebanon as an area in which Soviet forces would be used, and when
asked what would happen if a confrontation took place on Lebanese
territory said that "that situation would be different.... I spoke about
the aid with which we can defend Syria...."[48]

In two major areas of Syrian activity and interest Moscow and Damascus have differed, with the result that the latter has exercised its
independence of action. The Syrian sponsorship of a dissident movement within Fatah was not to the USSR's liking, but it had to bow to
circumstances. "The Soviet Union ... considers the PLO under the
leadership of Arafat the only legitimate representative of the Palestinian people," asserted Pavel Demchenko of *Pravda*. Asked which entity the USSR would choose if forced to such a choice, the PLO or
Syria, he said, "We totally support Syria, for it is the only regime in
the region which is confronting the Israeli-American aggression."[49]
The Soviets continue to favor reunification of the PLO, but have had
little success in pushing Syria in this direction and see little opportunity given the circumstances prevailing within the Palestinian organization.

The Soviet Union, however, does not limit its interests to Syria. It
has made overtures to Egypt, sold arms to Jordan, and supports Iraq
in many ways—and all three countries are ranged against Syria in
the mid-1980s Middle East lineup. The Assad regime is clearly aware
that the USSR's national interests dictate these relationships, but it
does not consider that its strong ties to the Kremlin require it to adopt
Moscow's attitudes on Arab issues. Syria does not approve of the
USSR's closeness to Iraq, a matter that has come up in bilateral
talks.[50] Soviet efforts to improve relations between Syria and Iraq
have born no fruit, as the Soviet ambassador to Kuwait admitted, adding that "the Soviet Union ... needs ... to work toward eliminating the
dispute and conflict between them."[51]

Inside Syria, the Soviet position has shown little change over the
past three years. The cabinet formed by Abd al-Ra'uf Kism on April 8,
1985, has two communist ministers (as Syrian cabinets have had for
the past dozen years).[52] The sixty-year-old communist party of Syria

(CPS) was denied seats in the People's Assembly chosen in 1981. The CPS is not pleased with the domestic policies of the Assad regime. Criticizing "the negative aspects of the socio-economic policy of our state," Politburo member Khaled Hammami asserted that "the parasitical bourgeoisie is growing and corruption is rife. The ruling quarters are suspicious and fearful of all initiative or independent activity on the part of the masses."[53] The reality of communist life, however, is that the CPS must subordinate its domestic desires to the benefits that Syrian external policy—described as "consistently anti-imperialist"—brings the USSR.[54] (If the Syrian communists were blessed with a sense of humor they might realize that this order of priority is precisely what "socialist realism" means for a Marxist-Leninist party in the Third World.)

The Syrian regime itself has from time to time called for stronger ties with the USSR. The Ba'ath party newspaper, while pointing out that "the Soviet Union's attitude ... does not extend to the point of making Syria's decisions," ran an article in March 1984 entitled "Qualitative and Quantitative Development of Syrian-Soviet Relations is an Urgent Revolutionary Task."[55] Both the party and government press frequently cite Soviet support for "anti-imperialist" and anti-Zionist forces in the Arab area. Syria and the USSR are in agreement on certain tactics, however. While Syria has long recognized the weight of U.S. influence in the Arab-Israeli dispute and keeps in contact with the United States, it has, during the past three years, used the Soviet desire for participation in any settlement process (through the mechanism of a general conference) as a means to pressure the United States and Jordan. At the same time, Syria pointedly reminds Moscow that it is an ally, not a puppet.[56]

In the contest for influence, each of the superpowers has advantages. The USSR's include its roles as arms supplier, political supporter, and major opponent of Israel's North American ally; the advantages of the United States (and of the West in general) are those of cultural affinity, technical superiority, and a Syrian predisposition for Western goods. Thus, although the Syrian press may wax effusive over Soviet aid in the economic, energy, and transportation areas, it was a U.S. company, Pecten, that found a new 35,000-barrel-a-day oil field in Syria in a concession it shares with Royal Dutch Shell and Deminex of West Germany. It may be worth as much as $300 million annually in foreign exchange when in full production.

Conclusions

From mid-1982 to mid-1985, the Assad regime survived the serious illness of its president, some rather undisciplined maneuvering for position on the part of would-be successors, and a military setback at the hands of Israel. The country has been virtually free of militant religious opposition, reasonably prosperous (although export earnings are down), and subject only to moderate inflation.[57] Externally, it has failed to move Jordan away from its close ties with Iraq and Egypt. Assad has contributed to Yasser Arafat's loss of the capability for independent action, but has seen him make common cause with King Hussein. The Syrian leader has weathered many crises in Lebanon, has outlasted the United States there, watched the Israelis withdraw almost completely, and has the traditional political leadership practically begging him to save them and the state. Hafiz al-Assad is the "master of Lebanon to the extent that anyone can be said to dominate the bewildering array of religious and political communities of which the country is composed."[59] Nonetheless, it is far from clear whether he—or anyone—is up to the herculean task of bringing order out of that chaos.

NOTES

1. John F. Devlin, "Syrian Policy," in Robert O. Freedman, ed., *The Middle East Since Camp David* (Boulder, Colo.: Westview Press, 1984), pp. 125–26.
2. For a descriptive analysis of Assad's system of government, see Devlin, "The Political Structure in Syria," *Middle East Review* 17, no. 1 (Fall 1984):15–21.
3. Alasdair Drysdale, "The Succession Question in Syria," *Middle East Journal* (hereafter *MEJ*) 39, no. 2 (Spring 1985):246–57. The following discussion draws heavily on Drysdale's excellent treatment of this issue.
4. Assad interview with *Le Point* (France) excerpted in *New York Times*, 28 December 1983. The six were the prime minister, ministers of foreign affairs and defense, speaker of the people's assembly, and "two party leaders"—presumably the assistant secretaries of the Ba'ath regional and national commands.
5. *New York Times*, 12 March 1984.
6. Drysdale, "Succession Question," p. 253.

7. Ibid., p. 257.

8. *Middle East Economic Digest* (hereafter *MEED*), 12 April 1985:36.

9. Devlin, "Syrian Policy," p. 137.

10. John F. Devlin, *Syria: Modern State in an Ancient Land* (Boulder, Colo.: Westview Press, 1983), pp. 97–99.

11. Speech to Fourth General Congress of Syria's Revolutionary Youth Organization, Damascus television, 15 April 1985 (*Foreign Broadcast Information Service/ Middle East* [hereafter *FBIS/ME*], 16 April 1985).

12. Ze'ev Schiff and Ehud Ya'ari, *Israel's Lebanon War* (New York: Simon and Schuster, 1984), ch. 3. Sharon's plans for war have also been mentioned by the retiring U.S. ambassador to Israel. For conduct of the war see, in addition to Schiff and Ya'ari, Itamar Rabinovich, *The War for Lebanon, 1970–1983* (Ithaca, N.Y.: Cornell University Press, 1984).

13. Syrian minister of information speaking on Radio Monte Carlo, 11 October 1982 (*FBIS/ME*, 12 October 1982). The Lebanese government's invitation was an after-the-fact arrangement. In his inaugural address on September 23, 1976, President Ilyas Sarkis stated that the "presence of Syrian troops on Lebanese soil . . . is in the hands of Lebanon's constitutional authorities. . . ." Excerpts of the address are in Walid Khalidi, *Conflict and Violence in Lebanon: Confrontation in the Middle East* (Cambridge: Harvard University Press, 1979), p. 195.

14. *New York Times*, 31 October 1982; and Hafiz al-Assad interview, Radio Damascus, 30 October 1982 (*FBIS/ME*, 2 November 1982).

15. Statement to Syrian People's Assembly, Damascus television, 1 February 1983 (*FBIS/ME*, 2 February 1983).

16. *New York Times*, 3 May 1983, quotes Assad as saying that "Syria . . . will oppose any gains which Israel is trying to achieve."

17. Jumblatt headed one of two principal Druze families in Lebanon. His preeminence was materially helped by the advanced age and illness of Amir Majid Arslan, head of the rival Druze family, who died in 1983.

18. Thomas L. Friedman, "American's Failure in Lebanon," *New York Times Magazine*, 8 April 1984, pp. 32–44 and 62–66, is an excellent treatment of the manner in which and the reasons why the United States got embroiled in military action in Lebanon. See also William B. Quandt, "Reagan's Lebanon Policy: Trial and Error," *MEJ* 38, no. 2 (Spring 1984):237–54.

19. Ja'ja' led the force that assassinated former president Franjiyah's son and family in 1978. (*Washington Post*, 19 March 1985.)

20. The Lebanese Forces' radio has said that moves in the southern area were aimed at creating separate Druze, Sunni, and Shi'a cantons. (*New York Times*, 29 April 1985.) Ja'ja' 's abortive move contributed to that process by bringing about an exodus of Christians from the area.

21. The Sunnis are the third largest community, but live mostly in cities—especially Tripoli, Beirut, and Sidon. Hence, a territorial canton would be hard to devise for this important element of the population.

22. There are a fair number of villages and towns in Lebanon with populations loyal to more than one religion. Hasbayya, near Mt. Hermon, is part Druze and part Greek Catholic, for example.

23. *New York Times*, 25 April 1985.

24. Interview on Radio Jerusalem, 25 April 1985 (*FBIS/ME*, 26 April 1985).

25. Among the many paradoxes of Lebanon is that the Shi'as of Amal are opposed both to a return of armed Palestinians to south Lebanon (which Israel also opposes, of course) and to the Israeli-armed force headed by Antoine Lahad in a strip along the Israeli border.

26. John Kifner, "Syria Finds It Also Lacks Lebanon Key," *New York Times*, 12 June 1985.

27. Naseer Aruri, "The PLO and the Jordan Option," *MERIP Reports*, no. 131, March–April 1985:8.

28. *MEJ*, "Chronology" 37, no. 4 (Autumn 1983):659, citing *Washington Post*, 23 May 1983. Schiff and Ya'ari, *Israel: Lebanon War*, p. 136, mentions some of the officers who fled the battlefield.

29. *MEJ*, "Chronology" 37, no. 4 (Autumn 1983):660, citing *Washington Post*, 30 May 1983.

30. *New York Times*, 25 June 1983, quoting Syria's press agency.

31. Ibid., 19 November 1984.

32. "Squaring the Circle," interview with Rashid Khalidi, *MERIP Reports*, no. 131 (March–April 1985):11.

33. Ibid., p. 12.

34. Aruri, "PLO and Jordan Option," and Khalidi, interview, *supra*, p. 14.

35. Devlin, "Syrian Policy," p. 132.

36. Interview on Radio Jerusalem, 25 April 1985 (*FBIS/ME*, 26 April 1985).

37. Ibid.

38. Syria was awarded $1.8 billion annually at the Baghdad Summit of April 1979. Iraq paid until 1981, while the Gulf oil states have gradually cut back. "In recent years, little, if any, of this [money] has actually been disbursed—because of recession in the main Arab oil-exporting countries, the demand for funds to back Iraq's war effort against Iran, and general Arab disaffection with Syria's regional policies" (*MEED*, 1 June 1985:23).

39. *New York Times*, 3 June 1985.

40. In February 1966, the founders and other leaders of the Ba'ath party then governing in Damascus were ousted and exiled in a coup in which Assad was a leader. After Iraqi Ba'athists seized power in Baghdad in 1968, many of these men went there where they were recognized as the legitimate Ba'ath leaders. Since then, there have been two Ba'ath parties.

41. Joint communiqué issued at the conclusion of a two-day meeting of the three states' foreign ministers, Radio Teheran, 23 January 1983 (*FBIS/ME*, 24 January 1983).

42. *MEED*, 3 August 1984:35.

43. For example, each is working on its part of a new highway between Damascus and Amman financed by the Arab Fund for Social and Economic Development, for completion in 1988. (OPECNA [Kuwait], 9 January 1984 [*FBIS/ME*, 11 January 1984].) The two countries and Saudi Arabia operate a microwave communications project and are studying a supplementary system. (PETRA-JNA [Amman], 20 May 1985 [*FBIS/ME*, 21 May 1985].)

44. *Newsweek*, 27 February 1984:26–27.

45. *MEJ* "Chronology" 37, no. 1 (Winter 1983):87, citing *Christian Science Monitor*, 10 October 1982.

46. The Syrian minister of information, in a statement reported by Kuwait News

Agency, 18 December 1982 (*FBIS/ME*, 20 December 1982), referred to losses of several billion without specifying the currency. *MEJ* "Chronology" 37, no. 2 (Spring 1983), cites the *Washington Post* of 19 December 1982 as its source for losses in the range of several billion dollars.

47. *New York Times*, 30 November 1982.

48. Radio Beirut, 2 March 1983 (*FBIS/ME*, 3 March 1983).

49. *Jerusalem Star* (Amman), 1 December 1983:1 (*FBIS/ME*, 2 December 1983).

50. *New York Times* report of Assad visit to Moscow, 19 October 1984.

51. Interview with Ambassador Akipov in *Al-Siyasah* (Kuwait), 13 December 1984 (*FBIS/ME*, 17 December 1984).

52. *MEED*, 12 April 1985:36.

53. *World Marxist Review* 27, no. 6 (June 1984):73.

54. Ibid.

55. *Al-Ba'th*, 23 March 1984 (*FBIS/ME*, 30 March 1984).

56. Ibid. See also Dimitri K. Simes, "Moscow, Damascus, and the Road to Peace," *New York Times*, 20 May 1983.

57. *MEED*, 1 June 1985:22.

58. John Newhouse, "A Small Window," *The New Yorker*, 11 March 1985:124.

II

Egyptian Policy under Mubarak: The Politics of Continuity and Change

Louis J. Cantori

The magnificent fact is that Egypt is ruled by Egyptians [applause], that Egypt's decision is the Egyptian people's decision, and that Egyptian willpower destroyed all foreign and domestic restrictions which used to direct its destiny and drain its strength. By right and reality, not by cheers and slogans, Egypt became owned by its sons. Egypt became a right for all the Egyptians....

　　Our people hold that it is the right and the duty of the other parties to seek sincerely and seriously to complete the links of peace, to achieve the liberation of Arab territory in the West Bank, in the Gaza sector and in the Syrian heights and to implement the commitment engendered by international law for the withdrawal of the invading forces from fraternal Lebanon.

> —President Husni Mubarak
> Speech of 21 July 1983, on the anniversary
> of the July 1952 Revolution.[1]

T HIS APPEAL to the intensity of Egyptian national identity and the linking of the peace process to the liberation of Arab territory accurately portrays both the key elements of President Mubarak's own foreign policy and the continuity of that policy vis-à-vis that of his predecessor, Anwar al-Sadat. In order to assess the question of the impact of the Israeli invasion of Lebanon upon Egyptian foreign policy, it is necessary to place these sentiments against the background of certain longterm, historically persistent features of Egyptian foreign policy. In addition, there are aspects of the Egyptian situation

323

that also have a bearing on general Arab state foreign-policy behavior, and on that of Third World nations in general.

There are certain geopolitical and other givens that have always characterized Egyptian foreign policy. The most important of these is that of the so-called landbridge connection to the east, across the Sinai Desert into the Levant. The primary issue here has been variously one of expansion of Egyptian influence or of defense against invaders. Second in importance is Egypt's policy toward the rest of Africa to the south. In recent history, this has centered mainly on the political control of the headwaters of the economic artery of Egypt, the Nile River. A third and less important geopolitical factor has been toward Libya and the West.

These historically transcendent geopolitical factors have been impacted upon in recent political history by three arenas and leadership roles that Egypt has been called upon to play. The first of these is pan-Arabism, which links Egypt to the eastern landbridge; the second is the Islamic world, which transcends the Middle East and links to the Third, nonaligned, developing world; and the third is pan-Africanism. Underlying all three of these roles has been the strong anti-imperialism that characterizes the modern history of Egypt and its relationship with outside powers—first the Ottoman Turks, then the British, then the Russians, and finally the Israelis.[2]

The geopolitical landbridge and pan-Arabism are the main emphases in Egyptian foreign policy. Since the revolution of 1952, this factor has had a variety of configurations and thrusts: Under Nasser (1952–1970), the direction was one of Egyptian domination and leadership; under Sadat, especially in the period that saw his visit to Jerusalem and the peace treaty with Israel that ensued (1977–1981), the policy was one of aloofness and separatism. Mubarak, on the other hand, has pursued a policy aimed at balancing the alienating effects of the peace treaty with Israel with continued efforts at rapprochement with the Arab state system. By way of contrast, under all three leaders, African and security policies to the south and security policies to the west have remained more constant and consistent. Egyptian African policy has been dominated by the two themes of guarding the headwaters of the Nile and supporting nonalignment and liberation in Africa. Thus Somalia is seen not only as a loyal Arab state that did not break off relations with Egypt, but also as a counterweight to Marxist Ethiopia and the latter's key position on the Nile's headwaters.

At the center of Egypt's African policy is the Sudan. Mubarak has continued Sadat's policy of fostering at least a symbolic merger of the two countries, via a joint parliament. On the other hand, the tottering Numeiry regime so long supported by Sadat was quickly abandoned at a crucial moment when his successor, General Siwar al-Dahab, was viewed as more acceptable to Egypt. In Chad, a longterm north-south civil war has found Egypt continuing to support President Hissein Habre against Libyan-backed elements in the north. Libya itself does not appear to be a major policy preoccupation for Egypt—possibly due to the fact that more than 200,000 Egyptians are regularly employed in Libya. On the other hand, the major portion of the Egyptian army is stationed in the western desert of Egypt, and in November of 1984 Egyptian intelligence thwarted a major assassination attempt on a Libyan political exile and in May 1985 an attempt to blow up the American embassy in Cairo.[3]

It is against the background of the preceding, then, that the impact of the June 1982 Israeli invasion of Lebanon must be considered. On the one hand, this event put the severest possible test upon the peace treaty (which has, remarkably, survived). On the other hand, it provided Egypt with the opportunity to combine its continued peace efforts with its effort to rejoin the Arab state system. This effort has been buoyed by the fact that among all the Arab states only Syria in fact took any direct action against the Israelis. Egypt's constraints under the peace treaty with Israel, therefore, did not look all that damning by way of comparison.

Egyptian foreign policy can be viewed from two additional Middle Eastern and Third World perspectives. The first is that the Middle East region is itself distinctive among Third World regions of the world in that the states making up that region vigorously interact with one another. (Many Third World states, by way of contrast, seldom do so.) A shared language and culture help explain this, and the ideological correlation is pan-Arabism. This has relevance to the present discussion, because President Mubarak's major policy task is the effort to break out of Egypt's diplomatic isolation in the Arab world, which was of course caused by his predecessor in the 1977–1981 period. Other Middle Eastern states share another unusual feature and that is the permeability of their national boundaries—that is, the manner in which leaderships, organizations, and cultural appeals cross national frontiers. In fact, Egypt tends to be an exception among Middle Eastern states in that its domestic politics are less affected by events in the region. This is the case because of the relatively homogeneous character of Egyptian society, the greater authority and depth of the state, and its ability to control and, when necessary, repress domestic opinion.[4]

Egypt Goes It Alone

Prior to 1977 Egypt was diplomatically dominant in the region. Looked at in terms of the landbridge/security factor in Egyptian foreign policy, Egypt was dominant from the early 1950s into the mid-1970s, whether in terms of the Arab cold war of competitive pan-Arabism or of the diplomacy *cum* war against Israel in the War of Attrition of 1969–1970, the October War of 1973, and afterwards.[5] When the Sinai II accord of 1975 failed to gain the support of the Syrians, and Egyptian dominance began to falter as a result, Sadat made his dramatic visit to Jerusalem in November of 1977. Motivated both by economic factors and by the need for military security assistance, Sadat pursued the two key objectives of the return of the occupied Sinai and a peace settlement for the Palestinians.

The Jerusalem visit enlisted the United States diplomatically. The results were the two Camp David accords or frameworks for peace of September 1978, which identified the Palestinian problem as being of first priority and a bilateral peace treaty between Egypt and Israel being of second priority. The manner in which the priorities were reversed in the Egyptian-Israeli Peace Treaty of March 1979 is too complex a question to be gone into in the present context. Suffice to say that, essentially, the treaty was very much second best for Sadat, a fact strongly felt by him; it resulted in the resignation of three top Egyptian foreign ministry personnel, and the outspoken criticism of the politically important intellectual elite in Egypt. Most important for the present discussion, however, was the absence in the text of the treaty of any strong linkage between the implementation of the peace process between Israel and Egypt and the Palestinian issue.[6] The absence of this linkage, and the seemingly total forsaking of the Palestinians by Egypt, caused even the moderate Arab states of Jordan, Saudi Arabia, and the Gulf states to join their radical brethren Syria, Libya, Algeria, and South Yemen in breaking relations with Egypt. With only Oman, Sudan, and Somalia continuing to maintain relations, and with the removal of the Arab league offices from Cairo, Egypt was effectively isolated.

The peace treaty did, however, significantly benefit Egypt. Not only was the entire Sinai regained by April 1982, but Egypt also regained control of Sinai oil resources. Perhaps even more important, however, was the fact that the United States emerged as an alternative to the USSR for arms supplies. Altogether, beginning in the 1980s Egypt began to receive in excess of two billion dollars a year in grants and loans for development purposes and military assistance from the United States.[7]

The inability of Sadat to address the Palestinian question had further domestic consequences. For one, the political opposition that had benefited from Sadat's policy of political liberalization became increasingly critical of the peace treaty, even though in general it received widespread popular support. This criticism, plus that conceived with widespread corruption, contributed significantly to the sentiment that motivated those who carried out Sadat's assassination on October 6, 1981.

Domestic Constraints upon Foreign Policy

Sadat acted as if domestic considerations in foreign policy were of little concern to him. Yet, in the last two years of his rule he had to resort to increasing political repression in order to contain the political criticism directed primarily at domestic political corruption but also at his foreign policy. Thus, in the summer of 1980 he enacted the so-called Law of Shame, which was intended to give him a legal basis for silencing critics, and in September 1981 he arrested and imprisoned 1500 leading religious and secular critics. While his death resulted from the act of a single conspiratorial group, it was greeted by a widespread sense of public relief reflecting increasing frustration over his domestic and foreign policies.[8]

Mubarak, by way of contrast, has concentrated his attention on domestic politics. The reasons for this have been twofold. The first is that he, unlike Nasser and Sadat (for reasons largely having to do with his fewer years), does not share the history of nationalist struggle against the British and a corrupt monarchy. With his more classic military background in the technological command structure of the air force, he has had to forge his own personal political legitimacy. Second, a significant avenue toward creating this legitimacy has been to rectify Sadat's relative neglect of domestic economic policy by, for example, continuing to support economic liberalization (that is, foreign private capital and an Egyptian private sector) but calling for a move from consumption to production. It follows from the preceding considerations, therefore, that Mubarak tends to gauge his foreign policy significantly in terms of its domestic implications.[9]

He is in turn constrained by three factors in the domestic situation. First and foremost is the role of the military—not as an active actor in the situation (as in the pre-1968 period), but rather more implicitly as the arbiter of policy. The military appears to remain committed to the peace treaty, while at least tolerant, if not actually supportive, of increasing alignment with the Arab state system. The military's support is assured to a degree by the continued generous supply of U.S. military equipment and training. The army's political influence is visible in the anomaly represented by the continuing vacancy of the presidentially appointed vice-presidency since Mubarak vacated that position to assume the presidency in October 1981. It is said that General Abu Ghazzala—minister of defense and deputy prime minister, and rumored to be a likely successor to Mubarak—has refused to accept the vice-presidency on the grounds that it would sidetrack him politically, but has not allowed anyone else (especially someone from the military) to be appointed to the position because he fears such a putative rival.

A second limiting factor is that of the legal opposition—the child of the limited multiparty system created by Sadat during his "liberal" period of the mid-1970s. Part of Sadat's increasing repression in the late 1970s was due to the criticism of these parties of his trip to Jerusalem and his progressively closer relationship with Israel. With the signing of the peace treaty in 1979, direct repudiation of that treaty by any political party is prohibited. It is also true, however, that the parties are not inclined toward that extreme position in any event. In June 1982, at the time of the invasion, they called for the recall of the Egyptian ambassador and for freezing the process of normalization. This is what, in fact, Mubarak proceeded to do after the Shatilla/Sabra massacres. The result is, that in the May 1984 elections to the parliament, foreign policy figured less importantly than it might have. Mubarak's twofold policy of serene relations with Israel and the continued pursuit of peace in alliance with the PLO effectively muted criticism. The results of the May 1984 elections had little bearing on foreign policy except that with the National Democratic Party gaining 392 seats and the New Wafd Party getting fifty-eight, the most severely critical political parties—the Socialist Labor Party (7.1% of the vote) and the National Union Progressivists (4.2% of the votes—were excluded from the parliament, and had to rely on their proprietary newspapers to express their points of view.[10] On balance, it would appear that Mubarak has been able to set the terms of the debate so that the peace treaty itself is not in question, but only the *tactics* of the peace process are open to debate. In fact, however, his aggressive policy of seeking to reenter the Arab state system has had the effect of preempting even this criticism.

A third constraining factor has been the role of the illegal opposition—an opposition that has taken an overwhelmingly religious form. From 1967 onwards, as a direct result of the magnitude of the defeat in that war, Egypt has been a part of the sea change of revitalized Islamic sentiment sweeping the Middle East. This has taken organizational expression in the form of clandestine, and sometimes religiously deviant, groups that are dangerous in terms of their potential for violence (although at present they lack significant popular support).[11] Being illegal and conspiratorial, these groups have—with one exception—been dealt with firmly by Mubarak through a series of arrests and trials. The exception is the Muslim Brotherhood, which was founded in 1928 and thus predates the recent revival of religious sentiment. While technically illegal, the Brotherhood's support was informally cultivated by Sadat, to the extent that he had even permitted the publication of their newspaper *al-Dawa* [*The Call*]. His forebearance may probably be ascribed to the fact that the Brotherhood did not publicly condemn the Camp David process. Other illegal, conspiratorial and violent groups such as al-Jihad (The Religious Struggle), which carried out the assassination of Sadat; Takfir wa al-Higra (Migration and Repentance); and Jund Allah (Soldiers of God) were totally condemnatory of what they regarded as a sellout to the Israelis.[12]

Mubarak has been careful to present himself as a devout modernist who, unlike Sadat, keeps his family affairs very private. By also bringing some of the most flagrantly corrupt individuals to trial, he has so far at least created an aura of uprightness that has permitted him to arrest large numbers of members of fringe groups without triggering adverse reactions. This, in turn, has strengthened his position in dealing with foreign-policy issues, including Egypt's relations with Israel.

The 1982 Israeli Invasion of Lebanon

From the outset, Israeli policy has put a strain upon the Egyptian-Israeli treaty. The outcome of the diplomacy leading to the 1979 Peace Treaty clearly signaled Israel's more limited view of the goals sought: the absence of linkage relating the peace treaty to the Camp David framework on the Palestinian question was major evidence of this. Further evidence of this was the Israeli minimalist interpretation of the meaning of autonomy for the Palestinians. Even more concrete evidence of the strain upon Egyptian-Israeli relations had to do with the Israeli settlements on the West Bank. Begin held the position that the peace treaty called for only a three-month freeze on such settlements, and not the five years understood by the United States and Egypt. Likud rushed ahead with its accelerated settlement policy, with the result that in the period 1977–1984, the number of settlements increased from thirty-six to more than 100 and the number of settlers from 5,000 to over 30,000.[13]

But Israeli provocations were not limited to interpretations of the peace treaty. In June 1981, only a few days after a meeting between Menachem Begin and Anwar al-Sadat, the Israelis bombed the Iraqi nuclear reactor—the time element making it look as if Sadat had foreknowledge of the event. This was followed in the next month by the Israeli bombing attack of PLO headquarters in Beirut, and in December 1981 by the annexation of the Golan Heights.[14] These events served to dramatize the changed power relationships of the Middle East: with Egypt removed from the Arab-Israeli power equation, Israel could take such actions with what amounted to impunity. This in turn served to increase the bitterness of the criticism directed toward Egypt by the other Arab states. Reinforcing Egypt's inability to act was the fact of the recency of Mubarak's accession to power and the further important consideration of the imminent return of Sinai. The latter was extremely important symbolically to the Egyptians and, until its actual April 1982 return as called for in the peace treaty, the Egyptian leadership was likely to be patient even in the face of the most provocative Israeli actions.

On April 25, 1982, to the accompaniment of great joy in Egypt, all of the Sinai was regained; less than a month and a half later, the Israelis invaded Lebanon (June 6, 1982). It is now known that, from the beginning, this was not meant to be the limited retaliatory strike it was proclaimed to be. Officially declared to be intended to secure a forty-kilometer strip in Lebanon on Israel's northern border, within days Israeli forces were beseiging Beirut. The real aim was to extirpate the Palestinian Liberation Organization, and to both impose a new political order on Lebanon and enforce a peace treaty between it and Israel.[15] The complexities of Israel's failure over a three-year period to accomplish these aims or to fully extricate itself from the Lebanon quagmire have a bearing on Egyptian foreign policy only in a very general (but nevertheless important) way.

The Egyptians appear to have been significantly caught by surprise by the invasion. On May 30, a National Democratic Party delegation headed by Deputy Prime Minister Mustafa Khalil visited with members of the Israeli Labour party in Israel.[16] The following day, the Israeli minister of industry visited Cairo,[17] and on June 2 Foreign Minister Kamal Hasan Ali returned from Israel after talks regarding Palestinian autonomy, a future possible meeting of Mubarak and Begin, and the boundary dispute over Taba (the small slice of land at the head of the Gulf of Aqaba).[18] On the sixth of June this pattern of seemingly constructive interaction was shattered by the invasion and the statement of the Egyptian government: "We demand that Israel stop all military operations and withdraw from Lebanese territory."[19] The following day, Mubarak met with his crisis group and announced that Egypt would take steps to counter the aggression. It is revealing of the most important feature of the peace treaty from the Israeli point of view—namely, the military neutralization of Egypt—that Egypt was limited to messages of protest to President Reagan, Prime Minister Begin, and the president of the European Economic Community and the sending of medical assistance.[20]

Mubarak faced strong protests against the Israeli invasion from within Egypt. This expressed itself in three areas. Quite possibly the most important of these was represented by the intellectuals, who, of course, in an elitist political system have an importance disproportionate to their numbers. Their criticism of U.S. policy in support of Israel was intense, especially when the United States vetoed a United Nations Security Council resolution condemning Israel.[21] In this group, as well as within the small political opposition group (Socialist Labor Party) in the Peoples Assembly (twenty of 390 members) and in street demonstrations, the protest was strongly stated.[22] Nevertheless, there were few calls for abolishing the peace treaty; instead, demands were made for recalling the Egyptian ambassador and curtailing relations. Prime Minister Fuad Muhyi al-Din in response to these demands noted the negligence and passivity of the other Arab states and stated that relations with Israel and the United States would not be broken because "we are not prepared to sell off Egyptian interests."[23]

Egypt did, however, continue to press the Lebanese, the Palestinian, and the larger Arab cases. Thus, Foreign Minister Kamal Hasan Ali, while pressing for a ceasefire and withdrawal in mid-June, disagreed strongly with the American policy position that such a withdrawal should include a Syrian withdrawal as well; he was insistent that it was the Israelis who should withdraw.[24] As the Israelis began to tighten the noose around Beirut, Egyptian policy began to be very supportive of the Palestinians. Thus, at the end of June, discussions took place with Palestine liberation representatives in Cairo at which the topics included an offer to have the Palestinians set up a provisional government.[25] The Shatilla and Sabra massacres of about 1,000 men, women, and children in September 1982 caused such violent outrage in Egypt that the withdrawal of the Egyptian ambassador from Tel Aviv was the absolute minimum Mubarak could do to demonstrate the strength of Egyptian feelings.

In general, then, Egyptian policy reacted to the 1982 invasion with a combination of low-level nonmilitary humanitarian assistance, vocal condemnation, and public support of the Palestinians. Even while critical of U.S. policy in Lebanon, relations with the United States were kept on an even keel. Even in the case of Israel, Foreign Minister Ali was in touch with Foreign Minister Shamir regarding new proposals on Taba.[26] In the midst of the stresses and strains of the situation, Egypt was being careful to preserve and pursue its own interests.

Relations with the United States

Mubarak inherited a relationship with the United States that under the impact of the charismatic personality of Anwar al-Sadat had become very special. Not only were there the concrete achievements of Sadat in having attracted the attention of the Americans with Egypt's strong performance in the 1973 war, but through his cumulative diplomatic achievements of Sinai I (1974), Sinai II (1975), Camp David (1978), and the Peace Treaty with Israel (1979) he pursued Egyptian interests that were significantly congruent with those of the United States. Thus, in light of Egypt's very recent experience, Mubarak could generally subscribe to the anti-Soviet motif of American policy (even though he probably could not agree that the Soviets lurked behind every dire event in the region). Furthermore, especially after the downfall of the shah in Iran in 1979, Sadat could only be supportive of the tendency of the United States to aid Egypt economically and militarily in order for it to become a substitute point of influence in the Middle East. From his perspective, the United States was helping Egypt maintain its regional hegemonic role. Furthermore, Sadat appreciated that if a comprehensive peace was to come to the Middle East it could only occur with an American commitment that would in turn bring Israel along. Sadat assumed that Egypt would continue to dominate this process, but the ability of the Israelis to remove the Palestinians from the diplomatic agenda in the 1979 peace treaty began to undermine his policy. This diplomatic reversal coincided with the advent of the expansionist foreign policy of the Israel Likud government. With the Reagan administration more supportive and even less critical of Israel from 1980 onward, Egypt under Sadat was predestined to be positioned on the margin of Middle Eastern international relations.

A further quality of Sadat's policy was the impact of his personality upon U.S. public opinion, thanks to his ability to project himself effectively in the media; more important, he was equally effective with American officials and elected representatives. Mubarak, his successor, possesses a more reserved and less outgoing personality. While this may be somewhat of a limiting factor, it has also had the effect of putting U.S.–Egyptian relations on a professionally more stable basis. The result has been more order and predictability in the relations of U.S.–Egyptian officials, including more authority and independence of point of view of the latter in its relations with the former. This has had the benefit of defusing somewhat the growing atmosphere of Egyptian intellectual criticism of the American official presence in Egypt.[27]

Mubarak has continued with this basic commitment to the relationship with the United States, but has modified it so as to make it more compatible with the principles of Sadat's more revolutionary predecessor, Gamal Abd al-Nasser. This blending was evident in his first annual address on the anniversary of the 1952 Revolution, when he announced ten principles of Egyptian foreign policy:

1. Adherence to the Egyptian national will
2. Rejection of all forms of subservience
3. Positive neutralism and nonalignment
4. Rejection of foreign alliances
5. Rejection of foreign bases
6. Support of international peace
7. Support of national liberation
8. Resistance to interference in Egypt's internal affairs
9. A halt to the armaments race and nuclear weapons
10. International cooperation[28]

Not only do these principles allow Mubarak to cloak himself in the familiar mantle of Nasser ("neutralism and nonalignment"; "no foreign bases" or "foreign alliances") and gain significant political legitimacy as a result, they also strike a strong theme "of Egyptianness" and Egyptian national pride.

The effort to assert greater Egyptian policy independence may be seen in the manner in which condemnation of Israel's invasion has been combined with a drawing closer to the PLO. But perhaps a more vivid example is the way in which in 1980, 1981, 1983, and 1984 joint maneuvers of American and Egyptian army units took place under the name "Operation Brightstar." By the time of the most recent maneuvers, there was a virtual news blackout, both abroad and inside Egypt, in the name of Egyptian political sensitivities.

Even more dramatic was the case of the Egyptian military base at Ras Banas, in the south of the country on the Red Sea coast. From 1981 onward, American policy had been clear in its desire to prepare the base as a logistical staging area for possible U.S. military activity in the Arabian peninsula and the Gulf. The subject was handled quietly, but when a U.S. congressional appropriation of 175 million dollars was made public the political opposition in Egypt made a great deal of the stationing of foreign troops on Egyptian soil. The project was officially cancelled in September 1984, but in October 1984 an advertisement for construction bids was published in error. This unleashed a flurry of criticism in Egypt, and President Mubarak found it necessary to offer to take groups of students and others to visit the base to verify that it was under Egyptian command and that no Americans were present.[29]

Symbolically, if not in substance, the clearest evidence of the

Egyptian intention to lessen its dependence upon the Americans is in the area of military procurement. A primary aim is to achieve self-sufficiency in weapons production and to diversify weapons purchased on the world market. Thus, while the Egyptian army has inevitably become dependent to a significant degree upon the Americans, it continues to strive for self-production or alternative international sources. Thus, for example, the Arab Military Industrial Organization (AMIO) weapons-production complex originally funded by Arab capital (which stopped in 1979) has regained growth and vitality in the last few years with apparent American assistance. Even with sizeable American military credits, the emphasis has been upon investment in production: jeeps, C-130 transport aircraft, armored personnel carriers. But, in addition, a deliberate effort has been made to use alternative technologies: British and Spanish ships, Rumanian tanks, French Mystere 2000 jets (under a coproduction agreement) and helicopters.[30] Finally, in July 1984, normal relations were resumed with the Soviet Union. (Sadat had expelled the Soviet ambassador in September 1981.) Clearly, Egypt has symbolically—and, even to a degree, in reality—become "non-aligned." These symbols have been useful to offset the appearance and reality of heavy economic and military dependence upon the United States.

Then Deputy Prime Minister Mustafa Khalil characterized Egypt's strategic relations with the United States in 1982 in a very succinct statement: "We have never said we are allied with the United States. Rather we said that Egypt's strategic objectives and interests coincide with U.S. strategic objectives." But, he pointed out:

> In evaluating its foreign policy the United States looks at things only within the context of its differences with the Soviet Union. We say to it: "There is only one threat to the area—Israel—and the invasion of Lebanon has categorically proved that Israel is the principal threat to the stability of the Arab countries."[31]

Reentering the Arab State System

Power relationships within the Arab state system had begun to shift even prior to Sadat's November 1977 visit to Jerusalem. This was due to the fact that Soviet policy had begun to shift political, economic, and military support to Syria. The decline of Egypt's hegemonic role, already in motion, was significantly accelerated by the events leading to its peace treaty with Israel in 1979 and its subsequent ostracism by practically all the Arab states. Almost from the outset of Mubarak's rule, however, Egypt began to edge out of isolation—although once again, the April 1982 Israeli evacuation of Sinai put a restraint upon this impulse. Already in that month, however, Egypt sent a delegation to a planning committee meeting in preparation for a meeting of the Conference on Non-Aligned States in Baghdad. In June 1982, Mubarak made a condolence visit to Saudi Arabia on the occasion of King Khalid's death, and had a prolonged discussion with the new king, Fahd. Even more important for the legitimacy of Mubarak's leadership domestically and for his visibility abroad in the Arab world was Egypt's readmission to the all-Muslim-nation Islamic Conference Organization in January 1984.

The Egyptian delegation in Baghdad in connection with the non-aligned nation conference signaled the growing closeness of its ties with Iraq. Due to Syria's support of Iran in the Iran-Iraq war (and the longterm animosity between Iraq and Iran in any event), Iraq has found a convenient ally in Egypt. Egypt has been able to make available what some analysts estimate to be billions of dollars in Soviet technology and military supplies, and possibly military advisors as well. In addition, thousands of Egyptian farmers are working in Iraqi agriculture, and it has also been claimed that Egyptians are working in the oil fields in order to relieve Iraqis for military service.[32] It is said that only Iraq's dependence upon Saudi Arabia and that nation's continuing reservations about Egypt have prevented Iraq from following in the footsteps of Jordan and resuming diplomatic relations.

The Israeli invasion of Lebanon created a diplomatic opportunity for Egypt in two respects. The first was that the Israeli decision created a situation in which Mubarak, for reasons of political survival, severely criticized Israel and eventually removed his ambassador; thereafter, Israeli-Egyptian relations slid into a "cold peace"—that is, scrupulously correct relations. At the same time, as already noted, Egypt came closer to the Palestinian Liberation Organization. This was the case early in the invasion, but as the internal dispute at the end of 1983 between Arafat (moderate) and Abu Musa (radical) factions of Fatah developed, Egypt rallied to the support of Arafat against the Syrian-supported radicals. (It has been reported that Egyptian ships aided Arafat's withdrawal from Tripoli.) Arafat was to reciprocate Egyptian support by visiting Cairo in December 1983, an action that contributed to the lessening of Egypt's isolation in the Arab and Muslim worlds: several weeks later, Egypt was readmitted to the Islamic Conference.

Reenergizing the Peace Process

The Israeli invasion provided an opportunity for reenergizing the peace process from within the region. Until then, the Camp David peace process had been externally stimulated by the United States. The onset of the Reagan administration seriously interrupted this process, and the next stimulus toward peace originated from within the region. Already in August 1981, there had emerged the Fahd plan which implicitly recognized Israel's right to exist. While largely stillborn, it was followed by the Reagan plan of September 1982, which seems to have been an American response to the Israeli invasion. In the same month, the Arab summit meeting in Fez, Morocco, incorporated the Fahd plan into its own communiqué.[33] Egypt immediately accepted the Reagan plan, and was clearly receptive to the Fez plan. Israel did not accept the Reagan plan, however, and what might have been a situation of diplomatic interaction and compromise was allowed to languish. The major reason for this was the manner in which the United States allowed itself to be sucked into the maelstrom of Lebanon. This served to divert attention and energy away from broader regional concerns and directed this energy to a deadly involvement that would lead to the death of U.S. officials and citizens, destruction of its facilities and the taking of American hostages. The abortive peace treaty of May 1983 between Lebanon and Israel without the involvement of Syria was a fitting comment on the policy diversion that Lebanon was to become.[34]

As a result of the American policy distraction (and in the pursuit of their own aims), Jordan and Egypt began to respond to the events in Lebanon by focusing increasingly upon the Palestinians. Jordan appears to have feared the possibility of a mass influx of Palestinians from Lebanon and from the West Bank. For Egypt, a new closeness with the Palestinians was useful, since they represented the most potent legitimizing factor available to Egypt for overcoming alienation from the Arab state system. With the growing internal moderate/radical rift in Fatah, Arafat found this attention useful and, as mentioned above, he visited Egypt in December 1983. There also developed a sig-

nificant pattern of Egyptian-Jordanian communication, leading finally to the reestablishment of diplomatic relations between the two
countries in September 1984. As a result, Husayn visited Cairo in December 1984, and Mubarak in turn visited Jordan the following
month. By February 11, 1985, there emerged an agreement between
Arafat and Husayn calling for the participation of both in organizing
a joint Jordanian-Palestinian delegation to negotiate the future of a
confederation of Jordan and the West Bank in an international conference, along with the Israelis and the five permanent members of
the United Nations Security Council and other interested parties.[35]

President Mubarak anticipated that the United States would be
reluctant to hold an international conference at which the Soviet Union would be present, so he made his own recommendation: that a
group made up of Egypt and a joint Palestinian-Jordanian delegation
have a preliminary meeting with officials of the American government in Washington. Mubarak also sought to get around the sticky
point of the U.S. policy of refusing to talk to the PLO until it recognized Israel, as spelled out in United Nations resolution 242. He attempted to do this by stipulating that the Palestinians on the delegation would be appointed by the PLO from the membership of the
Palestine National Council, a parliamentary body not technically
part of the PLO. (There had already been a series of behind-the-
scenes discussions with Prime Minister Peres of Israel in this regard,
and he subsequently voiced his public if cautious support for the idea
in principle.)[36] Mubarak made his visit to the United States in March
only to find that the death of the Soviet leader Konstantin Chernenko
reduced his visibility and impact upon American public opinion; his
proposal was politely declined, and his request for additional economic assistance significantly reduced. He was informed that the
United States chose not to be a mediator, and that the Arab states
themselves should engage in direct discussion with Israel, as the
"late" President Sadat had done.[37] (It is possible that the U.S. official
who used this term, in his eagerness to promote direct negotiations
between Israel and the Arabs, overlooked the possible relationship
between the direct talks Sadat had had with Israel and his death.)

More to the point, however, Mubarak's effort to finesse the February 11, 1985, agreement between the PLO and Jordan failed to ma-
terialize. The reasons are peculiar to each of the three major actors.
While Prime Minister Peres and Mubarak appear to have established
a reasonable working relationship, neither Foreign Minister Shamir

nor Minister of Industry Sharon of Likud would agree to either the international conference or to direct talks with anyone from the PNC. While Arafat had already made a major concession in adopting the Jordanian confederation option and in agreeing to direct talks with Israel, he insisted on the PLO's presence in the talks and on an international conference. Finally, it was clear that the United States had little initial enthusiasm for an initiative that was not its own, which would force it to review its agreement with Israel not to talk to the PLO, and which would draw the USSR into the peace process. In addition, as shown in the course of both Assistant Secretary for the Near East Richard Murphy's trip to the region in April and Secretary Shultz's the following month, it was clear that Mubarak did not have the agreement of Arafat for his compromise proposal.[38] While Mubarak's effort had at least temporarily failed, it did communicate to the United States the sincerity of his diplomatic intentions and this may have won him a degree of favor in Washington. King Husayn was told essentially the same thing on his visit to Washington at the end of May.[39] There the initiative was to stand at least temporarily, inasmuch as within two weeks the American TWA hostage issue was to burst upon the scene and monopolize diplomatic attention.

While this peace initiative that had originated from within the Middle East was at least temporarily stalled, there were signs that it might be resumed. The first such indication was that Mubarak's continuing interaction with Israel. In mid-May, an Israeli delegation consisting of the directors of the prime minister's and foreign minister's offices was in Cairo to discuss the Taba issue and—more important—to plan for a possible summer summit of President Mubarak and Prime Minister Peres. Mubarak stated that such a summit (and the return of the Egyptian ambassador to Tel Aviv) would depend on a solution being found for the Taba problem, on Israel's withdrawal from Lebanon, and on some "improvement" for the West Bank Palestinians.[40]

On each of these issues there appears to be room for compromise. Peres appears willing (as Likud of the Unity government is definitely not) to submit the Taba issue to the binding international arbitration desired by Egypt; the Israelis are all but out of Lebanon; and although the meaning of "improvement" for the West Bank is not entirely clear, it could refer to some sort of symbolic gesture—greater freedom for West Bankers to travel abroad and return, say. Yet another favorable omen for the possibility of movement toward negotiations and peace was the fact that the Jordanian-PLO-Egyptian initiative has presented Egypt with the opportunity to get out of the rut of the autonomy talk mode related to Camp David and to link its "Arab" policy to the peace effort. Enhancing this possibility is the fact that each of the actors now appears to have a political stake in the success of peace efforts: Mubarak, in order to defuse what is becoming an increasingly vocal opposition to Israel; Arafat, because of the further bludgeoning of Fatah in the April-May 1985 Shiite assaults on the Palestinian camps in Lebanon; and Peres, because as he attempts to lead a confused and divided post-Lebanon Israel his own electoral chances may be at stake.

Conclusion

The principal effect of the Israeli invasion of Lebanon from the Egyptian perspective has been to reinforce President Mubarak's policy since assuming office: that is, the reentry of Egypt into the Arab state system. The Israeli intention in invading Lebanon was to destroy the PLO. The ability of the PLO to successfully withstand the siege of Beirut by the Israelis in the summer weeks of 1982 indicates that what was achieved was a military weakening of the PLO, while at the same time it remained, at least for the moment, politically intact. This diminishing of the PLO provided Egypt with the opportunity to rally publicly to its support. The later Syrian support of PLO and Fatah radicals against Arafat and the PLO centrists at the end of 1983 politically weakened the PLO and Arafat's leadership and created a further opportunity for the Egyptians to rally supportively.

The Egyptian inclination to publicly support the PLO has had the effect of legitimizing Egypt's Arab credentials in the aftermath of its diplomatic isolation following and due to the 1979 treaty with Israel. This, combined with change in policy emphases in two key Arab states, has given impetus to Egypt's effort to rejoin the Arab state system. Iraq's need for military material assistance in its war with Iran (to augment declining Soviet aid) has been one such opportunity. Presently, diplomatic relations are conducted on a de facto basis that, in the Egyptian view, only Saudi Arabian objections prevent from becoming de jure. More important, Jordan's realization that renewed diplomatic action needs to be taken on the Palestinian issue has allowed Jordan and Egypt not only to resume diplomatic relations but also to begin work in concert on the peace process.

The foregoing indicates that Mubarak has been able to make significant progress toward realignment with the Arab states. Somalia, Sudan, Oman, and Jordan now have formal diplomatic relations with Egypt, and Morocco and Iraq have de facto relations. Saudi Arabia, North Yemen, and the remaining Gulf states, while their relations are more restrained, have continued important informal contacts as well as some meaningful commercial relationships—for example, the greater proportion of private foreign investment in Egypt has been from Kuwait, Saudi Arabia, and the Gulf states. Syria, South Yemen, Libya, and Algeria remain more steadfast in their opposition to Egypt's diplomatic relations with Israel. The distribution of power in the Arab world in the aftermath of the 1977 Sadat visit to Israel, however, has altered significantly, so that Syria and Iraq, for example, are presently more nearly on a par with Egypt. While Egypt remains culturally and militarily more dominant, it would not regain regional hegemony even if it were to reestablish relations with all Arab states. The Arab state system of the 1980s is one of more equal power, and thus potentially of more diplomatic fluidity. This degree of success in rejoining the Arab state system has had important benefits to Mubarak in terms of his domestic political stability. The result has been a defusing of criticism from the political opposition and a strengthening of his general political legitimacy.

This relative success has a bearing on relations with the United States as well, since as long as these relations are strong it is in American interest to have Egypt in a position of enhanced regional influence. Egyptian-American relations continue to have their stresses and strains, but in the Mubarak era they have been much less affected by personality and have therefore become more workmanlike. Likewise, the past tendency for U.S. economic assistance to be administered unilaterally appears to have changed to the point that there is now more consultation and interaction with Egyptian officials. Nonetheless, the very size of such assistance as well as the visibility of the American presence continue to present conditions that require careful management and sensitivity.

What might be called the "regionalization" of the peace process is a direct consequence of the Israeli invasion of Lebanon. Reference has already been made to Egypt's closeness to the Palestinians and to its diplomatic relations with Jordan. With the partial eclipse of the Likud alignment in Israel in the aftermath of its increasingly criticized policies in Lebanon (and Labor's greater prominence under Prime Minister Peres's leadership), the potential exists for greater Israeli accommodation towards peace. Nonetheless, the critical stumbling block represented by the Taba issue will have to be settled, as well as the issue of PLO participation in the peace process. Furthermore, it is unlikely that much of this will be accomplished under the present Unity government, whose Labor and Likud constituent elements are reasonably united on economic policy issues but are bitterly divided on foreign policy issues.

"Regionalization" is not, however, simply a matter of the diplomatic initiatives of regional actors. A further consequence of the invasion has been the bitterness of U.S. policy failures in Lebanon. As a result, American policy has appeared to have lost initiative and to have become more reactive. Thus, while Egyptian policy has shown significant success in taking steps to reestablish Egypt within the Arab state system, full membership will likely occur only with a peaceful settlement whose major impediments at present appear to rest with the immobility of American policy and the internal divisions of Israel and the PLO.

NOTES

1. Speech before National Democratic Party broadcast over the Cairo Domestic Service. Text in U.S. Government, *Foreign Broadcast Information Service/Middle East and Africa,* (hereafter cited as *FBIS/MEA*) 22 July 1983.

2. These themes recur frequently and regularly in most accounts of Egyptian foreign policy. See the important analytical article, Ali E. Hillal Dessouki, "The Primacy of Economics: The Foreign Policy of Egypt," in Bahgat Korany and Ali E. Hillal Dessouki, eds., *The Foreign Policies of Arab States* (Boulder, Colo.: Westview Press and The American University in Cairo Press, 1984), pp. 119–46. For an authoritative article by the minister of state for foreign affairs, see Boutrous Boutrous-Ghali, "The Foreign Policy of Egypt in the Post-Sadat Era," *Foreign Affairs* 60 (Spring 1982):769–88. For an article noting these same constants but very critical of Sadat's policy, see Mohamed Hassanein Heikal, "Egyptian Foreign Policy," *Foreign Affairs* 56 (Spring 1978):714–27. For an argument that the landbridge explains the cosmopolitan outlook of Egypt, see Fuad Ajami, *The Arab Predicament* (London: Cambridge University Press, 1981), p. 108, where the views of the Egyptian intellectual and diplomatist, Tahseen Bashir, are discussed.

3. On the subject of Mubarak's Sudan and African policy, see Boutrous-Ghali, "Foreign Policy," pp. 782–85; on the revolution in Sudan, see *New York Times,* 8 April 1985; and on Chad, see Middle East News Agency, *FBIS/MEA,* 8 January 1985, reporting on the visit of President Habre to Cairo.

4. On these points of contrast of Middle Eastern regional relations, see Korany and Dessouqi, *Foreign Policies,* p. 2; and Dessouqi in Korany and Dessouqi, *Foreign Policies,* p. 123.

5. See Malcolm Kerr, *The Arab Cold War: Gamal Abd al-Nasir and His Rivals 1958–1970,* 3rd ed. (London: Oxford University Press, 1971). For Egyptian accounts of the 1973 war, see Mohamed Hassanein Heikal, *The Road to Ramadan* (New York: Ballantine, 1975); Saad Al-Shazly *The Crossing of the Suez* (San Francisco: American Mideast Research, 1980); Ismail Fahmy, *Negotiating for Peace in the Middle East* (Cairo: American University in Cairo Press, 1983); and Anwar al-Sadat, *In Search of Identity* (New York: Harper, 1977).

6. See Louis J. Cantori, "Egyptian Policy," in Robert O. Freedman, ed., *The Middle East Since Camp David* (Boulder, Colo.: Westview, 1984), pp. 174–75 for a further discussion of this aspect.

7. For a critical treatment of the effects of the peace treaty and its impact upon Egypt, see Ibrahim Karawan, "Egypt and the Western Alliance: The Politics of Westomania?" in S. Spiegel, ed., *The Middle East and the Western Alliance* (London: Allen and Unwin, 1982), pp. 163–81.

8. On these events and their analysis, see John Waterbury, *The Egypt of Nasser and Sadat* (Princeton, N.J.: Princeton University Press, 1983), pp. 354–88.

9. On Mubarak, see ibid., pp. xiii–xvii.

10. On the role of these organizations and their internal dynamics in Egypt, see Saad Eddin Ibrahim, "Islamic Militancy as a Social Movement: The Case of Two Groups in Egypt," in Ali Hillal Dessouki, ed., *Islamic Resurgence in the Arab World* (New York: Praeger, 1982), pp. 117–37. More generally, see Louis J. Cantori, "Religion and Politics in Egypt," in M. Curtis, ed., *Religion and Politics in the Middle East* (Boulder, Colo.: Westview, 1982), pp. 92–122.

11. All political parties in the May 1984 elections had to receive 8% of the total vote before any of their elected representatives could be seated in the parliament. On this point (and on the elections in general) see Bertus Hendriks, "Egypt's Elections, Mubarak's Bind," *MERIP* 129 (January 1985), pp. 11–18; and Hamied Ansari, "Mubarak's Egypt," *Current History* 84 (January 1985):21.

12. On these groups, see Cantori, "Religion and Politics in Egypt."

13. Don Peretz, "Israel Confronts Old Problems," *Current History* 84 (January 1985):11.

14. Joel Beinin, "The Cold Peace," *MERIP* 129 (January 1985), pp. 3–19.

15. See the three-part series written by Arye Naor, former cabinet secretary to Prime Minister Begin, *Baltimore Sun,* 12–14 June 1985, in which he details the nature of this deception at the highest governmental level.

16. Cairo Daily Service, *FBIS,* 30 May 1982.

17. Middle East News Agency, *FBIS,* 31 May 1982.

18. Cairo Daily Service, *FBIS,* 3 June 1982.

19. Middle East News Agency, *FBIS,* 7 June 1982.

20. Ibid., *FBIS,* 8 June 1982.

21. See, for example, the editorial of Ibrahim Nafi in *al-Ahram,* 11 June 1982, where he sharply criticizes the "green light" that the U.S. must have given the Israelis, the illegal use of U.S. weapons, and the U.S. veto of the U.N. Security Council resolution; and the article by Egypt's leading short story writer, Yusuf Idris, also writing in *al-Ahram* (14 June 1982), where he makes similar points.

22. Agence France Presse, quoted in *FBIS,* 9 June 1982.

23. Ibid.

24. Middle East News Agency, *FBIS,* 16 June 1982.

25. Middle East News Agency, *FBIS,* 1 July 1982. It is noteworthy, however, that the invitation specifically said that no PLO military units would be allowed in Egypt. Thus, the invitation was one not likely to be picked up—and it was not.

26. The accusation by official Egyptians of the absence of good faith on the part of the Israelis in the peace process is repeated frequently in Egypt—for example, in a briefing by Ambassador Shafi Abd al-Hamid at the Egyptian foreign ministry on June 27, 1984. The Ambassador was just stepping down as a negotiator with the Israelis, and his frustration was evident.

Taba remains a sticky point in Israeli-Egyptian relations. Essentially, the boundary dispute involves a strip of land 700 yards in diameter just west of Eilath on the Gulf of Aqaba. The Egyptian accusation of "bad faith" is due to the fact that the Israeli government has permitted a major resort hotel to be constructed there while the area is still in dispute. The issue has become a symbolic one to the Egyptians.

27. Simon Ingram, "Mubarak's Problems with his U.S. Ally," *Middle East International* (25 January 1985):15–16. See also Michael Hudson, "Don't Take Egypt for Granted," *Middle East International* (22 July 1983):14–15.

28. Cairo Daily Service, *FBIS,* 28 July 1982.

29. David Ottaway, "Egypt's Mood Turns Against Close U.S. Ties," *Washington Post,* 30 January 1985.

30. Ibrahim A. Karawan, "Egypt's Defense Policy," in Sephanie Neuman, ed., *Defense Planning in Less-Industrialized States* (Lexington, Mass.: D. C. Heath, 1984), pp. 147–79. It includes valuable commentary by Professor Herman Eilts, former U.S. Ambassador to Egypt.

31. Mustafa Khalil *Mayu,* 5 July 1982.

32. Christine Moss Helms, *Iraq: Eastern Flank of the Arab World* (Washington, D.C.: Brookings, 1984), p. 185.

33. See Cantori, "Egyptian Policy," pp. 183–84, for a summary discussion of this process.

34. For a sharply critical treatment of U.S. policy in Lebanon, see George Ball, *Error and Betrayal in Lebanon* (Washington, D.C.: Foundation for Peace in the Middle East, 1984).

35. The text of the agreement appears in *New York Times,* 24 February 1985.

36. For an analysis of this sequence of events, see Judith Miller, "Mubarak Tries to Jump Start Stalled Mideast Peace Talks," *New York Times,* 3 March 1985.

37. Ibid., 12 March 1985.

38. Ibid., article by Judith Miller, 3 March 1985.

39. Ibid., 29 May 1985.

40. Ibid., 16 May 1985.

Bibliography

Books

Abdulghani, J. M. *Iraq and Iran: The Years of Crisis.* Baltimore: Johns Hopkins Press, 1984.

Ajami, Fuad. *The Arab Predicament.* London: Cambridge University Press, 1981.

Arian, Asher. *Politics in Israel.* London: Chatham House, 1985.

al Baharna, Husain. *The Arab Gulf States: Their Legal and Political Status and Their International Problems.* Beirut: Librairie du Liban, 1975.

Ball, George. *Error and Betrayal in Lebanon.* Washington, D.C.: Foundation for Peace in the Middle East, 1984.

Basic Petroleum Data Book. Vol. 5. Washington, D.C.: American Petroleum Institute, 1985.

Bazargan, Mohandes Mehdi. *Inqilab Dar Daw Harekat.* n.p. Chap, Naraqi, 1363.

Benvenisti, Meron. *The West Bank Data Project: A Survey of Israel's Policies.* Washington, D.C.: American Enterprise Institute for Public Policy Research, 1984.

Cassadio, J. P. *The Economic Challenge of the Arabs.* Farnborough, England: Westmead, 1976.

Cobban, Helena. *The Palestinian Liberation Organization: People, Power and Politics.* London: Cambridge University Press, 1984.

Curtis, Michael, ed. *Religion and Politics in the Middle East.* Boulder, Colo.: Westview Press, 1982.

Dawisha, Adeed, ed. *Islam in Foreign Policy.* Cambridge: Cambridge University Press, 1983.

———. Dawisha, Adeed and Dawisha, Karen, eds. *The Soviet Union in the Arab World.* New York: Holmes and Meier, 1982.

Day, Alan, ed. *Border and Territorial Disputes.* Detroit: Gale Research Company, 1982.

Devlin, John F. *Syria: Modern State in an Ancient Land.* Boulder, Colo.: Westview Press, 1983.

Donaldson, Robert H., ed. *The Soviet Union in the Third World: Successes and Failures.* Boulder, Colo.: Westview Press, 1981.

European Political Cooperation. Press and Information Office of the Federal Government of Germany, 1982.

Fahmy, Ismail. *Negotiating for Peace in the Middle East.* Cairo: American University of Cairo Press, 1983.

Freedman, Robert O. *Soviet Policy Toward the Middle East Since 1970.* 3rd ed. New York: Praeger, 1982.

Freedman, Robert O., ed. *Israel in the Begin Era.* New York: Praeger, 1982.

———. *The Middle East Since Camp David.* Boulder, Colo.: Westview Press, 1984.

Gabriel, Richard A. *Operation Peace for Galilee: The Israeli-PLO War in Lebanon.* New York: Hill and Wang, 1984.

Glassman, Jon D. *Arms for the Arabs: The Soviet Union and War in the Middle East.* Baltimore: Johns Hopkins University Press, 1975.

Golan, Galia. *Yom Kippur and After: The Soviet Union and the Middle East.* London: Cambridge University Press, 1977.

Hamid, Rashid. *Munadhamat al-tahrir al-filistiniyya [The Palestine Liberation Organization].* Beirut: Palestine Research Center, 1977.

Heikal, Mohamed. *The Road to Ramadan.* New York: Ballantine, 1975.

———. *The Sphinx and the Commissar.* New York: Harper and Row, 1978.

Helms, Christine Moss. *Iraq: Eastern Flank of the Arab World.* Washington, D.C.: Brookings, 1984.

Hunter, Shireen. *OPEC and the Third World: The Politics of Aid.* Bloomington, Ind.: Indiana University Press, 1984.

Ismael, Tareq. *Iraq and Iran: Roots of Conflict.* Syracuse, N.Y.: Syracuse University Press, 1982.

Israeli, Raphael, ed. *PLO in Lebanon: Selected Documents.* New York: St. Martin's Press, 1983.

Kahan, Yitzhak and Barak, Aharon. *The Beirut Massacre.* Translated by Bezalel Gordon. New York: Karz-Cohl Pub., 1983.

Kanet, Roger E., and Bahry, Donna, eds. *Soviet Economic and Political Relations with the Developing World.* New York: Praeger, 1975.

Kerr, Malcolm. *The Arab Cold War.* New York: Oxford University Press, 1971.

Khalidi, Rashid. *Under Siege: PLO Decisionmaking During the 1982 War.* New York: Columbia University Press, 1985.

Khalidi, Walid. *Conflict and Violence in Lebanon: Confrontation in the Middle East.* Cambridge: Harvard University Press, 1979.

Klinghoffer, Arthur. *Israel and the Soviet Union.* Boulder, Colo.: Westview Press, 1985.

Laqueur, Walter, and Rubin, Barry, eds. *The Israel-Arab Reader.* New York, 1984.

Lenczowski, George. *Soviet Advances in the Middle East.* Washington: American Enterprise Institute, 1972.

Liebman, Charles, and Don-Yehiya, Eliezer. *Religion and Politics in Israel.* Bloomington: Indiana University Press, 1984.

Lissak, Moshe. *Israeli Society and Its Defense Establishment.* Jerusalem: Biblio Distributors of Israel Universities Press, 1984.

Long, David, and Reich, Bernard, eds. *The Government and Politics of the Middle East and North Africa.* Boulder, Colo.: Westview Press, 1980.

Martin, Lenore. *The Unstable Gulf.* Lexington, Mass.: Lexington Books, 1984.

McLaurin, R. D., et al. *Middle East Foreign Policy: Issues and Processes.* New York: Praeger, 1982.

McLaurin, R. D., ed. *The Political Role of Minority Groups in the Middle East.* New York: Praeger, 1980.

Miller, Aaron David. *The PLO and the Politics of Survival.* Washington Paper No. 99. New York: Praeger, 1983.

Niblock, Tim, ed. *Iraq: The Contemporary State.* New York: St. Martin's Press, 1982.

Neuman, Stephanie, ed. *Defense Planning in Less-Industrialized States.* Lexington, Mass.: Lexington Books, 1984.

Oz, Amos. *In the Land of Israel.* Translated by Marie Goldberg-Bartura. New York: Harcourt Brace Jovanovich, 1983.

Penrose, Edith, and Penrose, E. F. *Iraq: International Relations and National Development.* Boulder, Colo.: Westview Press, 1978.

Pollock, David. *The Politics of Pressure: American Arms and Israeli Policy Since the Six Day War.* Westport, Conn.: Greenwood Press, 1982.

Porter, Bruce D. *The USSR in Third World Conflicts.* New York: Cambridge, 1984.

Primakov, E. M. *Anatomiia Blizhnevostochnogo Konflikta.* Moscow: Mysl', 1978.

Quandt, William B. *Saudi Security in the 1980s.* Washington, D.C.: Brookings Institution, 1981.

Rabinovich, Itamar, and Reinharz, Jehuda, eds. *Israel in the Middle East: Documents and Readings on Society, Politics, and Foreign Policy, 1948–Present.* New York: Oxford University Press, 1984.

Rabinovich, Itamar. *The War for Lebanon, 1970–1983.* Ithaca: Cornell University Press, 1984.

Ramazani, Rouhollah K. *The Foreign Policy of Iran, 1941–1973: A Study of Foreign Policy in Modernizing Nations.* Charlottesville: University Press of Virginia, 1975.

———. *The Northern Tier: Afghanistan, Iran and Turkey.* Princeton: Van Nostrand, 1966.

———. *The Persian Gulf: Iran's Role.* Charlottesville: University Press of Virginia, 1972.

———. *The Persian Gulf and the Strait of Hormuz*. The Netherlands: Alphen aan den Rijn, 1979.

———. *The United States and Iran: The Patterns of Influence*. New York: Praeger, 1982.

Randal, Jonathan C. *Going All the Way: Christian Warlords, Israeli Adventurers, and the War in Lebanon*. New York: Viking Press, 1983.

Reiser, Stuart. *The Politics of Leverage: The National Religious Party of Israel and Its Influence on Foreign Policy*. Harvard Middle East Papers, Modern Series, no. 2. Cambridge: Harvard University Center for Middle Eastern Studies, 1984.

Ro'i, Yaacov. *From Encroachment to Involvement: A Documentary Study of Soviet Policy in the Middle East*. Jerusalem: Israel Universities Press, 1974.

Ro'i, Yaacov, ed. *The Limits to Power*. London: Croom Helm, 1979.

Rubenberg, Cheryl. *The PLO: Its Institutional Infrastructure*. Belmont, Mass.: Institute for Arab Studies, 1983.

Rubinstein, Alvin Z., ed. *The Arab-Israeli Conflict: Perspectives*. New York: Praeger, 1984.

el-Sadat, Anwar. *In Search of Identity*. New York: Harper, 1977.

Sandler, Shmuel, and Frisch, Hillel. *Israel, the Palestinians, and the West Bank*. Lexington, Mass.: Lexington Books, 1984.

Schiff, Ze'ev, and Ya'ari, Ehud. *Israel's Lebanon War*. Translated by Ina Friedman. New York: Simon and Schuster, 1984.

Sella, Amnon. *Soviet Political and Military Conduct in the Middle East*. New York: St. Martin's, 1981.

Al-Shazly, Saad. *The Crossing of the Suez*. San Francisco: American Mideast Research, 1980.

Shultz, Richard H., and Godson, Roy. *Dezinformatsia: Active Measures in Soviet Strategy*. New York: Pergamon-Brassey's 1984.

Spiegel, Steven, ed. *The Middle East and the Western Alliance*. London: Allen and Unwin, 1982.

Sukhanraniha-ye Imam Khumayni Dar Shish Mah-ye Avval-e 1359. (Ayatollah Khomeini's speeches). Tehran: 1459.

Tahir-Kheli, Shirin, and Ayubi, Shaheen, eds. *The Iran-Iraq War: New Weapons, Old Conflicts*. New York: Praeger, 1983.

Waterbury, John. *The Egypt of Nasser and Sadat*. Princeton: Princeton University Press, 1983.

Articles

Ajami, Fouad. "The End of Pan Arabism." *Foreign Affairs* 57 (Winter 1978–1979):355–73.

Arian, Asher. "Elections 1981: Competitiveness and Polarization." *Jerusalem Quarterly,* no. 21 (Fall 1981):3–27.

Averick, Sara. "Pressure and Progress: Israel and West Beirut." *Near East Report* 26, no. 33 (August 13, 1982):162–63.

Baram, Amazia. "Saddam Hussain: A Political Profile," *The Jerusalem Quarterly* 17 (Fall 1980):115–44.

Batatu, Hanna. "Iraq's Underground Shi'a Movements: Characteristics, Causes and Prospects." *Middle East Journal* 35 (Autumn 1981):578–94.

Bengio, Ofra. "Iraq." *Middle East Contemporary Survey III: 1977–1978,* edited by Colin Legum. New York: Holmes and Meier, 1980:559–81.

Beinin, Joel. "The Cold Peace." *MERIP Reports,* January 1985, pp. 3–9.

Bialer, Uri. "The Iranian Connection in Israel's Foreign Policy, 1948–1951." *The Middle East Journal,* Spring 1985, pp. 292–315.

Cantori, Louis J. "Egyptian Policy." In Robert O. Freedman, ed., *The Middle East Since Camp David.* Boulder, Colo.: Westview Press, 1984, pp. 174–75.

Cohen, Elliot A. "Peace for Galilee: Success or Failure?" *Commentary* 78, no. 5 (November 1984):24–30.

Cohen, Raymond. "Israel and the Soviet-American Statement of October 1, 1977: The Limits of Patron-Client Influence." *Orbis* 22, no. 3 (Fall 1978):613–33.

Cooley, John K. "The Shifting Sands of Arab Communism." *Problems of Communism* 24, no. 2 (1975):22–42.

Dawisha, Adeed. "Invoking the Spirit of Arabism: Islam in the Foreign Policy of Saddam's Iraq." In Adeed Dawisha, ed., *Islam in Foreign Policy.* New York: Cambridge University Press, 1983, pp. 117–22.

———. "Iraq: The West's Opportunity." *Foreign Policy* 41 (Winter 1980–1981):134–53.

———. "The Soviet Union in the Arab World: The limits to Superpower Influence." In Adeed Dawisha and Karen Dawisha, eds., *The Soviet Union in the Arab World.* New York: Holmes and Meier, 1982, pp. 8–23.

Dawisha, Karen. "The USSR in the Middle East: Superpower in Decline?" *Foreign Affairs* 61 (Winter 1982–1983):438–52.

Demant, Peter. "Israeli Settlement Policy Today." *MERIP Reports,* July/August 1983, pp. 3–13.

Dessouki, Ali E. Hillal. "The Primacy of Economics: The Foreign Policy of Egypt." In Bahgat Korany and Ali E. Hillal Dessouki, eds., *The Foreign Policies of Arab States.* Boulder, Colo.: Westview Press and The American University of Cairo Press, 1984, pp. 119–46.

Devlin, John F. "The Policial Structure in Syria." *Middle East Review* 18, no. 1 (Fall 1984):15–21.

———. "Syrian Policy." In Robert O. Freedman, ed., *The Middle East Since Camp David.* Boulder, Colo.: Westview Press, 1984, pp. 125–26.

Dishon, Daniel, and Maddy-Weitzman, Bruce. "Inter-Arab Affairs." In *Middle East Contemporary Survey IV: 1979–1980,* edited by Colin Legum. New York: Holmes and Meier, 1981, pp. 169–225.

Dowty, Alan. "Israel: From Ideology to Reality." In Alvin Z. Rubinstein, ed., *The Arab-Israeli Conflict: Perspectives.* New York: Praeger, 1984, pp. 107–44.

Drysdale, Alasdair. "The Succession Question in Syria." *Middle East Journal* 39, no. 2 (Spring 1985):246–57.

Falk, Gloria. "Israeli Public Opinion: Looking Toward a Palestinian Solution." *The Middle East Journal* 39, no. 3 (Summer 1985):247–69.

Feuerwerger, Marvin. "Iraq: An Opportunity for the West?" *Middle East Review* (Fall/Winter 1981–1982):26–30.

Freedman, Robert O. "Soviet Policy Toward the Middle East Since Camp David." In Robert O. Freedman, ed., *The Middle East Since Camp David.* Boulder, Colo.: Westview Press, 1984, pp. 9–57.

———. "Soviet Policy Toward Ba'athist Iraq: 1968–1979." In Robert H. Donaldson, ed., *The Soviet Union in the Third World: Successes and Failures.* Boulder, Colo.: Westview Press, 1981, pp. 161–91.

———. "Soviet Policy Toward Syria Since Camp David." *Middle East Review* (Fall/Winter 1981–1982):31–42.

———. "The Soviet Union and the Communist Parties of the Arab World: An Uncertain Relationship." In Roger E. Kanet and Donna Bahry, eds., *Soviet Economic and Political Relations with the Developing World.* New York: Praeger, 1975, pp. 100–134.

Friedman, Thomas L. "America's Failure in Lebanon." *The New York Times Magazine,* 8 April 1984, pp. 32–44, 62–66.

Garfinkle, Adam M. "Jordanian Foreign Policy." *Current History,* January 1984:21–24, 38–39.

Ghali, Boutrous Boutrous. "The Foreign Policy of Egypt in the Post-Sadat Era." *Foreign Affairs* 60 (Spring 1982):769–88.

Hallabra, Saad Allah. "The Euro-Arab Dialogue." *American-Arab Affairs,* no. 10, Fall 1984:44–59.

Heikal, Mohamed Hassanein. "Egyptian Foreign Policy." *Foreign Affairs* 56 (Spring 1978):714–27.

Horowitz, Dan. "Israel's War in Lebanon: New Patterns of Strategic Thinking and Civilian-Military Relations." In Moshe Lissak, ed., *Israeli Society and Its Defense Establishment* (Jerusalem: Biblio Distributors of Israel Universities Press, 1984), pp. 83–101.

Hudson, Michael. "Don't Take Egypt for Granted." *Middle East International,* 22 July 1983:14–15.

Hunter, Shireen T. "Arab-Iranian Relations and Stability in the Persian Gulf." *Washington Quarterly* 7, no. 3 (Summer 1984):67–76.

———. "Syrian-Iranian Relations: An Alliance of Convenience or More?" *Middle East Insight,* May/June 1984.

Hunter, Shireen T., and Hunter, Robert E. "The Post Camp David Arab World." In Robert O. Freedman, ed., *The Middle East Since Camp David* (Boulder, Colo.: Westview Press, 1984), pp. 79–99.

Ibrahim, Saad Eddin. "Islamic Militancy as a Social Movement: The Case of Two Groups in Egypt." In Ali Hillal Dessouki, ed., *Islamic Resurgence in the Arab World* (New York: Praeger, 1982), pp. 117–37.

Ingram, Simon. "Mubarak's Problems with his U.S. Ally." *Middle East International,* 25 January 1985, pp. 15–16.

Karawan, Ibrahim A. "Egypt's Defense Policy." In Stephanie Neuman, ed., *Defense Planning in Less-Industrialized States* (Lexington, Mass.: D. C. Heath, 1984), pp. 147–79.

———. "Egypt and the Western Alliance: The Politics of Westomania?" In Steven Spiegel, ed., *The Middle East and the Western Alliance* (London: Allen and Unwin, 1982), pp. 163–81.

Khalidi, Rashid. "The Palestinians in Lebanon: The Social Repercussions of Israel's Invasion." *Middle East Journal* 38, no. 2 (Spring 1984):255–66.

Khourfy, Nabeel. "The Pragmatic Trend in Inter-Arab Politics." *Middle East Journal* 368 (Summer 1982):374–88.

Komarov, V. "Highways and Byways." *New Times* (Moscow), no. 2, 1984, pp. 18–21.

Krauthammer, Charles. "Who Won Lebanon?" *The New Republic,* 24 June 1985:15–16.

Lesch, Ann M. "Israeli Settlement in the West Bank: Mortgaging the Future." *Journal of South Asian and Middle Eastern Studies* 7, no. 1 (Fall 1983):3–23.

Long, David, and Hearty, John. "Republic of Iraq." In David Long and Bernard Reich, eds., *The Government and Politics of the Middle East and North Africa* (Boulder, Colo.: Westview Press, 1980), pp. 107–28.

Miller, Aaron David. "Palestinians in the 1980s." *Current History,* January 1984:17–20, 34–36.

Moisi, Dominique. "La France de Mitterrand Et Le Conflict Du Proche Orient: Comment Concilier Emotion et Politique." *Politiques Étrangères* 2 (June 1982):395–402.

Mullen, Thomas. "Will Saddam Outlast the Iran-Iraq War?" *Middle East Insight* 3 (1984):33–34.

Niblock, Tim. "Iraqi Politics Towards the Arab States of the Gulf, 1958–1981." In Tim Niblock, ed., *Iraq: The Contemporary State* (New York: St. Martin's Press, 1982), pp. 125ff.

Oweiss, Ibrahim M. "The Israeli Economy and Its Military Liability." *American-Arab Affairs,* no. 8 (Spring 1984):31–40.

Perera, Judith. "Hammering Out a Compromise." *The Middle East,* no. 101 (March 1983):8–9.

Peretz, Don. "Israeli Policy." In Robert O. Freedman, ed., *The Middle East*

Since Camp David (Boulder, Colo.: Westview Press, 1984), pp. 143–70.

Peretz, Don, and Smooha, Sammy. "Israel's Eleventh Knesset Election." *The Middle East Journal* 39, no. 1 (Winter 1984):86–104.

Pipes, Daniel. "A Border Adrift: Origins of the Conflict." In Shirin Tahir-Kheli and Shaheen Ayubi, eds., *The Iran-Iraq War: New Weapons, Old Conflicts* (New York: Praeger, 1983), pp. 3–26.

Pollock, David. "Jordan: Option or Optical Illusion?" *Middle East Insight*, March/April 1985:19–26.

Quandt, William B. "Reagan's Lebanon Policy: Trial and Error." *Middle East Journal* 138, no. 2 (Spring 1984):237–54.

Ramazani, Rouhollah K. "Emerging Patterns of Regional Relations in Iranian Foreign Policy." *Orbis* 18, no. 4 (Winter 1975):143–U.S.69.

———. "Iran's Islamic Revolution and the Persian Gulf." *Current History,* January 1985:5–8, 40–41.

———. "Khumayni's Islam in Iran's Foreign Policy." In Adeed Dawisha, ed., *Islam in Foreign Policy* (Cambridge: Cambridge University Press, 1983).

———. "Who Lost America? The Case of Iran." *The Middle East Journal,* Winter 1982:5–21.

Roberts, Cynthia A. "Soviet Arms-Transfer Policy and the Decision to Upgrade Syrian Air Defenses." *Survival,* July/August 1983:154–64.

Rouleau, Eric. "The Future of the PLO." *Foreign Affairs,* Fall 1983:138–56.

Rubenberg, Cheryl A. "The PNC and the Reagan Initiative." *American-Arab Affairs* 4 (April 1983):53–69.

Rubin, Barry. "The Reagan Administration and the Middle East." In Ken A. Oye et al., *The Eagle Defiant* (Boston: Little, Brown & Co., 1982), pp. 367–89.

Schiff, Ze'ev. "Lebanon: Motivations and Interests in Israel's Policy." *The Middle East Journal* 38, no. 2 (Spring 1984):220–27.

———. "The Specter of Civil War in Israel." *The Middle East Journal* 39, no. 2 (Spring 1985):231–45.

Sciolino, Elaine. "The Big Brother: Iraq under Saddam Husayn." *New York Times Magazine,* 3 February 1983, pp. 16ff.

Seliktar, Ofira. "Ethnic Stratification and Foreign Policy in Israel: The Attitudes of Oriental Jews Towards the Arabs and the Arab-Israeli Conflict." *The Middle East Journal* 38, no. 1 (Winter 1984):34–50.

Simon, Reeva. "Iraq." In *World Encyclopedia of Political Systems and Parties* 1, edited by George Dalvey (New York: Facts on File, 1983), pp. 493–500.

Smolansky, Oles. "The Kremlin and the Iraqi Ba'ath, 1968–1982: An Influence Relationship." *Middle East Review* 15 (Spring/Summer 1983):622–28.

Snyder, Jed. "The Road to Osiraq: Baghdad's Quest for the Bomb?" *Middle East Journal* 37 (Autumn 1983):565–93.

Stepanov, A. "Consistent Support." *New Times* (Moscow), no. 42 (1983):13.

———. "To Safeguard Palestinian Unity." *New Times* (Moscow), no. 28 (1983):14–15.

Tinnin, David. "Iraq and the New Arab Alliance." *Fortune* 3 (November 1980):44–46.

Tomasek, Robert. "The Resolution of Major Controversies between Iran and Iraq." *World Affairs* 139 (Winter 1976–1977):206–230.

Wright, Claudia. "Iraq–New Power in the Middle East." *Foreign Affairs* 58 (Winter 1979–1980):257–77.

Ya'ari, Ehud. "Israel's Dilemma in Lebanon." *Middle East Insight* 3, no. 4 (April/May 1984):18–23.

Yaniv, Avner, and Lieber, Robert J. "Personal Whim or Strategic Imperative? The Israeli Invasion of Lebanon." *International Security* 8, no. 2 (Fall 1983).117–42.

Yishai, Yael. "Dissent in Israel: Opinions on the Lebanon War." *Middle East Review* 168, no. 2 (Winter 1983/84):38–44.

Yuryev, V. "Kuwait Facing the Future." *International Affairs* (Moscow), March 1984:141–47.

Index

THE MIDDLE EAST AFTER THE ISRAELI INVASION OF LEBANON

was composed in 10½-point Mergenthaler Linotron 202 Caslon and leaded 2½ points
by Partners Composition;
with display type in Remarkable by Arnold & Debel Inc.,
and Caslon No. 224 Medium by Rochester Mono/Headliners;
and ornaments provided by Jōb Litho Services;
printed by sheet-fed offset on 50-pound, acid-free Eggshell Cream,
Smyth-sewn and bound over binder's boards in Joanna Arrestox B,
also adhesive bound with paper covers
by Maple-Vail Book Manufacturing Group, Inc.;
with dust jackets and paper covers printed in 2 colors by Philips Offset Company, Inc.;
designed by Shawn Lewis;
and published by

SYRACUSE UNIVERSITY PRESS

SYRACUSE, NEW YORK 13244-5160